Vauxhall/Opel Vivaro & Renault Trafic Diesel
Owners Workshop Manual

Euan Doig

Models covered

(6439 - 272)

Vivaro & Trafic panel vans with 1.9 litre (1870cc) and 2.0 litre (1995cc) turbo-diesel engines

Also covers major features of Nissan Primastar
Does NOT cover petrol models, 2.5 litre diesel engine, 'Quickshift'/'Tecshift' auto-shift transmission
or features specific to specialist bodywork/conversions
Does NOT cover new ranges introduced May 2014

© Haynes Group Limited 2018

A book in the **Haynes Owners Workshop Manual Series**

ABCDE
FGHIJ
KLMNO

ISBN **978 1 78521 439 4**

British Library Cataloguing in Publication Data
A catalogue record for this book is available from the British Library.

Printed in India

Haynes Group Limited
Sparkford, Yeovil, Somerset BA22 7JJ, England

Haynes North America, Inc
2801 Townsgate Road, Suite 340, Thousand Oaks, CA 91361

Disclaimer

There are risks associated with automotive repairs. The ability to make repairs depends on the individual's skill, experience and proper tools. Individuals should act with due care and acknowledge and assume the risk of performing automotive repairs.

The purpose of this manual is to provide comprehensive, useful and accessible automotive repair information, to help you get the best value from your vehicle. However, this manual is not a substitute for a professional certified technician or mechanic.

This repair manual is produced by a third party and is not associated with an individual vehicle manufacturer. If there is any doubt or discrepancy between this manual and the owner's manual or the factory service manual, please refer to the factory service manual or seek assistance from a professional certified technician or mechanic.

Even though we have prepared this manual with extreme care and every attempt is made to ensure that the information in this manual is correct, neither the publisher nor the author can accept responsibility for loss, damage or injury caused by any errors in, or omissions from, the information given.

Contents

LIVING WITH YOUR VAUXHALL VIVARO/RENAULT TRAFIC

Contents

The Vauxhall Vivaro and Renault Trafic II were introduced in 2001; the product of collaboration between the two companies. These stylish vans set new standards for performance, economy, passenger protection and comfort levels. They share the same body and mechanical equipment, using well-proven turbo-diesel engines used elsewhere in the Renault range, and built at Vauxhall's Luton factory. The body was available in several different configurations, including SWB, LWB, high-roof, low-roof, Combi (minibus) and tipper. These front-wheel drive models where given a 'soft' facelift in 2006, including minor changes to the front and rear bumpers, headlights, radiator grille, etc.

The diesel engines are all turbocharged, direct injection, in-line, 4-cylinder units of 1870 cc or 1995 cc displacement. The 1.9 litre engines are single overhead camshaft design with 8 valves, whereas the 2.0 litre engines are double overhead camshaft design, with 16 valves. The engines feature a comprehensive engine management system with extensive emission control equipment.

Transmissions are either 5- or 6-speed manual with a hydraulically operated clutch.

Braking is by discs all round, with a load-sensing valve fitted to non-ABS models to regulate the rear braking pressure in relation to the payload. Power-assisted steering is standard on all models, with anti-lock braking (ABS) and ESP (Electronic Stability Program) available as an option. All models are equipped with independent front McPherson strut type suspension, and a beam-type rear axle, incorporating separate dampers and coil springs.

A wide range of standard and optional equipment is available within the range, with driver's airbag as standard equipment, and passenger's airbag and side airbags available as an option.

Provided that regular servicing is carried out in accordance with the manufacturer's recommendations, the Vauxhall Vivaro and Renault Trafic should provide reliable, spacious, comfortable transport.

Your Vauxhall/Renault manual

The aim of this manual is to help you get the best value from your vehicle. It can do so in several ways. It can help you decide what work must be done (even should you choose to get it done by a garage). It will also provide information on routine maintenance and servicing, and give a logical course of action and diagnosis when random faults occur. However, it is hoped that you will use the manual by tackling the work yourself. On simpler jobs it may even be quicker than booking the vehicle into a garage and going there twice, to leave and collect it. Perhaps most important, a lot of money can be saved by avoiding the costs a garage must charge to cover its labour and overheads.

The manual has drawings and descriptions to show the function of the various components so that their layout can be understood. Tasks are described and photographed in a clear step-by-step sequence. The illustrations are numbered by the Section number and paragraph number to which they relate – if there is more than one illustration per paragraph, the sequence is denoted alphabetically.

References to the 'left' or 'right' of the vehicle are in the sense of a person in the driver's seat, facing forwards.

Acknowledgements

Thanks are due to Draper Tools Limited, who provided some of the workshop tools, and to all those people at Sparkford who helped in the production of this manual.

We take great pride in the accuracy of information given in this manual, but vehicle manufacturers make alterations and design changes during the production run of a particular vehicle of which they do not inform us. No liability can be accepted by the authors or publishers for loss, damage or injury caused by any errors in, or omissions from the information given.

Working on your car can be dangerous. This page shows just some of the potential risks and hazards, with the aim of creating a safety-conscious attitude.

General hazards

Scalding

• Don't remove the radiator or expansion tank cap while the engine is hot.

• Engine oil, transmission fluid or power steering fluid may also be dangerously hot if the engine has recently been running.

Burning

• Beware of burns from the exhaust system and from any part of the engine. Brake discs and drums can also be extremely hot immediately after use.

Crushing

• When working under or near a raised vehicle, always supplement the jack with axle stands, or use drive-on ramps.

Never venture under a car which is only supported by a jack.

• Take care if loosening or tightening high-torque nuts when the vehicle is on stands. Initial loosening and final tightening should be done with the wheels on the ground.

Fire

• Fuel is highly flammable; fuel vapour is explosive.

• Don't let fuel spill onto a hot engine.

• Do not smoke or allow naked lights (including pilot lights) anywhere near a vehicle being worked on. Also beware of creating sparks (electrically or by use of tools).

• Fuel vapour is heavier than air, so don't work on the fuel system with the vehicle over an inspection pit.

• Another cause of fire is an electrical overload or short-circuit. Take care when repairing or modifying the vehicle wiring.

• Keep a fire extinguisher handy, of a type suitable for use on fuel and electrical fires.

Electric shock

• Ignition HT and Xenon headlight voltages can be dangerous, especially to people with heart problems or a pacemaker. Don't work on or near these systems with the engine running or the ignition switched on.

• Mains voltage is also dangerous. Make sure that any mains-operated equipment is correctly earthed. Mains power points should be protected by a residual current device (RCD) circuit breaker.

Fume or gas intoxication

• Exhaust fumes are poisonous; they can contain carbon monoxide, which is rapidly fatal if inhaled. Never run the engine in a confined space such as a garage with the doors shut.

• Fuel vapour is also poisonous, as are the vapours from some cleaning solvents and paint thinners.

Poisonous or irritant substances

• Avoid skin contact with battery acid and with any fuel, fluid or lubricant, especially antifreeze, brake hydraulic fluid and Diesel fuel. Don't syphon them by mouth. If such a substance is swallowed or gets into the eyes, seek medical advice.

• Prolonged contact with used engine oil can cause skin cancer. Wear gloves or use a barrier cream if necessary. Change out of oil-soaked clothes and do not keep oily rags in your pocket.

• Air conditioning refrigerant forms a poisonous gas if exposed to a naked flame (including a cigarette). It can also cause skin burns on contact.

Asbestos

• Asbestos dust can cause cancer if inhaled or swallowed. Asbestos may be found in gaskets and in brake and clutch linings. When dealing with such components it is safest to assume that they contain asbestos.

Special hazards

Hydrofluoric acid

• This extremely corrosive acid is formed when certain types of synthetic rubber, found in some O-rings, oil seals, fuel hoses etc, are exposed to temperatures above 4000C. The rubber changes into a charred or sticky substance containing the acid. *Once formed, the acid remains dangerous for years. If it gets onto the skin, it may be necessary to amputate the limb concerned.*

• When dealing with a vehicle which has suffered a fire, or with components salvaged from such a vehicle, wear protective gloves and discard them after use.

The battery

• Batteries contain sulphuric acid, which attacks clothing, eyes and skin. Take care when topping-up or carrying the battery.

• The hydrogen gas given off by the battery is highly explosive. Never cause a spark or allow a naked light nearby. Be careful when connecting and disconnecting battery chargers or jump leads.

Air bags

• Air bags can cause injury if they go off accidentally. Take care when removing the steering wheel and trim panels. Special storage instructions may apply.

Diesel injection equipment

• Diesel injection pumps supply fuel at very high pressure. Take care when working on the fuel injectors and fuel pipes.

⚠ *Warning: Never expose the hands, face or any other part of the body to injector spray; the fuel can penetrate the skin with potentially fatal results.*

Remember...

DO

• Do use eye protection when using power tools, and when working under the vehicle.

• Do wear gloves or use barrier cream to protect your hands when necessary.

• Do get someone to check periodically that all is well when working alone on the vehicle.

• Do keep loose clothing and long hair well out of the way of moving mechanical parts.

• Do remove rings, wristwatch etc, before working on the vehicle – especially the electrical system.

• Do ensure that any lifting or jacking equipment has a safe working load rating adequate for the job.

DON'T

• Don't attempt to lift a heavy component which may be beyond your capability – get assistance.

• Don't rush to finish a job, or take unverified short cuts.

• Don't use ill-fitting tools which may slip and cause injury.

• Don't leave tools or parts lying around where someone can trip over them. Mop up oil and fuel spills at once.

• Don't allow children or pets to play in or near a vehicle being worked on.

The following pages are intended to help in dealing with common roadside emergencies and breakdowns. You will find more detailed fault finding information at the back of the manual, and repair information in the main chapters.

If your vehicle won't start and the starter motor doesn't turn

- ☐ Slide the passenger's seat rearwards, fold the carpet forward, undo the fasteners, remove the cover, and make sure that the battery terminals are clean and tight.
- ☐ Switch on the headlights and try to start the engine. If the headlights go very dim when you're trying to start, the battery is probably flat. Get out of trouble by jump starting (see next page) using a friend's car.

If your vehicle won't start even though the starter motor turns as normal

- ☐ Is there fuel in the tank?
- ☐ Is there moisture on electrical components under the bonnet? Switch off the ignition, then wipe off any obvious dampness with a dry cloth. Spray a water-repellent aerosol product (WD-40 or equivalent) on ignition and fuel system electrical connectors like those shown in the photos.

A Check the mass airflow sensor wiring connector for security.

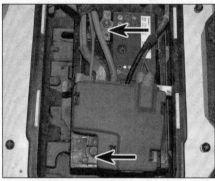

B Check the security of the battery connections (under the passenger compartment floor).

C Check the security of the preheating system control unit.

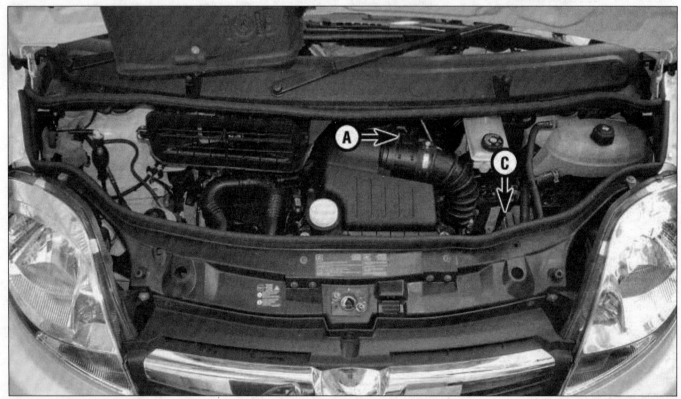

Check that electrical connections are secure (with the ignition switched off) and spray them with a water-dispersant spray like WD-40 if you suspect a problem due to damp.

Jump starting

When jump-starting a vehicle using a booster battery, observe the following precautions:

✔ Before connecting the booster battery, make sure that the ignition is switched off.

Caution: Remove the key in case the central locking engages when the jump leads are connected

✔ Ensure that all electrical equipment (lights, heater, wipers, etc) is switched off.

✔ Take note of any special precautions printed on the battery case.

✔ Make sure that the booster battery is the same voltage as the discharged one in the vehicle.

✔ If the battery is being jump-started from the battery in another vehicle, the two vehicles MUST NOT TOUCH each other.

✔ Make sure that the transmission is in neutral (or PARK, in the case of automatic transmission).

HAYNES HiNT *Jump starting will get you out of trouble, but you must correct whatever made the battery go flat in the first place. There are three possibilities:*

1 The battery has been drained by repeated attempts to start, or by leaving the lights on.

2 The charging system is not working properly (alternator drivebelt slack or broken, alternator wiring fault or alternator itself faulty).

3 The battery itself is at fault (electrolyte low, or battery worn out).

1 Slide the passenger's seat fully rearwards, and fold the floor carpet forwards to access the battery cover.

2 Remove the battery cover.

3 Connect one end of the red lead to the positive (+) terminal of the discharged battery.

4 Connect the other end of the red lead to the positive (+) terminal of the booster battery.

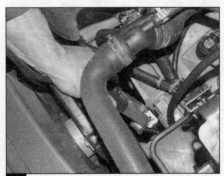
5 Connect one end of the black jump lead to a bolt or bracket on the engine block on the vehicle providing the jump start.

6 Connect the other end of the black jump lead to the negative (-) terminal of the discharged battery.

7 Make sure that the jump leads will not come into contact with the cooling fan, drivebelts or other moving parts on the engine.

8 Start the engine, then with the engine running at fast idle speed disconnect the jump leads in the reverse order of connection.

Wheel changing

 Warning: Do not change a wheel in a situation where you risk being hit by other traffic. On busy roads, try to stop in a lay-by or a gateway. Be wary of passing traffic while changing the wheel – it is easy to become distracted by the job in hand.

Preparation

☐ When a puncture occurs, stop as soon as it is safe to do so.

☐ Park on firm level ground, if possible, and well out of the way of other traffic.

☐ Use hazard warning lights if necessary.

☐ If you have one, use a warning triangle to alert other drivers of your presence.

☐ Apply the handbrake and engage first or reverse gear.

☐ Chock the wheel diagonally opposite the one being removed – a couple of large stones will do for this.

☐ If the ground is soft, use a flat piece of wood to spread the load under the jack.

Changing the wheel

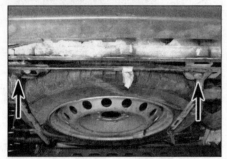

1 The jack and tools are stored under the driver's seat, whilst the spare wheel is located under the rear of the vehicle.

2 Slacken the wheel carrier left-hand security bolt a few turns, using the tool provided in the kit, then unscrew the carrier right-hand bolt completely.

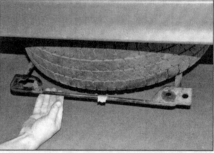

3 Push the carrier to the left-hand side a little until it clears the security bolt. Lower the carrier and wheel – it's heavy!

4 Prise off the punctured wheel cover/hub cap, slacken each wheel bolt by a half turn, using the tool provided. If the bolts are too tight, DON'T stand on the brace to undo them – call for assistance.

5 Place the jack under the lifting point nearest the wheel, then raise the jack until the spigot on the head engages with the hole in the lifting point.

6 Raise the vehicle until the wheel is raised clear of the ground, then unscrew the wheel bolts and remove the wheel.

7 Fit the spare wheel, and screw in the bolts. Lightly tighten the bolts, then lower the vehicle to the ground.

Finally . . .

☐ Remove the wheel chocks.

☐ Position the spare wheel on the carrier, then lift the carrier into place, engaging it with the security bolt. Refit the remaining carrier bolt and tighten them both securely.

☐ Stow the jack and tools back in the vehicle.

☐ Check the tyre pressure on the wheel just fitted. If it is low, or if you don't have a pressure gauge with you, drive slowly to the nearest garage and inflate the tyre to the right pressure. In the case of the space-saver spare wheel, this pressure is much higher than for a normal tyre.

☐ The wheel bolts should be slackened and retightened to the specified torque (140 Nm/ 103 lbf ft) at the earliest possible opportunity.

☐ Have the damaged tyre or wheel repaired as soon as possible.

8 Securely tighten the wheel bolts in a criss-cross pattern sequence, then refit the wheel trim or hub cap, as applicable.

Identifying leaks

Puddles on the garage floor or drive, or obvious wetness under the bonnet or underneath the car, suggest a leak that needs investigating. It can sometimes be difficult to decide where the leak is coming from, especially if an engine undershield is fitted. Leaking oil or fluid can also be blown rearwards by the passage of air under the car, giving a false impression of where the problem lies.

 Warning: Most automotive oils and fluids are poisonous. Wash them off skin, and change out of contaminated clothing, without delay.

 The smell of a fluid leaking from the car may provide a clue to what's leaking. Some fluids are distinctively coloured. It may help to remove the engine undershield, clean the car carefully and to park it over some clean paper overnight as an aid to locating the source of the leak.
Remember that some leaks may only occur while the engine is running.

Sump oil

Engine oil may leak from the drain plug...

Oil from filter

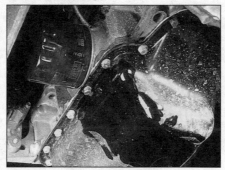

...or from the base of the oil filter.

Gearbox oil

Gearbox oil can leak from the seals at the inboard ends of the driveshafts.

Antifreeze

Leaking antifreeze often leaves a crystalline deposit like this.

Brake fluid

A leak occurring at a wheel is almost certainly brake fluid.

Power steering fluid

Power steering fluid may leak from the pipe connectors on the steering rack.

Towing

When all else fails, you may find yourself having to get a tow home – or of course you may be helping somebody else. Long-distance recovery should only be done by a garage or breakdown service. For shorter distances, DIY towing using another vehicle is easy enough, but observe the following points:

☐ Use a proper tow-rope – they are not expensive. The vehicle being towed must display an ON TOW sign in its rear window.
☐ Always turn the ignition key to the 'on' position when the vehicle is being towed, so that the steering lock is released, and the direction indicator and brake lights work.

☐ A towing eye socket is provided in the front bumper, and a towing eye is located below the rear bumper. The front socket is hidden behind a cover panel at the right-hand end of the front bumper **(see illustration)**.
☐ Before being towed, release the handbrake and select neutral on the transmission.
☐ Note that greater-than-usual pedal pressure will be required to operate the brakes, since the vacuum servo unit is only operational with the engine running.
☐ On models with power steering, greater-than-usual steering effort will also be required.
☐ Make sure that both drivers know the route before setting off.

☐ The driver of the vehicle being towed must keep the tow-rope taut at all times to avoid snatching.
☐ Only drive at moderate speeds and keep the distance towed to a minimum. Drive smoothly and allow plenty of time for slowing down at junctions.

Introduction

There are some very simple checks which need only take a few minutes to carry out, but which could save you a lot of inconvenience and expense.

These *Weekly checks* require no great skill or special tools, and the small amount of time they take to perform could prove to be very well spent, for example:

☐ Keeping an eye on tyre condition and pressures, will not only help to stop them wearing out prematurely, but could also save your life.

☐ Many breakdowns are caused by electrical problems. Battery-related faults are particularly common, and a quick check on a regular basis will often prevent the majority of these.

☐ If your vehicle develops a brake fluid leak, the first time you might know about it is when your brakes don't work properly. Checking the level regularly will give advance warning of this kind of problem.

☐ If the oil or coolant levels run low, the cost of repairing any engine damage will be far greater than fixing the leak, for example.

Underbonnet check points

◄ **1.9 litre engine**

A *Engine oil level filler cap/ dipstick*

B *Coolant expansion tank*

C *Brake (and clutch) fluid reservoir*

D *Power steering fluid reservoir*

E *Screen washer fluid reservoir*

◄ **2.0 litre engine**

A *Engine oil level dipstick*

B *Engine oil filler cap*

C *Coolant expansion tank*

D *Brake (and clutch) fluid reservoir*

E *Power steering fluid reservoir*

F *Screen washer fluid reservoir*

Engine oil level

Before you start
✔ Make sure that the vehicle is on level ground.
✔ Check the oil level before the vehicle is driven, or at least 15 minutes after the engine has been switched off.

 HAYNES HINT *If the oil is checked immediately after driving the vehicle, some of the oil will remain in the upper engine components, resulting in an inaccurate reading on the dipstick.*

The correct oil
Modern engines place great demands on their oil. It is very important that the correct oil for your vehicle is used (see *Lubricants and fluids*).

Vehicle care
● If you have to add oil frequently, you should check whether you have any oil leaks. Place some clean paper under the vehicle overnight, and check for stains in the morning. If there are no leaks, then the engine may be burning oil.
● Always maintain the level between the upper and lower dipstick marks (see photo 3). If the level is too low, severe engine damage may occur. Oil seal failure may result if the engine is overfilled by adding too much oil.

1 The dipstick top is brightly-coloured for easy identification (see *Underbonnet check points* for exact location). Withdraw the dipstick; on 1.9 litre models, the dipstick is integral with the filler cap.

2 Using a clean rag or paper towel, remove all oil from the dipstick. Insert the clean dipstick into the tube as far as it will go, then withdraw it again.

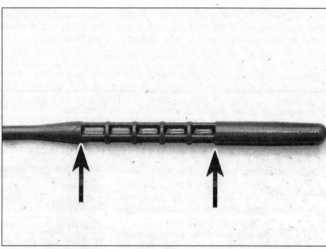

3 Note the oil level on the end of the dipstick, which should be in the hatched area between the upper (MAX) mark and lower (MIN) mark. Approximately 1.5 litres of oil will raise the level from the lower mark to the upper mark.

4 Oil is added through the filler cap. Unscrew the cap and top-up the level; a funnel may help to reduce spillage. Add the oil slowly, checking the level on the dipstick often. Don't overfill (see *Vehicle care*).

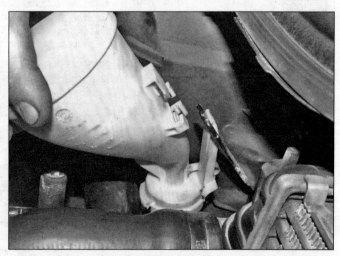

5 Note that on 1.9 litre models, a funnel is stored at the front of the engine compartment.

Coolant level

Warning: Do not attempt to remove the expansion tank pressure cap when the engine is hot, as there is a very great risk of scalding. Do not leave open containers of coolant about, as it is poisonous.

Vehicle care

● With a sealed-type cooling system, adding coolant should not be necessary on a regular basis. If frequent topping-up is required, it is likely there is a leak. Check the radiator, all hoses and joint faces for signs of staining or wetness, and rectify as necessary.

● It is important that antifreeze is used in the cooling system all year round, not just during the winter months. Don't top-up with water alone, as the antifreeze will become diluted.

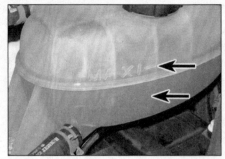

1 The coolant reservoir is located on the left-hand inner wing. The coolant level is visible through the reservoir body. The coolant level varies with engine temperature. When cold, the coolant level should be between the MAXI and MINI marks. When the engine is hot, the level may rise slightly above the MAXI mark.

2 If topping-up is necessary, wait until the engine is cold. Slowly unscrew the expansion tank cap, to release any pressure present in the cooling system, and remove it. Add a mixture of water and antifreeze to the expansion tank until the coolant is at the correct level. Refit the cap and tighten it securely.

Brake and clutch fluid level

Warning:
• Brake fluid can harm your eyes and damage painted surfaces, so use extreme caution when handling and pouring it.
• Do not use fluid that has been standing open for some time, as it absorbs moisture from the air, which can cause a dangerous loss of braking effectiveness.

HAYNES HiNT
• Make sure that your vehicle is on level ground.
• The fluid level in the reservoir will drop slightly as the brake pads wear down, but the fluid level must never be allowed to drop below the MINI mark.

Safety first!

● If the reservoir requires repeated topping-up this is an indication of a fluid leak somewhere in the system, which should be investigated immediately.
● If a leak is suspected, the vehicle should not be driven until the braking system has been checked. Never take any risks where brakes are concerned.

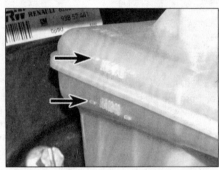

1 The MAXI and MINI marks are indicated on the reservoir. The fluid level must be kept between the marks at all times.

2 If topping-up is necessary, first wipe clean the area around the filler cap to prevent dirt entering the hydraulic system.

3 Unscrew the reservoir cap and carefully lift it out of position. Inspect the reservoir, if the fluid is dirty, the hydraulic system should be drained and refilled (see Chapter 1).

4 Carefully add fluid, taking care not to spill it onto the surrounding components. Use only the specified fluid; mixing different types can cause damage to the system. After topping-up to the correct level, securely refit the cap and wipe off any spilt fluid. Reconnect the fluid level wiring connector.

Power steering fluid level

✔ Park the vehicle on level ground.
✔ Set the steering wheel straight-ahead.
✔ The engine should be turned off.

Safety first!

● The need for frequent topping-up indicates a leak, which should be investigated immediately.

 For the check to be accurate, the steering must not be turned once the engine has been stopped.

1 The reservoir is mounted on the right-hand inner wing. The fluid level should be between the MINI and MAXI marks when the fluid is cold.

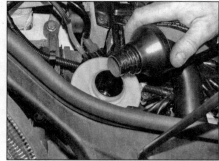

2 Wipe clean the area around the reservoir filler neck, and unscrew the filler cap. When topping-up, use the specified type of fluid – do not overfill the reservoir. When the level is correct, securely refit the cap.

Screen washer fluid level

● On models so equipped, the screen washer fluid is also used to clean the headlights.

● Screenwash additives not only keep the windscreen clean during foul weather, they also prevent the washer system freezing in cold weather – which is when you are likely to need it most. Don't top-up using plain water as the screenwash will become too diluted, and will freeze during cold weather.

 Warning: On no account use coolant antifreeze in the washer system – this could discolour or damage paintwork.

1 The washer fluid reservoir filler is located at the front right-hand side of the engine compartment. Release the cap and observe the level in the reservoir by looking down the filler neck.

2 When topping-up the reservoir, a screenwash additive should be added in the quantities recommended on the bottle.

Wiper blades

Note: *Fitting details for wiper blades vary according to model, and according to whether genuine Vauxhall or Renault wiper blades have been fitted. Use the procedures and illustration shown as a guide for your vehicle.*

✔ Check the condition of the wiper blades; if they are cracked or show any signs of deterioration, or if the glass swept area is smeared, renew them. Wiper blades should be renewed annually.

1 Pull the arm fully away from the glass until it locks. Swivel the blade through 90°, and slide the blade out of the arm's hooked end.

Tyre condition and pressure

It is very important that tyres are in good condition, and at the correct pressure - having a tyre failure at any speed is highly dangerous. Tyre wear is influenced by driving style - harsh braking and acceleration, or fast cornering, will all produce more rapid tyre wear. As a general rule, the front tyres wear out faster than the rears. Interchanging the tyres from front to rear ("rotating" the tyres) may result in more even wear. However, if this is completely effective, you may have the expense of replacing all four tyres at once!

Remove any nails or stones embedded in the tread before they penetrate the tyre to cause deflation. If removal of a nail does reveal that the tyre has been punctured, refit the nail so that its point of penetration is marked. Then immediately change the wheel, and have the tyre repaired by a tyre dealer.

Regularly check the tyres for damage in the form of cuts or bulges, especially in the sidewalls. Periodically remove the wheels, and clean any dirt or mud from the inside and outside surfaces. Examine the wheel rims for signs of rusting, corrosion or other damage. Light alloy wheels are easily damaged by "kerbing" whilst parking; steel wheels may also become dented or buckled. A new wheel is very often the only way to overcome severe damage.

New tyres should be balanced when they are fitted, but it may become necessary to re-balance them as they wear, or if the balance weights fitted to the wheel rim should fall off. Unbalanced tyres will wear more quickly, as will the steering and suspension components. Wheel imbalance is normally signified by vibration, particularly at a certain speed (typically around 50 mph). If this vibration is felt only through the steering, then it is likely that just the front wheels need balancing. If, however, the vibration is felt through the whole car, the rear wheels could be out of balance. Wheel balancing should be carried out by a tyre dealer or garage.

1 *Tread Depth - visual check*
The original tyres have tread wear safety bands (B), which will appear when the tread depth reaches approximately 1.6 mm. The band positions are indicated by a triangular mark on the tyre sidewall (A).

2 *Tread Depth - manual check*
Alternatively, tread wear can be monitored with a simple, inexpensive device known as a tread depth indicator gauge.

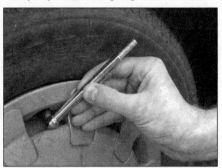

3 *Tyre Pressure Check*
Check the tyre pressures regularly with the tyres cold. Do not adjust the tyre pressures immediately after the vehicle has been used, or an inaccurate setting will result.

Tyre tread wear patterns

Shoulder Wear

Underinflation (wear on both sides)
Under-inflation will cause overheating of the tyre, because the tyre will flex too much, and the tread will not sit correctly on the road surface. This will cause a loss of grip and excessive wear, not to mention the danger of sudden tyre failure due to heat build-up.
Check and adjust pressures
Incorrect wheel camber (wear on one side)
Repair or renew suspension parts
Hard cornering
Reduce speed!

Centre Wear

Overinflation
Over-inflation will cause rapid wear of the centre part of the tyre tread, coupled with reduced grip, harsher ride, and the danger of shock damage occurring in the tyre casing.
Check and adjust pressures

If you sometimes have to inflate your car's tyres to the higher pressures specified for maximum load or sustained high speed, don't forget to reduce the pressures to normal afterwards.

Uneven Wear

Front tyres may wear unevenly as a result of wheel misalignment. Most tyre dealers and garages can check and adjust the wheel alignment (or "tracking") for a modest charge.
Incorrect camber or castor
Repair or renew suspension parts
Malfunctioning suspension
Repair or renew suspension parts
Unbalanced wheel
Balance tyres
Incorrect toe setting
Adjust front wheel alignment
Note: *The feathered edge of the tread which typifies toe wear is best checked by feel.*

Battery

Caution: Before carrying out any work on the vehicle battery, read the precautions given in 'Safety first!' at the start of this manual.

✔ Make sure that the battery tray is in good condition, and that the clamp is tight. Corrosion on the tray, retaining clamp and the battery itself can be removed with a solution of water and baking soda. Thoroughly rinse all cleaned areas with water. Any metal parts damaged by corrosion should be covered with a zinc-based primer, then painted.

✔ Periodically (approximately every three months), check the charge condition of the battery as described in Chapter 5.
✔ On batteries which are not of the maintenance-free type, periodically check the electrolyte level in the battery – see Chapter 5.
✔ If the battery is flat, and you need to jump start your vehicle, see *Roadside Repairs*.

 Battery corrosion can be kept to a minimum by applying a layer of petroleum jelly to the clamps and terminals after they are reconnected.

1 The battery is located under the passenger compartment floor. Slide the passenger's seat fully rearwards, and lift the carpet in front of the seat.

2 Using the tool provided in the vehicle tool kit, undo the fasteners and remove the cover over the battery.

3 Check the tightness of battery clamps to ensure good electrical connections. You should not be able to move them. Also check each cable for cracks and frayed conductors.

4 If corrosion (white, fluffy deposits) is evident, remove the cables from the battery terminals, clean them with a small wire brush, then refit them. Automotive stores sell a tool for cleaning the battery post . . .

5 . . . as well as the battery cable clamps.

Bulbs and fuses

✔ Check all external lights and the horn. Refer to the appropriate Sections of Chapter 12 for details if any of the circuits are found to be inoperative.

✔ Visually check all accessible wiring connectors, harnesses and retaining clips for security, and for signs of chafing or damage.

> **HAYNES HiNT**
> *If you need to check your brake lights and indicators unaided, back up to a wall or garage door and operate the lights. The reflected light should show if they are working properly.*

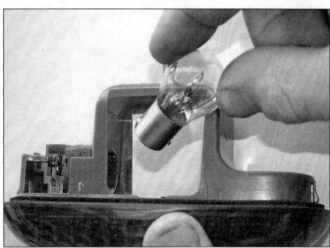

1 If a single indicator light, brake light or headlight has failed, it is likely that a bulb has blown and will need to be renewed. Refer to Chapter 12 for details. If both brake lights have failed, it is possible that the brake light switch is faulty (see Chapter 9).

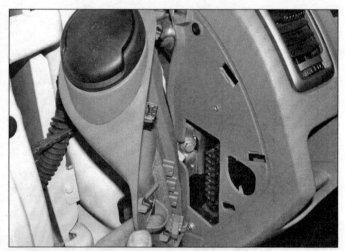

2 If more than one indicator light or headlight has failed, it is likely that either a fuse has blown or that there is a fault in the circuit (see Chapter 12). The fuses are located in the fusebox situated at the passenger's end of the facia. Pull open the fusebox cover.

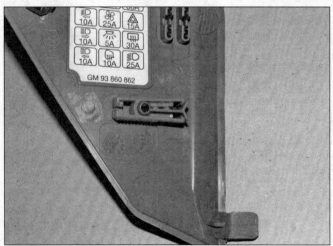

3 To renew a blown fuse, simply pull it out using the plastic tweezers provided.

4 Fit a new fuse of the same rating (see Chapter 12). If the fuse blows again, it is important that you find out why – a complete checking procedure is given in Chapter 12.

Lubricants and fluids

Engine† . . . .   Multigrade engine oil, viscosity SAE 5W/30 to
ACEA A3/B4, or ACEA C3 for models with a
particulate filter (M9R 630 engine)

Cooling system . . . .   Vauxhall/Renault coolant

Manual transmission . . . .   TransElf TRX 75W80 API GL-5*

Brake and clutch systems . . . .   Hydraulic fluid to DOT 4+

Power steering . . . .   Dexron II

*† Certain models have a decal in the engine compartment which details the engine oil specification.
Where no decal is fitted, follow the above recommendations.*

* Consult a dealer or specialist for latest recommendation.

Tyre pressures

Note: *These pressures apply to original-equipment tyres, and may vary if any other make or type of tyre is fitted; check with the tyre manufacturer or supplier for correct pressures if necessary. The pressures should be checked only when the tyres are cold.*

Size	Front	Rear
195/65 x 16	3.4 bar (49 psi)	3.7 bar (54 psi)
195/75 x 16	3.8 bar (55 psi)	4.2 bar (61 psi)
205/65 x 16	3.8 bar (55 psi)	4.2 bar (61 psi)
215/65 x 16	3.1 bar (45 psi)	3.4 bar (49 psi)

Chapter 1
Routine maintenance and servicing

Contents

Degrees of difficulty

 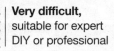

Easy, suitable for novice with little experience	Fairly easy, suitable for beginner with some experience	Fairly difficult, suitable for competent DIY mechanic	Difficult, suitable for experienced DIY mechanic	Very difficult, suitable for expert DIY or professional

1 Servicing specifications

Lubricants and fluids
Refer to *Weekly checks* on page 0•17

Capacities

Engine oil (including filter)
1.9 litre engines	4.6 litres
2.0 litre engines	7.7 litres
Difference between MAX and MIN dipstick marks	1.5 to 2.0 litres

Cooling system
All engines except M9R 630	6.4 litres
M9R 630 engine (2.0 litre with particulate filter)	8.5 litres

Transmission .... 2.7 litres

Fuel tank .... 90 litres

Brakes

Front disc brakes:
Pad thickness (including backplate):
New	18.0 mm
Minimum thickness	9.0 mm

Rear disc brakes:
Pad thickness (including backing):
New	17.0 mm
Minimum thickness	9.0 mm

Remote control battery
Type CR1220

Torque wrench settings

	Nm	lbf ft
Auxiliary drivebelt guide roller (2.0 litre only)	44	32
Auxiliary drivebelt tensioner assembly (2.0 litre only)	25	18
Engine oil drain plug:		
1.9 litre engines	20	15
2.0 litre engines	18	13
Engine oil filter cover (2.0 litre only)	25	18
Roadwheel bolts	140	103

2 Maintenance schedule

The maintenance intervals in this manual are provided with the assumption that you, not the dealer, will be carrying out the work. These are the minimum maintenance intervals recommended by us for vehicles driven daily. If you wish to keep your vehicle in peak condition at all times, you may wish to perform some of these procedures more often. We encourage frequent maintenance, because it enhances the efficiency, performance and resale value of your vehicle.

If the vehicle is driven in dusty areas, used to tow a trailer, or driven frequently at slow speeds (idling in traffic) or on short journeys, more frequent maintenance intervals are recommended.

When the vehicle is new, it should be serviced by a dealer service department (or other workshop recognised by the vehicle manufacturer as providing the same standard of service) in order to preserve the warranty. The vehicle manufacturer may reject warranty claims if you are unable to prove that servicing has been carried out as and when specified, using only original equipment parts or parts certified to be of equivalent quality.

Every 250 miles or weekly

☐ Refer to *Weekly checks*

Every 9000 miles or 12 months

☐ Renew the engine oil and filter (Section 6)*
☐ Drain any water from the fuel filter (Section 7)

* Note: *Frequent oil and filter changes are good for the engine and we recommend that the oil and filter be renewed at the interval specified here (or at least once every 12 months), especially if the vehicle is used on a lot of short journeys or covers a small annual mileage.*

Every 18 000 miles or 2 years

In addition to all the items listed previously, carry out the following:

☐ Check the brake pad thickness – front and rear (Section 8)
☐ Check the operation of the handbrake (Section 9)
☐ Check the operation of the clutch (Section 10)
☐ Check the condition of the auxiliary drivebelts (Section 11 or 12)
☐ Check the condition of the seat belts (Section 13)
☐ Check the operation of all electrical systems (Section 14)
☐ Check the condition of the exhaust system and mountings (Section 15)
☐ Check the suspension and steering components (Section 16)
☐ Check the tightness of the roadwheel bolts (Section 17)
☐ Check the operation of the air conditioning system (Section 18)

Every 18 000 miles or 2 years (continued)

☐ Renew the air filter element (Section 19)*
☐ Renew the fuel filter (Section 20)
☐ Check the manual transmission oil level (Section 21)
☐ Check all underbonnet components and hoses for fluid leaks (Section 22)
☐ Renew the pollen filter (Section 23)
☐ Carry out a road test (Section 24)

* Note: *Although the manufacturers recommend this task to be carried out on 2.0 litre models every 36 000 miles we recommend that the filter be renewed more frequently, perhaps every 18 000 miles or every two years, especially if the vehicle is used in a dusty environment.*

Every 2 years

☐ Renew the remote control batteries (Section 25)

Every 36 000 miles or 4 years

In addition to all the items listed previously, carry out the following:
☐ Renew the timing belt (Section 26)*
☐ Renew the brake fluid (Section 27)
☐ Renew the coolant (Section 28)

* Note: *Although the normal interval for timing belt renewal is 72 000 miles, it is strongly recommended that the interval is reduced to 36 000 miles on vehicles which are subjected to intensive use, ie, mainly short journeys or a lot of stop-start driving. The actual belt renewal interval is therefore very much up to the individual owner, but bear in mind that severe engine damage may result if the belt breaks.*

3 Component location

Underbonnet view of a 1.9 litre model

1 Fuel filter
2 Power steering fluid reservoir
3 Air cleaner housing
4 Brake/clutch fluid reservoir
5 Coolant expansion tank
6 Engine oil filler cap
7 Pollen filter housing

Underbonnet view of a 2.0 litre model

1 Fuel filter
2 Power steering fluid reservoir
3 Air cleaner housing
4 Brake/clutch fluid reservoir
5 Coolant expansion tank
6 Engine oil filler cap
7 Pollen filter housing

Front underbody view (1.9 litre model shown – others similar)

1 Engine oil drain plug
2 Transmission oil drain plug
3 Steering track rod end
4 Control arm
5 Rear/lower engine
  mounting
6 Power steering pump
7 Front subframe

Rear underbody view

1 Shock absorber
2 Rear silencer
3 Handbrake cables
4 Lateral control rod
5 Axle mounting bushes
6 Handbrake adjustment nut
7 Rear axle

Maintenance procedures

4 Introduction

This Chapter is designed to help the home mechanic maintain his/her vehicle for safety, economy, long life and peak performance.

The Chapter contains a master maintenance schedule, followed by Sections dealing specifically with each task in the schedule. Visual checks, adjustments, component renewal and other helpful items are included. Refer to the accompanying illustrations of the engine compartment and the underside of the vehicle for the locations of the various components.

Servicing your vehicle in accordance with the mileage/time maintenance schedule and the following Sections will provide a planned maintenance programme, which should result in a long and reliable service life. This is a comprehensive plan, so maintaining some items but not others at the specified service intervals will not produce the same results.

As you service your vehicle, you will discover that many of the procedures can – and should – be grouped together, because of the particular procedure being performed, or because of the close proximity of two otherwise-unrelated components to one another. For example, if the vehicle is raised for any reason, the exhaust can be inspected at the same time as the suspension and steering components.

The first step in this maintenance programme is to prepare yourself before the actual work begins. Read through all the Sections relevant to the work to be carried out, then make a list and gather together all the parts and tools required. If a problem is encountered, seek advice from a parts specialist, or a dealer service department.

5 Regular maintenance

If, from the time the vehicle is new, the routine maintenance schedule is followed closely, and frequent checks are made of fluid levels and high-wear items, as suggested throughout this manual, the engine will be kept in relatively good running condition, and the need for additional work will be minimised.

It is possible that there will be times when the engine is running poorly due to the lack of regular maintenance. This is even more likely if a used vehicle, which has not received regular and frequent maintenance checks, is purchased. In such cases, additional work may need to be carried out, outside of the regular maintenance intervals.

If engine wear is suspected, a compression test or leakdown test (refer to Chapter 2A or 2B) will provide valuable information regarding the overall performance of the main internal components. Such a test can be used as a basis to decide on the extent of the work to be carried out. If, for example, a compression test indicates serious internal engine wear, conventional maintenance as described in this Chapter will not greatly improve the performance of the engine, and may prove a waste of time and money, unless extensive overhaul work is carried out first.

The following series of operations are those most often required to improve the performance of a generally poor-running engine:

Primary operations

a) Clean, inspect and test the battery (see 'Weekly checks').
b) Check all the engine-related fluids (see 'Weekly checks').
c) Check the condition and tension of the auxiliary drivebelt (Sections 11 and 12).
d) Check the condition of the air filter element, and renew if necessary (Section 19).
e) Check the fuel filter – drain off any water and renew filter if necessary (Sections 7 and 20).
f) Check the condition of all hoses, and check for fluid leaks (Section 22).

If the above operations do not prove fully effective, carry out the following secondary operations:

Secondary operations

All items listed under *Primary operations*, plus the following:

a) Check the charging system (Chapter 5).
b) Check the preheating system (Chapter 5).
c) Check the fuel system (Chapter 4A).

Every 9000 miles or 12 months

6 Engine oil and filter renewal

1 Frequent oil and filter changes are the most important preventive maintenance procedures that can be undertaken by the DIY owner. As engine oil ages, it becomes diluted and contaminated, which leads to premature engine wear.
2 Before starting this procedure, gather together all the necessary tools and materials.

Also make sure that you have plenty of clean rags and newspapers handy, to mop-up any spills. Ideally, the engine oil should be warm, as it will drain more easily, and more built-up sludge will be removed with it.
3 Take care not to touch the exhaust or any other hot parts of the engine when working under the vehicle. To avoid any possibility of scalding, and to protect yourself from possible skin irritants and other harmful contaminants in used engine oils, it is advisable to wear gloves when carrying out this work.
4 Firmly apply the handbrake then jack up

the front of the vehicle and support it on axle stands (see *Jacking and vehicle support*). Undo the retaining screws and remove the plastic undertray from underneath the engine/ transmission (where fitted).
5 Remove the oil filler cap. On 1.9 litre engines the dipstick is part of the oil filler cap. On 2.0 litre engines, the dipstick is on the front of the engine.
6 Slacken the drain plug about half a turn, position the draining container under the drain plug, and then remove the plug completely **(see illustration)**. Note that on some engines an 8 mm square section drain plug key will be needed to unscrew the drain plug.
7 Allow some time for the oil to drain, noting that it may be necessary to reposition the container as the oil flow slows to a trickle.
8 After all the oil has drained; wipe the drain plug and the sealing washer with a clean rag. Examine the condition of the sealing washer, and renew it if it shows signs of scoring or other damage that may prevent an oil-tight seal. Clean the area around the drain plug opening, and refit the plug complete with the washer and tighten it securely **(see illustration)**.
9 Move the container into position under the

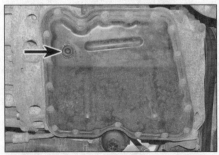

6.6 Use an 8 mm square section key/bit to undo the drain plug (arrowed – 2.0 litre model shown)

6.8 Engine oil drain plug and sealing washer

6.10 1.9-litre model oil filter (arrowed – viewed from beneath)

6.12 Apply a little clean engine oil to the filter seal

6.13 Unscrew the filter housing cap (arrowed) using a 27 mm socket

oil filter, which is located on the front of the cylinder block.

1.9 litre engines

10 Use an oil filter removal tool to slacken the filter initially, then unscrew it by hand the rest of the way **(see illustration)**. Position it with its open end uppermost to prevent further spillage of oil, then empty the oil from the old filter into the container.

11 Use a clean rag to remove any oil, dirt and sludge from the filter sealing area on the engine. Check the old filter to make sure that the rubber sealing ring has not stuck to the engine. If it has, carefully remove it.

12 Apply a light coating of clean engine oil to the sealing ring on the new filter, then screw the filter into position on the engine **(see illustration)**. Tighten the filter firmly by hand only – do not use any tools.

2.0 litre engines

13 The filter is a cartridge inside the oil filter housing. Unscrew the filter housing cap using a 27 mm socket, and withdraw the filter cartridge, draining the oil into the container**(see illustration)**.

14 Use a clean rag to remove any oil, dirt and sludge from inside the oil filter housing. Remove any old rubber seals from the oil filter housing and filter cap, and fit the new seals, which should be supplied with the filter **(see illustration)**.

15 Insert the filter cartridge, then apply a light coating of clean engine oil to the sealing ring **(see illustrations)**. Screw the filter cap into position on the engine. Tighten the filter cap firmly by hand at first, then use socket to tighten it to the specified torque.

All models

16 Refit the undertray and securely tighten its retaining screws. Remove the old oil and all tools from under the vehicle then lower the vehicle to the ground.

17 Fill the engine through the filler hole, using the correct grade and type of oil (refer to *Weekly checks* for details of topping-up). Pour in half the specified quantity of oil first, and then wait a few minutes for the oil to drain into the sump. Continue to add oil, a small quantity at a time, until the level is up to the lower mark on the dipstick. Adding

approximately a further 1.5 litres will bring the level up to the upper mark on the dipstick. Refit the oil filler cap. **Note:** *On 1.9 litre engines, it can take some time for the oil to fully reach the sump.*

18 Start the engine and run it for a few minutes, checking that there are no leaks around the oil filter seal and the sump drain plug. Note that when the engine is first started, there will be a delay of a few seconds before the oil pressure warning light goes out while the new filter fills with oil. Do not race the engine while the warning light is on.

19 Stop the engine, and wait a few minutes for the oil to settle in the sump once more. With the new oil circulated and the filter now completely full, recheck the level on the dipstick, and add more oil as necessary. **Note:** *It's recommended to allow 15 minutes for the engine oil level to settle before rechecking.*

20 Dispose of the used engine oil safely with reference to *General repair procedures*.

Engine oil life monitor

21 On models with an 'Engine oil life monitor' integral with the instrument panel display, reset the monitor as follows:
- a) *Switch on the ignition (without starting the engine), and fully depress and hold the accelerator pedal.*
- b) *Apply the brake pedal 3 times, and hold down on the last depression.*
- c) *Release the accelerator pedal.*
- d) *Release the brake pedal.*
- e) *Turn off the ignition.*
- f) *Wait 5 seconds for the monitor to illuminate.*
- g) *Turn off the ignition, then on again within 3 seconds. The monitor should be reset.*
- h) *The complete procedure described must be completed within 100 seconds of switching on the ignition.*

6.14 Renew the filter housing cap O-ring seal

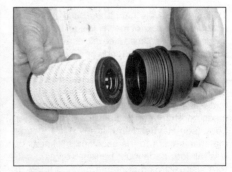

6.15a Insert the new filter cartridge...

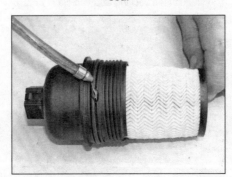

6.15b... and apply a little clean engine oil to the seal

6.15c Refit the filter cartridge and cap to the housing

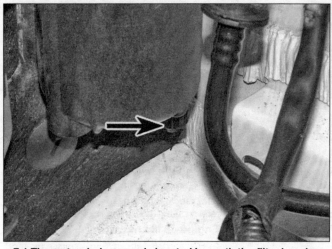

7.1 The water drain screw is located beneath the filter housing (arrowed)

7.2 Slacken the bleed screw (arrowed)

7 Fuel filter water draining

1 Place a suitable container beneath the drain screw **(see illustration)**.

2 Loosen the fuel filter bleed screw, then open the drain screw by turning it anti-clockwise. On fuel systems with a hand priming pump, this may need to be operated a couple of times to allow the fuel to flow **(see illustration)**.

3 Allow the entire contents of the filter to drain into the container, and then securely tighten the drain screw and the bleed screw.

4 Prime and bleed the fuel system as described in Chapter 4A, Section 4.

5 Dispose of the used fuel safely with reference to *General repair procedures*.

Every 18 000 miles or 2 years

8 Brake pad check

1 Firmly apply the handbrake, and then jack up the front or rear of the vehicle and support it securely on axle stands (see *Jacking and vehicle support*). Remove the roadwheels as required. Remember, the vehicle has disc brakes all round, so all four calipers should be checked.

2 For a quick check, the thickness of friction material remaining on each brake pad can be measured through the aperture in the caliper body **(see Haynes Hint)**. If any pad's friction material is worn to the specified thickness or less, all four pads must be renewed as a set. Pad wear warning contacts may be fitted to the inboard pads, but this should not be used as an excuse for omitting a visual check.

Haynes Hint: For a quick check, the thickness of the friction material remaining on each brake pad can be seen through the aperture in the caliper body.

3 For a comprehensive check, the brake pads should be removed and cleaned. This will allow the operation of the caliper to be checked, and the brake disc itself to be fully examined for condition on both sides. Refer to Chapter 9 for further information.

4 On completion refit the roadwheels and lower the vehicle to the ground. Tighten the roadwheel bolts to the specified torque.

9 Handbrake check

1 The handbrake is kept in adjustment by the self-adjusting action of the rear disc calipers.

2 Chock the front wheels, then jack up the rear of the vehicle, and support securely on axle stands (see *Jacking and vehicle support*).

9.5 Slacken the handbrake adjuster nut

3 Fully release the handbrake and check that the wheels can be rotated easily by hand. The wheels may drag slightly, but there should be no binding.

4 If the wheels bind, it is likely that the handbrake mechanism or cables are partially seized. If the operation of the mechanism is not satisfactory, proceed as follows.

5 Working underneath the rear of the vehicle, slacken the adjuster nut until there is no tension in the handbrake cables **(see illustration)**.

6 Remove the rear roadwheels.

7 Check that the handbrake cables slide freely in their sheaths, and that the operating levers on the calipers move freely (see Chapter 9 for further information).

8 Push the handbrake operating levers on the calipers as far as they will go against their bottom stops.

9 If all the parts move freely, adjust the handbrake mechanism as described in Chapter 9.

10 Refit the roadwheels, and lower the vehicle to the ground. Tighten the roadwheel bolts to the specified torque.

10 Clutch check

Check that the clutch pedal moves smoothly and easily through its full travel, and that the clutch itself functions correctly, with no trace of slip or drag. If the clutch

11.7 Use a spanner on the hexagonal section (arrowed) to rotate the tensioner anti-clockwise

11.9 Auxiliary drivebelt routing – 1.9-litre engines without air conditioning

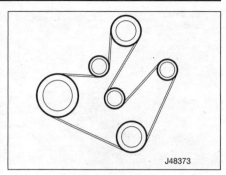

J48373

11.13 Auxiliary drivebelt routing – 1.9-litre engines with air conditioning

action is less than precise, this may indicate the need for bleeding the system – it could also indicate the presence of a fluid leak (see Chapter 6).

11 Auxiliary drivebelt check and renewal – 1.9 litre engines

Note: *The manufacturer recommends that a belt be renewed whenever it is slackened or removed.*

Checking

1 The auxiliary drivebelt is located at the right-hand side of the engine.
2 Two different drivebelt configurations may be encountered, depending on model.
3 Due to their function and material makeup, drivebelts are prone to failure after a period of time and should therefore be inspected.
4 Since the drivebelt is located very close to the right-hand side of the engine compartment, it is possible to gain better access by raising the front of the vehicle (see *Jacking and vehicle support*) and removing the right-hand wheel, then removing the splash shield from inside the wheel arch.
5 With the engine switched off, inspect the full length of the drivebelt for cracks and separation of the belt plies. It will be necessary to turn the crankshaft (using a socket or spanner on the crankshaft pulley bolt) in order to move the belt from the pulleys so that the full length of the belt can be inspected thoroughly. Twist the belt between the pulleys so that both sides can be viewed. Also check for fraying, and glazing which gives the belt a shiny appearance. Check the pulleys for nicks, cracks, distortion and corrosion.

Tensioning

6 A spring-loaded tensioner is fitted to automatically maintain the correct tension on the belt. If problems with belt squeal or slip are encountered, the belt should be renewed. If the problem continues, it will be necessary to renew the tensioner assembly.

Renewal

Models without air conditioning

7 To remove the belt use a spanner to move the tensioner anti-clockwise (as viewed from the right-hand side of the vehicle) **(see illustration)**. Lock the tensioner in this position using a 2.0 mm diameter pin or drill bit.
8 Note the routing of the belt, and then slip the belt off the pulleys.
9 Fit the new belt ensuring that it is routed correctly **(see illustration)**.
10 With the belt in position, hold the tensioner in position, then remove the locking pin, and carefully release the force on the spanner so the belt will automatically become tensioned.
11 Refit the splash shield, roadwheel, and lower the vehicle to the ground. Tighten the roadwheel bolts to the specified torque.

Models with air conditioning

12 To remove the belt use a spanner to move the tensioner clockwise (as viewed from the right-hand side of the vehicle) **(see illustration 11.7)**.
13 Note the routing of the belt, and then slip the belt off the pulleys **(see illustration)**.
14 Fit the new belt ensuring that it is routed correctly.
15 With the belt in position, hold the tensioner in position, then remove the locking pin, and carefully release the force on the spanner so the belt will automatically become tensioned.
16 Refit the splash shield, roadwheel, and lower the vehicle to the ground. Tighten the roadwheel bolts to the specified torque.

12 Auxiliary drivebelt check and renewal – 2.0 litre engines

Note: *The manufacturer recommends that the belt should be renewed whenever it is slackened or removed, along with the tensioner and guide rollers.*

Checking

1 The auxiliary drivebelt is located at the right-hand side of the engine.
2 Due to their function and material makeup, drivebelts are prone to failure after a period of time and should therefore be inspected, and if necessary adjusted periodically.
3 Since the drivebelt is located very close to the right-hand side of the engine

compartment, it is possible to gain better access by raising the front of the vehicle and removing the right-hand wheel, then removing the splash shield from inside the wheel arch, and the engine undertray.
4 With the engine stopped, inspect the full length of the drivebelt for cracks and separation of the belt plies. It will be necessary to turn the engine (using a spanner or socket and bar on the crankshaft pulley bolt) in order to move the belt from the pulleys so that the belt can be inspected thoroughly. Twist the belt between the pulleys so that both sides can be viewed. Also check for fraying, and glazing which gives the belt a shiny appearance. Check the pulleys for nicks, cracks, distortion and corrosion.

Tensioning

5 A spring-loaded tensioner is fitted to automatically maintain the correct tension on the belt. If problems with belt squeal or slip are encountered, the belt, tensioner and guide rollers should be renewed.

Renewal

6 To remove the belt, use a spanner to move the tensioner clockwise (as viewed from the right-hand side of the vehicle). A 4.0 mm Allen key or drill bit can be inserted into a hole in the tensioner body to hold it in the released position **(see illustration)**.
7 Note the routing of the belt, then slip the belt off the pulleys.

12.6 Rotate the tensioner clockwise, and lock it in place using a 4.0 mm drill bit/rod (arrowed)

12.8 Tensioner mounting bolts (arrowed)

12.9 Prise off the cap and undo the guide roller retaining bolt

12.12 Auxiliary drivebelt routing – 2.0 litre engines

8 Remove the locking pin, undo the mounting bolts and remove the tension roller assembly from the engine **(see illustration)**.

9 Prise off the cap, then undo the guide roller mounting bolt, and remove the roller **(see illustration)**.

10 Position the new guide roller, tighten the mounting bolt to the specified torque, and refit the cap.

11 Fit the new tensioner assembly, and tighten the mounting bolts to the specified torque. Reset the tensioner position as described in paragraph 6.

12 Fit the new belt ensuring that it is routed correctly **(see illustration)**.

13 With the belt in position, use the spanner to hold the tensioner in position while the 4 mm Allen key is removed, then carefully release the spanner anti-clockwise so the belt will automatically become tensioned.

14 Refit the wheel arch liner/splash shield and roadwheel, and then lower the vehicle to the ground. Tighten the roadwheel bolts to the specified torque.

13 Seat belt check

1 Carefully examine the seat belt webbing for cuts, or any signs of serious fraying or deterioration. If the belt is of the retractable type, pull the belt all the way out of the inertia reel, and examine the full extent of the webbing.

2 Fasten and unfasten the belt, ensuring

that the locking mechanism holds securely, and releases properly when intended. If the belt is of the retractable type, check also that the retracting mechanism operates correctly when the belt is released.

3 Check the security of all seat belt mountings and attachments that are accessible without removing any trim or other components.

14 Electrical systems check

1 Check the operation of all electrical equipment, ie, lights, direction indicators, horn, etc. Refer to the appropriate Sections of Chapter 12 for details if any of the circuits are found to be inoperative.

2 Note that brake light switch adjustment is described in Chapter 9, Section 18.

3 Visually check all accessible wiring connectors, harnesses and retaining clips for security, and for signs of chafing or damage. Rectify any faults found.

15 Exhaust system check

1 With the engine cold (at least an hour after the vehicle has been driven), check the complete exhaust system from the engine to the end of the tailpipe. The exhaust system is most easily checked with the vehicle raised on a hoist, or suitably supported on axle stands,

so that the exhaust components are readily visible and accessible.

2 Check the exhaust pipes and connections for evidence of leaks, severe corrosion and damage. Make sure that all brackets and mountings are in good condition, and that all relevant nuts and bolts are tight. Leakage at any of the joints or in other parts of the system will usually show up as a black sooty stain in the vicinity of the leak.

3 Rattles and other noises can often be traced to the exhaust system, especially the brackets and mountings. Try to move the pipes and silencers. If the components are able to come into contact with the body or suspension parts, secure the system with new mountings. Otherwise separate the joints (if possible) and twist the pipes as necessary to provide additional clearance.

16 Suspension and steering check

Front suspension and steering

1 Raise the front of the vehicle, and securely support it on axle stands (see *Jacking and vehicle support*).

2 Visually inspect the balljoint dust covers and the steering rack-and-pinion gaiters for splits, chafing or deterioration **(see illustrations)**. Any wear of these components will cause loss of lubricant, together with dirt and water entry, resulting in rapid deterioration of the balljoints or steering gear.

3 Check the power steering fluid hoses for chafing or deterioration, and the pipe and hose unions for fluid leaks. Also check for signs of fluid leakage under pressure from the steering gear rubber gaiters, which would indicate failed fluid seals within the steering gear.

4 Grasp the roadwheel at the 12 o'clock and 6 o'clock positions, and try to rock it **(see illustration)**. Very slight free play may be felt, but if the movement is appreciable, further investigation is necessary to determine the source. Continue rocking the wheel while an assistant depresses the footbrake. If the movement is now eliminated or significantly

16.2a Check the condition of the steering rack gaiters...

16.2b ... and the various balljoint dust covers (arrowed)

reduced, it is likely that the hub bearings are at fault. If the free play is still evident with the footbrake depressed, then there is wear in the suspension joints or mountings.

5 Now grasp the wheel at the 9 o'clock and 3 o'clock positions, and try to rock it as before. Any movement felt now may again be caused by wear in the hub bearings or the steering track rod balljoints. If the outer balljoint is worn, the visual movement will be obvious. If the inner joint is suspect, it can be felt by placing a hand over the rack-and-pinion rubber gaiter and gripping the track rod. If the wheel is now rocked, movement will be felt at the inner joint if wear has taken place.

6 Using a large screwdriver or flat bar, check for wear in the suspension mounting bushes by levering between the relevant suspension component and its attachment point. Some movement is to be expected, as the mountings are made of rubber, but excessive wear should be obvious. Also check the condition of any visible rubber bushes, looking for splits, cracks or contamination of the rubber.

7 With the vehicle standing on its wheels, have an assistant turn the steering wheel back-and-forth, about an eighth of a turn each way. There should be very little, if any, lost movement between the steering wheel and roadwheels. If this is not the case, closely observe the joints and mountings previously described. In addition, check the steering column universal joints for wear, and also check the rack-and-pinion steering gear itself.

Rear suspension

8 Chock the front wheels, then jack up the rear of the vehicle and support securely on axle stands (see *Jacking and vehicle support*).
9 Working as described previously for the front suspension, check the rear hub bearings, the suspension bushes and the shock absorber mountings for wear.

Shock absorber

10 Check for any signs of fluid leakage around the shock absorber body, or from the rubber gaiter around the piston rod. Should any fluid be noticed, the shock absorber is defective internally, and should be renewed.
Note: *Shock absorbers should always be renewed in pairs on the same axle.*

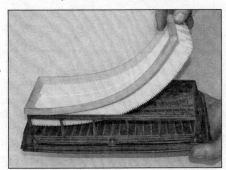
19.2 Lift the filter element from the housing cover

16.4 Grasp the wheel at the 6 o'clock and 12 o'clock positions

11 The efficiency of the shock absorber may be checked by bouncing the vehicle at each corner. Generally speaking, the body will return to its normal position and stop after being depressed. If it rises and returns on a rebound, the shock absorber is probably suspect. Also examine the shock absorber upper and lower mountings for any signs of wear.

17 Roadwheel bolt check

1 Where applicable, remove the wheel trims, and slacken the roadwheel bolts slightly.
2 Tighten the bolts to the specified torque, using a torque wrench.

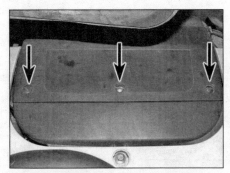
19.3 Undo the screws (arrowed) and detach the oil filler cap assembly

18 Air conditioning system check

A dealer or suitably-equipped repairer using dedicated test equipment must check the air conditioning system.

19 Air filter element renewal

Removal

1.9 litre models
1 Undo the 3 retaining screws, and remove the air filter housing cover **(see illustrations)**.
2 Lift out the air filter element and wipe clean the filter housing **(see illustration)**.

2.0 litre models
3 Undo the 2 screws and detach the engine oil filler cap from the air cleaner assembly **(see illustration)**.
4 Slacken the clamp and disconnect the air hose from the mass airflow sensor **(see illustration)**.
5 Disconnect the wiring plug from the mass airflow sensor.
6 Undo the 2 retaining screws and remove the upper part of the air cleaner housing **(see illustrations)**.
7 Noting its fitted location, remove the air filter element **(see illustration)**.

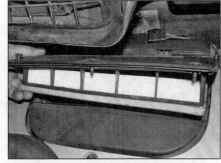
19.1b... and lift up the air filter cover

19.4 Slacken the clamp and disconnect the air hose

19.6a Undo the screws (arrowed)...

19.6b... and lift up the front of the air cleaner housing cover

19.7 Remove the air filter element

Refitting

8 Clean the inside of the air cleaner body and housing/cover, being careful not to get dirt into the inlet duct.

9 Fit the new filter element, making sure it is correctly located, securing it in position with the retaining screws.

10 The remainder of refitting is a reversal of removal.

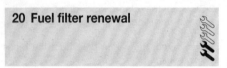

20 Fuel filter renewal

Caution: Do not allow dirt to enter the fuel system during this procedure.

Locking-ring filter assembly

1 Depress the release buttons and disconnect

the fuel pipes from the top of the filter. Take care not to damage the fuel lines as they are removed; cover the ends of the fuel lines to prevent any dirt ingress.

2 Disconnect the fuel heater wiring connector from the top of the filter housing, and the water sensor (where fitted).

3 Release the retaining clip and slide the fuel filter assembly upwards from the support bracket.

4 Rotate the locking ring anti-clockwise and remove the filter cover. Discard the O-ring seal.

5 Lift the filter element from the housing.

6 Clean the filter housing, then locate the new fuel filter in position.

7 Renew the O-ring seal, refit the filter cover (ensuring it's correctly aligned) and secure it with the locking ring.

8 Slide the filter assembly into place on the support bracket, then reconnect the fuel pipes

and wiring plugs. Prime the fuel system as described in Chapter 4A, Section 4.

Through-bolt filter assembly

9 Depress the release button and disconnect the fuel pipe from the top of the filter assembly (see illustration). Take care not to damage the fuel lines as they are removed; cover the ends of the fuel lines to prevent any dirt ingress.

10 Disconnect the fuel heater wiring connector from the top of the filter housing, and the water sensor (where fitted) (see illustration).

11 Release the retaining clip at the front edge of the bracket, then slide the fuel filter assembly upwards from the support bracket (see illustration).

12 Rotate the protective cover lockring (where fitted) anti-clockwise and remove the cover from the filter assembly (see illustrations).

13 Depress the release button and disconnect the remaining fuel pipe from the filter assembly. Plug the openings to prevent contamination.

14 With the fuel filter assembly removed from the vehicle, slacken and remove the retaining bolt from the centre of the top of the filter housing (see illustration).

15 Note the fitted position of the top of the filter housing in relation to the lower housing bowl, then release the lower bowl to access the filter. Remove the fuel filter and recover the fuel filter sealing ring, a new seal will be required for refitting.

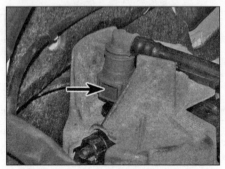

20.9 Depress the release button (arrowed) and disconnect the fuel pipe

20.10 Disconnect the heater wiring plug (arrowed)

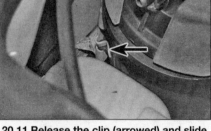

20.11 Release the clip (arrowed) and slide the filter housing upwards

20.12a Rotate the lockring anticlockwise...

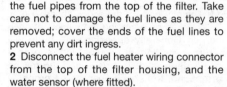

20.12b... and remove the protective cover

16 Fit the new filter into the filter housing bowl, then smear the new sealing ring with fuel and fit it to the housing **(see illustrations)**.
17 Align the top of the filter housing (in position, noted on removal) and fit the lower bowl to the top of the filter housing **(see illustration)**.
18 Fit a new seal to the retaining bolt and tighten it securely.
19 Where applicable, make sure the drain plug in the bottom of the fuel filter housing is tight.
20 Refit the filter assembly to its mounting bracket and reconnect the fuel line to the top of the housing, taking care not to damage the pipes. Refit the protective cover (where fitted), then reconnect the remaining fuel line.
21 Reconnect the fuel heater wiring connector to the top of the filter housing, and the water sensor wiring plug (where fitted).
22 Prime the fuel system as described in Chapter 4A, Section 4.

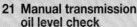
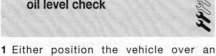

21 Manual transmission oil level check

1 Either position the vehicle over an inspection pit, or jack up the front and rear of the vehicle and support it on axle stands (see *Jacking and vehicle support*). The vehicle must be level for the check to be accurate. Refer to Chapter 7 for information on transmission identification.
2 Undo the retaining screws and remove the undertray from beneath the engine/transmission.
3 Clean the area around the filler/level plug on the end of the transmission, then slacken and remove the plug from the transmission **(see illustration)**. Check the condition of the filler plug seal, and obtain a new one if necessary.

1.9 litre models – PK5 and PK6 transmissions

Note: *This check can only be carried out by using the special Vauxhall tool/dipstick KM-6400 or Renault tool/dipstick BVi 1675. The dipstick is curved and its main section must be kept horizontal after inserting through the filler/level plug hole. There are two pairs of 'min' and 'max' level marks (A and B) on one*

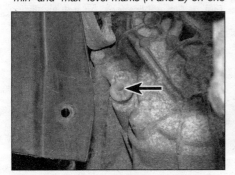

21.3 Transmission oil filler/level plug (arrowed)

20.14 Undo the central retaining bolt

20.16b Renew the sealing ring

side of the dipstick and a single pair (C) on the other (ie, six marks in all). The C marks must be used.
4 Insert the dipstick through the filler plug recess. Make sure the slot in the top of the dipstick bracket is located on the rib on the transmission housing **(see illustration)**.
5 Slide the dipstick out of the filler plug and check the oil level. Note the oil level on the end of the dipstick: it should be between the upper and lower marks **(see illustration)**. With the oil up to the maximum mark there will be approximately 2.4 litres in the transmission. With the oil up to the minimum mark there will be approximately 2.0 litres in the transmission. The target level is midway between the two.
6 Top-up the transmission oil level with the specified type of lubricant via the filler hole. Once the level is up to the correct level, refit the filler plug and sealing washer and tighten it

21.4 Insert the dipstick into the filler/level hole

20.16a Fit the new filter element

20.17 Align the top part of the filter housing with the lower part

securely. Where necessary, refit the undertray and securely tighten its retaining screws. Note that frequent need for topping-up indicates a leakage, possibly through an oil seal. The cause should be investigated and rectified.

2.0 litre models – PF6 transmission

7 The transmission oil level should be up to the lower edge of the filler/level plug aperture.
8 If necessary, top-up using the specified type of lubricant until the transmission oil level is correct. Fill the transmission until oil starts to flow out and allow excess oil to drain.
9 Once the transmission oil level is correct, refit the filler/level plug and tighten it securely.
10 Refit the engine undertray then lower the vehicle to the ground. Note that frequent need for topping-up indicates a leakage, possibly through an oil seal. The cause should be investigated and rectified.

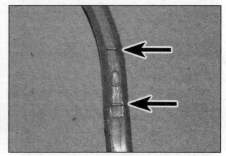

21.5 Maximum and minimum level marks (arrowed) on the side of the dipstick labelled C

23.2 Release the clips (arrowed) and lower the pollen filter from the housing

22 Hose and fluid leak check

1 Visually inspect the engine joint faces, gaskets and seals for any signs of water or oil leaks. Pay particular attention to the areas around the cylinder head cover, cylinder head, oil filter and sump joint faces. Bear in mind that, over a period of time, some very slight seepage from these areas is to be expected – what you are really looking for is any indication of a serious leak. Should a leak be found, renew the offending gasket or oil seal by referring to the appropriate Chapters in this manual.

2 Also check the security and condition of all the engine-related pipes and hoses, and all braking system pipes and hoses. Ensure that all cable-ties or securing clips are in place, and in good condition. Clips that are broken or missing can lead to chafing of the hoses, pipes or wiring, which could cause more serious problems in the future.

3 Carefully check the radiator hoses and heater hoses along their entire length. Renew any hose that is cracked, swollen or deteriorated. Cracks will show up better if the hose is squeezed. Pay close attention to the hose clips that secure the hoses to the cooling system components. Hose clips can pinch and puncture hoses, resulting in cooling system leaks.

4 Inspect all the cooling system components (hoses, joint faces, etc) for leaks. Where any problems are found on system components, renew the component or gasket with reference to Chapter 3.

5 With the vehicle raised, inspect the fuel tank and filler neck for punctures, cracks

and other damage. The connection between the filler neck and tank is especially critical. Sometimes a rubber filler neck or connecting hose will leak due to loose retaining clamps or deteriorated rubber.

6 Carefully check all rubber hoses and metal fuel lines leading away from the fuel tank. Check for loose connections, deteriorated hoses, crimped lines, and other damage. Pay particular attention to the vent pipes and hoses, which often loop up around the filler neck and can become blocked or crimped. Follow the lines to the front of the vehicle, carefully inspecting them all the way. Renew damaged sections as necessary. Similarly, whilst the vehicle is raised, take the opportunity to inspect all underbody brake fluid pipes and hoses.

7 From within the engine compartment, check the security of all fuel, vacuum and brake hose attachments and pipe unions, and inspect all hoses for kinks, chafing and deterioration.

8 Where applicable, check the condition of the power steering fluid pipes and hoses.

23 Pollen filter renewal

1 The pollen filter is located on the underside of the bonnet. It is fitted in the air inlet housing, and filters the air to ensure it is completely clean before entering the passenger compartment.

2 Open the bonnet, release the 2 clips and remove the element from the air intake housing **(see illustration)**.

3 Refitting is a reversal of removal.

24 Road test

Instruments and electrical equipment

1 Check the operation of all instruments and electrical equipment.

2 Make sure that all instruments read correctly, and switch on all electrical equipment in turn, to check that it functions properly.

Steering and suspension

3 Check for any abnormalities in the steering, suspension, handling or road 'feel'.

4 Drive the vehicle, and check that there are no unusual vibrations or noises.

5 Check that the steering feels positive, with no excessive 'sloppiness', or roughness, and check for any suspension noises when cornering and driving over bumps.

Drivetrain

6 Check the performance of the engine, clutch, transmission and driveshafts.

7 Listen for any unusual noises from the engine, clutch and transmission.

8 Make sure that the engine runs smoothly when idling, and that there is no hesitation when accelerating.

9 Check that, where applicable, the clutch action is smooth and progressive, that the drive is taken up smoothly, and that the pedal travel is not excessive. Also listen for any noises when the clutch pedal is depressed.

10 Check that all gears can be engaged smoothly without noise, and that the gear lever action is smooth and not abnormally vague or 'notchy'.

11 Listen for a metallic clicking sound from the front of the vehicle, as the vehicle is driven slowly in a circle with the steering on full-lock. Carry out this check in both directions. If a clicking noise is heard, this indicates wear in a driveshaft joint (see Chapter 8).

Braking system

12 Make sure that the vehicle does not pull to one side when braking, and that the wheels do not lock when braking hard.

13 Check that there is no vibration through the steering when braking.

14 Check that the handbrake operates correctly, without excessive movement of the lever, and that it holds the vehicle stationary on a slope.

15 Test the operation of the brake servo unit as follows. Depress the footbrake four or five times to exhaust the vacuum, and then start the engine. As the engine starts, there should be a noticeable 'give' in the brake pedal as vacuum builds-up. Allow the engine to run for at least two minutes, and then switch it off. If the brake pedal is now depressed again, it should be possible to detect a hiss from the servo as the pedal is depressed. After about four or five applications, no further hissing should be heard, and the pedal should feel considerably harder.

25.2a Use a coin...

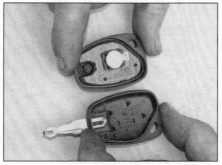

25.2b... to prise apart the remote control housing

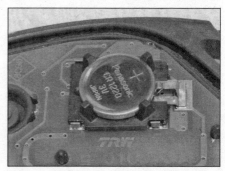

25.4 Fit the battery with the negative side as noted on removal

Every 2 years

25 Remote control battery renewal

1 The battery must be renewed when the range of the remote control starts to become reduced. We consider it prudent to renew the battery every 2 years regardless of its range.
2 The battery cover may be held by a screw, or simply clipped into place. Undo the screw (where applicable), then insert a coin into the slot provided, and prise the cover away **(see illustrations)**.

3 Note its fitted position, then carefully remove the battery.
4 Insert the new battery and refit the cover **(see illustration)**. Where applicable, refit the retaining screw.

Every 36 000 miles or 4 years

26 Timing belt renewal – 1.9 litre engines

Refer to Chapter 2A, Section 5.

27 Brake fluid renewal

⚠ *Warning: Brake hydraulic fluid can harm your eyes and damage painted surfaces, so use extreme caution when handling and pouring it. Do not use fluid that has been standing open for some time, as it absorbs moisture from the air. Excess moisture can cause a dangerous loss of braking effectiveness.*

1 The procedure is similar to that for the bleeding of the hydraulic system as described in Chapter 9, Section 2, except that the brake fluid reservoir should be emptied by siphoning, using a clean poultry baster or similar before starting, and allowance should be made for the old fluid to be expelled when bleeding a section of the circuit.
2 Working as described in Chapter 9, open the first bleed screw in the sequence, and pump the brake pedal gently until nearly all the old fluid has been emptied from the master cylinder reservoir. Top-up to the MAXI level with new fluid, and continue pumping until only the new fluid remains in the reservoir, and new fluid can be seen emerging from the bleed screw. Tighten the screw, and top the reservoir level up to the MAXI

level line. **Note:** *Vauxhall and Renault recommend that, where possible, a pressure bleeding method should be used, as described in Chapter 9. If the manual (basic) method described above is used, and the results are less than satisfactory, try the pressure-bleeding method.*
3 Work through all the remaining bleed screws in the sequence until new fluid can be seen at all of them. Be careful to keep the master cylinder reservoir topped-up to above the MINI level at all times, or air may enter the system and greatly increase the length of the task.
4 When the operation is complete, check that all bleed screws are securely tightened, and that their dust caps are refitted. Wash off all traces of spilt fluid, and recheck the master cylinder reservoir fluid level.
5 Check the operation of the brakes before taking the vehicle on the road.
6 Dispose safely of the used brake fluid with reference to *General repair procedures*.

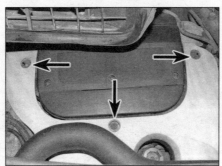

28.2a Prise out the caps, undo the screws (arrowed)...

28 Coolant renewal

⚠ *Warning: Wait until the engine is cold before starting this procedure. Do not allow antifreeze to come in contact with your skin, or with the painted surfaces of the vehicle. Rinse off spills immediately with plenty of water. Never leave antifreeze lying around in an open container, or in a puddle in the driveway or on the garage floor. Children and pets are attracted by its sweet smell, but antifreeze can be fatal if ingested.*
Note: *The manufacturers do not specify renewal intervals for the coolant on some models, but it is advisable to drain and refill the system every four years to ensure that the corrosion inhibiting properties of the coolant are maintained.*

Cooling system draining

1 With the engine completely cold, remove the expansion tank filler cap. Turn the cap anti-clockwise, wait until any pressure remaining in the system is released, then unscrew it and lift it off.
2 On 1.9 litre engines, prise out the caps, undo the 3 retaining screws, remove the plastic cover from the top of the engine, then unclip and remove the air intake ducting from the air cleaner housing **(see illustrations)**.
3 On 2.0 litre engines, remove the air cleaner assembly as described in Chapter 4A.
4 On 2.0 litre models with the M9R 630 engine (water-cooled turbocharger), release the clip

28.2b... and remove the plastic cover

28.6 Release the clamp (arrowed) and disconnect the radiator bottom hose

28.7a Coolant bleed screws for the 2.0 litre models are located on the heater hose beneath the servo (arrowed)...

28.7b... on the heater hose to the right-hand side of the servo (arrowed)...

28.7c... and on the thermostat housing (arrowed)

and remove the air hose from the turbocharger air intake pipe. Unclip the wastegate vacuum pipe as the hose is withdrawn.

5 Raise the front of the vehicle and support it securely on axle stands (see *Jacking and vehicle support*). Undo the fasteners and remove the engine undertray (where fitted).

6 Unclip the lower radiator hose from the cooling fan shroud, then position a suitable container beneath the radiator bottom hose connection. Slacken the hose clip, pull off the hose and allow the coolant to drain into the container **(see illustration)**.

7 To assist draining, open the cooling system bleed screws. These are located in the thermostat/coolant housing, turbocharger coolant hose (M9R 630 engine only) and heater hoses, depending on engine type **(see illustrations)**.

8 Refit the bottom hose. Use a new hose clip if necessary, and reclip the hose to the fan shroud.

Cooling system filling

9 Before attempting to fill the cooling system, make sure that all hoses and clips are in good condition, and that the clips are tight. Note that an antifreeze mixture must be used all year round, to prevent corrosion of the engine components.

10 Remove the expansion tank filler cap.

11 Open the cooling system bleed screws (see paragraph 7).

12 Place a container under the vehicle, below the expansion tank, to catch any coolant that may be spilt during the topping-up procedure. Also place a wad of rags around the expansion tank.

13 Slowly fill the system until the coolant level reaches the top of the expansion tank filler neck.

14 Where applicable, close the bleed screws when coolant free from air bubbles emerges.

Close the screws in sequence, starting with the lowest screw in the system.

15 Refit the expansion tank cap.

16 Refit the engine cover, air intake ducting and air cleaner assembly as applicable.

17 Switch off the air conditioning (where applicable), and set the heating to full heat and airflow.

18 Start the engine, and run it at a fast idle speed (do not exceed 2500 rpm) until the cooling fan cuts in.

19 Stop the engine and check the coolant level, which should be up to the MAXI mark on the side of the tank. Check that the expansion tank filler cap is tight.

20 Allow the engine to cool, and then recheck the coolant level with reference to *Weekly checks*. Top-up the level if necessary and refit the expansion tank filler cap. Refit the engine undertray, and lower the vehicle to the ground.

Antifreeze mixture

21 The antifreeze should always be renewed at the specified intervals. This is necessary not only to maintain the antifreeze properties, but also to prevent corrosion that would otherwise occur as the corrosion inhibitors become progressively less effective.

22 Always use Vauxhall or Renault long-life coolant antifreeze, which is orange in colour and silicate-free. The quantity of antifreeze is recommended at a mixture of 50% antifreeze and 50% clear tap water.

23 Before adding antifreeze, the cooling system should be completely drained, preferably flushed, and all hoses checked for condition and security.

24 After filling with antifreeze, a label should be attached to the expansion tank, stating the type and concentration of antifreeze used, and the date installed. Any subsequent topping-up should be made with the same type and concentration of antifreeze.

25 Dispose safely of the used coolant with reference to *General repair procedures*.

Caution: Do not use engine antifreeze in the windscreen/tailgate washer system, as it will cause damage to the vehicle paintwork. A screenwash additive should be added to the washer system in the quantities stated on the bottle.

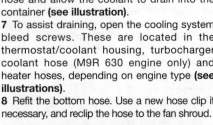
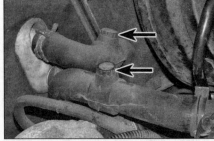

28.7d Coolant bleed screws for the 1.9-litre models are located on the heater hoses (arrowed)...

28.7e... and on the thermostat housing (arrowed)

Chapter 2 Part A:
1.9 litre engine in-car repair procedures

Contents

Degrees of difficulty

| **Easy,** suitable for novice with little experience 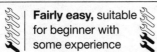 | **Fairly easy,** suitable for beginner with some experience | **Fairly difficult,** suitable for competent DIY mechanic | **Difficult,** suitable for experienced DIY mechanic | **Very difficult,** suitable for expert DIY or professional |

Specifications

General

Type	Four-cylinder, in-line, 8-valve single overhead camshaft, direct common-rail injection
Designation	F9Q 760 and 762
Bore	80.0 mm
Stroke.	93.0 mm
Capacity.	1870 cc
Compression ratio	18.3:1
Firing order.	1-3-4-2 (No 1 cylinder at flywheel end of engine)
Direction of crankshaft rotation	Clockwise, viewed from timing belt end

Output:
Power:

F9Q 760	74 kW @ 3500 rpm
F9Q 762	60 kW @ 3500 rpm

Torque:

F9Q 760	240 Nm @ 2000 rpm
F9Q 762	190 Nm @ 2000 rpm

Valve clearances (engine cold)

Inlet.	0.15 to 0.25 mm
Exhaust.	0.35 to 0.45 mm

Timing belt tension value

Pretension	95 ± 3 Hz
Tension	90 ± 3 Hz

Camshaft

Drive	Toothed belt
Endfloat	0.045 to 0.135 mm

Piston

Protrusion	0.56 ± 0.06 mm

Lubrication system

Minimum oil pressure at 80°C:
    At 1000 rpm . . . . 1.2 bars
    At 3500 rpm . . . . 3.5 bars
Oil pump clearances:
    Gear-to-body:
        Minimum . . . . 0.10 mm
        Maximum . . . . 0.24 mm
    Gear endfloat:
        Minimum . . . . 0.020 mm
        Maximum . . . . 0.085 mm

Torque wrench settings

	Nm	lbf ft
Auxiliary belt tensioner	44	32
Auxiliary belt guide roller (air conditioned models only)	21	15
Camshaft bearing cap beam	20	15
Camshaft sprocket bolt	60	44
Connecting rod (big-end) cap bolts:*		
Stage 1	20	15
Stage 2	Angle-tighten a further 40° ± 6°	
Crankshaft pulley bolt:*		
Stage 1	20	15
Stage 2	Angle-tighten a further 115° ± 15°	
Cylinder head bolts:*		
Stage 1	30	22
Stage 2	Angle-tighten a further 230°	
Cylinder head cover bolts:		
Stage 1 – centre bolt	12	9
Stage 2 – two outer bolts	12	9
Stage 3 – retighten centre bolt	12	9
Engine/transmission mountings:		
Right-hand engine mounting:		
Mounting bracket-to-cylinder head bracket bolts	62	46
Engine stabiliser	105	77
Engine damping block to inner wing	44	32
Engine damping block to mounting bracket	44	32
Mounting support bracket to cylinder head	35	26
Left-hand transmission mounting:		
Mounting stud nut	44	32
Rubber mounting bracket-to-body bolts	62	46
Rear mounting bracket/tie-rod:		
Tie-rod link-to-subframe bolt	105	77
Tie-rod link to mounting bracket	180	133
Mounting bracket-to-sump bolts	62	46
Exhaust manifold nut	28	21
Flywheel bolts*	55	41
Front crossmember	44	32
Fuel pump rear bracket	25	18
Fuel pump sprocket nut	50	37
Intake manifold nut	28	21
Main bearing caps (cap tightening order 3, 4, 2, 5, 1)	65	48
Oil level sensor	30	22
Oil pressure switch	38	28
Oil pump bolts	24	18
Roadwheel bolts	140	103
Sump bolts:		
Stage 1	8	6
Stage 2	15	11
Sump drain plug	20	15
Timing belt tensioner nut	50	37
Timing belt tensioner plate bolts	10	7
Vacuum pump bolt	23	17

* New nuts/bolts must be used

1 General information

How to use this Chapter

This Part of Chapter 2 is devoted to in-car repair procedures for the 1.9 litre engine. Similar information covering the 2.0 litre engine will be found in Chapter 2B. All procedures concerning engine removal and refitting, and engine block/cylinder head overhaul can be found in Chapter 2C.

Most of the operations included in this Chapter are based on the assumption that the engine is still installed in the car. Therefore, if this information is being used during a complete engine overhaul, with the engine already removed, many of the steps included here will not apply.

Engine description

The engine is of four-cylinder, in-line, single overhead camshaft type, mounted transversely at the front of the vehicle with the transmission bolted to the left-hand side.

The crankshaft is supported in five shell-type main bearings. Thrustwashers are fitted to No 2 main bearing to control crankshaft endfloat.

The connecting rods are attached to the crankshaft by horizontally split shell-type big-end bearings and to the pistons by gudgeon pins. The gudgeon pins are fully-floating and are retained by circlips. The aluminium alloy pistons are of the slipper type and are fitted with three piston rings: two compression rings and a scraper-type oil control ring.

The single overhead camshaft is mounted in five plain bearings machined directly in the aluminium alloy cylinder head and is driven by the crankshaft via a toothed timing belt.

The camshaft operates the valves via inverted bucket-type followers, which operate in bores machined directly in the cylinder head. Valve clearance adjustment is by different thickness followers. The inlet and exhaust valves are mounted vertically in the cylinder head and are each closed by a single valve spring.

The fuel injection pump is driven by the timing belt and is described in further detail in Chapter 4A.

A semi-closed crankcase ventilation system is employed and crankcase fumes are drawn from an oil separator on the cast iron cylinder block and passed via a hose (and in certain cases, a second oil separator) to the inlet tract (see Chapter 4B for further details).

The lubrication system is of the full-flow, pressure-feed type. Oil is drawn from the sump by a chain-driven gear-type oil pump located beneath the crankshaft. Engine oil is fed through an externally-mounted oil filter to the main oil gallery feeding the crankshaft and camshaft. Oil spray jets are fitted to the cylinder block to supply oil to the underside of

the pistons. Certain models are fitted with an oil cooler mounted on the cylinder block.

Operations with engine in car

The following operations can be carried out without having to remove the engine from the vehicle:
a) Removal and refitting of the cylinder head.
b) Removal and refitting of the timing belt and sprockets.
c) Renewal of the camshaft oil seals.
d) Removal and refitting of the camshaft.
e) Removal and refitting of the sump.
f) Removal and refitting of the connecting rods and pistons.*
g) Removal and refitting of the oil pump.
h) Renewal of the crankshaft oil seals.
i) Renewal of the engine mountings.
* Note: Although the operation marked with an asterisk can be carried out with the engine in the vehicle after removal of the sump, it is better for the engine to be removed in the interests of cleanliness and improved access. For this reason, the procedure is described in Chapter 2C.

2 Compression and leakdown tests – description and interpretation

Compression test

Note: A compression tester specifically designed for diesel engines must be used for this test, because of the higher pressures involved.

1 When engine performance is down, or if misfiring occurs which cannot be attributed to a fault in the fuel system, a compression test can provide diagnostic clues as to the engine's condition. If the test is performed regularly it can give warning of trouble before any other symptoms become apparent.

2 The tester is connected to an adapter that screws into the glow plug or injector hole (see illustration). It is unlikely to be worthwhile buying such a tester for occasional use, but it may be possible to borrow or hire one – if not, have the test performed by a garage.

3 Unless specific instructions to the contrary are supplied with the tester, observe the following points:
a) The battery must be in a good state of charge, the air filter must be clean and the engine should be at normal operating temperature.
b) All the injectors or glow plugs should be removed before starting the test. If removing the injectors, also remove the fire seal washers (which must be renewed when the injectors are refitted – see Chapter 4A), otherwise they may be blown out.
c) Where applicable, it is advisable to disconnect the stop solenoid on the pump to reduce the amount of fuel discharged as the engine is cranked.

2.2 Carrying out a compression test

4 The actual compression pressures measured are not as important as the balance between cylinders.

5 The cause of poor compression is less easy to establish on a diesel engine than on a petrol engine. The effect of introducing oil into the cylinders ('wet' testing) is not conclusive, because there is a risk that the oil will sit in the swirl chamber or in the recess on the piston crown instead of passing to the rings. However, the following can be used as a rough guide to diagnosis.

6 All cylinders should produce very similar pressures; any cylinders that have a great difference indicates the existence of a fault. Note that the compression should build-up quickly in a healthy engine; low compression on the first stroke, followed by gradually increasing pressure on successive strokes, indicates worn piston rings. A low compression reading on the first stroke, which does not build-up during successive strokes, indicates leaking valves or a blown head gasket (a cracked head could also be the cause).

7 A low reading from two adjacent cylinders is almost certainly due to the head gasket having blown between them.

Leakdown test

8 A leakdown test measures the rate at which compressed air fed into the cylinder is lost. It is an alternative to a compression test and in many ways it is better, since the escaping air provides easy identification of where pressure loss is occurring (piston rings, valves or head gasket).

9 The equipment needed for leakdown testing is unlikely to be available to the home mechanic. If poor compression is suspected, have the test performed by a suitably-equipped garage.

3 Top Dead Centre (TDC) for No 1 piston – locating

Caution: Timing pins are intended SOLELY for the purpose of checking the position of the crankshaft during various engine overhaul procedures. DO NOT use them as locking tools to prevent crankshaft rotation while the pulley or flywheel bolts are unscrewed or tightened.

3.4 Remove the blanking plug from the cylinder block

1 Top Dead Centre (TDC) is the highest point in the cylinder that each piston reaches as the crankshaft turns. Each piston reaches TDC at the end of the compression stroke and again at the end of the exhaust stroke; however, for the purpose of timing the engine, TDC refers to the position of No 1 piston at the end of its compression stroke. No 1 piston is at the flywheel end of the engine.

2 When No 1 piston is at TDC, the timing mark on the camshaft sprocket should be aligned with the pointer on the timing belt outer cover (the sprocket mark can be viewed through the cut-out in the cover, below the pointer). Additionally, a crankshaft positioning pin (Vauxhall tool no KM-6031 or Renault tool MOT 1054) can be inserted through a hole in the cylinder block into a cut-out in the crankshaft.

3 To align the timing marks, the crankshaft must be turned. This should be done by using a spanner on the crankshaft pulley bolt. Improved access to the pulley bolt can be obtained by jacking up the front right-hand corner of the vehicle and removing the roadwheel and the wheel arch lower liner (secured by screws). Unclip the washer hose from the support clip (where fitted). If desired, to enable the engine to be turned more easily, remove the glow plugs (Chapter 5) or the fuel injectors (Chapter 4A).

4 The crankshaft position should be checked by inserting a timing pin – Vauxhall tool KM-6031 or Renault tool MOT 1054 **(see Tool Tip)**. To do this, unscrew the blanking plug from the front left-hand end of the cylinder block, next to the base of the oil level dipstick tube **(see illustration)**.

> **TOOL TiP** *If the special tool mentioned in this Section is not available, an 8 mm diameter rod or drill bit can be used instead. On some engines, however, an 8 mm diameter rod may be too slack a fit in the cylinder block plug aperture for the crankshaft position to be determined accurately – it will therefore be necessary in such cases to have a stepped pin made up, with an 8 mm diameter at its tip to engage in the crankshaft slot and a larger diameter as necessary to fit precisely in the cylinder block aperture.*

5 Prise out the caps, unscrew the 3 retaining nuts, and withdraw the engine sound-insulating cover **(see illustration)**.

6 Check that the timing mark on the camshaft sprocket is aligned with the hole on the timing belt outer cover **(see illustration)**. The engine is now positioned with No 1 piston at TDC on its compression stroke.

7 Turn the engine slightly anti-clockwise (against the normal direction of rotation), so that the camshaft sprocket is half a tooth out of alignment with the cover pointer.

8 Insert the timing pin fully into the hole in the front of the engine, then carefully turn the engine clockwise, keeping light pressure on the end of the timing pin. At the TDC position, the pin should enter a slot in the crankshaft web, and the engine should be locked in position (rock the engine very slightly backwards or forwards to achieve engagement). In this position, the camshaft sprocket marks should also come into alignment **(see illustrations)**.

9 Once in place it should be impossible to turn the crankshaft – if the crankshaft will still move to-and-fro slightly, then the timing pin has entered the balance hole instead of the timing slot. **Note:** *Do not attempt to rotate the engine whilst the timing pin is in place. If the engine is to be left in this state for a long period of time, it is a good idea to place warning notices inside the vehicle and in the engine compartment. This will reduce the possibility of the engine being accidentally cranked on the starter motor, which will cause severe damage if done with the timing pin in place.*

10 On completion, remove the timing pin and refit all removed components.

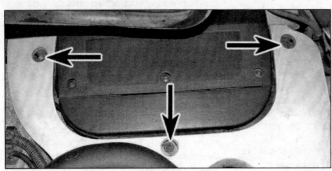

3.5 Prise out the caps, undo the nuts (arrowed) and remove the cover from the engine

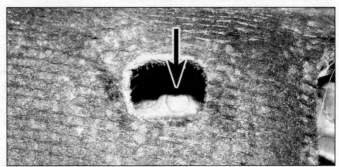

3.6 The circular mark on the camshaft sprocket (arrowed) should be visible through the hole in the timing belt cover

3.8a Insert a suitable drill bit...

3.8b... or a purpose-made timing pin to check the crankshaft position

3.8c When the crankshaft is at TDC, the pin (arrowed) will go fully home

4.3 Undo the coolant heater bracket nut/ bolt (arrowed)

4.4 Unclip the wiring harness (arrowed) from the cylinder head cover

4.10 Measure the valve clearances using a feeler gauge

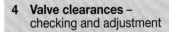

4 Valve clearances – checking and adjustment

Note: *This operation is not part of the maintenance schedule. It should be undertaken if noise from the valve gear becomes evident, or if loss of performance gives cause to suspect that the clearances may be incorrect. A new cylinder head cover gasket may be required on refitting.*

Checking

1 Prise out the caps, undo the nuts and withdraw the engine sound-insulating cover.
2 Remove the air cleaner housing as described in Chapter 4A.
3 Undo the nut/bolt and detach the coolant heater support bracket from the engine lifting eye **(see illustration)**.
4 Disconnect the wiring plugs from the fuel injectors, and the camshaft sensor, then unclip the wiring loom from the cylinder head cover **(see illustration)**.
5 Remove the glow plugs as described in Chapter 5.
6 During the following procedure, the crankshaft must be turned, using a spanner on the crankshaft pulley bolt. Improved access to the pulley bolt can be obtained by jacking up the front right-hand corner of the vehicle (see *Jacking and vehicle support*) and removing the roadwheel and the wheel arch lower liner.
7 Unscrew the bolts from the cylinder head cover and withdraw the cover from the engine. Recover the gasket.
8 Draw the valve positions on a piece of paper, numbering them 1 to 8 from the flywheel end of the engine. Identify them as inlet or exhaust (ie, 1I, 2E, 3I, 4E, 5I, 6E, 7I, 8E).
9 Turn the crankshaft until the valves of No 1 cylinder (flywheel end) are 'rocking' – the exhaust valve will be closing and the inlet valve will be opening. The piston of No 4 cylinder will be at the top of its compression stroke, with both valves fully closed – the clearances for both valves of No 4 cylinder may now be checked.
10 Insert a feeler gauge of the correct thickness (see Specifications) between the cam lobe and the cam follower and check

that it is a firm sliding fit **(see illustration)**. If it is not, use the feeler gauges to ascertain the exact clearance and record this for use when calculating the new follower thickness required. Note that the inlet and exhaust valve clearances are different (see Specifications).
11 With No 4 cylinder valve clearances checked, turn the engine through half a turn so that No 3 valves are 'rocking', then check the valve clearances of No 2 cylinder in the same way. Similarly check the remaining valve clearances in the sequence shown **(see illustration)**. **Note:** *There are NO shims fitted to the cam followers. If the valve clearance is not within tolerance the complete cam follower (bucket) will need to be substituted with one of the correct thickness. A Vauxhall or Renault parts department can supply 25 different thicknesses of cam followers to suit your requirements.*

Adjustment

Note: *A micrometer will be required for this operation.*
12 Remove the camshaft as described in Section 8, and lift out the followers. Note the fitted position of the followers to calculate the correct thickness for refitting.
13 Where a valve clearance differs from the specified value, then the follower for that valve must be substituted with a thinner or thicker one accordingly **(see illustration)**. **Note:** *It is not permissible to swap the followers around between valves.*
14 The thickness of follower required is calculated as follows. If the measured clearance is less than specified, subtract the measured clearance from the specified clearance and deduct the result from the thickness of the existing follower. For example:

Sample calculation – clearance too small

Clearance measured (A) = 0.15 mm
Desired clearance (B) = 0.20 mm
Difference (B – A) = 0.05 mm
Follower thickness fitted = 3.70 mm
Follower required = 3.70 – 0.05 = 3.65 mm
15 If the measured clearance is greater than specified, subtract the specified clearance from the measured clearance and add the

VALVES ROCKING ON CYLINDER	CHECK CLEARANCE ON CYLINDER
1	4
3	2
4	1
2	3

4.11 Valve clearance checking sequence

result to the thickness of the existing follower. For example:

Sample calculation – clearance too big

Clearance measured (A) = 0.50 mm
Desired clearance (B) = 0.40 mm
Difference (A – B) = 0.10 mm
Follower thickness fitted = 3.45 mm
Follower required = 3.45 + 0.10 = 3.55 mm

Refitting

16 When all followers have been selected

4.13 Check the follower thickness using a micrometer

5.5 Undo the auxiliary drivebelt tensioner bolt (arrowed)

with the correct thickness, refit the followers and camshaft as described in Section 8. **Note:** *When the camshaft is fitted back in position, check through the valve clearances again to make sure they are within the tolerance given, before refitting all other components.*

17 Refitting is a reversal of removal, but where applicable carry out the following procedures:
  a) *If not already done, remove the spanner from the crankshaft pulley bolt and the timing pin from the crankshaft.*
  b) *Refit the cylinder head cover, using a new gasket where necessary – tighten the cover retaining bolts evenly to the specified torque wrench setting.*
  c) *Refit the glow plugs (Chapter 5).*
  d) *Reconnect any hoses that were moved for access on removal. If fuel lines were disconnected, reconnect them, then prime and bleed the fuel system as described in Chapter 4A.*
  e) *Refit the engine sound insulating cover.*

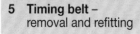

5 Timing belt –
removal and refitting

Note: *Vauxhall and Renault specify the use of special electronic tools to correctly set the timing belt tension. If access to this equipment cannot be obtained, an approximate setting can be achieved using the method described below. If this method described is used, the tension must be checked using the special electronic tool at the earliest possible*

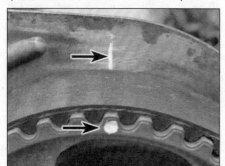

5.12a Make a mark on the timing belt inner cover to align with the mark on the camshaft sprocket (arrowed)

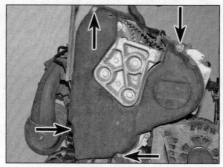

5.11 Timing belt outer cover bolts (arrowed)

opportunity. Do not drive the vehicle over large distances, or use high engine speeds, until the belt tension is known to be correct. Refer to a dealer for advice.
Note: *The timing belt should be renewed whenever it is disturbed; never refit a belt that has already been used.*

Removal

1 Disconnect the battery negative terminal as described in Chapter 5.
2 Apply the handbrake, then jack up the front of the vehicle and support it on axle stands (see *Jacking and vehicle support*). Remove the right-hand front roadwheel, the undo the retaining screws and remove the engine undercover and the splash shield from the right-hand end of the engine. Release the washer hose from the retaining clips (where fitted).
3 Prise out the caps, unscrew the retaining nuts/screws and withdraw the engine sound-insulating cover.
4 Position an engine hoist, or an engine lifting beam across the engine compartment and attach the jib to the right-hand engine lifting eyelet. Raise the lifting gear to take up the slack, so that it is just supporting the weight of the engine.
5 Remove the auxiliary drivebelt as described

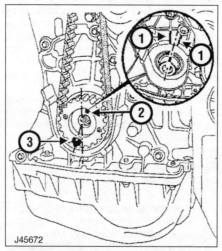

J45672

5.12b The crankshaft groove (2) should be between the ribs (1), and the timing mark (3) should be one tooth offset at TDC

in Chapter 1, then undo the bolt and remove the auxiliary belt tensioner **(see illustration)**. On models with air conditioning, undo the bolt and remove the guide roller from above the compressor.
6 Release the wiring harness and fuel hose from the engine damping block bracket at the right-hand end of the cylinder head.
7 Unclip the power steering reservoir from the front panel.
8 Undo the three bolts securing the right-hand engine mounting bracket to the cylinder head bracket. Similarly, undo the bolts securing the rubber mounting to the body, and the engine stabiliser bolt, with reference to Section 14. Release the relevant cable clips and remove the complete mounting assembly.
9 Using a socket and extension bar, slacken the crankshaft pulley bolt. Hold the crankshaft stationary while the bolt is unscrewed by engaging a screwdriver with the flywheel ring gear teeth through the opening at the lower rear of the cylinder block. Unscrew the bolt and remove the washer and crankshaft pulley.
10 Temporarily refit the crankshaft pulley bolt. Turn the crankshaft so that No 1 piston is at TDC on the compression stroke and insert a timing pin to check the crankshaft position, as described in Section 3.
11 Unscrew the securing bolts and withdraw the outer timing belt cover **(see illustration)**.
12 With No 1 piston at TDC on the compression stroke (see paragraph 10), note the position of any timing marks on the camshaft, fuel injection pump and crankshaft sprockets. Make a mark on the timing belt inner cover in line with the mark on the camshaft sprocket **(see illustrations)**.
13 Loosen the retaining nut, and then push back the tensioner to relieve the tension on the timing belt **(see illustration)**. Retighten the nut.
14 Release the belt from the camshaft sprocket first, then from the fuel injection pump sprocket, idler pulley and crankshaft sprocket, and remove it from the engine.
15 **Do not** turn the camshaft or the crankshaft whilst the timing belt is removed, as there is a risk of piston-to-valve contact. If it is necessary to turn the camshaft for any reason, before doing so, remove the timing

5.13 Slacken the timing belt tensioner nut (arrowed)

pin and turn the crankshaft anti-clockwise (viewed from the timing belt end of the engine) by a quarter-turn to position all four pistons halfway down their bores.

16 Clean the sprockets, idler pulley and tensioner and wipe them dry – **do not** apply excessive amounts of solvent to the idler pulley and tensioner otherwise the bearing lubricant may be removed. Also clean the timing belt inner cover and the related surfaces of the cylinder head and block.

Refitting

17 Ensure that the crankshaft is at the TDC position for No 1 cylinder, with the timing pin in place to ensure complete accuracy, as described previously. If the pistons have been positioned halfway down their bores (see paragraph 15), turn the crankshaft clockwise (viewed from the timing belt end of the engine) until the timing pin can be refitted. To enable the tensioner to be adjusted, screw a 6 mm bolt into the threaded hole provided in the timing belt inner cover. The bolt will bear against the rear of the tensioner pulley and enable adjustments of the belt tension to be made **(see illustration)**.

18 Where applicable, align any markings on the belt with the timing marks on the crankshaft and camshaft sprockets, ensuring that the running direction arrows (where applicable) on the belt are pointing clockwise (viewed from the timing belt end of the engine) **(see illustrations)**. Fit the timing belt over the crankshaft sprocket first, followed by the coolant pump sprocket, fuel injection pump sprocket, camshaft sprocket and tensioner.

19 Check that all the timing marks are still aligned and remove all slack from the timing belt by tightening the bolt fitted to the timing belt inner cover.

20 The belt tension must now be checked – this can be set or checked accurately **only** by using the manufacturer's special tools to pretension the belt and measure its vibration frequency. If this equipment is not available, set the belt's tension as carefully as possible **(see Haynes Hint)**, then take the vehicle to a dealer as soon as possible for the tension to be checked by qualified personnel using the special equipment. Do not take the vehicle on any long journeys or rev the engine to high speeds until the timing belt's tension has been checked and is known to be correct.

21 If the adjustment is incorrect, the tensioner will have to be repositioned by loosening the tensioner nut and by screwing the bolt fitted to the timing belt inner cover in or out.

22 With the correct tension applied, retighten the tensioner nut to the specified torque. This torque is critical, since if the nut were to come loose, considerable engine damage would result. Loosen the bolt fitted to the timing belt inner cover so that it no longer bears on the tensioner roller bracket.

5.17 An M6 bolt (arrowed) fitted to the timing belt tensioner backplate to adjust the tension

5.18a Align the mark on the new belt with the mark on the crankshaft sprocket...

5.18b... and the camshaft sprocket

5.18c Ensure the arrows point in the direction of rotation (clockwise)

23 Remove the crankshaft timing pin, then refit the crankshaft pulley and new securing bolt. Prevent the crankshaft turning using the method described previously and tighten the bolt to the specified torque **(see illustration)**.

24 Check that the crankshaft is still positioned with No 1 piston at TDC (by temporarily refitting the crankshaft timing pin), then remove the timing pin and turn the crankshaft two complete turns in the normal direction of rotation, returning it to the TDC position again. Re-insert the timing pin in the cylinder block.

25 Temporarily refit the timing belt outer cover, which covers the camshaft sprocket, and check that the sprocket timing mark still aligns with the pointer on

the cover, as noted before removal (see Section 3).

26 Recheck the belt tension as described previously. If the tension is incorrect, the setting and checking procedure must be repeated until the correct tension is achieved.

27 With the belt tensioned correctly, remove the M6 bolt from the timing belt inner cover and remove the timing pin from the cylinder block, if not already done. Refit the blanking plug to the cylinder block and tighten it securely, also tighten the tensioner retaining bolt.

28 Refit the timing belt upper outer covers, ensuring that any brackets secured by the bolts are in position as noted before removal.

29 Locate the right-hand engine mounting

 HAYNES HiNT *With experience, timing belt tension may be judged to be approximately correct when the belt can be twisted 45 to 90° with moderate pressure between the finger and thumb midway between the sprockets on the belt's longest run. If the special tool is not available, and there is any doubt about the tension of the belt, the vehicle should be taken to a dealer or suitably-equipped repairer as soon as possible for the tension to be checked.*

5.23 Angle-tighten the crankshaft pulley bolta

6.2 Slide the sprocket from the crankshaft

assembly into position and refit the bolts securing the mounting bracket to the cylinder head. Tighten the bolts to the specified torque. Refit the three bolts securing the rubber mounting to the body. Ensure that the movement limiter is positioned centrally over the mounting rubber then tighten the three bolts to the specified torque.

30 Tighten the engine stabiliser bolt to the specified torque.

31 Remove the engine hoist or lifting beam used to support the engine.

32 The remainder of refitting is a reversal of removal.

6 Timing belt sprockets and tensioner – removal and refitting

Note: *A new timing belt must be used on refitting.*

Crankshaft sprocket

Removal

1 Remove the timing belt as described in Section 5.

2 It should be possible simply to pull the sprocket off the crankshaft **(see illustration)**. However in some cases a puller may be required to draw off the sprocket – one can easily be made up as shown **(see Tool tip)**.

3 Recover the Woodruff key if it is loose. Examine the oil seal for signs of oil leakage and, if necessary, renew it as described in Section 12.

It is easy to make up a puller for the crankshaft sprocket using two bolts, a strip of metal and the existing crankshaft pulley bolt. By unscrewing the pulley bolt against the metal strip, the sprocket is drawn off the crankshaft.

Refitting

4 Refitting is a reversal of removal. Refit the Woodruff key to the crankshaft keyway and slide on the sprocket, making sure it is correctly engaged with the key and with its flange against the cylinder block/timing belt inner cover.

5 Fit the new timing belt as described in Section 5.

Fuel injection pump sprocket

Note: *A puller will be required to remove the sprocket from the pump shaft, Vauxhall use special tool KM 6240 and Renault use special tool MOT 1525 to withdraw the sprocket.*

Removal

6 Remove the timing belt as described in Section 5.

7 Use a homemade tool to prevent the injection pump sprocket from rotating **(see illustration)**.

8 Unscrew the sprocket retaining nut, then fit a suitable puller to the sprocket to withdraw it from the pump shaft **(see illustration)**. Take care not to damage the end of the pump shaft as the sprocket is removed.

9 Remove the sprocket and, where applicable, recover the Woodruff key from the end of the pump shaft if it is loose.

Refitting

10 Refitting is a reversal of removal, bearing in mind the following points:
a) *Tighten the sprocket nut to the specified torque wrench setting.*
b) *Fit and tension the new timing belt as described in Section 5.*

Camshaft sprocket

Note: *A suitable puller may be will be required for this operation.*

Removal

11 Remove the timing belt as described in Section 5. If it is necessary to turn the camshaft for any reason, remove the timing pin and turn the crankshaft anti-clockwise (viewed from the timing belt end of the engine) by a quarter-turn to position all four pistons halfway down their bores.

12 On vehicles up to 2006 model year, disconnect the air hose from the right-hand side of the intercooler, release the support bracket from the front panel, and move the hose to one side.

13 On vehicles from 2007 model year, release the clamp and disconnect the air hose from the intake manifold to the intercooler.

14 Ensure the area around the rear of the high-pressure fuel pump is clean and free from debris (using a vacuum cleaner if possible), then disconnect the wiring plug from the pump fuel pressure regulator, then disconnect the fuel feed and return hoses from the pump **(see illustration)**. Plug the openings to prevent contamination.

15 Undo the unions and remove the high-pressure fuel pipe between the common rail and the pump. Note that a new pipe must be fitted.

16 Undo the bolts securing the support bracket to the rear of the fuel pump **(see illustration)**.

17 Slacken the 3 bolts securing the engine mounting support bracket to the right-hand end of the engine, and move the bracket/fuel pump approximately 12 mm forwards **(see illustrations)**.

18 Unscrew the camshaft sprocket bolt. The sprocket can be held by making up a sprocket holding tool **(see illustration)**.

19 Remove the bolt, washer and sprocket

6.7 Use a homemade tool to prevent the pump sprocket from rotating

6.8 Use a puller to withdraw the pump sprocket

6.14 Depress the release buttons and disconnect the fuel feed and return hoses (arrowed)

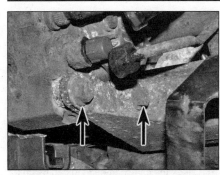

6.16 Undo the bolts (arrowed) securing the bracket to the pump

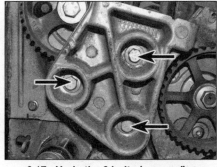

6.17a Undo the 3 bolts (arrowed)...

6.17b... and move the bracket/pump 12 mm forwards

from the camshaft. A suitable puller may be required, in which case ensure that the legs of the puller act on the holes in the sprocket, **not** on the sprocket teeth.

Refitting

20 Refit the sprocket with its projecting hub towards the cylinder head and ensuring that the key engages correctly with the keyway.

21 Ensure that the washer is in place, then refit the sprocket bolt and tighten it to the specified torque, holding the pulley as during removal.

22 Refit the engine right-hand mounting support bracket to the engine and tighten the securing bolts.

23 Refit the bolts securing the pump rear support bracket, and tighten the bolts to the specified torque.

24 Reconnect the fuel pump feed/return hoses, and the pressure regulator wiring plug.

25 Fit the new timing belt as described in Section 5.

Tensioner

Removal

26 Remove the timing belt as described in Section 5.

27 Remove the securing nut and its washer, unscrew the retaining bolts, and then withdraw the tensioner assembly **(see illustration)**.

Refitting

28 Refitting is a reversal of removal, but check that the roller spins freely without binding or excessive play. Ensure that the peg on the

6.18 Take care not to damage the camshaft position sensor (arrowed) when removing the sprocket

backing plate engages with the hole in the tensioner bracket, and apply a little thread-locking compound to the bolts threads.

29 Fit the new timing belt as described in Section 5.

7	Camshaft oil seals – renewal

Timing belt end oil seal

1 Remove the camshaft sprocket as described in Section 6.

2 Make a note of the fitted depth of the old seal then, using a small screwdriver, prise it out of the cylinder head, taking care not to damage the surface of the camshaft. Alternatively, the

6.27 Timing belt tensioner retaining bolts (arrowed)

oil seal can be removed by drilling a small hole and inserting a self-tapping screw. A pair of grips can then be used to pull out the oil seal, by pulling on the screw **(see illustrations)**. If difficulty is experienced, insert two screws diagonally opposite each other.

3 Wipe clean the oil seal seating in the cylinder head, then dip the new seal in fresh engine oil and locate it over the camshaft with its closed side facing outwards. Make sure that the oil seal lip is not damaged as it is located on the camshaft **(see illustration)**.

4 Using a tube of suitable diameter, drive the oil seal squarely into the housing to the previously-noted depth. A block of wood cut to pass over the end of the camshaft may be used instead **(see illustration)**.

5 Refit the camshaft sprocket as described in Section 6.

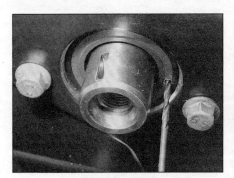

7.2a Drill a small hole...

7.2b... insert a screw and use pliers to extract the seal

7.3 Wrap some insulating tape around the end of the camshaft to prevent damage to the oil seal

7.4 Use a suitable socket to drive the new oil seal into the cylinder head

Transmission end oil seal

6 No oil seal is fitted to the transmission end of the camshaft. The sealing is provided by a gasket between the cylinder head and the brake vacuum pump housing and, on certain models, by an O-ring fitted between the pump and the housing. The gasket and the O-ring, where applicable, can be renewed after unbolting the pump from the cylinder head (see Chapter 9).

8 Camshaft and followers – removal, inspection and refitting

Note: *A new camshaft timing belt end oil seal should be fitted and a new cylinder head cover gasket may be required on refitting. Suitable sealant will be required for the camshaft bearing caps and thread-locking compound for the bearing cap bolts.*

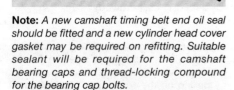

8.7b... and the camshaft cover

8.11 Lift the camshaft bearing cap retainer from the cylinder head

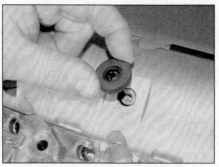

8.7a Remove the sealing washers...

Removal

1 Remove the camshaft sprocket as described in Section 6.
2 Remove the timing belt tensioner as described in Section 6.
3 Unscrew the bolts securing the timing belt upper inner cover to the end of the cylinder head.
4 Manipulate the timing belt inner cover from the camshaft end and withdraw the cover from the engine.
5 Remove the brake vacuum pump from the transmission end of the cylinder head, as described in Chapter 9.
6 Where necessary for improved access, unclip any hoses that are routed across the top of the cylinder head cover and move them to one side out of the way. If any fuel lines are disconnected, cover the open unions to prevent dirt ingress.
7 Unscrew the cylinder head cover bolts and

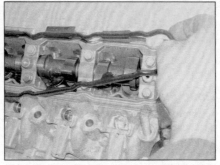

8.7c Recover the rubber gasket

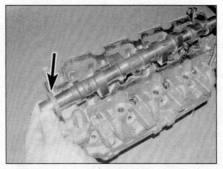

8.12 Lift out the camshaft with the oil seal (arrowed)

withdraw the cover. Recover the gasket **(see illustrations)**.
8 At this point it may be useful to measure the camshaft endfloat, using a dial gauge. Compare with the value given in the Specifications **(see illustration)**. This will give an indication of the amount of wear present on the thrust surfaces.
9 If the original camshaft is to be refitted, it is advisable to measure the valve clearances at this stage, as described in Section 4, so that any followers required can be obtained before the camshaft is refitted.
10 Check the camshaft bearing cap beam for identification marks and, if none are present, make identifying marks so that it can be refitted in its original position.
11 Progressively slacken the bolts from the bearing cap retainer, until the valve spring pressure is relieved. Remove the bolts (noting their locations to ensure correct refitting), and lift the bearing cap retainer from the camshaft **(see illustration)**.
12 Lift out the camshaft with the oil seal still in position on the end of the camshaft **(see illustration)**.
13 Remove the followers. Place them in a compartmented box, or on a sheet of card marked into eight sections, so that they can be refitted to their original locations. Write down the follower thicknesses – this will be needed later if any of the valve clearances are incorrect. The follower thickness is usually etched on the top of the follower, but it is prudent to use a micrometer to measure the true thickness of any follower removed, as it may have been reduced by wear **(see illustration)**.

8.8 Measure the camshaft endfloat using a DTI gauge

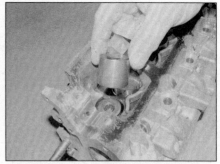

8.13 Lift out the camshaft followers

8.20 Lubricate the followers before fitting

8.21a Lubricate the camshaft bearing surfaces...

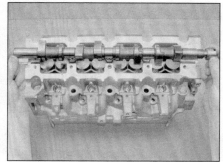
8.21b... and refit the camshaft

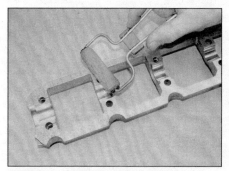
8.22 Apply sealant to the camshaft bearing cap retainer with a roller

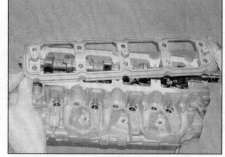
8.23 Refit the camshaft bearing cap retainer

8.24 Tighten the bolts progressively to the specified torque

Inspection

14 Examine the camshaft bearing surfaces and cam lobes for wear ridges, pitting or scoring. Renew the camshaft if evident.
15 Renew the oil seal at the timing belt end of the camshaft as a matter of course. Store the camshaft so that its weight is not resting on the seal.
16 Examine the camshaft bearing surfaces in the cylinder head and bearing cap beam. Deep scoring or other damage means that the cylinder head must be renewed.
17 Inspect the followers for scoring, pitting and wear ridges. Renew as necessary.
18 Clean the sealant from the cylinder head to bearing cap beam mating surfaces.

Refitting

19 Ensure that the pistons are positioned halfway down their bores, as described for sprocket removal in Section 6.
20 Refer to paragraphs 9 and 13, and Section 4, to correct the valve clearances. Oil the followers and fit them to the bores from which they were removed **(see illustration)**.
21 Oil the camshaft bearings **(see illustrations)**. Place the camshaft onto the cylinder head. The oil seal can be fitted at this stage, but it must be positioned so that it is flush with the cylinder head face.
22 Apply sealant (Loctite 518, available from dealers) to the cylinder head mating face of the camshaft bearing cap retainer **(see illustration)**. Use a roller to get an even layer along its length, making sure no sealant goes inside the camshaft bearing surfaces.
23 Refit the camshaft bearing cap retainer

(see illustration), ensuring that the camshaft oil seal is correctly located in the end of the cylinder head.
24 Apply a few drops of thread-locking compound to the threads of the bolts for the bearing cap beam. Fit the bolts and tighten them progressively to the specified torque **(see illustration)**.
25 If a new camshaft has been fitted, measure the endfloat using a dial gauge and check that it is within the specified limits.
26 Refit the brake vacuum pump with reference to Chapter 9.
27 Refit the timing belt upper inner cover, then refit and tighten the bolts securing it to the cylinder head.
28 Refit the timing belt tensioner, ensuring that the peg on the cylinder block engages with the hole in the tensioner bracket.
29 Refit the camshaft sprocket as described in Section 6.
30 Check the valve clearances as described

9.7 Slide out the locking catch (arrowed) and disconnect the blower motor resistor wiring plug

in Section 4 and take any corrective action necessary.
31 Refit the cylinder head cover, using a new gasket – tighten the cover retaining bolts, in the correct sequence, to the specified torque wrench setting.
32 Refit/reconnect any hoses that were moved for access. If fuel lines were disconnected, reconnect them, then prime and bleed the fuel system as described in Chapter 4A.
33 Reconnect the battery negative terminal as described in Chapter 5.

9 Cylinder head – removal, inspection and refitting

Removal

1 Disconnect the battery negative terminal as described in Chapter 5.
2 Prise up the caps, unscrew the retaining bolts and withdraw the engine sound-insulating cover.
3 Drain the cooling system as described in Chapter 1.
4 Remove the auxiliary drivebelt as described in Chapter 1.
5 Remove the timing belt as described in Section 5 and the timing belt tensioner as described in Section 6.
6 The engine must now be supported from below so that the engine hoist or lifting beam used for timing belt removal can be removed for access to the top of the engine.
7 Disconnect the heater fan resistor wiring plug **(see illustration)**.

9.8a The blower motor housing is secured by a nut (arrowed) on the right-hand side...

9.8b... a nut (arrowed) on the left-hand side...

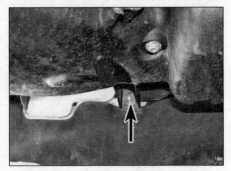

9.8c... a nut underneath (arrowed)...

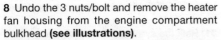

9.8d... and a bolt (arrowed) at the upper, right-hand edge

9.10 Undo the thermoplunger bracket nut/bolt (arrowed)

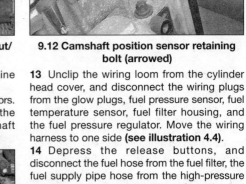

9.12 Camshaft position sensor retaining bolt (arrowed)

8 Undo the 3 nuts/bolt and remove the heater fan housing from the engine compartment bulkhead **(see illustrations)**.
9 Remove the air cleaner assembly as described in Chapter 4A.
10 Undo the nut/bolt and detach the thermo-

plunger housing bracket from the engine lifting eye **(see illustration)**.
11 Disconnect the plugs from the fuel injectors.
12 Disconnect the wiring plug, undo the retaining bolt and remove the camshaft position sensor **(see illustration)**.

13 Unclip the wiring loom from the cylinder head cover, and disconnect the wiring plugs from the glow plugs, fuel pressure sensor, fuel temperature sensor, fuel filter housing, and the fuel pressure regulator. Move the wiring harness to one side **(see illustration 4.4)**.
14 Depress the release buttons, and disconnect the fuel hose from the fuel filter, the fuel supply pipe hose from the high-pressure pump, and the fuel return hose from the fuel temperature sensor **(see illustrations)**. Plug the openings to prevent contamination.
15 Disconnect the wiring plugs from the thermoplunger, EGR valve, and coolant temperature sensor.
16 Disconnect the vacuum hose from the brake vacuum pump **(see illustration)**.
17 Slacken and disconnect the oil supply pipe from the top of the turbocharger unit and the cylinder block, disconnect the pipe mounting bracket from the rear of the manifold **(see illustrations)**.

9.14a Depress the release button (arrowed) and disconnect the fuel hose from the filter...

9.14b... the high-pressure pump, and the fuel temperature sensor (arrowed)

9.16 Squeeze together the sides of the collar (arrowed) and disconnect the hose from the vacuum pump

9.17a Turbocharger oil feed pipe unit (arrowed) and pipe bracket bolt (arrowed)

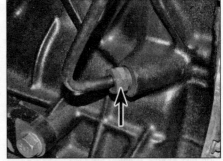

9.17b Turbocharger oil feed connection on the cylinder block (arrowed)

18 Remove the exhaust front section/catalytic converter as described in Chapter 4A.

19 Disconnect the oil return pipe from the bottom of the turbocharger.

20 Disconnect the breather hose from the air intake hose to the turbocharger.

21 Release the clamps and disconnect the air intake/outlet hoses and wastegate vacuum hose from the turbocharger.

22 Release the retaining clips and disconnect the hoses from the coolant housing on the transmission end of the cylinder head.

23 Unbolt the EGR valve from the intake manifold. Recover the gasket.

24 If not already done, remove the timing pin from the cylinder block and turn the crankshaft anti-clockwise (viewed from the timing belt end of the engine) by a quarter-turn to position all four pistons halfway down their bores.

25 Working in the **reverse** of the sequence shown in illustration 9.39, progressively slacken the cylinder head bolts by half a turn at a time until all bolts can be unscrewed by hand and removed. Note that new bolts must be used for refitting.

26 The cylinder head assembly complete with ancillaries is heavy and it is advisable to attach a hoist and suitable lifting tackle.

27 Lift the cylinder head (complete with manifolds, injection pump and timing belt upper inner cover) upwards and off the cylinder block. If it is stuck, tap it upwards using a hammer and block of wood (taking care not to damage the fuel injection pump). **Do not** try to rotate the cylinder head (it is located by two dowels), nor attempt to prise it free using a screwdriver inserted between the block and head faces. If the locating dowels are a loose fit, remove them and store them with the head for safe-keeping **(see illustration)**.

28 If desired, the manifolds, turbocharger and fuel injection pump can be removed from the cylinder head with reference to the relevant Sections of Chapter 4A.

Inspection

29 The mating faces of the cylinder head and block must be perfectly clean before refitting the head. Use a cleaning agent to dissolve any remains of gasket still on the mating faces. Take particular care with the aluminium cylinder head, as the soft metal is damaged easily. Also, make sure that debris is not allowed to enter the oil and water channels – this is particularly important for the oil circuit, as carbon could block the oil supply to the camshaft or crankshaft bearings. Using adhesive tape and paper, seal the water, oil and bolt holes in the cylinder block. Clean the piston crowns in the same way.

30 Check the block and head for nicks, deep scratches and other damage. If there is more serious damage, then it may need to be repaired by machining, but this is a specialist job.

31 If warpage of the cylinder head is suspected, use a straight-edge to check it for distortion. Refer to Chapter 2C if necessary.

> ⚠ **Warning: If the cylinder head is warped more than the stated specification a new cylinder head will be required, as regrinding of the cylinder head is NOT permitted.**

32 Clean out the cylinder head bolt holes in the block using a pipe cleaner, or a rag and screwdriver. Make sure that all oil is removed, otherwise there is a possibility of the block being cracked by hydraulic pressure when the bolts are tightened.

33 Examine the cylinder head bolt threads in the cylinder block for damage – if necessary, use the correct-size tap to chase out the threads in the block. The manufacturers recommend that the cylinder head bolts are renewed, regardless of their apparent condition.

Refitting

34 Where applicable, refit the manifolds, turbocharger and fuel injection pump to the cylinder head, with reference to the relevant Sections of Chapter 4A.

35 Turn the crankshaft clockwise (viewed from the timing belt end) until Nos 1 and 4 pistons pass bottom dead centre (BDC) and begin to rise, then position them halfway up their bores (this is to prevent the possibility of piston-to-valve contact). Nos 2 and 3 pistons will also be at their midway positions, but descending their bores. Do not turn the crankshaft again until the timing belt is to be refitted.

36 Ensure that the cylinder head locating dowels are fitted to the cylinder block, then fit the correct gasket the right way round on the cylinder block with the identification mark(s) at the front corner of the engine at the flywheel end.

37 Lower the cylinder head onto the block. Ensure that the timing belt upper inner cover engages correctly with the lower inner cover on the cylinder block. Where applicable, disconnect the lifting tackle and hoist.

38 Lubricate the new cylinder head bolts with clean engine oil, then insert the bolts, with their washers, and tighten them finger-tight.

39 Tighten the cylinder head bolts to the specified torques in the sequence shown and in the stages given in the Specifications at the beginning of this Chapter **(see illustration)**. When angle-tightening the bolts, it is recommended that an angle-tightening gauge be used to ensure accuracy. Note that provided the bolts are tightened exactly as specified, there will be no need to retighten them once the engine has been started and run after reassembly.

> ⚠ **Warning: The final tightening stages involve very high forces. Ensure that the tools used are in good condition. If the engine has been removed from the vehicle, it is recommended that the final tightening stages be carried out with the engine refitted to the vehicle (it may be necessary to remove the engine right-hand mounting upper bracket for access to one of the bolts with the engine in the vehicle).**

9.27 Locating dowel (arrowed) in the cylinder block

40 Fit a new timing belt with reference to Section 5.

41 The remainder of refitting is a reversal of removal, noting the following points:

a) Tighten all fasteners to their specified torque where given.

b) Refit all wiring looms disturbed to their original routing.

c) Change the engine oil and filter as described in Chapter 1.

d) Refill and bleed the cooling system as described in Chapter 1.

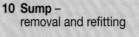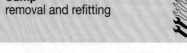

10 Sump –
removal and refitting

Removal

1 Apply the handbrake, then jack up the front of the vehicle and support it on axle stands (see *Jacking and vehicle support*). Undo the retaining screws and remove the plastic undercover from beneath the engine/transmission.

2 Drain the engine oil as described in Chapter 1, then refit and tighten the drain plug.

3 Undo the bolts securing the rear engine stabiliser bracket to the sump, and the stabiliser arm **(see illustration)**.

4 Unscrew the bolts securing the left-hand end of the sump to the transmission bellhousing flange.

5 Unscrew the bolts securing the sump to the cylinder block. Tap the sump with a hide or plastic mallet to break the seal, and then remove the sump along with its gasket.

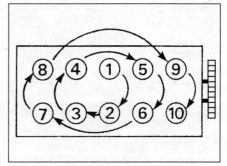

9.39 Cylinder head bolt tightening sequence

10.3 Undo the bolts (arrowed) securing the stabiliser bracket to the sump

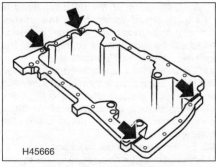

10.7 Apply sealant in the areas shown before refitting the sump

10.9 Use a straight-edge to align the sump and the cylinder block

Discard the gasket; a new one must be used on refitting.

Refitting

6 Remove all traces of dirt and oil from the mating surfaces of the sump and cylinder block.

7 Apply a bead of Rhodorseal 5661 sealant (from Vauxhall dealers, part no 93 160 951) or Mastixo sealant (from Renault dealers) to the join between the crankshaft oil seal housing and cylinder block, and to the join between the main bearing cap and cylinder block **(see illustration)**.

8 Locate the new gasket on the top of the sump and lift the sump into position.

9 Insert the bolts and initially tighten them all to the Stage 1 torque setting given in the Specifications. If the engine is in the car, ensure that the left-hand end of the sump is in contact with the transmission bellhousing flange. If the engine is removed from the car,

use a straight-edge to maintain the alignment between the left-hand end of the sump and cylinder block **(see illustration)**.

10 Progressively tighten the bolts to the Stage 2 torque setting in an anti-clockwise spiral pattern starting at the centre and working outwards.

11 The remainder of refitting is a reversal of removal, remembering to fill the engine with fresh oil, with reference to Chapter 1.

11 Oil pump – removal, inspection and refitting

Removal

Oil pump alone

1 To remove the oil pump alone, first remove the sump, referring to Section 10.

2 Unscrew bolts securing the anti-emulsion plate to the crankcase and the oil pump mounting bolts **(see illustrations)**. Withdraw the anti-emulsion plate from the cylinder block.

3 Tilt the pump to disengage its sprocket from the drive chain and lift away the pump **(see illustration)**. If the locating dowels are displaced, refit them in their locations.

Oil pump with chain and sprockets

4 To remove the oil pump complete with its drive chain and sprockets, first remove the sump (Section 10), then unbolt the crankshaft timing belt end oil seal housing, as described in Section 12 **(see illustration)**. Note the presence of the chain guide block and of its two locating dowels.

5 Unscrew the bolts securing the sprocket to the oil pump hub. Use a screwdriver through one of the holes in the sprocket to hold it stationary.

6 Slide the drive sprocket from the crankshaft and the driven sprocket from the oil pump. Withdraw both sprockets and the chain **(see illustration)**. Note that the drive sprocket is not keyed to the crankshaft, but relies on the pulley bolt being tightened correctly to clamp the sprocket. It is most important that the pulley bolt is correctly tightened otherwise there is the possibility of the oil pump not functioning.

7 Unbolt the oil pump as described in paragraph 2 above.

Inspection

8 Unscrew the retaining bolts and lift off the

11.2a Unscrew the bolts...

11.2b... remove the anti-emulsion plate...

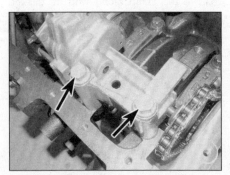

11.2c... then undo the pump mounting bolts (arrowed)

11.3 Disengage the oil pump sprocket from the drive chain

11.4 Remove the timing belt end oil seal housing

11.6 Remove the oil pump sprockets and chain

11.9 Withdraw the retaining clip and remove the oil pressure relief valve components

11.11a Measure the oil pump gear-to-body clearance

11.11b Measure the oil pump gear endfloat

11.11c Check the flatness of the oil pump cover

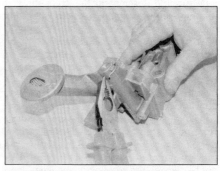

11.12 Bend the end of the retaining clip to ensure it remains in position

pump cover. Withdraw the idler gear and the drivegear/shaft. Mark the idler gear before removal, so that it can be refitted in its original position.

9 Extract the retaining clip and remove the oil pressure relief valve spring retainer, spring, spring seat and plunger (see illustration).

10 Clean the components and carefully examine the gears, pump body and relief valve plunger for any signs of scoring or wear. Renew the complete pump assembly if excessive wear is evident (no spare parts are available).

11 If the components appear serviceable, measure the clearance between the pump body and the gears using feeler gauges. Also measure the gear endfloat and check the flatness of the end cover (see illustrations). If the clearances exceed the specified tolerances, the pump must be renewed. There should be no discernible wear or distortion of the end cover.

12 If the pump is satisfactory, reassemble the components in the reverse order of removal (see illustration). Fill the pump with oil, then refit the cover and tighten the bolts securely. Prime the oil pump by filling it with clean engine oil whilst rotating the driveshaft.

Refitting

13 Wipe clean the oil pump and cylinder block mating surfaces.

14 Check that the two locating dowels are fitted in the cylinder block, and then position the oil pump on them and insert the two mounting bolts. Tighten the bolts to their specified torque.

15 Engage the sprockets on the chain (if

removed), and then refit both sprockets and the chain as an assembly. Slide the drive sprocket fully onto the crankshaft and locate the driven sprocket on the oil pump hub.

16 Align the holes, then insert the sprocket bolts and tighten them securely while holding the sprocket stationary with a screwdriver.

17 Refit the anti-emulsion plate and secure with the retaining bolt(s).

18 Refit the oil seal housing as described in Section 12 – do not forget the chain guide block and its two locating dowels – and the sump (refer to Section 10).

12 Crankshaft oil seals – renewal

Note: There are two types of seals that may be used on this engine, these are not interchangeable and should only be renewed with the same type.
a) Early type, which has a spring inside the V-shaped lip of the seal.
b) Later type, which has a flat sealing lip with no spring and comes with a plastic protector, which is also a fitting sleeve.

⚠ **Warning: Both manufacturers recommend that the later elastomer seals should only be fitted using a special tool, to prevent any damage to the seal. The seal should not be touched as it is very fragile; when handling, only touch the plastic protector sleeve which is supplied with the seal.**

Timing belt end oil seal

1 Remove the crankshaft sprocket, as described in Section 6.

2 Note the fitted position of the old seal, then prise it out of the oil seal housing using a screwdriver or suitable hooked instrument (see illustration). An alternative method of removing the oil seal is to carefully drill two small holes opposite each other in the oil seal and insert self-tapping screws, then pull on the screws with grips. Take care not to damage the surface of the crankshaft or spacer or the seal housing. **Note:** *On some models it may be necessary to remove the timing belt lower inner cover to allow the seal to be withdrawn. If this is the case, remove the idler pulley then unbolt the cover.*

3 Clean the seal housing and polish off any burrs or raised edges, which may have caused the seal to fail in the first place. Inspect the

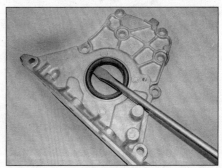

12.2 Removing the timing belt end oil seal with the timing cover removed

12.5 Use a socket to drive the new seal into place

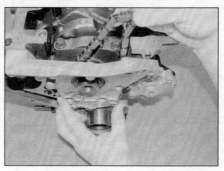

12.6 Refit the oil seal housing

seal rubbing surface on the crankshaft. If it is grooved or rough in the area where the old seal was fitted, the new seal should be fitted slightly less deeply, so that it rubs on an unworn part of the crankshaft surface.

4 Wipe clean the oil seal seating, then dip the new seal in fresh engine oil and locate it over the crankshaft with its closed side facing outwards. Make sure that the oil seal lip is not damaged, as it is located on the crankshaft.

5 Using a tube of suitable diameter, drive the oil seal squarely into the housing to the previously-noted position – take great care not to damage the seal lips during fitting **(see illustration)**. Note that if the surface of the shaft was noted to be badly scored, press the new seal slightly further into its housing so that its lip is running on an unmarked area of the shaft.

6 Where necessary, refit the timing belt lower inner cover **(see illustration)** and install the idler pulley. Refit the crankshaft sprocket as described in Section 6 and fit the new timing belt as described in Section 5.

Timing belt end oil seal housing

7 Remove the timing belt as described in Section 5, and the crankshaft sprocket and idler pulley with reference to Section 6. Remove the Woodruff key from the crankshaft keyway, and then unbolt the timing belt lower inner cover from the cylinder block.

8 Unscrew the bolts securing the sump to the oil seal housing.

9 Unscrew the retaining bolts and carefully withdraw the oil seal housing, noting the locating dowels around its two lower bolt

holes. If it is stuck in place a leverage point is provided on its upper edge (near the timing belt idler pulley) to allow a screwdriver or similar to be used gently to prise the housing away from the cylinder block without risking damage to the delicate mating surfaces of either. If the sump gasket is damaged, the sump will have to be removed to renew it. Note the presence of the oil pump drive chain guide block and of its two locating dowels – check that the guide block is fit for further use and renew it if there is any doubt about its condition.

10 The oil seal should be renewed whenever the housing is removed. Note the fitted position of the old seal, then prise it out with a screwdriver and wipe clean the seating. Smear the outer perimeter of the new seal with fresh engine oil and locate it squarely on the housing with its closed side facing outwards. Place the housing on a block of wood, then use a socket or metal tube to drive in the oil seal.

11 On refitting, clean all traces of sealant from the housing, sump and block mating faces. Check that the chain guide block is correctly fitted and that the housing's locating dowels are in place.

12 Apply a 1.5 mm diameter bead of Rhodorseal 5661 (available from dealers) to the housing's gasket surfaces, around the inner edges of the bolt holes and apply a smear of sealant to the threads of the two bolts (nearest the oil seal) which project inside the cylinder block. Do **NOT** allow sealant to foul the oil gallery at the upper end of the housing. Refit the housing to the cylinder

block and sump, tightening the bolts securely and evenly. **Note:** *On some models a steel gasket may be fitted, check with your dealer.*

13 Refit the Woodruff key to the crankshaft keyway, then refit the timing belt lower inner cover to the cylinder block, tightening securely its retaining bolts.

14 Refit the crankshaft sprocket and the idler pulley, and fit the new timing belt with reference to Sections 6 and 5.

Transmission end oil seal

15 Remove the flywheel as described in Section 13.

16 Prise out the old oil seal using a small screwdriver, taking care not to damage the surface of the crankshaft. Alternatively, the oil seal can be removed as described in paragraph 2.

17 Inspect the seal rubbing surface on the crankshaft. If it is grooved or rough in the area where the old seal was fitted, the new seal should be fitted slightly less deeply, so that it rubs on an unworn part of the surface.

18 Wipe clean the oil seal seating. Locate it over the crankshaft; making sure its sealing lip is facing inwards. Make sure that the oil seal lip is not damaged, as it is located on the crankshaft.

19 Using a metal tube, drive the oil seal squarely into the bore until flush. A block of wood cut to pass over the end of the crankshaft may be used instead.

20 Refit the flywheel with reference to Section 13.

13 Flywheel – removal, inspection and refitting

Note: *New flywheel retaining bolts will be required on refitting.*

Removal

1 Remove the transmission as described in Chapter 7, then remove the clutch assembly as described in Chapter 6.

2 Prevent the flywheel from turning by locking the ring gear teeth with a screwdriver. Alternatively a home-made tool similar to that shown can be used **(see illustration)**. Make alignment marks between the flywheel and crankshaft using paint or a suitable marker pen.

3 Slacken and remove the flywheel retaining bolts and remove the flywheel. Do not drop it, as it is very heavy. If the locating dowel (where fitted) is a loose fit in the crankshaft end, remove and store it with the flywheel for safe-keeping. Discard the bolts, as they should be renewed whenever they are disturbed **(see illustration)**.

Inspection

4 If the flywheel-to-clutch mating surface is deeply scored, cracked or otherwise damaged, then the flywheel must be renewed, unless it is possible to have it surface ground. Seek

13.2 Use a fabricated tool (arrowed) to prevent the flywheel from turning

13.3 The flywheel bolts (arrowed) are unequally spaced for refitting

the advice of a dealer or engine reconditioning specialist.

5 If the ring gear is badly worn or has missing teeth, then the complete flywheel must be renewed. The ring gear is not available as a separate item.

Refitting

6 Clean the mating surfaces of the flywheel and crankshaft.

7 Ensure that the locating dowel is in position (where fitted) and offer up the flywheel, locating it on the dowel, and fit the new retaining bolts. If the original is being refitted align the marks made prior to removal.

8 Lock the flywheel using the method employed on dismantling, and tighten the retaining bolts to the specified torque.

9 Refit the clutch as described in Chapter 6.

10 Remove the locking tool, and refit the transmission as described in Chapter 7.

14 Engine/transmission mountings – renewal
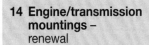

Inspection

1 If improved access is required, apply the handbrake, then jack up the front of the vehicle and support it on axle stands (see *Jacking and vehicle support*).

2 Check the mounting rubber to see if it is cracked, hardened or separated from the metal at any point; renew the mounting if any such damage or deterioration is evident.

3 Check that all the mounting's fasteners are securely tightened; use a torque wrench to check if possible.

4 Using a large screwdriver or a crowbar, check for wear in the mounting by carefully levering against it to check for free play. Where this is not possible, enlist the aid of an assistant to move the engine/transmission back-and-forth, or from side-to-side, while you watch the mounting. While some free play is to be expected even from new components, excessive wear should be obvious. If excessive free play is found, check first that the fasteners are correctly secured, and then renew any worn components as described below.

Renewal

Right-hand mounting

5 Place a jack beneath the engine, with a block of wood on the jack head (remove the undercover to improve access to the sump). Raise the jack until it is supporting the weight of the engine. Alternately, attach an engine support bar to the lifting brackets and support the weight of the engine with the bar.

6 Where fitted, undo the two retaining bolts and withdraw the acoustic mass unit (metal weight) from the engine mounting assembly.

7 Slacken the rear mounting bolt for the tie-rod at the rear of the mounting, remove the

14.7a Slacken the bolt at the rear of the tie-rod (arrowed)

front bolt to the engine mounting and swivel the tie-rod to one side (see illustrations).

8 Undo the bolt securing the rubber mounting to the engine mounting bracket.

9 Slacken and remove the three bolts securing the engine mounting bracket to the cylinder head, and withdraw it from the engine. Where applicable, release any cables or wiring from the top of the engine mounting bracket.

10 Unscrew the retaining bolts and remove the rubber mounting from the body (see illustration).

11 Check carefully for signs of wear or damage on all components, and renew them where necessary.

12 On reassembly, fit the rubber mounting and movement limiter to the body, insert the retaining bolts but tighten them finger-tight only at this stage.

13 Refit the upper part of the bracket to the cylinder head, locating it on the stud for the rubber mounting. Tighten the mounting bolts to the cylinder head to the specified torque.

14 Refit the nut securing the rubber mounting to the engine mounting bracket and tighten it to the specified torque.

15 Centralise the movement limiter around the rubber mounting then tighten the three bolts to the specified torque.

16 Swivel the tie-rod at the rear of the mounting bracket back into place and refit the front bolt to the engine mounting, tighten the bolts to the specified torque.

17 Refit the acoustic mass unit to the engine mounting assembly (where fitted) and tighten the retaining bolts to the specified torque.

18 Remove the jack from underneath

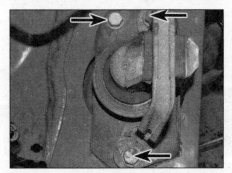
14.10 Undo the bolts (arrowed) and remove the rubber mounting

14.7b Remove the bolt (arrowed) securing the tie-rod to the mounting bracket

the engine or the engine support bar (as applicable).

Left-hand mounting

19 Place a jack beneath the transmission, with a block of wood on the jack head. Raise the jack until it is supporting the weight of the transmission.

20 Slacken and remove the mounting rubber's centre nut, and two retaining bolts and remove the mounting from the engine compartment (see illustration).

21 If necessary, undo the retaining bolts and remove the mounting bracket from the top of the transmission housing. The mounting stud can be separated from the bracket once its lower retaining nut has been undone.

22 Check carefully for signs of wear or damage on all components, and renew them where necessary.

23 Refit the stud to the mounting bracket and tighten its to the specified torque.

24 Refit the bracket to the transmission, tightening its mounting bolts to the specified torque.

25 Fit the mounting rubber to the bracket and tighten its retaining bolts and centre nut to the specified torque.

26 Remove the jack from underneath the transmission.

Rear mounting

27 If not already done, apply the handbrake, then jack up the front of the vehicle and support it on axle stands (see *Jacking and vehicle support*).

28 Position a jack with a block of wood on its head underneath the sump. Raise the jack until it is supporting the weight of the engine.

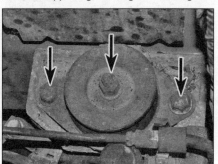
14.20 Undo the nut/bolts (arrowed) and remove the left-hand mounting

14.29 Undo the bolts and remove the rear mounting link (arrowed)

29 Slacken and remove the nut and bolt from each end of the mounting link and remove the link from underneath the vehicle. If necessary, undo the retaining nuts and bolts and remove the mounting bracket from the engine **(see illustration)**.

30 Check carefully for signs of wear or damage on all components, and renew them where necessary.

31 On reassembly, fit the mounting bracket (where removed) to the rear of the engine and tighten its retaining bolts to the specified torque.

32 Fit the mounting link, and tighten both its bolts to their specified torque settings.

33 Lower the vehicle to the ground and reconnect the battery negative terminal.

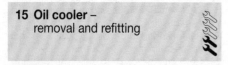

15 Oil cooler –
removal and refitting

Removal

1 Drain the cooling system as described in Chapter 1.

2 Remove the oil filter (refer to Chapter 1).

3 Loosen the clips and disconnect the coolant hoses from the oil cooler.

4 Unscrew the oil filter mounting stud, which also secures the oil cooler, and withdraw the oil cooler from the engine. Recover the sealing ring **(see illustrations)**.

Refitting

5 Refitting is a reversal of removal, but use a new sealing ring.

16.6 Disconnect the oil pressure warning light switch wiring plug

15.4a Remove the oil filter mounting stud...

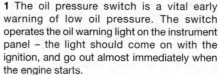

16 Oil pressure switch –
removal and refitting

1 The oil pressure switch is a vital early warning of low oil pressure. The switch operates the oil warning light on the instrument panel – the light should come on with the ignition, and go out almost immediately when the engine starts.

2 If the light does not come on, there could be a fault on the instrument panel, the switch wiring, or the switch itself. If the light does not go out, low oil level, worn oil pump (or sump pick-up blocked), blocked oil filter, or worn main bearings could be to blame – or again, the switch may be faulty.

3 If the light comes on while driving, the best advice is to turn the engine off immediately, and not to drive the vehicle until the problem has been investigated – ignoring the light could mean expensive engine damage.

Removal

4 The oil pressure switch is located on the front face of the engine, next to the oil filter.

5 Jack up the front of the car, and support it on axle stands (see *Jacking and vehicle support*), then undo the fasteners and remove the engine undertray.

6 Disconnect the wiring plug from the switch **(see illustration)**.

7 Unscrew the switch from the block, and remove it together with its sealing washer. There should only be a very slight loss of oil when this is done.

17.2 Disconnect the oil level sensor wiring plug

15.4b... then withdrawn the oil cooler and recover the sealing ring

Inspection

8 Examine the switch for signs of cracking or splits. If the top part of the switch is loose, this is an early indication of impending failure.

9 Check that the wiring terminals at the switch are not loose, then trace the wire from the switch connector until it enters the main loom – any wiring defects will give rise to apparent oil pressure problems.

Refitting

10 Refitting is the reverse of the removal procedure, noting the following points:

a) *Clean the switch threads before fitting. Tighten the switch securely.*

b) *Reconnect the switch connector, making sure it clicks home properly. Ensure that the wiring is routed away from any hot or moving parts.*

c) *Lower the vehicle to the ground, then check the engine oil level and top-up if necessary (see 'Weekly checks').*

d) *Check for signs of oil leaks once the engine has been restarted and warmed-up to normal operating temperature.*

17 Oil level sensor –
removal and refitting

Removal

1 The sensor is fitted at the front of the engine, next to the oil filter. Access to the sensor may be easiest from under the vehicle, jack up the front of the car, and support it on axle stands (see *Jacking and vehicle support*). Undo the retaining bolts and remove the engine undertray.

2 Disconnect the wiring plug, then unscrew and withdraw the sensor from the engine block **(see illustration)**.

Refitting

3 Refitting is a reversal of removal. Tighten the sensor securely, to prevent leaks.

Chapter 2 Part B:
2.0 litre engine in-car repair procedures

Contents

Degrees of difficulty

Easy, suitable for novice with little experience | **Fairly easy,** suitable for beginner with some experience | **Fairly difficult,** suitable for competent DIY mechanic | **Difficult,** suitable for experienced DIY mechanic | **Very difficult,** suitable for expert DIY or professional

Specifications

General

Type	Four-cylinder, in-line, double overhead camshaft, 16-valve
Designation	M9R 630, 692, 780, 782, 784, 786 or 788
Output:	
Power	66 or 84 kW @ 3500 rpm
Torque	240, 260, 290 or 300 Nm @ 1600 rpm
Bore	84.0 mm
Stroke	90.0 mm
Capacity	1995 cc
Compression ratio	15.6:1
Firing order	1-3-4-2 (No 1 cylinder at timing chain end of engine)
Direction of crankshaft rotation	Clockwise, viewed from timing chain end

Camshafts

Drive	Timing chain to exhaust camshaft sprocket
Number of bearings on each	6
Camshaft endfloat	0.05 to 0.13 mm

Lubrication system

Minimum oil pressure at 80°C:	
At 800 rpm	0.9 bars
At 3000 rpm	4.0 bars

Torque wrench settings

	Nm	lbf ft
Anti-roll bar link arm	44	32
Auxiliary support bracket to engine	44	32
Camshaft bearing caps	10	7
Camshaft housing	12	9
Connecting rod (big-end) cap bolts:*		
Stage 1	25	18
Stage 2	Angle-tighten a further 55° ± 6°	
Crankshaft main bearing cap bolts:		
Stage 1	20	15
Stage 2	Angle-tighten a further 70° ± 6°	
Crankshaft oil seal:		
Stage 1	5	4
Stage 2	10	7
Crankshaft position ring to crankshaft:		
Stage 1	3	2
Stage 2	20	15
Crankshaft pulley bolt:*		
Stage 1	50	37
Stage 2	Angle-tighten a further 85° ± 6°	
Cylinder block baseplate	25	18
Cylinder head bolts:*		
Stage 1	5	4
Stage 2	30	22
Stage 3	Angle-tighten a further 300° ± 6°	
Driveshaft intermediate bearing bracket	60	44
Engine/transmission mountings:		
Right-hand engine mounting:		
Upper plate to engine bracket	25	18
Rubber pad/lower bracket to engine bracket	100	74
Bracket to engine (M8):*	25	18
Bracket to engine (M10):*		
Stage 1	30	22
Stage 2	Angle-tighten a further 54°	
Rubber pad to inner wing	44	32
Upper engine stabiliser bar:		
To engine bracket	44	32
To body	100	74
Left-hand mounting:		
Mounting to body	44	32
Mounting to transmission	60	44
Rear engine mounting:		
Tie-bar to bracket	280	207
Tie-bar to subframe	100	74
Exhaust camshaft sprocket to timing gear:		
Stage 1	10	7
Stage 2	Angle-tighten a further 40° ± 6°	
Flywheel bolts:*		
Stage 1	35	26
Stage 2	Angle-tighten a further 40° ± 6°	
Front crossmember	44	32
Fuel pump drivegear to camshaft:*		
Stage 1	40	30
Stage 2	Angle-tighten a further 34°	
Intake camshaft timing gear:		
Stage 1	20	15
Stage 2	Angle-tighten a further 35° ± 6°	
Intake manifold	25	18
Oil cooler/filter housing to block:		
Stage 1	5	4
Stage 2	25	18
Oil level dipstick guide tube	10	7
Oil level sensor	25	18
Oil pressure sensor	30	22
Oil pump strainer	10	7
Oil pump to cylinder block:		
Stage 1	5	4
Stage 2	25	18

Torque wrench settings (continued)

	Nm	lbf ft
Oil separator	12	9
Oil splash plate to oil pump	10	7
Power steering high-pressure pipe mounting	25	18
Steering track rod end nut	37	27
Sump:		
Stage 1	5	4
Stage 2	16	12
TDC setting pin hole plug	25	18
Timing chain hydraulic tensioner*	10	7
Timing chain guides to engine*	25	18
Timing cover bolts:		
Stage 1	5	4
Stage 2:		
M8 bolt	18	13
M6 bolt	16	12

* Do not re-use.

1 General information

How to use this Chapter

This Part of Chapter 2 is devoted to in-car repair procedures for the 2.0 litre engine. Similar information covering the 1.9 litre engine will be found in Chapter 2A. Some procedures involve the removal of the engine, however, and overhaul procedures and engine removal and refitting can be found in Chapter 2C.

If certain information in this Chapter is being used during a complete engine overhaul, with the engine already removed, many of the steps included here will not apply.

Engine description

The 2.0 litre engine is a four-cylinder overhead camshaft 16-valve design, mounted transversely at the front of the vehicle with the transmission bolted to the left-hand side. The power steering pump, coolant pump, alternator and air conditioning compressor are driven by the auxiliary drivebelt. The brake servo vacuum pump is driven directly by the exhaust camshaft at the flywheel end.

The crankshaft is supported in five shell-type main bearings. Thrustwashers are fitted to No 2 main bearing to control crankshaft endfloat. The connecting rods are attached to the crankshaft by horizontally split shell-type big-end bearings, and to the pistons by gudgeon pins. The gudgeon pins are a sliding fit in the connecting rods and are retained by circlips. The aluminium alloy pistons are of the slipper type, and are fitted with three piston rings – two compression rings and a scraper-type oil control ring.

The double overhead camshafts are mounted in the cylinder head, and are driven by a timing chain direct from the crankshaft to the exhaust camshaft sprocket. The intake camshaft is driven by gear direct from the exhaust camshaft at the timing chain end. The high-pressure fuel pump is gear-driven from the flywheel end of the intake camshaft.

The camshafts operate the 16 valves, which are mounted in the cylinder head, through rocker arms situated directly above the camshaft. Automatic adjustment of the valve-to-rocker arm clearance is provided by hydraulic lifters located in the cylinder head.

A dual-mass flywheel is fitted to reduce engine vibration and transmission noise.

Engine lubrication is by pressure feed from a gear-type oil pump, chain-driven off the timing chain end of the crankshaft. Engine oil is fed through an externally mounted oil filter and oil cooler to the main oil gallery feeding the crankshaft and camshaft. The oil cooler helps keep the oil temperature constant under arduous operating conditions.

Operations with engine in car

The following operations can be carried out without having to remove the engine from the vehicle:

a) *Removal and refitting of the crankshaft pulley.*
b) *Removal and refitting of the sump.*
c) *Removal and refitting of the oil pump.*
d) *Removal and refitting of the cylinder block baseplate.*
e) *Removal and refitting of the big-end bearings, connecting rods, and pistons.**
f) *Removal and refitting of the balancer shaft unit.*
g) *Renewal of the crankshaft oil seals.*
h) *Removal and refitting of the flywheel.*
i) *Renewal of the engine/transmission mountings.*

* Although the operation marked with an asterisk can be carried out with the engine in the vehicle after removal of the sump and baseplate, it is better for the engine to be removed, in the interests of cleanliness and improved access. For this reason, the procedure is described in Chapter 2C.

2 Compression test – description and interpretation

Refer to Chapter 2A, Section 2.

3 Top Dead Centre (TDC) for No 1 piston – locating

1 Top dead centre (TDC) is the highest point in the cylinder that each piston reaches as the crankshaft turns. Each piston reaches TDC at the end of the compression stroke and again at the end of the exhaust stroke. However, for the purpose of timing the engine, TDC refers to the position of No 1 piston at the end of its compression stroke.

2 Apply the handbrake, and then jack up the front of the vehicle and support it on axle stands (see *Jacking and vehicle support*). Remove the right-hand roadwheel.

3 Remove the engine undertray (where fitted) and the right-hand wheel arch liner in order to gain access to the crankshaft pulley bolt. Where applicable, unclip the screen washer hose.

4 To facilitate turning the engine easily, remove the glow plugs as described in Chapter 5.

5 With the help of an assistant and using a socket on the crankshaft pulley bolt, turn the engine clockwise until pressure can be felt in the No 1 glow plug hole, indicating that the No 1 piston is rising on its compression stroke.

6 Continue to turn the crankshaft clockwise until the pressure in No 1 cylinder ceases, then turn the crankshaft an additional quarter turn so the piston is approximately midway down its bore.

7 Unscrew the TDC plug from the front of the cylinder block and insert Vauxhall TDC tool EN-48330 or Renault tool TDC MOT 1766, tightening it securely **(see illustrations)**.

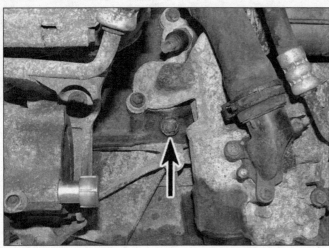

3.7a Unscrew the TDC plug (arrowed)...

3.7b... and insert the crankshaft TDC setting tool

8 Turn the crankshaft anti-clockwise until it just contacts the TDC tool.

9 The engine is now positioned with No 1 piston at TDC on its compression stroke. For further information on setting the timing up, see timing chain removal and refitting in Section 5.

Caution: Do not attempt to rotate the engine whilst the crankshaft TDC tool is in position. If the engine is to be left in this state for a long period of time, it is a good idea to place warning notices inside the vehicle, and in the engine compartment. This will reduce the possibility of the engine being accidentally cranked on the starter motor.

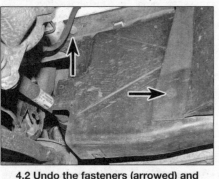

4.2 Undo the fasteners (arrowed) and remove the wheel arch splash shield

4 Crankshaft pulley – removal and refitting

Removal

1 Disconnect the battery negative lead as described in Chapter 5. Apply the handbrake, and then jack up the front of the vehicle and support it on axle stands (see *Jacking and vehicle support*). Remove the right-hand roadwheel.

2 Unbolt and remove the plastic undertray from the beneath the engine/transmission and the splash shield from within the right-hand

4.4 The tool engages with the slots in the pulley spacer to hold the crankshaft

wheel arch **(see illustration)**. Where applicable, release the washer hose from the retaining clip.

3 Remove the auxiliary drivebelt as described in Chapter 1.

4 Slacken the crankshaft pulley retaining bolt. To prevent crankshaft rotation whilst the retaining bolt is slackened, select 4th gear and have an assistant apply the brakes firmly. If this fails to prevent rotation, lock the flywheel ring gear; the starter motor may need to be removed to access the flywheel ring gear. *Do not* be tempted to use the crankshaft timing pin to prevent the crankshaft from rotating (see Section 3). Note that there is a Vauxhall/Renault tool available to hold the crankshaft **(see illustration)**.

5 Remove the retaining bolt, spacer and pulley from the end of the crankshaft **(see illustrations)**. Discard the bolt – a new one must be fitted.

Refitting

6 Remove all traces of locking compound from the crankshaft threads.

7 Refit the pulley to the crankshaft followed by the spacer, then screw in the new retaining bolt. Tighten the bolt first to the specified Stage 1 torque and then through the specified Stage 2 angle, using the method employed on removal to prevent rotation **(see illustration)**.

4.5a Unscrew the pulley bolt, remove it with the spacer...

4.5b... then remove the pulley

4.7 Use an angle gauge to accurately tighten the crankshaft pulley bolt

5.4 Undo the bolts (arrowed) and remove the auxiliary drivebelt tensioner

5.5 Prise off the cover and remove the guide roller bolt

5.8 Squeeze the clip (arrowed) towards the reservoir and slide it upwards from the bracket

8 Refit the auxiliary drivebelt as described in Chapter 1.
9 Refit the splash shield, undertray and road-wheel, and lower the vehicle to the ground.
10 Reconnect the battery negative lead as described in Chapter 5.

5 Timing chain, sprockets and guides – removal, inspection and refitting

Note: *Although it is possible to carry out this procedure with the engine in situ, access is limited. If greater access is required, remove the engine and transmission as described in Chapter 2C.*

Removal

1 Drain the engine oil as described in Chapter 1.
2 Disconnect the battery negative lead as described in Chapter 5.
3 Remove the crankshaft pulley as described in Section 4. **Note:** *Before removing the auxiliary drivebelt, slacken but do not remove the coolant pump pulley bolts.*
4 Undo the bolts and remove the auxiliary drivebelt tensioner from the engine **(see illustration)**.
5 Prise up the cover, and undo the bolt securing the auxiliary drivebelt guide roller **(see illustration)**.
6 Completely unscrew the bolts and remove the coolant pump pulley.
7 Support the engine with a trolley jack from below or an engine hoist from above, as it's

now necessary to remove the right-hand engine mounting assembly.
8 Release the retaining clip and slide the power steering pump fluid reservoir upwards from the bracket, and move to one side **(see illustration)**.
9 Release the wiring loom and fuel pipes from the right-hand engine mounting bracket.
10 Undo the 6 retaining bolts and remove the right-hand engine mounting and bracket assembly **(see illustration)**.
11 Undo the 4 bolts and remove the upper plate from the right-hand engine mounting bracket **(see illustration)**.
12 Undo the bolts and remove the upper stabiliser arm and engine mounting support bracket from the right-hand end of the engine **(see illustrations)**.
13 A new crankshaft oil seal will be required for refitting, so it is recommended that the old

one is removed from the timing cover now as described in Section 13.
14 Progressively unscrew the bolts securing the timing cover to the engine, including the bolt concealed in the hole where the engine mounting bracket was fitted. Note the location of the M8 bolt at the bottom of the engine.
15 Ease the timing cover away while cutting the silicone sealant/adhesive to release it **(see illustration)**. This is a very difficult and time-consuming job, however methodical use of a suitable spatula or thin knife will eventually release the cover.
16 Where fitted, unbolt the air conditioning compressor, and tie it to one side. There's no need to disconnect the refrigerant pipes.
17 If fitted, remove the crankshaft/flywheel locking device used in the crankshaft pulley removal procedure.
18 Using a spanner on the crankshaft nose

5.10 Undo the bolts (arrowed) and remove the mounting with the bracket

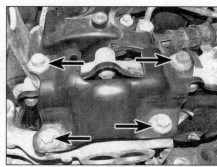

5.11 Upper plate bolts (arrowed)

5.12a Stabiliser arm retaining bolt (arrowed)

5.12b Undo the bolts (arrowed) and remove the engine mounting bracket

5.15 Use a sharp knife to cut through the timing cover sealant

5.18 Turn the crankshaft clockwise until the mark (arrowed) on the crankshaft boss is just after the 6 o'clock position

5.20 The reference hole (arrowed) in the camshaft sprocket should be approximately at the 12 o'clock position

5.21 Undo the intake camshaft timing gear bolt (arrowed)

5.23 Compress the timing chain tensioner and lock it in place by inserting a 3.0 mm diameter rod

flats, turn the crankshaft **clockwise** until the reference mark on the crankshaft boss/ sprocket is positioned just after the 6 o'clock position, and the reference hole in the

camshaft sprocket is just past the 12 o'clock position **(see illustration)**.
19 Unscrew the TDC plug/bolt from the front of the cylinder block and insert Vauxhall TDC

tool EN-48330 or Renault tool TDC MOT 1766, tightening it securely **(see illustrations 3.7a and 3.7b)**.
20 Turn the crankshaft **anti-clockwise** until it just contacts the TDC tool. The engine is now set with No 1 piston at TDC on its compression stroke. Check that the reference mark on the crankshaft is at the 6 o'clock position, and the reference hole in the camshaft sprocket is at the 12 o'clock position **(see illustration)**.
21 Unscrew and remove the bolt securing the timing gear to the intake camshaft **(see illustration)**.
22 If the timing chain is to be re-used, mark it with a dab of paint to ensure it is refitted the same way round. Loosen the 3 exhaust camshaft sprocket retaining bolts.
23 Compress the timing chain hydraulic tensioner piston by pressing the guide, then lock it by inserting a 3.0 mm diameter Allen key or pin in the hole provided **(see illustration)**.
24 Unscrew the bolts and remove the tensioner **(see illustration)**.
25 Unscrew the single bolt and remove the dynamic tensioner guide **(see illustrations)**.
26 Completely remove the 3 exhaust camshaft sprocket bolts, remove the special washer and withdraw the sprocket and chain from the camshaft **(see illustrations)**.
27 Withdraw the sprocket from the nose of the crankshaft, and remove the timing chain **(see illustration)**.
28 Unbolt and remove the static timing chain guide **(see illustration)**.
29 Unscrew and remove the TDC tool from the cylinder block.

5.24 Undo the bolts and remove the tensioner

5.25a Undo the bolt...

5.25b... and remove the dynamic tensioner guide

5.26a Undo the bolts...

5.26b... remove the special washer...

5.26c... then withdraw the exhaust camshaft sprocket

Inspection

30 Thoroughly clean then visually inspect all parts for wear and damage. Check the timing chain for loose pins, cracks, worn rollers and side plates. Check the sprockets for hook-shaped, chipped and broken teeth. Also check the timing chain for wear by extending it horizontally, holding each end and attempting to flex the chain. Renew the timing chain and sprockets as a set if the engine has high mileage or fails inspection. Check the chain guides for excessive wear and scoring and renew them if necessary. Note that some scoring is normal but if they are deeply grooved they must be renewed. Vauxhall and Renault recommend the tensioner (and retaining bolts) is renewed regardless of condition.

Refitting

31 Carefully clean the surfaces of the timing cover, cylinder block and cylinder head, taking care not to damage the surfaces.
32 Check that the engine is still set to its TDC position as described in Section 3 using the TDC setting tools EN-48330 or TDC MOT 1766.
33 Position the timing mark on the intake camshaft timing gear at 12 o'clock and align it with the boss on the camshaft housing. Make sure that the groove on the exhaust camshaft is horizontal with the larger offset uppermost **(see illustration)**.
34 Locate the timing chain on the crankshaft sprocket so that the copper link is aligned with the timing mark, then locate the sprocket on the nose of the crankshaft. Raise the chain to keep it engaged with the crankshaft sprocket while locating it onto the rigid tensioner guide, then locate the exhaust camshaft sprocket in the upper loop so that the copper link aligns with the TDC hole in the sprocket **(see illustrations)**. **Note:** *A new timing chain may be fitted either way round, however a re-used chain should be fitted in its original orientation as noted during removal.*
35 Fit the exhaust camshaft sprocket onto its timing gear.
36 Refit the static timing chain guide and tighten the new bolts to the specified torque.
37 Locate the new special washer and bolts on the exhaust camshaft timing gear and finger-tighten the bolts at this stage. The sprocket must be free to rotate within the elongated holes

5.27 Withdraw the sprocket from the crankshaft

5.28 Remove the static timing chain guide

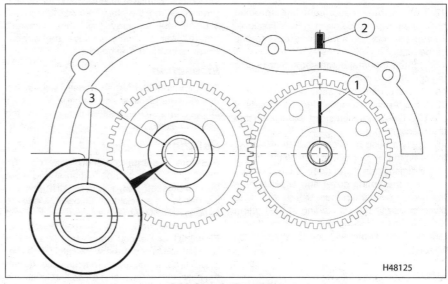

5.33 Camshaft settings

1 *TDC mark on intake camshaft timing gear*
2 *Boss on the camshaft housing*
3 *Exhaust camshaft offset at TDC*

38 Locate the dynamic tensioner guide in position and tighten the new single bolt to the specified torque.
39 Fit the new hydraulic tensioner together with locking Allen key, insert the new bolts and tighten to the specified torque. Make sure the tensioner is in contact with the cylinder block before tightening the bolts.
40 Remove the locking Allen key or pin to allow the tensioner piston to tension the timing chain.

41 At this stage Vauxhall tool EN-48332 or Renault tool MOT 1769 is required to set the gears and sprocket in position while the sprocket/gear bolts are tightened. Engage the tool with the slot on the end of the exhaust camshaft then turn the tool until it is possible to locate the dowels in the intake camshaft timing gear **(see illustrations)**. Insert the bolt through the top of the tool and tighten into the hole in the camshaft housing.

5.34a Align the copper link with the mark on the crankshaft sprocket (arrowed)...

5.34b... then fit the exhaust camshaft sprocket with the copper link aligned with the reference hole

5.41a Engage the tool with the holes in the intake camshaft timing gear and the slot in the exhaust sprocket (arrowed)

5.41b Secure the tool to the camshaft housing with a bolt (arrowed)

42 Tighten the exhaust camshaft sprocket bolts in the two stages given in Specifications. The special tool has a hole for access to one of the bolts.

43 Tighten the intake camshaft gear bolt to the specified torque.

44 Remove camshaft setting tool and the TDC tool. Apply locking fluid to the threads of the TDC hole plug, then insert and tighten it to the specified torque.

45 Apply a bead of silicone adhesive/sealant to the timing cover contact face on the engine of the dimensions shown **(see illustrations)**.

46 Refit the timing cover and finger-tighten the bolts, then tighten them in the two stages given in Specifications starting at the bottom right M8 bolt and working in an anti-clockwise direction so that the final bolt to tighten is the M6 bolt.

47 The remainder of refitting is a reversal of removal, noting the following points:

a) *Tighten all fasteners to their specified torque where given.*

b) *Refill the engine with clean oil as described in Chapter 1.*

c) *Reconnect the battery negative lead as described in Chapter 5.*

---

6 Timing gears –
removal, inspection and refitting

Removal

1 Remove the timing chain, sprockets and guides as described in Section 5.

2 Insert a screwdriver in the intake camshaft timing gear special hole, and compress the wear compensation spring by lifting the screwdriver in order to release it from the exhaust camshaft timing gear.

3 Slide the exhaust camshaft timing gear from the exhaust camshaft extension and release the screwdriver from the intake camshaft timing gear.

4 Completely unscrew the intake camshaft timing gear bolt and remove the spacer followed by the timing gear.

Inspection

5 Thoroughly clean then visually inspect the timing gears for wear and damage. Check for chipped and broken gear teeth and renew the gears if necessary.

Refitting

6 Before the intake timing gear can be refitted, the wear compensation spring must be compressed and a 4.0 mm diameter pin inserted in the special hole to lock it. Moderate force is necessary to compress the spring and it is recommended that Vauxhall bench tool EN-48331 or Renault bench tool MOT 1763 be used to carry out the work safely, however a similar home-made tool may be used. Clamp the baseplate of the tool in a vice and locate the intake camshaft timing gear on it making sure that the key is engaged to lock it. Now locate the tool lever on its pivot and tighten the wing nut. Engage the lever teeth with the lower wear compensation teeth and turn the lever anti-clockwise until the wear compensation teeth are aligned with the gear teeth. Lock the two gear sections in this position using a 4.0 mm

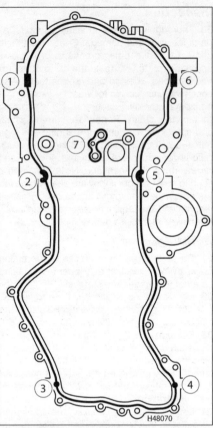

5.45a Sealant application for the timing cover

Bead diameter 5 ± 2 mm from points 1 to 6 passing around the lower part of the engine

Bead diameter 11 ± 2 mm for a length of 10 to 15 mm on points 1, 2, 3, 4, 5 and 6

Bead diameter 3.5 ± 1 mm from points 6 to 1 passing around the upper part of the cylinder head

Bead diameter 3.5 ± 1 mm around the inner edge 7

5.45b Apply a bead of silicone sealant/adhesive to the timing cover contact face...

5.45c... including the central 'island'

6.6 Use the bench tool to set the wear compensator on the intake camshaft timing gear

6.7 Locate the timing gear on the intake camshaft...

6.8... then fit the spacer and bolt

6.10a Locate the timing gear on the exhaust camshaft...

6.10b... so that the mounting holes (arrowed) are centre within the gear elongated slots

6.11 Remove the locking pin from the intake camshaft timing gear

diameter pin inserted in the special hole (see illustration). Note: *New intake camshaft timing gears are supplied with a plastic locking pin already fitted.*

7 Remove the intake camshaft timing gear from the tool and locate it on the intake camshaft (see illustration).

8 Refit the spacer and finger-tighten the bolt (see illustration).

9 Position the timing mark on the intake camshaft timing gear at 12 o'clock position. Make sure that the groove on the exhaust camshaft is horizontal with the larger offset uppermost.

10 Offer the exhaust camshaft timing gear onto the camshaft so that the mounting holes are central within the gear elongated slots, then engage the gear teeth with the intake camshaft timing gear and press it fully into position (see illustrations).

11 Check the alignment of the intake camshaft

timing gear (12 o'clock), and the exhaust camshaft timing gear with the camshaft slots, then remove the locking pin from the intake camshaft timing gear (see illustration).

12 Refit the timing chain, sprockets and guides as described in Section 5.

7 Camshafts – removal, inspection and refitting

Removal

1 Disconnect the battery negative lead as described in Chapter 5.

2 Remove the front bumper, bonnet and radiator grille as described in Chapter 11.

3 Pull the rubber seal from the top edge of the bonnet slam panel.

4 Remove both front headlights as described in Chapter 12.

5 Undo the bolts, drill out the rivets and remove the front impact absorbers/air deflector assembly (see illustrations).

6 Release the retaining clip and slide the power steering fluid reservoir upwards from the front panel (see illustration 5.8). There's no need to disconnect the pipes. Position the reservoir to one side.

7 Release the clamps and remove the intercooler hoses.

8 Undo the bolts securing the air cleaner support frame to the bonnet slam panel (see illustration).

9 Make alignment marks between the bonnet lock and the slam panel, then undo the bolts, manoeuvre the lock from place, prise off the cover and disconnect the release cable (see illustrations). Release the cable/wiring loom from the retaining clips on the slam panel.

10 Undo the bolts and release the engine

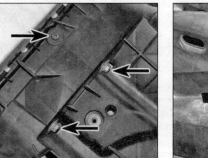

7.5a Drill out the rivets, undo the bolts (arrowed) at the side...

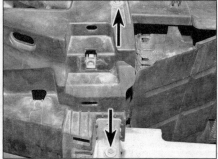

7.5b... and front of the impact absorber (arrowed)

7.8 Support frame-to-bonnet slam panel bolts (arrowed)

7.9a Bonnet lock bolts (arrowed)

7.9b Slide off the plate and disconnect the release cable

7.10 Undo the bolt (arrowed) securing the ECM bracket

management ECM bracket and bonnet alarm contact switch bracket (where fitted) from the slam panel (see illustration).

11 Release the clips, undo the bolts, and remove the complete front/slam panel from the vehicle (see illustrations).

12 Release the clip and remove the right-hand air deflector panel adjacent to the radiator.

13 Remove the air cleaner assembly and fuel injectors as described in Chapter 4A. On M9R 630 engines, remove the turbocharger air hoses as described in Chapter 4A.

14 Remove the fuel injectors as described in Chapter 4A.

15 Remove the timing chain, sprockets and gears as described in Sections 5 and 6.

16 Remove the brake vacuum pump as described in Chapter 9.

17 Unscrew the bolts and remove the fuel collector outlet pipe from the rear of the cylinder head.

18 Undo the 2 bolts and remove the rear lifting eye from the cylinder head.

19 Progressively unscrew the camshaft housing retaining bolts then carefully remove the housing complete with camshafts from the top of the cylinder head. If necessary, use a screwdriver and block of wood to lever the housing but take care not to damage the joint faces of the housing and cylinder head. There is no need to remove the camshaft followers and hydraulic lifters from the cylinder head.

20 With the housing upside down on the workbench, note the location of the intake and exhaust camshafts, and the marks on the bearing caps to identify their position. The caps are marked ADM1 and ADM2 for the intake camshaft, and ECH1 and ECH2 for the exhaust camshaft (see illustrations).

21 Progressively unscrew the bolts, remove the bearing caps and lift the camshafts from the housing (see illustrations).

22 If the exhaust camshaft is to be renewed, remove the high-pressure fuel pump drivegear from it as follows (see illustration). Grip the gear in a vice equipped with soft metal plates to protect the gear, then loosen the bolt, support the camshaft and fully unscrew the bolt.

7.11a The front panel is secured by 2 bolts (arrowed) at the right-hand edge...

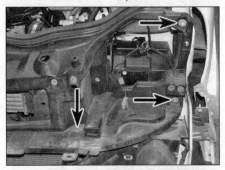

7.11b... 3 bolts (arrowed) on the left-hand side...

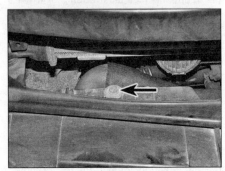

7.11c... 1 bolt (arrowed) to the right of centre...

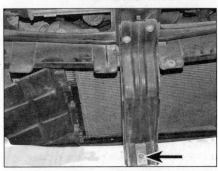

7.11d... and 1 bolt (arrowed) at the base of the central bracket

7.11e Lift the entire front panel from place

7.20a Intake camshaft bearing cap marking

7.20b Exhaust camshaft bearing cap marking

7.21a Remove the camshaft bearing caps

7.21b Remove the intake camshaft...

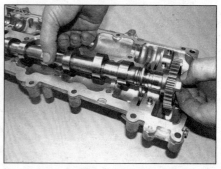

7.21c... and the exhaust camshaft

7.22 High-pressure pump drivegear on the exhaust camshaft

7.26 Lubricate the bearing surfaces before fitting the camshafts

7.28 Camshafts set to their TDC positions (arrowed)

Inspection

23 Thoroughly clean all components taking care to remove all traces of sealant from the joint faces.

24 Examine the camshaft bearing surfaces and cam lobes for signs of wear ridges and scoring. Renew the camshaft if any of these conditions are apparent. Examine the condition of the bearing surfaces, both on the camshaft journals and in the cylinder head/bearing caps/housing. If the bearing surfaces are worn excessively, the cylinder head, camshafts and housing will need to be renewed. Check the teeth of the high-pressure pump drivegear for wear and chipping, and if necessary renew the gear.

Refitting

25 If removed, refit the high-pressure pump drivegear by gripping it in the soft-metal-jawed vice, locating the camshaft from beneath, then screwing on new the bolt. Tighten the bolt in the stages given in Specifications.

26 Lubricate the bearing surfaces with clean engine oil then locate the camshafts in the housing in their previously-noted positions **(see illustration)**.

27 Refit the bearing caps, making sure they make contact with the housing before inserting the bolts finger-tight. Finally, tighten the bolts to their specified torque.

28 The camshafts must now be set to their TDC positions. Temporarily place the housing on the bench in its normal position with the camshafts facing downward. Turn the exhaust camshaft as necessary so that the timing

end grooves are horizontal with the larger offset uppermost. Turn the inlet manifold side camshaft as necessary so that the timing mark is at 12 o'clock position **(see illustration)**.

29 Ensure the contact faces are clean, then apply a bead of silicone 1.5 ± 1.0 mm in diameter around the edges and central 'islands' of the cylinder head upper face. Make sure the bead runs on the inner side of the outer bolt holes **(see illustrations)**.

30 To assist in locating the camshaft housing correctly on the cylinder head, temporarily screw two M6 studs, 60 mm long in the diagonally-opposite holes **(see illustration)**.

31 Set the crankshaft in its TDC position with pistons 1 and 4 at the top of their cylinders.

32 Carefully locate the camshaft housing complete with camshafts onto the top of the

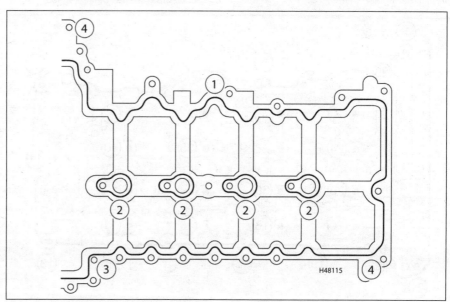

7.29a Silicone adhesive/sealant application to the cylinder head

1 Exhaust side bead   *2 Central 'islands'*   *3 Inlet side bead*   *4 Guide stud location*

7.29b Apply sealant to the edges...

7.29c... and central 'islands' of the cylinder head upper face

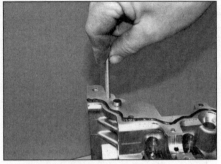

7.30 Use two M6 studs as guides when refitting the camshaft housing

7.32 Locate the camshaft housing on the cylinder head

cylinder head, making sure that the guide studs enter the correct holes before lowering it into position **(see illustration)**.
33 Referring to the diagram **(see illustration 7.36)** first insert then progressively tighten bolts 2, 20, 7 and 14 to the specified torque. Remove the two guide studs.
34 Insert the remaining retaining bolts and finger-tighten them at this stage.
35 Completely loosen bolts 2, 20, 7 and 14, then finger-tighten them.

36 Tighten the camshaft housing bolts to the specified torque in the sequence shown **(see illustration)**. Wipe away excess sealant from the outer joint face.
37 The remainder of refitting is a reversal of removal.
38 On completion check the engine oil level as described in *Weekly checks*. Start the engine and check for any noises. **Note:** *Do not run the engine at high speeds until the correct oil pressure has been reached.*

8 Cylinder head – removal and refitting

Note 1: *The cylinder head is removed with the inlet and exhaust manifold/turbocharger still attached. The aid of an assistant will be required, and the assembly is very heavy.*
Note 2: *Before restarting the engine, it may be necessary to use a diagnostic tool to clear any faults that may be stored in the injection ECU.*

Removal

1 Disconnect the battery negative lead as described in Chapter 5, then drain the cooling system with reference to Chapter 1.
2 Remove the camshaft housing as described in Section 7, paras 1 to 19.
3 Disconnect the wiring plug, then undo the bolts and remove the heater blower motor housing from the engine compartment bulkhead **(see illustrations)**.
4 Disconnect the air hoses from the turbocharger.
5 According to version, remove the particulate filter or the catalytic converter from the turbocharger outlet as described in Chapter 4A. Remove the turbocharger oil feed and return pipes as described in Chapter 4A. Plug the openings to prevent contamination.
6 Release the clamp and disconnect the upper coolant hose from the engine **(see illustration)**.
7 Note their fitted positions, then release the clamps and disconnect the coolant hoses from the thermostat housing at the left-hand end of the cylinder head, then undo the bolts and remove the thermostat housing **(see illustration)**.
8 Remove the oil level dipstick/filler cap then unbolt and remove the guide tube. Renew the O-ring seal.
9 Remove the throttle valve (also referred to as a damper valve) as described in Chapter 4A.
10 Remove the exhaust gas recirculation rigid pipes with reference to Chapter 4B.
11 Progressively slacken the cylinder head bolts by half a turn at a time until all bolts can be unscrewed by hand and removed.
12 Lift the cylinder head upwards and

8.3a The heater blower motor housing is secured by a nut (arrowed) on the right-hand side...

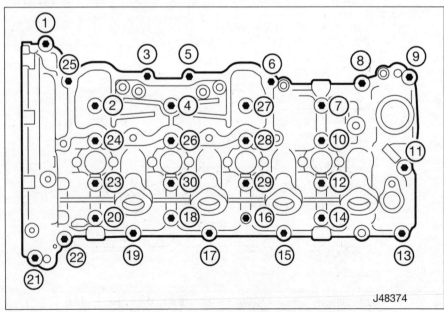

7.36 Camshaft housing bolt tightening sequence

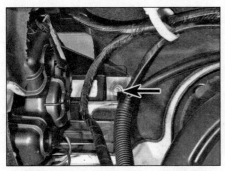

8.3b... a nut (arrowed) on the left-hand side...

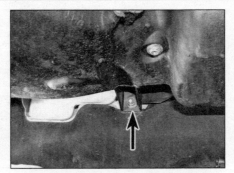

8.3c... a nut (arrowed) underneath...

8.3d... and a bolt (arrowed) at the upper edge

off the cylinder block. If it is stuck, tap it upwards using a hammer and block of wood. *Do not* try to rotate it (it is located by two dowels), nor attempt to prise it free using a screwdriver inserted between the block and head faces. If the locating dowels are a loose fit, remove them and store them with the head for safe-keeping. As the head is removed, check around the cylinder head to make sure everything has been disconnected.

13 Remove the cylinder head gasket.

14 Before removing the hydraulic lifters and rockers, have ready a container with 16 compartments and fill the container with engine oil to the depth of the lifters. **Note:** *The lifters must remain immersed in oil during the period they are removed from the cylinder head to prevent air entering them.*

15 Remove each hydraulic lifter and follower assembly and place in the container so that they can each be identified for location in the cylinder head. It is important they are each refitted to their correct bore on reassembly **(see illustrations)**.

Inspection

16 The mating faces of the cylinder head and block must be perfectly clean before refitting the head. Use a scraper (taking care not to damage the surface of the head) to remove all traces of gasket and carbon, and also clean the tops of the pistons. Take particular care with the aluminium cylinder head, as the soft metal is damaged easily. Also, make sure that

8.6 Upper coolant hose retaining clip (arrowed)

debris is not allowed to enter the oil and water channels – this is particularly important for the oil circuit, as carbon could block the oil supply to the camshaft or crankshaft bearings. Using adhesive tape and paper, seal the water, oil and bolt holes in the cylinder block. To prevent carbon entering the gap between the pistons and bores, smear a little grease in the gap. After cleaning the piston, rotate the crankshaft so that the piston moves down the bore, and then wipe out the grease and carbon with a cloth rag. Clean the piston crowns in the same way.

17 Check the block and head for nicks, deep scratches and other damage. If slight, they may be removed carefully with a file. More serious damage may be repaired by machining – Check with a dealer or engine reconditioning specialist.

18 If warpage of the cylinder head is

8.7 Thermostat housing bolts (arrowed)

suspected, use a straight-edge to check it for distortion. Refer to Chapter 2C if necessary.

19 Ensure that the cylinder head bolt holes in the block are clean and free of oil. Syringe or soak up any oil left in the bolt holes. This is most important in order that the correct bolt tightening torque can be applied and to prevent the possibility of the block being cracked by hydraulic pressure when the bolts are tightened.

20 Examine the cylinder head bolt threads in the cylinder block for damage. If necessary, use the correct-size tap to chase out the threads in the block, and use a die to clean the threads on the bolts. The cylinder head bolts must be discarded and renewed, regardless of their apparent condition. Also, check that the locating dowels are in good condition and correctly located in the cylinder block **(see illustration)**.

8.15a Hydraulic lifter and follower assembly in position

8.15b Remove the lifter and follower assembly

8.15c Keep the lifter and follower assemblies immersed in clean oil, and identified so they can be refitted to their original positions

8.20 Head locating dowel (arrowed) in the cylinder block

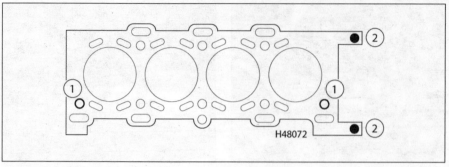

8.22 Ensure the locating dowels (1) are correctly fitted, then apply sealant to the areas (2) shown

8.23a Locate the cylinder head gasket on the block...

8.23b... and apply silicone adhesive/sealant to the timing end extremities

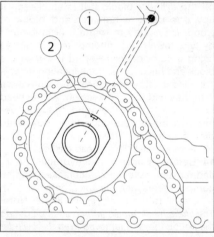

8.24 Align the groove (2) in the crankshaft nose with the bolt hole (1) on the cylinder block

Refitting

21 Ensure that the mating faces of the cylinder block and head are spotlessly clean, that the retaining bolt threads are also clean and dry, and that they screw easily in and out of their locations.

22 Ensure that the locating dowels are correctly fitted to the block, then apply 2 drops of silicone adhesive/sealant (5 to 7 mm diameter) to the surface of the two extremities at the timing end of the block (see illustration).

23 Locate the new cylinder head gasket on the block, then again apply 2 drops of silicone adhesive/sealant (5 to 7 mm diameter) to the timing end extremities of the gasket (see illustrations).

24 Using a spanner on the crankshaft nose flats, turn the crankshaft clockwise until the groove is aligned with the bolt hole on the cylinder block (see illustration). This will position the pistons halfway up the cylinder bores.

25 Carefully lower the cylinder head onto the block, engaging it over the dowels. Insert the cylinder new head bolts and finger-tighten them at this stage (see illustrations). Do not lubricate the bolt threads.

26 Working progressively, starting from the centre bolts and working outwards in a spiral motion, tighten the cylinder head bolts to their Stage 1 torque setting, using a torque wrench and suitable socket.

27 Using the same sequence, tighten the cylinder head bolts to their Stage 2 torque setting.

28 Once all bolts are tightened to the Stage 2 torque setting, using the same sequence, tighten each bolt through its specified final Stage 3 angle, using a socket and extension bar (see illustration). It is recommended that an angle-measuring gauge be used during this stage of the tightening, to ensure accuracy.

29 Clean away any excess sealant from the timing end of the head gasket.

30 If the hydraulic lifters and rockers have remained immersed in oil, no air will have entered them, however if there is any doubt, compress the piston head of the lifter and check that it does not move. If it does, the lifter may be re-primed by immersing it in clean oil. Also, check that the rocker-to-lifter clips are correctly in place.

31 Lubricate the lifter bores in the cylinder head with engine oil, then refit each hydraulic lifter and rocker assembly to its previously-noted location making sure that the rockers are correctly positioned on the valves.

8.25a Lower the cylinder head onto the block...

8.25b... and insert the new retaining bolts

8.28 Use an angle-gauge to accurately tighten the cylinder head bolts

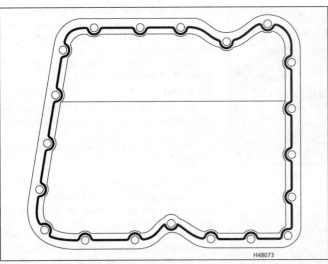

9.7a Apply silicone sealant/adhesive to the sump perimeter as shown

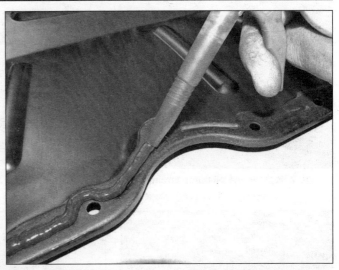

9.7b Apply silicone sealant/adhesive to the sump

32 The remainder of refitting is a reversal of removal, noting the following points:
a) *Tighten all fasteners to their specified torque where given.*
b) *Reconnect the battery negative lead as described in Chapter 5.*
c) *Refill the cooling system as described in Chapter 1.*
d) *Change the oil filter and fill the engine with clean engine oil as described in Chapter 1.*

9 Sump –
removal and refitting

Removal

1 Apply the handbrake, then jack up the front of the vehicle and support it on axle stands (see *Jacking and vehicle support*). Undo the retaining screws and remove the undertray from beneath the engine/transmission.

2 Drain the engine oil as described in Chapter 1, then refit and tighten the drain plug, using a new sealing washer. Ensure all the oil is completely drained.
3 Remove the engine oil level dipstick.
4 Unscrew and remove the bolts securing the sump to the cylinder block baseplate.
5 The sump is sealed to the cylinder block baseplate with strong silicone adhesive/sealant which is very difficult to cut, however methodical use of a suitable spatula or thin knife will release the sump. Take care not to distort or damage the mating surfaces of the sump and baseplate, and take adequate precautions to catch any oil remaining in the sump.

Refitting

6 Thoroughly clean the mating surfaces of the sump and cylinder block baseplate, taking care not to damage their surfaces.
7 Apply a 5 ± 2 mm diameter bead of silicone adhesive/sealant to the sump as shown **(see illustrations)**.

8 Lift the sump into position making sure it is correctly aligned with the holes in the baseplate, then insert the bolts and finger-tighten them **(see illustration)**.
9 Tighten the sump bolts to the Stage 1 torque given in Specifications using the sequence shown **(see illustration)**.
10 Tighten the sump bolts to the Stage 2 torque using the same sequence.
11 Refit the undertray and lower the vehicle to the ground.
12 Fill the engine with fresh oil with reference to Chapter 1.

10 Oil pump, drive chain and sprocket – removal, inspection and refitting

Removal

Oil pump

1 Remove the sump as described in Section 9.

9.8 Lift the sump into position

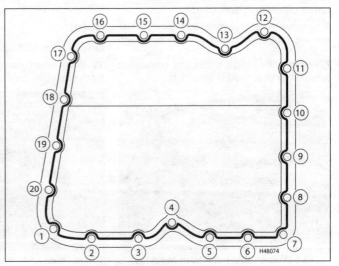

9.9 Sump bolt tightening sequence

10.2 Remove the oil pump strainer

10.4a Undo the mounting bolts...

10.4b... then unhook the drive chain and remove the oil pump

10.5 Oil pump splash plate (arrowed)

2 Unscrew the two bolts and remove the oil pump strainer from the baseplate **(see illustration)**.

3 Unscrew the bolt securing the splash plate to the oil pump. The bolt goes through the oil pump housing to the splash plate located on the crankshaft side of the oil pump.

4 Unscrew the mounting bolts then release the drive sprocket from the drive chain and withdraw the oil pump **(see illustrations)**. If necessary, a length of bent wire may help to unhook the chain from the sprocket.

5 If necessary, remove the splash plate through the access aperture – this is quite difficult as there is limited room **(see illustration)**.

Drive chain and sprocket

6 To remove the drive chain and sprocket first remove the oil pump as previously described in this Section.

7 Remove the timing chain and crankshaft sprocket as described in Section 5.

10.8 Unhook the chain from the drive sprocket...

8 Unhook the drive chain from the drive sprocket on the crankshaft and remove the chain **(see illustration)**.

9 Slide the drive sprocket from the nose of the crankshaft, while noting its fitted position **(see illustration)**.

Inspection

10 Clean the components and carefully examine the chain, sprockets and pump for any signs of excessive wear. If evident, it is recommended that all the components are renewed as a set.

11 Before refitting the oil pump, prime it by filling with clean engine oil whilst rotating the sprocket clockwise.

Refitting

Drive chain and sprocket

12 Wipe clean the oil pump and cylinder block mating surfaces.

10.9... then slide the drive sprocket from the nose of the crankshaft

13 Slide the drive sprocket fully onto the crankshaft as previously-noted, then feed the chain through the baseplate aperture and onto the sprocket.

14 Refit the timing chain and crankshaft sprocket as described in Section 5.

Oil pump

15 Lift the oil pump into position on the cylinder block, then engage it with the drive chain.

16 Insert the oil pump mounting bolts and the splash plate-to-pump bolt finger-tight at this stage.

17 Tighten the oil pump mounting bolts in the two stages given in the Specifications.

18 Tighten the splash plate-to-pump bolt to the specified torque.

19 Refit the oil pump strainer together with a new seal and finger-tighten the bolts, then fully tighten the bolts to the specified torque.

20 Refit the sump as described in Section 9.

11 Cylinder block baseplate – removal and refitting

Note: *Removal of the engine is not essential to carry out this procedure, however, given the amount of work involved, and the restricted access, It may well be preferable to remove the engine and transmission as described in Chapter 2C.*

Removal

1 Remove the timing cover with reference to Section 5.

2 Remove the transmission as described in Chapter 7. Ensure the engine is well-supported during this and subsequent procedures in this Section.

3 Remove the clutch assembly as described in Chapter 6.

4 Remove the flywheel as described in Section 12.

5 Remove the transmission end crankshaft oil seal housing as described in Section 13.

6 Remove the sump as described in Section 9.

7 Unscrew the two bolts and remove the oil pump strainer from the baseplate. It is not necessary to remove the oil pump.

8 The baseplate bolt access holes at the transmission end may be fitted with blanking covers. If so, drill and cut them out using a 13 mm drill bit so that a socket can be inserted onto the bolts. The outer covers will have to be cut with a cold chisel, and the inner covers driven out using a suitable tube or drift **(see illustrations)**. Obtain new covers for refitting. Where blanking covers are not fitted, extra long bolts are used instead.

9 Progressively unscrew and remove the 16 baseplate bolts.

10 The baseplate is sealed to the crankcase with silicone adhesive/sealant and is likely to be difficult to remove. To help break the seal, insert two long studs into the outer bolt holes at the transmission end, and fit a nut and

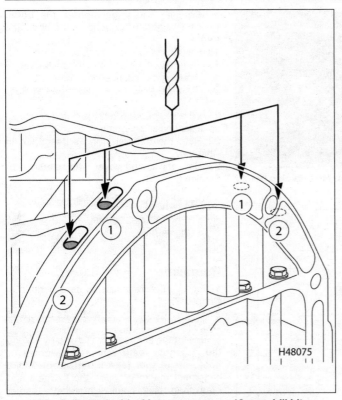

11.8a Drill out the blanking covers use a 13 mm drill bit...

1 Inner cover locations   *2 Outer cover locations*

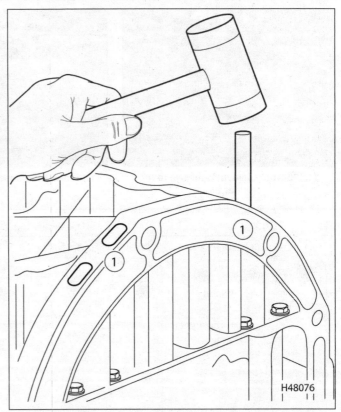

11.8b... then drive out the inner covers using a suitable drift

washer to each stud as shown. Progressively tighten the nuts to force the baseplate off of the crankcase **(see illustration)**. On completion, remove the studs.

Refitting

11 Thoroughly clean the mating surfaces of the baseplate, crankcase and timing cover, taking care not to damage their surfaces.

12 Apply a 5 ± 2 mm diameter bead of silicone adhesive/sealant to the cylinder block as shown **(see illustrations)**.

13 If necessary, the studs used to separate the baseplate from the crankcase may be used without their nuts and washers as guides during refitting. Locate the baseplate on the crankcase making sure the bolt holes are correctly aligned, then insert the bolts and finger-tighten them **(see illustration)**.

14 Tighten the baseplate bolts to the specified torque, working in sequence from the

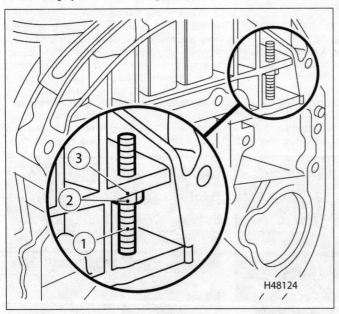

11.10 Use two studs to release the baseplate from the crankcase

1 Stud   *2 Nut*   *3 Washer*

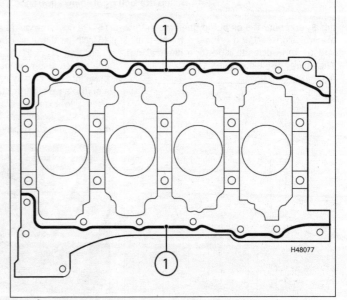

11.12a Apply silicone sealant/adhesive to the cylinder block/ crankcase as shown (1)

11.12b Apply sealant/adhesive to the cylinder block

11.13 Insert the baseplate retaining bolts

a new seal and finger-tighten the bolts, then fully-tighten the bolts to the specified torque.
18 Refit the sump as described in Section 9.
19 Fit a new transmission end crankshaft oil seal housing as described in Section 13.
20 Refit the flywheel as described in Section 12.
21 Where applicable, refit the clutch assembly as described in Chapter 6.
22 Refit the transmission as described in Chapter 7.
23 Refit the timing cover with reference to Section 5.

12 Flywheel –
removal, inspection and refitting

Removal

1 Remove the transmission as described in Chapter 7.
2 Remove the clutch assembly as described in Chapter 6.
3 Prevent the flywheel from turning by locking the ring gear teeth with a screwdriver or home-made tool **(see illustration)**. Make alignment marks between the flywheel and crankshaft using paint or a suitable marker pen.
4 Slacken and remove the retaining bolts and remove the flywheel from the crankshaft flange **(see illustrations)**. Do not drop it, as it is very heavy. If the locating dowel (where fitted) is a loose fit in the crankshaft end, remove and store it with the flywheel for safe-keeping. Discard the bolts, as they should be renewed whenever they are disturbed.

Inspection

5 Examine the flywheel for scoring of the clutch face, and for wear or chipping of the ring gear teeth. If the clutch face is scored, the flywheel may be surface-ground, but renewal is preferable. Seek the advice of a dealer or engine-reconditioning specialist to see if machining is possible. If the ring gear is worn or damaged, the flywheel must be renewed, as it is not possible to renew the ring gear separately. Clean the bolt hole threads in the crankshaft – an old retaining bolt with three

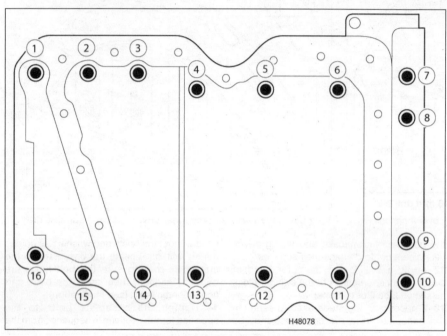

11.14 Baseplate bolt tightening sequence

timing end near the oil pump, then around the transmission end and returning to the timing end on the opposite side **(see illustration)**. Wipe away any excess sealant.

15 Remove the guide studs.
16 Where blanking covers are fitted, apply a 5 ± 2 mm diameter bead of silicone adhesive/ sealant to the new covers before pressing them into position by hand initially. Finally, use a suitable tube or drift to drive in new blanking covers to a depth of 3.0 mm from the lower edge of the holes **(see illustration)**.
17 Refit the oil pump strainer together with

11.16 Apply sealant to the new covers (1) before driving them into the holes (2)

12.3 Home-made tool for locking the flywheel

12.4a Unscrew and remove the bolts...

12.4b... then withdraw the flywheel from the crankshaft flange

12.5 Old flywheel bolts with 3 hacksaw cuts on the threads is ideal to clean the threads in the crankshaft

12.7a Turn the flywheel secondary element anti-clockwise and mark the limit of its travel on the starter ring gear teeth...

12.7b... then turn the secondary element clockwise, and mark its travel limit again

12.9a Attach a length of steel strip to the flywheel secondary element (drive surface)...

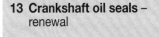

12.9b... and mount a DTI gauge in-line with the edge of the secondary element

cuts on the threads is ideal for doing this (see illustration).

6 Some of these vehicles are fitted with dual mass flywheels. While neither Vauxhall nor Renault publish any checking procedures, some clutch and flywheel manufacturers do publish some information concerning rotational and lateral movement.

7 In order to check the rotational movement, lock the flywheel in place as previously described. Rotate the flywheel secondary element (drive surface) by hand anti-clockwise, mark its position in relation to the primary flywheel element (bolted to the crankshaft), then rotate it by hand clockwise and mark its position. Bear in mind, that the *free* rotational movement is being measured here – do not use excessive force to rotate the secondary element. Mark the limits of the rotational movement is relation to the number of flywheel starter ring gear teeth (see illustrations).

8 The number of starter ring gear teeth

12.12 Mark the bolts and holes to ensure correct angle-tightening of the flywheel bolts

travelled by the flywheel secondary element, should be noted and compared to the flywheel manufacturer's specification. The permissible travel varies enormously, and differs from one flywheel part number to the next. If in any doubt, consult a dealer or transmission specialist as to whether a new unit is needed.

9 In order to check the lateral movement of the flywheel, attach a length of steel strip to the flywheel secondary element (drive surface), and mount a DTI gauge so that it measures in-line with the edge of the secondary flywheel element (see illustrations). Pull the steel strip away from the flywheel, zero the DTI gauge, then push the strip towards the flywheel and read off the measurement. Again, the permissible amount of lateral movement varies from one flywheel part number to the next. Compare the measurement taken with the manufacturer's specification. If in any doubt, consult a dealer or transmission specialist as to whether a new unit is needed.

Refitting

10 Clean the mating surfaces of the flywheel and crankshaft.

11 Ensure that the locating dowel is in position (where fitted) and offer up the flywheel, locating it on the dowel, and fit the new retaining bolts. If the original is being refitted, align the marks made prior to removal.

12 Lock the flywheel using the method employed on dismantling, and tighten the retaining bolts to the specified torque and angle. To ensure all the bolts are tightened to the correct angle, make marks on the bolts and flywheel bolt holes (see illustration).

13 Refit the clutch as described in Chapter 6.
14 Refit the transmission as described in Chapter 7.

13 Crankshaft oil seals – renewal

Timing end oil seal

1 Remove the crankshaft pulley as described in Section 4.

2 A socket adapter is provided with the new crankshaft oil seal. Using the adapter, unscrew the old oil seal from the timing cover by rotating it anti-clockwise approximately 30°.

3 Clean the crankshaft and timing cover.

4 The new oil seal must not be lubricated during fitting. First, position the seal with its three raised segments aligned with the cut-outs in the timing cover and push the seal

13.4 Locate the new seal on the timing cover with the raised segments aligned with the cut-outs

13.5 Fit the adapter and tighten the seal securely

13.8 Remove the transmission end oil seal and housing

13.10 Use 3 bolts to act as guides when fitting the new oil seal housing

13.11 Press the housing into position and remove the seal protector

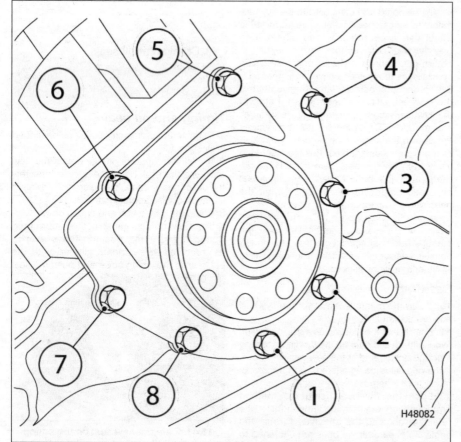

13.12 Tightening sequence for the transmission end oil seal housing bolts

H48082

into the cover using hand pressure only. This will force the plastic protector from the centre of the oil seal **(see illustration)**.

5 Using the adapter, tighten the oil seal securely **(see illustration)**.

6 Refit the crankshaft pulley as described in Section 4.

Transmission end oil seal

Note: *The transmission end oil seal is supplied together with the oil seal housing and cannot be renewed separately.*

7 Remove the flywheel as described in Section 12.

8 Unscrew the bolts and remove the oil seal housing from the cylinder block/baseplate **(see illustration)**.

9 Clean the contact faces of the cylinder block and baseplate. Do not remove the protector or touch the lip of the new oil seal during fitting as this will result in oil leakage.

10 Carefully locate the oil seal and housing onto the crankshaft and insert three 90 mm long M6 bolts loosely to act as guides **(see illustration)**. Do not press the housing into position at this stage.

11 Apply even pressure to the housing and press it into position until it contacts the cylinder block. Now remove the protector and the 3 guide bolts **(see illustration)**.

12 Insert the retaining bolts and finger-tighten, then tighten them to the initial torque given in the Specifications in the sequence shown **(see illustration)**.

13 Tighten the bolts to their final torque using the same sequence.

14 Refit the flywheel as described in Section 12.

14 Engine/transmission mountings – inspection and renewal

Inspection

1 If improved access is required, apply the handbrake, then jack up the front of the vehicle and support it on axle stands (see *Jacking and vehicle support*).

2 Check the mounting rubber to see if it is cracked, hardened or separated from the metal at any point; renew the mounting if any such damage or deterioration is evident.

3 Check that all the mounting's fasteners are securely tightened; use a torque wrench to check if possible.

4 Using a large screwdriver or a crowbar, check for wear in the mounting by carefully levering against it to check for free play. While some free play is to be expected, even from new components, excessive wear should be obvious. If excessive free play is found, check first that the fasteners are correctly secured, and then renew any worn components as described below.

5 Where this is not possible, enlist the aid of an assistant to move the engine/transmission

14.8 Unclip the fuel pipes and wiring from the engine mounting bracket

14.9 Undo the engine mounting bolts (arrowed)

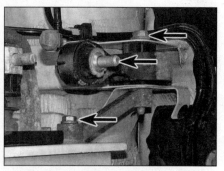

14.14 Upper stabiliser bolts (arrowed – shown with the engine remove for clarity)

back-and-forth, or from side-to-side, while you watch the mounting.

Renewal

Right-hand mounting

6 Remove the engine undertray, then place a jack beneath the engine baseplate (NOT the sump) with a block of wood on the jack head. Raise the jack until it is supporting the weight of the engine. Alternately, attach an engine support bar to the lifting brackets and support the weight of the engine with the bar. **Note:** *DO NOT support the engine directly beneath the sump as it may be distorted causing the strainer to be blocked and resulting in an incorrect high oil level with a risk of engine racing.*

7 Unclip the power steering fluid reservoir from the bonnet slam panel and move it to one side. There's no need to disconnect the fluid pipes.

8 Unclip the fuel pipes and wiring harness from the right-hand engine mounting **(see illustration)**.

9 Undo the bolt securing the mounting to the engine bracket, then undo the 3 bolts and remove the mounting assembly **(see illustration)**.

10 Locate the new mounting on the body and tighten the bolts to the specified torque.

11 Refit the mounting-to-bracket bolt and tighten it to the specified torque.

12 Re-attach the diesel fuel pipes and wiring harness to the mounting.

13 Remove the jack from underneath the engine or the engine support bar (as applicable), then refit the undertray.

Upper stabiliser bar

14 Undo the bolts securing the stabiliser bar to the engine bracket and the vehicle body. Remove the stabiliser bar **(see illustration)**.

15 Refit the stabiliser bar, and tighten the retaining bolts to the specified torque.

Left-hand mounting

16 Remove the engine undertray, then place a jack beneath the transmission with a block of wood on the jack head. Raise the jack until it is supporting the weight of the transmission.

17 Undo the 2 bolts and one nut, then remove

the left-hand mounting from the gearbox **(see illustration)**.

18 Check carefully for signs of wear or damage on all components, and renew them where necessary.

19 Refit the mounting to the gearbox and tighten the nut and bolts to the specified torque.

20 Lower the jack and refit the engine undertray.

Rear mounting stabiliser bar

21 If not already done, apply the handbrake, then jack up the front of the vehicle and support it on axle stands (see *Jacking and vehicle support*). Remove the engine undertray.

22 Unscrew and remove the bolts from each end of the rear mounting stabiliser bar and remove the bar from underneath the vehicle **(see illustration)**.

23 Check for signs of wear or damage on all components, and renew them as necessary.

24 Fit the stabiliser bar to the bracket and subframe and align the bolt holes. Insert the bolts and tighten to the specified torque.

25 Refit the engine undertray, then lower the vehicle to the ground.

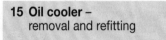

15 Oil cooler –
removal and refitting

Note: *The oil cooler is part of the oil filter housing; it would be good practice to renew the oil and oil filter whenever the oil cooler is removed.*

Removal

1 Disconnect the battery negative lead as described in Chapter 5.

2 Remove the front bumper, bonnet and radiator grille as described in Chapter 11.

3 Pull the rubber seal from the top edge of the bonnet slam panel.

4 Remove both front headlights as described in Chapter 12.

5 Undo the bolts, drill out the rivets and remove the front impact absorbers/air deflector assembly **(see illustrations 7.5a and 7.5b)**.

6 Release the retaining clip and move the power steering fluid reservoir to one side. There's no need to disconnect the pipes.

7 Release the clamps and remove the intercooler hoses.

8 Undo the bolts securing the air cleaner support frame to the bonnet slam panel **(see illustration 7.8)**.

9 Make alignment marks between the bonnet lock and the slam panel, then undo the bolts, manoeuvre the lock from place and disconnect the release cable **(see illustrations 7.9a and 7.9b)**. Release the cable/wiring loom from the retaining clips on the slam panel.

10 Undo the bolts and release the engine management ECM bracket and bonnet alarm contact switch bracket from the slam panel **(see illustration 7.10)**.

11 Release the clips, undo the bolts, and remove the complete front/slam panel from the vehicle **(see illustrations 7.11a to 7.11e)**.

12 Drain the engine oil and remove the oil filter as described in Chapter 1, then refit and tighten the drain plug.

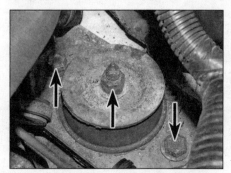

14.17 Left-hand engine/transmission mounting bolts/nut (arrowed)

14.22 Rear mounting stabiliser bar bolts (arrowed)

15.15 Pull out the clip (arrowed) and recover the washer

15.19 Disconnect the lower hose (arrowed) from the oil cooler

15.23a Remove the oil cooler/filter housing...

15.23b... and recover the gasket

13 Drain the cooling system as described in Chapter 1. Alternatively, clamp the oil cooler coolant hoses as close to the cooler as possible, and be prepared for some coolant loss as the hoses are disconnected.

14 Apply the handbrake, then jack up the front of the vehicle and support it on axle stands (see *Jacking and vehicle support*). Remove the engine/transmission undertray.

15 Pull out the 2 clips securing the radiator and condenser (where fitted) to the radiator support crossmember, and recover the washers **(see illustration)**.

16 Release the retaining clips and remove the air deflector panel from each side of the radiator.

17 On models with air conditioning, disconnect the pressure sensor wiring plug.

18 Lift the radiator and condenser (where fitted) assembly upwards from the support crossmember, and secure the assembly to the front crossmember using cable-ties, etc.

19 Release the clip and disconnect the lower coolant hose from the oil filter/cooler housing **(see illustration)**.

20 Undo the bolt and release the power steering hose from the filter/cooler housing, and move it to one side.

21 Disconnect the oil pressure sensor wiring plug.

22 Release the clip and disconnect the upper coolant hose from the oil filter/cooler housing.

23 Unscrew the four mounting bolts and remove the oil cooler/filter housing from the front of the cylinder block. Discard the gasket, as a new one must be used on refitting **(see illustrations)**.

Refitting

24 Fit a new gasket to the oil cooler/filter housing, then offer the housing to the cylinder block. Ensure that the housing is correctly positioned then refit the mounting bolts and finger-tighten initially.

25 Tighten the bolts in diagonal sequence to the Stage 1 torque, then tighten them to the Stage 2 torque using the same sequence.

26 The remainder of refitting is a reversal of removal.

16 Oil pressure sensor – removal and refitting

1 The oil pressure sensor gives a vital early warning of low oil pressure. The sensor operates the oil warning light on the instrument panel – the light should come on with the

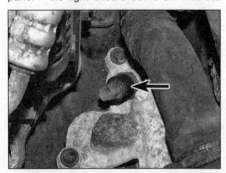

16.7 The oil pressure sensor (arrowed) is on the front face of the cylinder block

ignition, and go out almost immediately when the engine starts.

2 If the light does not come on, there could be a fault on the instrument panel, the switch wiring, or the switch itself. If the light does not go out, low oil level, worn oil pump (or sump pick-up blocked), blocked oil filter, or worn main bearings could be to blame – or again, the switch may be faulty.

3 If the light comes on while driving, the best advice is to turn the engine off immediately, and not to drive the vehicle until the problem has been investigated – ignoring the light could mean expensive engine damage.

Removal

Models without air conditioning

4 The oil pressure sensor is located on the front of the engine, in the oil filter housing.

5 It may be easier to access the sensor from underneath the vehicle, jack up the front of the car, and support it on axle stands (see *Jacking and vehicle support*). Undo the retaining bolts and remove the engine undertray.

6 Disconnect the wiring plug from the sensor.

7 Unscrew the sensor from the housing, and remove it together with its sealing washer **(see illustration)**. There should only be a very slight loss of oil when this is done.

Models with air conditioning

8 Disconnect the battery negative lead as described in Chapter 5.

9 Remove the radiator grille and front bumper as described in Chapter 11.

10 Undo the bolts and remove the central impact absorber.

11 Release the clip and remove the air deflector panel from the right-hand side of the radiator.

12 Disconnect the wiring plug, then unscrew the oil pressure warning switch from the housing.

Inspection

13 Examine the sensor for signs of cracking or splits. If the top part of the sensor is loose, this is an early indication of impending failure.

14 Check that the wiring connector terminals are good, then trace the wire from the switch connector until it enters the main loom – any wiring defects will give rise to apparent oil pressure problems.

Refitting

15 Refitting is the reverse of the removal procedure, noting the following points:

a) *Clean the sensor threads before fitting. Tighten the switch to the specified torque.*

b) *Reconnect the sensor wiring, making sure it is routed away from any hot or moving parts.*

c) *Lower the vehicle to the ground, then check the engine oil level and top-up if necessary (see 'Weekly checks').*

d) *Check for signs of oil leaks once the engine has been restarted and warmed-up to normal operating temperature.*

17 Oil level sensor –
removal and refitting

Removal

1 The oil level sensor is located at the rear, right-hand side of the engine, above the right-hand driveshaft intermediate bearing.
2 Access to the sensor may be easiest from under the right-hand front wheel arch. First, jack up the front of the car, and support it on axle stands (see *Jacking and vehicle support*). Remove the front right-hand roadwheel.

3 Undo the fasteners and remove the wheel arch liner.
4 The oil level sensor wiring may be fitted with heat-resisting insulating material. Cut the clip and move the material to one side.
5 Disconnect the wiring plug, then unscrew the oil level sensor from the cylinder block **(see illustration)**.

Refitting

6 Refitting is a reversal of removal. Tighten the sensor, track rod and link arm to their specified torques.

17.5 Unscrew the oil level sensor

Notes

Chapter 2 Part C:
Engine removal and overhaul procedures

Contents

Degrees of difficulty

Easy, suitable for novice with little experience | **Fairly easy,** suitable for beginner with some experience | **Fairly difficult,** suitable for competent DIY mechanic | **Difficult,** suitable for experienced DIY mechanic | **Very difficult,** suitable for expert DIY or professional

Specifications

1.9 litre engines

Cylinder head

Maximum gasket face distortion	0.05 mm
Cylinder head height	162.75 ± 1.75 mm
Valve seat angle	89.5°
Valve seat width	1.8 mm

Valves

	Intake	Exhaust
Valve head diameter	35.200 to 35.450 mm	32.500 to 35.750 mm
Valve stem diameter	6.974 to 6.996 mm	6.960 to 6.982 mm
Valve length	110.79 to 111.19 mm	110.59 to 110.79 mm
Valve lift (max)	8.866 mm	10.344 mm

Valve springs

Free length	44 to 48 mm
External diameter	29.5 mm
Internal diameter	21.5 ± 0.1 mm

Pistons

Piston diameter (nominal)	79.866 ± 0.0075 mm

Piston rings

End gap (measured in cylinder):
Top compression	0.2 to 0.35 mm
Second compression (sealing)	0.7 to 0.9 mm
Oil control (scraper)	0.25 to 0.5 mm

Crankshaft

Main bearing journal diameter:
Size group 1 (blue)	54.785 to 54.795 mm
Size group 2 (red)	54.795 to 54.805 mm
Main bearing running clearance	0.027 to 0.086 mm
Big-end bearing journal diameter	48.01 mm +0.01 mm
Big-end bearing running clearance	0.027 to 0.086 mm
Crankshaft endfloat	0.067 to 0.233 mm

Torque wrench settings .... Refer to Chapter 2A Specifications

2.0 litre engines

Cylinder head
Maximum gasket face distortion	0.05 mm	
Cylinder head height	132.5 mm	
Valve seat angle (included)	N/A	

Valves
	Intake	Exhaust
Valve head diameter	27.7 ± 0.12 mm	26.0 ± 0.12 mm
Valve stem diameter	5.97 to 5.99 mm	5.96 to 5.97 mm
Valve length	103.89 mm	103.78 mm
Valve lift (maximum)	N/A	

Valve springs
Free length	46.90 mm	46.90 mm
External diameter	19.70 ± 0.2 mm	19.70 ± 0.2 mm
Internal diameter	14.10 ± 0.2 mm	14.10 ± 0.2 mm

Cylinder block
Maximum gasket face distortion	0.05 mm

Gudgeon pin
Length	64.7 to 65.0 mm
External diameter	31.99 to 32.0 mm

Pistons
Piston diameter	83.79 to 83.80 mm
Piston protrusion	0.335 to 0.489 mm

Piston rings
End gap (measured in cylinder):
Top compression	0.23 to 0.38 mm
Second compression (sealing)	0.6 to 0.8 mm
Oil control (scraper)	0.25 to 0.50 mm

Crankshaft
Main bearing journal diameter	59.998 to 60.012 mm
Main bearing running clearance	0.03 to 0.07 mm
Big-end bearing journal diameter	52.00 to 52.02 mm
Big-end bearing running clearance	0.05 to 0.10 mm
Crankshaft endfloat	0.05 to 0.70 mm

Torque wrench settings ... Refer to Chapter 2B Specifications

1 General information

Included in this Part of Chapter 2 are details of removing the engine/transmission from the vehicle and general overhaul procedures for the cylinder head, cylinder block and all other engine internal components.

The information given ranges from advice concerning preparation for an overhaul and the purchase of parts, to detailed step-by-step procedures covering removal, inspection, renovation and refitting of engine internal components.

After Section 5, all instructions are based on the assumption that the engine has been removed from the car. For information concerning in-car engine repair, as well as the removal and refitting of those external components necessary for full overhaul, refer to Part A or B of this Chapter and to Section 5. Ignore any preliminary dismantling operations described in Parts A or B that are no longer relevant once the engine has been removed from the car.

Apart from torque wrench settings, which are given at the beginning of Parts A or B (as applicable), all specifications relating to engine overhaul are at the beginning of this Chapter.

2 Engine overhaul – general information

It is not always easy to determine when, or if, an engine should be completely overhauled, as a number of factors must be considered.

High mileage is not necessarily an indication that an overhaul is needed, while low mileage does not preclude the need for an overhaul. Frequency of servicing is probably the most important consideration. An engine which has had regular and frequent oil and filter changes, as well as other required maintenance, should give many thousands of miles of reliable service. Conversely, a neglected engine may require an overhaul very early in its life.

Excessive oil consumption is an indication that piston rings, valve seals and/or valve guides are in need of attention. Make sure that oil leaks are not responsible before deciding that the rings and/or guides are worn. Perform a compression test, as described in Part A or B of this Chapter, to determine the likely cause of the problem.

Check the oil pressure with a gauge fitted in place of the oil pressure switch, and compare it with that specified. If it is extremely low, the main and big-end bearings, and/or the oil pump, are probably worn out.

Loss of power, rough running, knocking or metallic engine noises, excessive valve gear noise, and high fuel consumption may also point to the need for an overhaul, especially if they are all present at the same time. If a complete service does not remedy the situation, major mechanical work is the only solution.

An engine overhaul involves restoring all internal parts to the specification of a new engine. During an overhaul, the pistons and the piston rings are renewed. New main and big-end bearings are generally fitted; if necessary, the crankshaft may need to be renewed also. The valves are serviced as well, since they are usually in less-than-perfect condition at this point. While the engine is being overhauled, other components, such as the starter and alternator, can be overhauled as well. The end result should be an as-new engine that will give many trouble-free miles.

Note: *Critical cooling system components such as the hoses, thermostat and coolant pump should be renewed when an engine is overhauled. The radiator should be checked carefully, to ensure that it is not clogged or leaking. Also, it is a good idea to renew the oil pump whenever the engine is overhauled.*

Before beginning the engine overhaul, read through the entire procedure, to familiarise yourself with the scope and requirements of the job. Overhauling an engine is not difficult if you follow carefully all of the instructions, have the necessary tools and equipment, and pay close attention to all specifications. It can, however, be time-consuming. Plan on the vehicle being off the road for a minimum of two weeks, especially if parts must be taken to an engineering works for repair or reconditioning. Check on the availability of parts and make sure that any necessary special tools and equipment are obtained in advance. Most work can be done with typical hand tools, although a number of precision measuring tools are required for inspecting parts to determine if they must be renewed. Often the engineering works will handle the inspection of parts and offer advice concerning reconditioning and renewal. **Note:** *Always wait until the engine has been completely dismantled, and until all components (especially the cylinder block and the crankshaft) have been inspected, before deciding what service and repair operations must be performed by an engineering works. The condition of these components will be the major factor to consider when determining whether to overhaul the original engine, or to buy a reconditioned unit. Do not, therefore, purchase parts or have overhaul work done on other components until they have been thoroughly inspected.* As a general rule, time is the primary cost of an overhaul, so it does not pay to fit worn or sub-standard parts.

As a final note, to ensure maximum life and minimum trouble from a reconditioned engine, everything must be assembled with care, in a spotlessly-clean environment.

3 Engine removal – methods and precautions

If you have decided that the engine must be removed for overhaul or major repair work, several preliminary steps should be taken.

Locating a suitable place to work is extremely important. Adequate workspace, along with storage space for the car, will be needed. If a workshop or garage is not available, at the very least, a flat, level, clean work surface is required.

Cleaning the engine compartment and engine/transmission before beginning the removal procedure will help keep tools clean and organised.

An engine hoist or A-frame will also be necessary. Make sure the equipment is rated in excess of the combined weight of the

engine and transmission. Safety is of primary importance, considering the potential hazards involved in lifting the engine/transmission out of the car.

If this is the first time you have removed an engine, an assistant should ideally be available. Advice and aid from someone more experienced would also be helpful. There are many instances when one person cannot simultaneously perform all of the operations required when lifting the engine out of the vehicle.

Plan the operation ahead of time. Before starting work, arrange for the hire of or obtain all of the tools and equipment you will need. Some of the equipment necessary to perform engine/transmission removal and installation safely and with relative ease (in addition to an engine hoist) is as follows: a heavy duty trolley jack, complete sets of spanners and sockets as described in the reference section of this manual, wooden blocks, and plenty of rags and cleaning solvent for mopping-up spilled oil, coolant and fuel. If the hoist must be hired, make sure that you arrange for it in advance, and perform all of the operations possible without it beforehand. This will save you money and time.

Plan for the vehicle to be out of use for quite a while. An engineering works will be required to perform some of the work, which the do-it-yourself person cannot accomplish without special equipment. These places often have a busy schedule, so it would be a good idea to consult them before removing the engine, in order to accurately estimate the amount of time required to rebuild or repair components that may need work.

During the engine removal procedure, it is advisable to make notes of the locations of all brackets, cable ties, earthing points, etc, as well as how the wiring harnesses, hoses and electrical connections are attached and routed around the engine and engine compartment. An effective way of doing this is to take a series of photographs of the various components before they are disconnected or removed. A digital or simple inexpensive disposable camera is ideal for this and the resulting photographs will prove invaluable when the engine is refitted.

Always be extremely careful when lifting

the engine/transmission assembly from the engine bay. Serious injury can result from careless actions. If help is required, it is better to wait until it is available rather than risk personal injury and/or damage to components by continuing alone. By planning ahead and taking your time, a job of this nature, although major, can be accomplished successfully and without incident.

4 Engine and transmission – removal, separation, connection and refitting

Caution: Be careful not to allow dirt into the injection pump or injector pipes during this procedure.
Note: *On models with air conditioning, it is necessary to have the refrigerant circuit evacuated prior to removing the engine/transmission, and have it recharged upon completion.*

Removal

1 Disconnect the battery negative lead as described in Chapter 5.
2 Remove the bonnet and front bumper as described in Chapter 11.
3 On 1.9 litre engines, prise up the caps, undo the 3 bolts and remove the plastic cover from the top of the engine.
4 Undo the bolt securing the hose support bracket (where fitted) to the bonnet slam panel.
5 Remove the intercooler and air cleaner housing as described in Chapter 4A.
6 Apply the handbrake, then jack up the front of the vehicle and support it on axle stands (see *Jacking and vehicle support*). Remove both front roadwheels.
7 Undo the fasteners and remove the engine/transmission undertray (where fitted), then undo the screws and remove the inner splash shield from the right-hand inner wheel arch liner.
8 Drain the engine oil and coolant as described in Chapter 1.
9 On 2.0 litre models, note their fitted locations, then detach the various components from the support frame in the engine compartment, then undo the 2 nuts/bolts and remove the support frame **(see illustrations)**.

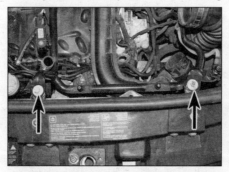

4.9a The air filter support frame is secured by 2 bolts at the front (arrowed)...

4.9b... and 2 nuts (arrowed) at the engine compartment bulkhead

4.10 Undo the expansion tank retaining bolt (arrowed)

4.16a Drill out the rivets, undo the bolts (arrowed) at the side...

4.16b... and front of the impact absorber (arrowed)

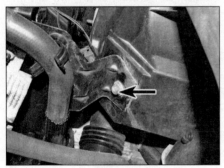

4.16c Undo the bolt (arrowed) securing the ECM bracket

4.16d The front panel is secured by 2 bolts (arrowed) at the right-hand edge...

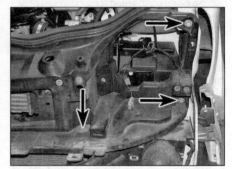

4.16e... 3 bolts (arrowed) on the left-hand side...

10 Undo the retaining bolt and remove the coolant expansion tank. Disconnect the various coolant hoses and remove the expansion tank from the engine compartment **(see illustration)**.
11 Pull up and remove the rubber seal at the top of the bonnet slam panel.

12 Remove both headlights as described in Chapter 12.
13 Disconnect the bonnet switch wiring plug (where fitted), then release the wiring loom from the slam panel.
14 Make alignment marks between the

bonnet lock and the slam panel, then undo the retaining bolts, pull the lock from place and disconnect the release cable. Release the cable from the clips on the slam panel.
15 Release the clip and slide the power steering fluid reservoir upwards from the mounting. Place it to one side.
16 Unclip the air deflector panels, drill out the rivets, remove the impact absorbers (2.0 litre models only), then on all models, undo the bolts and remove the complete front panel **(see illustrations)**.
17 Remove the radiator and cooling fan shroud as described in Chapter 3.
18 Where applicable, remove the air conditioning condenser and compressor as described in Chapter 3.
19 Disconnect the heater resistor wiring plug, unclip the wiring loom, then undo the nuts/bolt and remove the heater blower motor housing from the engine compartment bulkhead.

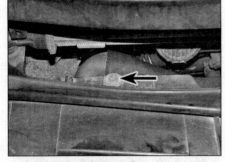

4.16f... 1 bolt (arrowed) to the right of centre...

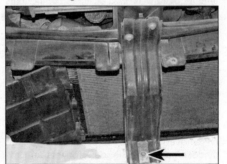

4.16g... and 1 bolt (arrowed) at the base of the central bracket

4.16h Lift the entire front panel from place

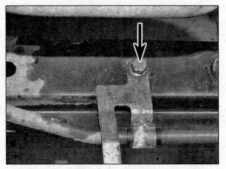

4.20a Undo the power steering bracket bolt (arrowed)...

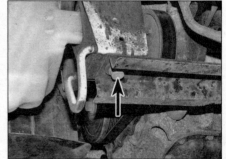

4.20b... then undo the bolt (arrowed) at each end of the radiator crossmember

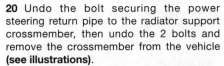

4.22 Release the clips (arrowed) and disconnect the coolant hoses at the engine compartment bulkhead

4.24a Thermoplunger assembly – 2.0 litre engines...

4.24b... and 1.9 litre engines

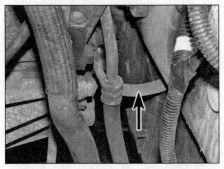

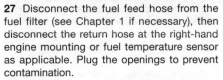

4.26a Disconnect the earth strap (arrowed) from the end of the transmission casing...

4.26b... and the starter motor (arrowed) – 2.0 litre models

20 Undo the bolt securing the power steering return pipe to the radiator support crossmember, then undo the 2 bolts and remove the crossmember from the vehicle **(see illustrations)**.

21 Release the retaining clip and disconnect the clutch hydraulic hose from the transmission as described in Chapter 6 and position it clear. Cover or cap the ends of the pipe and connector to prevent any dirt ingress.

22 Release the clips and disconnect the coolant hoses from the heater matrix connections at the engine compartment bulkhead **(see illustration)**.

23 Disconnect the hose(s) from the vacuum pump on the cylinder head.

24 Disconnect the engine loom wiring by unplugging the various engine components, unclipping/unbolting the loom from the engine/transmission, and laying the loom to one side. Label the wiring plugs and note the harness routing to aid refitting. Disconnect the wiring plugs from the following (where fitted) **(see illustrations)**:

a) Fuel filter water sensor.
b) Common rail regulator and sensor.
c) Glow plugs.
d) Throttle valve.
e) EGR valve.
f) Camshaft position sensor.
g) Fuel injectors.
h) Fuel temperature sensor.
i) Thermoplunger assembly.
j) High-pressure fuel pump.
k) Reversing light switch.
l) Coolant temperature sensor.
m) Alternator.
n) Starter motor.
o) Oil pressure warning switch.
p) Crankshaft position sensor.
q) Oil level sensor.
r) Vehicle speed sensor (non-ABS only) – above the differential on the transmission casing.

25 Note their fitted positions and disconnect any remaining vacuum hoses attached to the engine.

26 Disconnect the earth strap connections at the end of the transmission, and starter motor bolt (2.0 litre models) or catalytic converter bracket (1.9 litre models) as applicable **(see illustrations)**.

27 Disconnect the fuel feed hose from the fuel filter (see Chapter 1 if necessary), then disconnect the return hose at the right-hand engine mounting or fuel temperature sensor as applicable. Plug the openings to prevent contamination.

28 Release the fuel hose and wiring loom from the right-hand engine mounting bracket and move them to one side.

29 Disconnect the gearchange cables from the transmission as described in Chapter 7.

30 Undo the bolts and detach the power steering pipe support brackets from the transmission casing/mounting.

31 Working as described in Chapter 8, remove both driveshafts.

32 Disconnect the exhaust pipe from the catalytic converter/particulate filter as described in Chapter 4A.

33 Apply a clamp to the power steering fluid supply hose from the reservoir to the pump, then release the clip and disconnect the hose.

34 From underneath the vehicle, undo the bolt and disconnect the power steering pipes from the steering rack. Plug the openings to prevent contamination. Be prepared for fluid spillage.

35 Undo the retaining bolts and remove the rear stabiliser link, connecting the engine/transmission mounting to the body.

36 Undo the nut, and detach the thermoplunger housing from the engine lifting bracket (where applicable) **(see illustration)**.

37 Manoeuvre the engine hoist into position, and attach it to the lifting brackets bolted onto the cylinder head, and cast into the top surface of the transmission casing. Raise the

hoist until it is supporting the weight of the engine/transmission.

38 Unscrew the nut from the transmission left-hand mounting stud then undo the bolts securing the rubber mounting assembly and remove it from the bracket on the vehicle body.

39 Undo the bolt securing the stabiliser arm to the end of the cylinder head or mounting bracket.

40 Undo the mounting bolts/nut securing the right-hand engine mounting bracket and remove it from the vehicle. Slacken the rubber mounting bolts to the body to allow for settlement movement when refitting.

41 Make a final check that any components which would prevent the removal of the engine/transmission from the vehicle have been removed or disconnected. Ensure that components such as the gearchange linkage/cables and driveshafts are secured so that they cannot be damaged on removal.

4.36 Undo the bolt (arrowed) securing the thermoplunger housing to the bracket

4.42 Undo the crossmember bolts each side (arrowed – one hidden underneath)

42 Undo the retaining bolts and remove the front crossmember from the vehicle **(see illustration)**. **Note:** *The front crossmember must be reinstalled as soon as the engine/ transmission have been removed, to prevent possible chassis distortion. Refit the nuts/ bolts and tighten them to the specified torque.*

43 With the help of an assistant, raise the hoist and lift the engine/transmission slightly, ensuring that nothing is trapped or damaged. Once the engine is high enough, turn it slightly as necessary and withdraw it forwards, out of the engine compartment and clear of the vehicle.

Separation

44 With the engine/transmission assembly removed, support the assembly on suitable blocks of wood, on a workbench (or failing that, on a clean area of the workshop floor).
45 Undo the retaining bolts, and remove the starter motor from the transmission (see Chapter 5).
46 Ensure that both engine and transmission are adequately supported, then slacken and remove the remaining bolts securing the transmission housing to the engine. Note the correct fitted positions of each bolt (and the relevant brackets) as they are removed, to use as a reference on refitting.
47 Carefully withdraw the transmission from the engine, ensuring that the weight of the transmission is not allowed to hang on the input shaft while it is engaged with the clutch friction plate.
48 Once the transmission is free, remove the locating dowels from the engine or trans- mission, and keep them in a safe place.

Refitting

49 Make sure that the clutch is correctly centred and that the clutch release components are fitted to the bellhousing. Do not apply any grease to the transmission input shaft, the guide sleeve, or the release bearing itself, as these components have a friction- reducing coating which does not require lubrication.
50 Manoeuvre the transmission squarely into position, and engage it with the engine dowels. Refit the bolts securing the transmission to

the engine, and tighten them to the specified torque. Refit the starter motor.
51 The remainder of refitting is essentially a reversal of removal, noting the following points:
  a) *Tighten all fastenings to the specified torque and, where applicable, torque angle. Refer to the relevant Chapters of this manual for torque wrench settings not directly related to the engine.*
  b) *Reconnect and if necessary, adjust the manual transmission selector cables as described in Chapter 7.*
  c) *Refit the air cleaner assembly as described in Chapter 4A.*
  d) *Refit the auxiliary drivebelt(s), then refill the engine with coolant and oil as described in Chapter 1.*
  e) *Refill the transmission with lubricant if necessary as described in Chapter 1 or 7 as applicable.*
  f) *Refer to Section 19 before starting the engine.*

5 Engine overhaul – dismantling sequence

It is much easier to dismantle and work on the engine if it is mounted on a portable engine stand. These stands can often be hired from a tool hire shop. Before the engine is mounted on a stand, the flywheel should be removed so that the stand bolts can be tightened into the end of the cylinder block.

If a stand is not available, it is possible to dismantle the engine with it suitably- supported on a sturdy, workbench or on the floor. Be careful not to tip or drop the engine when working without a stand.

If you intend to obtain a reconditioned engine, all ancillaries must be removed first, to be transferred to the new engine (just as they will if you are doing a complete engine overhaul yourself). These components include the following.
  a) *Engine mountings and brackets (Chap- ter 2A or 2B).*
  b) *Alternator including auxiliary components mounting bracket (Chapter 5).*
  c) *Power steering pump and bracket(s) (Chapter 10).*
  d) *Coolant pump, thermostat and housing, and coolant outlet chamber/elbow (Chapter 3).*
  e) *Oil filter (Chapter 1).*
  f) *Oil cooler housing (Chapter 2A or 2B).*
  g) *Braking system vacuum pump (Chapter 9).*
  h) *Dipstick tube.*
  i) *Fuel system components (Chapter 4A).*
  j) *Wiring harness and all electrical switches and sensors.*
  k) *Intake and exhaust manifolds (Chapter 4A).*
  l) *Clutch components (Chapter 6).*
  m) *Flywheel (Chapter 2A or 2B).*
Note: *When removing the external components from the engine, pay close*

attention to details that may be helpful or important during refitting. Note the fitting positions of gaskets, seals, washers, bolts and other small items.

If you are obtaining a short engine (cylinder block, crankshaft, pistons and connecting rods all assembled), then the cylinder head, timing belt/chain (together with tensioner, tensioner and idler pulleys and covers) and auxiliary drivebelt tensioner will have to be removed also (as applicable).

If a complete overhaul is planned, the engine can be dismantled in the order given below.
  a) *Intake and exhaust manifolds.*
  b) *Timing belt or chain, sprockets, tensioner, pulleys and covers.*
  c) *Cylinder head.*
  d) *Flywheel.*
  e) *Sump.*
  f) *Oil pump.*
  g) *Pistons/connecting rods.*
  h) *Crankshaft.*

6 Cylinder head – dismantling

Note: *New and reconditioned cylinder heads are available from the manufacturer, and from engine overhaul specialists. Be aware that some specialist tools are required for the dismantling and inspection procedures, and new components may not be readily available. It may therefore be more practical and economical for the home mechanic to purchase a reconditioned head, rather than dismantle, inspect and recondition the original head.*

1 Remove the cylinder head as described in Chapter 2A or 2B (as applicable).
2 Remove the camshaft, rockers and followers/lifters (as applicable) as described in Chapter 2A or 2B.
3 Place the cylinder head on wooden blocks and tap each valve stem smartly, using a light hammer and drift, to free the spring and associated items.
4 Using a valve spring compressor, compress each valve spring in turn until the split collets can be removed. Lift out the collets; a small screwdriver, a magnet or a pair of tweezers may be useful. Carefully release the spring compressor and remove it.
5 Remove the valve spring upper seat and the valve spring. Pull the valve out of its guide.
6 Pull off the valve stem oil seal with a pair of long-nosed pliers. Alternatively, a valve stem oil seal removal tool can be obtained from automotive accessory shops. The tool is basically a pair of pliers with specially shaped ends that grip the seal.
7 It is essential that each valve is stored together with its collets, spring and seats **(see illustration)**. The valves should also be kept in their correct sequence, unless they are so badly worn or burnt that they are to be

renewed. If they are going to be kept and used again, place each valve assembly in a labelled polythene bag or similar container.

8 Continue removing all the remaining valves in the same way.

7 Cylinder head and valves – cleaning and inspection

1 Thorough cleaning of the cylinder head and valve components, followed by a detailed inspection, will enable you to decide how much valve service work must be carried out during the engine overhaul. **Note:** *If the engine has been severely overheated, it is best to assume that the cylinder head is warped – check carefully for signs of this.*

Cleaning

2 Scrape away all traces of old gasket material from the cylinder head.
3 Scrape away the carbon from the combustion chambers and ports, then wash the cylinder head thoroughly with paraffin or a suitable solvent.
4 Scrape off any heavy carbon deposits that may have formed on the valves, then use a power-operated wire brush to remove deposits from the valve heads and stems.

Inspection

Note: *Be sure to perform all the following inspection procedures before concluding that the services of a machine shop or engine overhaul specialist are required. Make a list of all items that require attention.*

Cylinder head

5 Inspect the head very carefully for cracks, evidence of coolant leakage, and other damage. If cracks are found, a new cylinder head should be obtained.
6 Use a straight-edge and feeler blade to check that the cylinder head surface is not distorted **(see illustration)**. Vauxhall and Renault state that no resurfacing of the cylinder head surface is possible.
7 Examine the valve seats in each of the combustion chambers. If they are severely pitted, cracked, or burned, they will need to be recut by an engine overhaul specialist. If they

6.7 Place each valve and its associated components in a labelled plastic bag

are only slightly pitted, this can be removed by grinding-in the valve heads and seats with fine valve-grinding compound, as described below.
8 Check the valve guides for wear by inserting the relevant valve, and checking for side-to-side motion of the valve. A very small amount of movement is acceptable. If the movement seems excessive, remove the valve. Measure the valve stem diameter (see below), and renew the valve if it is worn. If the valve stem is not worn, the wear must be in the valve guide, and the guide must be renewed. The renewal of valve guides is best carried out by a dealer, or engine overhaul specialist, who will have the necessary tools available.
9 If renewing the valve guides, the valve seats should be reground only *after* the guides have been fitted.

Valves

10 Examine the head of each valve for pitting, burning, cracks, and general wear. Check the valve stem for scoring and wear ridges. Rotate the valve, and check for any obvious indication that it is bent. Look for pits or excessive wear on the tip of each valve stem. Renew any valve that shows any such signs of wear or damage.
11 If the valve appears satisfactory at this stage, measure the valve stem diameter at several points using a micrometer **(see illustration)**. Any significant difference in the readings obtained indicates wear of the valve stem. Should any of these conditions be apparent, the valve(s) must be renewed.
12 If the valves are in satisfactory condition,

they should be ground (lapped) into their respective seats, to ensure a smooth, gas-tight seal. If the seat is only lightly pitted, or if it has been recut, fine grinding compound *only* should be used to produce the required finish. Coarse valve-grinding compound should *not* be used, unless a seat is badly burned or deeply pitted. If this is the case, the cylinder head and valves should be inspected by an expert, to decide whether seat recutting, or even the renewal of the valve or seat insert (where possible) is required.
13 Valve grinding is carried out as follows. Place the cylinder head upside-down on a bench.
14 Smear a trace of (the appropriate grade of) valve-grinding compound on the seat face, and press a suction grinding tool onto the valve head. With a semi-rotary action, grind the valve head to its seat, lifting the valve occasionally to redistribute the grinding compound **(see illustration)**. A light spring placed under the valve head will greatly ease this operation.
15 If coarse grinding compound is being used, work only until a dull, matt even surface is produced on both the valve seat and the valve, then wipe off the used compound, and repeat the process with fine compound. When a smooth unbroken ring of light grey matt finish is produced on both the valve and seat, the grinding operation is complete. *Do not* grind-in the valves any further than absolutely necessary, or the seat will be prematurely sunk into the cylinder head.
16 When all the valves have been ground-in, carefully wash off *all* traces of grinding compound using paraffin or a suitable solvent, before reassembling the cylinder head.

Valve components

17 Examine the valve springs for signs of damage and discoloration and also measure their free length using vernier calipers or a steel rule or by comparing the existing spring with a new component.
18 Stand each spring on a flat surface, and check it for squareness. If any of the springs are damaged, distorted or have lost their tension, obtain a complete new set of springs. It is normal to renew the valve springs as a matter of course if a major overhaul is being carried out.
19 Renew the valve stem oil seals regardless of their apparent condition.

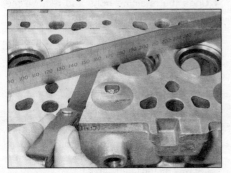

7.6 Check the cylinder head gasket face for distortion

7.11 Use a micrometer to measure the valve stem diameter

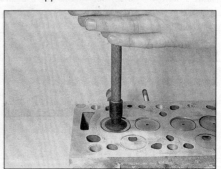

7.14 Grinding-in a valve

8.2 Press on the valve guide oil seal using a socket

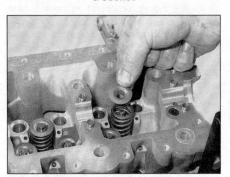

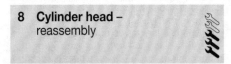

8.3b... and the spring retainer...

8.3a Fit the valve spring...

8.4... then compress the valve spring and fit the collets

1.9 litre engines, but at the timing chain end of the engine on 2.0 litre engines.

4 Turn the crankshaft to bring pistons 1 and 4 to BDC (bottom dead centre).

5 Unscrew the bolts from No 1 piston big-end bearing cap. Take off the cap, noting its correct fitted position, and recover the bottom half bearing shell. If the bearing shells are to be re-used, tape the cap and the shell together. **Note:** *On the 2.0 litre engine, the shells do not have location tabs, so identify them for orientation.*

6 Using a hammer handle, push the piston up through the bore, and remove it from the top of the cylinder block. **Note:** *On the 2.0 litre engine it will be necessary to slightly turn the piston and connecting rods in their bores to prevent the connecting rods damaging the piston oil splash jets.* Recover the bearing shell, and tape it to the connecting rod for safe-keeping.

7 Loosely refit the big-end cap to the connecting rod, and secure with the bolts – this will help to keep the components in their correct order.

8 Remove No 4 piston assembly in the same way.

9 Turn the crankshaft through 180° to bring pistons 2 and 3 to BDC (bottom dead centre), and remove them in the same way.

8 Cylinder head – reassembly

1 Lubricate the stems of the valves, and insert the valves into their original locations. If new valves are being fitted, insert them into the locations to which they have been ground.

2 Refit the spring seat then, working on the first valve, dip the new valve stem seal in fresh engine oil. Carefully locate it over the valve and onto the guide. Take care not to damage the seal as it is passed over the valve stem. Use a suitable socket or metal tube to press the seal firmly onto the guide **(see illustration)**.

3 Locate the valve spring on top of its seat, and then refit the spring retainer **(see illustrations)**.

4 Compress the valve spring, and locate the split collets in the recess in the valve stem

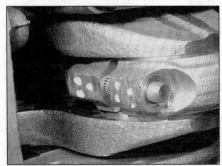

9.3 Identify the connecting rods and bearing caps using quick-drying paint

(see illustration). Release the compressor, then repeat the procedure on the remaining valves.

5 With all the valves installed, place the cylinder head on blocks on the bench and, using a hammer and interposed block of wood, tap the end of each valve stem to settle the components.

6 Refit the camshaft, followers and shims/hydraulic tappets (as applicable) as described in Chapter 2A or 2B.

7 The cylinder head can then be refitted as described in Chapter 2A or 2B.

9 Piston/connecting rod assemblies – removal

1 Remove the cylinder head, sump and oil pump as described in Part A or B of this Chapter as applicable. On the 2.0 litre engine, also remove the cylinder block baseplate.

2 If there is a pronounced wear ridge at the top of any bore, it may be necessary to remove it with a scraper or ridge reamer, to avoid piston damage during removal. Such a ridge indicates excessive wear of the cylinder bore.

3 Using quick-drying paint, mark each connecting rod and big-end bearing cap with its respective cylinder number on the flat machined surface provided; if the engine has been dismantled before, note carefully any identifying marks made previously **(see illustration)**. Note that No 1 cylinder is at the transmission (flywheel) end of the engine on

10 Crankshaft – removal

1.9 litre engines

1 Remove the timing belt, the crankshaft sprocket, the oil pump and the flywheel as described in Part A of this Chapter. If the piston and connecting rod assemblies are also to be removed, remove the cylinder head.

2 Check the crankshaft endfloat as described in Section 13, then proceed as follows.

3 Remove the piston and connecting rod assemblies as described in Section 9. If no work is to be done on the pistons and connecting rods, unbolt the caps and push the pistons far enough up the bores that the connecting rods are positioned clear of the crankshaft journals.

4 Undo the retaining bolts and remove the timing belt lower cover from the cylinder block.

5 Slacken and remove the retaining bolts securing the crankshaft oil seal housing to the cylinder block and remove the housing from the crankshaft end. If the cover locating dowels are a loose fit, remove and store them with the cover for safe-keeping.

6 The main bearing caps should be numbered 1 to 5 from the transmission (flywheel) end of the engine **(see illustration)**. If not, mark them accordingly using quick-drying paint in the same way as the connecting rods.

7 Unscrew and remove the main bearing cap retaining bolts, and withdraw the caps **(see**

10.6 The main bearing caps should be numbered from 1 to 5 from the flywheel end of the engine

10.7 Unscrew and remove the retaining bolts, and withdraw the main bearing caps

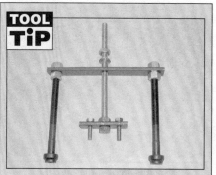

TOOL TiP

To make a main bearing cap removal tool, obtain a length of steel strip about 6 mm thick by 30 mm wide, and long enough to straddle the main bearing cap. Drill three holes in the strip as shown. Attach two suitable lengths of threaded rod, using two nuts each, to the outer two holes in the strip, or alternatively two old cylinder head bolts can be used instead. Make a lifting plate by cutting a second length of steel strip, long enough to fit over the bearing cap. Drill a hole in the centre, then mark and drill a hole each side so that the plate can be bolted to the holes in the cap. Attach a threaded rod to the lifting plate using two nuts and screw on another nut at the top.

illustration). Recover the lower main bearing shells, and tape them to their respective caps for safe-keeping. Note that No 1 main bearing cap is sealed to the sides of the cylinder block with a semi-permanent silicone-based sealant. As there is very little clearance between the crankshaft and cylinder block in this area in which to tap or prise the cap free, it may be necessary to use Vauxhall special tool KM-6405 or Renault tool MOT 1423 for removal. Alternatively, fabricate a home-made alternative as shown **(see Tool tip)**.
8 Carefully lift out the crankshaft, taking care not to displace the upper main bearing shells, and discard the oil seal **(see illustration)**.
9 Recover the upper bearing shells from the cylinder block, and tape them to their respective caps for safe-keeping. Remove the thrustwasher halves from the side of crankcase main bearing, and store them with the bearing cap.

2.0 litre engines

10 Remove the flywheel, transmission end crankshaft oil seal housing, timing cover, cylinder block baseplate, oil pump and splash plate as described in Chapter 2B. Unbolt the oil deflector from the front of the crankcase **(see illustration)**. If the piston and connecting rod assemblies are also to be removed, remove the timing chain and cylinder head.
11 Check the crankshaft endfloat as described in Section 13, then proceed as follows.
12 Remove the piston and connecting rod assemblies as described in Section 9. If no work is to be done on the pistons and

connecting rods, unbolt the caps and push the pistons far enough up the bores that the connecting rods are positioned clear of the crankshaft journals.
13 The main bearing caps should be numbered 1 to 5 from the timing chain end of the engine. If not, mark them accordingly using quick-drying paint in the same way as the connecting rods.
14 Unscrew and remove the main bearing cap retaining bolts, and withdraw the caps. Recover the lower main bearing shells, and tape them to their respective caps for safe-keeping.
15 Carefully lift out the crankshaft, taking care not to displace the upper main bearing shells.
16 Recover the upper bearing shells from the cylinder block, and tape them to their respective caps for safe-keeping. Remove the thrustwasher halves from the side of the centre crankcase main bearing, and store

them with the bearing cap. If necessary, unbolt the crankshaft position ring and remove the spigot bearing using a puller/slide hammer **(see illustrations)**.

10.8 Lift the crankshaft from the crankcase

10.10 Oil deflector (arrowed) on the front of the crankcase

10.16a Crankshaft position ring

10.16b Use a slide hammer...

10.16c... to remove the spigot bearing from the crankshaft

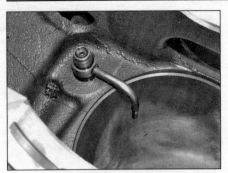

11.2 Piston oil jet spray tube (2.0 litre engine)

11 Cylinder block – cleaning and inspection

Cleaning

1 Remove all external components and electrical switches/sensors from the block. For complete cleaning, the core plugs should ideally be removed. Drill a small hole in the plugs, and then insert a self-tapping screw into the hole. Pull out the plugs by pulling on the screw with a pair of grips, or by using a slide hammer.

2 On 1.9 litre engines, undo the retaining bolts and remove the piston oil jet spray tubes from inside the cylinder block. On 2.0 litre engines the piston oil jet spray tubes must **not** be removed **(see illustration)**.

3 Scrape all traces of gasket from the cylinder block, and from the main bearing casting (where fitted), taking care not to damage the gasket/sealing surfaces.

4 Remove all oil gallery plugs (where fitted). The plugs are usually very tight – they may have to be drilled out, and the holes retapped. Use new plugs when the engine is reassembled.

5 If any of the castings are extremely dirty, all should be steam-cleaned.

6 After the castings are returned, clean all oil holes and oil galleries one more time. Flush all internal passages with warm water until the water runs clear. Dry thoroughly, and apply

a light film of oil to all mating surfaces, to prevent rusting. Also oil the cylinder bores. If you have access to compressed air, use it to speed up the drying process, and to blow out all the oil holes and galleries.

> 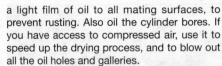 **Warning: Wear eye protection when using compressed air.**

7 If the castings are not very dirty, you can do an adequate cleaning job with hot (as hot as you can stand), soapy water and a stiff brush. Take plenty of time, and do a thorough job. Regardless of the cleaning method used, be sure to clean all oil holes and galleries very thoroughly, and to dry all components well. Protect the cylinder bores as described above, to prevent rusting.

8 All threaded holes must be clean, to ensure accurate torque readings during reassembly. To clean the threads, run the correct-size tap into each of the holes to remove rust, corrosion, thread sealant or sludge, and to restore damaged threads. If possible, use compressed air to clear the holes of debris produced by this operation.

> **Warning: Wear eye protection when cleaning out these holes in this way.**

9 Apply suitable sealant to the new oil gallery plugs, and insert them into the holes in the block. Tighten them securely. Similarly apply a suitable sealant to new core plugs and tap them into the block using a socket or tube.

10 Where applicable, refit the piston oil jet spray tubes to the cylinder block, making sure their locating pegs are correctly engaged, and securely tighten the retaining bolts **(see illustrations)**.

11 If the engine is not going to be reassembled right away, cover it with a large plastic bag to keep it clean; protect all mating surfaces and the cylinder bores as described above, to prevent rusting.

Inspection

12 Visually check the castings for cracks and corrosion. Look for stripped threads in the threaded holes. If there has been any history of internal water leakage, it may be worthwhile having an engine overhaul specialist check the cylinder block with special equipment.

If defects are found, have them repaired if possible, or renew the assembly.

13 Check each cylinder bore for scuffing and scoring. Check for signs of a wear ridge at the top of the cylinder, indicating that the bore is excessively worn.

14 Oversize pistons are not available for any of the diesel engines. If the bores are worn, it will be necessary to obtain a new cylinder block, together with new standard size pistons.

15 Seek the advice of a dealer or engine overhaul specialist regarding standard size cylinder bore size groups and the availability of matching pistons.

12 Piston/connecting rod assemblies – inspection

1 Before the inspection process can begin, the piston/connecting rod assemblies must be cleaned, and the original piston rings removed from the pistons.

2 Carefully expand the old rings over the top of the pistons. The use of two or three old feeler blades will be helpful in preventing the rings dropping into empty grooves. Be careful not to scratch the piston with the ends of the ring. The rings are brittle, and will snap if they are spread too far. They're also very sharp – protect your hands and fingers. Note that the third ring may incorporate an expander. Always remove the rings from the top of the piston. Keep each set of rings with its piston if the old rings are to be re-used.

3 Scrape away all traces of carbon from the top of the piston. A hand-held wire brush (or a piece of fine emery cloth) can be used, once the majority of the deposits have been scraped away, the piston identification markings should be visible.

4 Remove the carbon from the ring grooves in the piston, using an old ring. Break the ring in half to do this (be careful not to cut your fingers – piston rings are sharp). Be careful to remove only the carbon deposits – do not remove any metal, and do not nick or scratch the sides of the ring grooves.

5 Once the deposits have been removed, clean the piston/connecting rod assembly with paraffin or a suitable solvent, and dry thoroughly. Make sure that the oil return holes in the ring grooves are clear.

6 If the pistons and cylinder bores are not damaged or worn excessively, the original pistons can be refitted. Normal piston wear shows up as even vertical wear on the piston thrust surfaces, and slight looseness of the top ring in its groove. New piston rings should always be used when the engine is reassembled.

7 Carefully inspect each piston for cracks around the skirt, around the gudgeon pin holes, and at the piston ring 'lands' (between the ring grooves).

8 Look for scoring and scuffing on the piston

11.10a Refit the piston oil jets, ensuring the locating pegs are correctly located in the block holes (arrowed)...

11.10b... then refit the retaining bolts

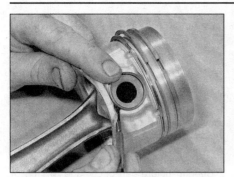

12.12a Carefully prise out the circlip...

12.12b... then press out the gudgeon pin and separate the piston and connecting rod

skirt, holes in the piston crown, and burned areas at the edge of the crown. If the skirt is scored or scuffed, the engine may have been suffering from overheating, and/or abnormal combustion, which caused excessively high operating temperatures. The cooling and lubrication systems should be checked thoroughly. Scorch marks on the sides of the pistons show that blow-by has occurred. A hole in the piston crown, or burned areas at the edge of the piston crown, indicates that abnormal combustion has been occurring. If any of the above problems exist, the causes must be investigated and corrected, or the damage will occur again. The causes may include incorrect injection pump timing, or a faulty injector.

9 Corrosion of the piston, in the form of pitting, indicates that coolant has been leaking into the combustion chamber and/or the crankcase. Again, the cause must be corrected, or the problem may persist in the rebuilt engine.

10 Examine each connecting rod carefully for signs of damage, such as cracks around the big-end and small-end bearings. Check that the rod is not bent or distorted. Damage is highly unlikely, unless the engine has been seized or badly overheated. Detailed checking of the connecting rod assembly can only be carried out by a dealer or engine repair specialist with the necessary equipment.

11 The gudgeon pins are of the floating type, secured in position by two circlips. If necessary, the pistons and connecting rods can be separated as follows.

12 Using a small flat-bladed screwdriver, prise out the circlips, and push out the gudgeon pin **(see illustrations)**. Hand pressure should be sufficient to remove the pin. Identify the piston and rod to ensure correct reassembly. Discard the circlips – new ones *must* be used on refitting.

13 Examine the gudgeon pin and connecting rod small-end bearing for signs of wear or damage. Wear will mean both the pin and connecting rod will have to be renewed.

14 The connecting rods themselves should not be in need of renewal, unless seizure or some other major mechanical failure has occurred. Check the alignment of the connecting rods visually, and if the rods are not straight, take them to an engine overhaul specialist for a more detailed check.

15 Examine all components, and renew any worn parts. If new pistons are purchased, they will be supplied complete with gudgeon pins and circlips. Circlips can also be purchased individually.

16 If the pistons and/or connecting rods are to be renewed, seek the advice of a dealer or engine overhaul specialist regarding cylinder bore/piston size groups.

17 On 1.9 litre engines, locate the piston on the connecting rod so that the oil hole in the rod faces away from the combustion chamber in the piston crown **(see illustration)**. Apply a smear of clean engine oil to the gudgeon pin. Slide it into the piston and through the connecting rod small-end. Check that the piston pivots freely on the rod, then secure the gudgeon pin in position with two new circlips. Ensure that each circlip is correctly located in its groove in the piston.

18 On 2.0 litre engines locate the piston on the connecting rod so that the V marking on the piston crown is opposite the machined bosses on the connecting rod big-end **(see illustration)**. Apply a smear of clean engine oil to the gudgeon pin. Slide it into the piston and through the connecting rod small-end. Check that the piston pivots freely on the rod, then secure the gudgeon pin in position with two new circlips. Ensure that each circlip is correctly located in its groove in the piston with the gap at the top.

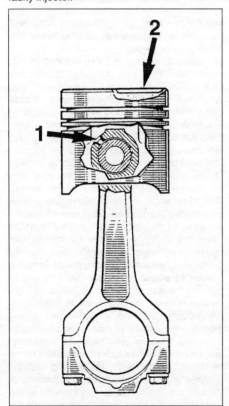

12.17 On 1.9 litre engines, the oil hole (1) in the connecting rod small end should face away from the combustion chamber (2) in the piston crown

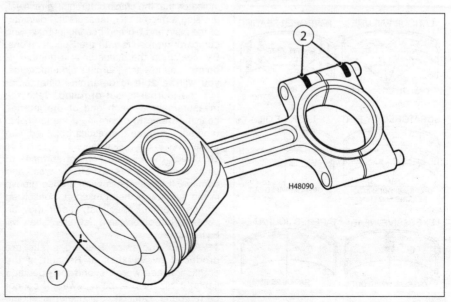

H48090

12.18 The V marking (1) on the piston crown must be opposite the machined bosses (2) on the big end

13.2 Measure the crankshaft endfloat using a dial gauge...

13.3... or feeler gauge

13 Crankshaft – inspection

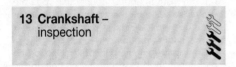

Checking endfloat

1 If the crankshaft endfloat is to be checked, this must be done when the crankshaft is still installed in the cylinder block, but is free to move (see Section 10).

2 Check the endfloat using a dial gauge in contact with the end of the crankshaft. Push the crankshaft fully one way, and then zero the gauge. Push the crankshaft fully the other way, and check the endfloat **(see illustration)**. The result can be compared with the specified amount, and will give an indication as to whether new thrustwashers are required.

3 If a dial gauge is not available, feeler blades can be used. First push the crankshaft fully towards the flywheel end of the engine, then use feeler blades to measure the gap between the web of the crankpin and the thrustwasher **(see illustration)**.

Inspection

4 Clean the crankshaft using paraffin or a suitable solvent, and dry it, preferably with compressed air if available. Be sure to clean the oil holes with a pipe cleaner or similar probe, to ensure that they are not obstructed.

 Warning: Wear eye protection when using compressed air.

5 Check the main and big-end bearing journals for uneven wear, scoring, pitting and cracking.

6 Big-end bearing wear is accompanied by distinct metallic knocking when the engine is running (particularly noticeable when the engine is pulling from low speed) and some loss of oil pressure.

7 Main bearing wear is accompanied by severe engine vibration and rumble – getting progressively worse as engine speed increases – and again by loss of oil pressure.

8 Check the bearing journal for roughness by running a finger lightly over the bearing surface. Any roughness (which will be accompanied by obvious bearing wear) indicates that the crankshaft requires renewal.

9 Using a micrometer, measure the diameter of the main and big-end bearing journals, and compare the results with the Specifications. By measuring the diameter at a number of points around each journal's circumference, you will be able to determine whether or not the journal is out-of-round. Take the measurement at each end of the journal, near the webs, to determine if the journal is tapered. Compare the results obtained with those given in the Specifications.

10 Check the oil seal contact surfaces at each end of the crankshaft for wear and damage. If the seal has worn a deep groove in the surface of the crankshaft, consult an engine overhaul specialist; repair may be possible, but otherwise a new crankshaft will be required.

11 As no undersize bearing shells are produced by Vauxhall or Renault, if the crankshaft has worn beyond the specified limits, it will have to be renewed; it cannot be reground. Consult your dealer or engine specialist for further information on parts availability.

14 Main and big-end bearings – inspection and selection

Inspection

1 Even though the main and big-end bearings should be renewed during the engine overhaul, the old bearings should be retained for close examination, as they may reveal valuable information about the condition of the engine.

2 Bearing failure can occur due to lack of lubrication, the presence of dirt or other foreign particles, overloading the engine, or corrosion **(see illustration)**. Regardless of the cause of bearing failure, the cause must be corrected (where applicable) before the engine is reassembled, to prevent it from happening again.

3 When examining the bearing shells, remove them from the cylinder block, the main bearing caps, the connecting rods and the connecting rod big-end bearing caps. Lay them out on a clean surface in the same general position as their location in the engine. This will enable you to match any bearing problems with the corresponding crankshaft journal.

4 Dirt and other foreign matter gets into the engine in a variety of ways. It may be left in the engine during assembly, or it may pass through filters or the crankcase ventilation system. It may get into the oil, and from there into the bearings. Metal chips from machining operations and normal engine wear are often present. Abrasives are sometimes left in engine components after reconditioning, especially when parts are not thoroughly cleaned using the proper cleaning methods. Whatever the source, these foreign objects often end up embedded in the soft bearing material, and are easily recognised. Large particles will not embed in the bearing, and will score or gouge the bearing and journal. The best prevention for this cause of bearing failure is to clean all parts thoroughly, and keep everything spotlessly clean during engine assembly. Frequent and regular engine oil and filter changes are also recommended.

5 Lack of lubrication (or lubrication breakdown) has a number of interrelated causes. Excessive heat (which thins the oil), overloading (which squeezes the oil from the bearing face) and oil leakage (from excessive bearing clearances, worn oil pump or high engine speeds) all contribute to lubrication breakdown. Blocked oil passages, which usually are the result of misaligned oil holes in a bearing shell, will also oil-starve a bearing, and destroy it. When lack of lubrication is the cause of bearing failure, the bearing material is wiped or extruded from the steel backing of the bearing. Temperatures may increase to the point where the steel backing turns blue from overheating.

6 Driving habits can have a definite effect on bearing life. Full-throttle, low-speed operation (labouring the engine) puts very high loads

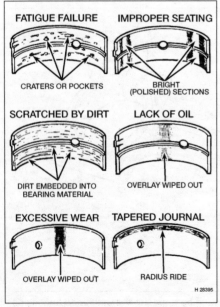

FATIGUE FAILURE — CRATERS OR POCKETS

IMPROPER SEATING — BRIGHT (POLISHED) SECTIONS

SCRATCHED BY DIRT — DIRT EMBEDDED INTO BEARING MATERIAL

LACK OF OIL — OVERLAY WIPED OUT

EXCESSIVE WEAR — OVERLAY WIPED OUT

TAPERED JOURNAL — RADIUS RIDE

H 28395

14.2 Typical bearing failures

on bearings, tending to squeeze out the oil film. These loads cause the bearings to flex, which produces fine cracks in the bearing face (fatigue failure). Eventually, the bearing material will loosen in pieces, and tear away from the steel backing.

7 Short-distance driving leads to corrosion of bearings, because insufficient engine heat is produced to drive off the condensed water and corrosive gases. These products collect in the engine oil, forming acid and sludge. As the oil is carried to the engine bearings, the acid attacks and corrodes the bearing material.

8 Incorrect bearing installation during engine assembly will lead to bearing failure as well. Tight-fitting bearings leave insufficient bearing running clearance, and will result in oil starvation. Dirt or foreign particles trapped behind a bearing shell result in high spots on the bearing, which lead to failure.

Selection

9 The main and big-end bearing shells supplied by the manufacturer are only available in one standard size. Therefore, if the relevant crankshaft journals are all within tolerance, and new bearing shells are fitted, the bearing running clearances should then be correct. Before obtaining new bearing shells, consult a dealer or engine reconditioning specialist as to the latest recommendations concerning bearing shell selection.

15 Engine overhaul – reassembly sequence

1 Before reassembly begins, ensure that all new parts have been obtained, and that all necessary tools are available. Read through the entire procedure to familiarise yourself with the work involved, and to ensure that all items necessary for reassembly of the engine are at hand. In addition to all normal tools and materials, thread-locking compound will be needed. A suitable tube of liquid sealant will also be required for the joint faces that are fitted without gaskets. It is recommended that Vauxhall's and Renault's own producta(s) are used, which are specially formulated for this purpose; the relevant product names are quoted in the text of each Section where they are required.

2 In order to save time and avoid problems, engine reassembly can be carried out in the following order:
  a) Crankshaft.
  b) Piston/connecting rod assemblies.
  c) Oil pump.
  d) Sump.
  e) Flywheel.
  f) Cylinder head.
  g) Timing belt/chain tensioner and sprockets.
  h) Engine external components.

3 At this stage, all engine components should

be absolutely clean and dry, with all faults repaired. The components should be laid out (or in individual containers) on a completely clean work surface.

16 Piston rings – refitting

1 Before refitting the rings to the pistons, check their end gaps by inserting each of them in their cylinder bores. Use the piston to make sure that they are square. Manufacturer rings are supplied pregapped; no attempt should be made to adjust the gaps by filing.

2 Refit the piston rings as follows. Where the original rings are being refitted, use the marks or notes made on removal, to ensure that each ring is refitted to its original groove and the same way up. New rings generally have their top surfaces identified by markings (often an indication of size, such as STD, or the word TOP) – the rings must be fitted with such markings uppermost **(see illustration)**. Note: *Always follow any instructions supplied with the new piston ring sets – different manufacturers may specify different procedures. Do not mix up the top and second compression rings, as they have different cross-sections.*

3 The oil control ring (lowest one on the piston) should be installed first, and is composed of three separate elements. Slip the spacer/expander into the groove. Next, install the lower side rail. Place one end of the side rail into the groove between the spacer/expander and the ring land, hold it firmly in place, and slide a finger around the piston while pushing the rail into the groove. Next, install the upper side rail in the same manner. After the three oil ring components have been installed, check that both the upper and lower side rails can be turned smoothly in the ring groove.

4 The second compression (middle)

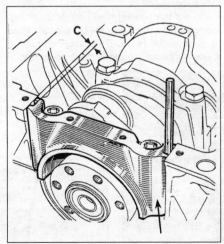

17.2a Measure the No 1 main bearing cap side seal groove using a dowel rod

Bearing cap (arrowed) C Seal groove measurement

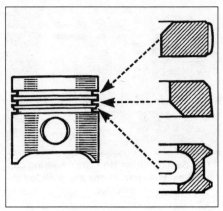

16.2 Piston ring fitting details

ring is installed next, followed by the top compression ring – ensure their marks are uppermost. Do not expand either ring any more than necessary to slide it over the top of the piston.

5 With all the rings in position, space the ring gaps (including the elements of the oil control ring) uniformly around the piston at 120° intervals. Repeat the procedure for the remaining pistons and rings.

17 Crankshaft – refitting

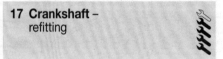

Note: *To obtain the correct main bearing running clearance, new main bearing shells should always be fitted regardless of the condition of the original ones.*

1 Crankshaft refitting is the first stage of engine reassembly following overhaul. It is assumed at this point that the cylinder block/crankcase and crankshaft have been cleaned, inspected and repaired or reconditioned as necessary. Position the cylinder block on a clean level work surface, with the crankcase facing upwards. The crankshaft can now be refitted as described in the following sub-Sections according to engine type.

1.9 litre engines

2 Before fitting the crankshaft and main bearings, decide whether the No 1 main bearing cap is to be sealed using butyl seals or silicone sealant. If butyl seals are to be used, it is necessary to determine the correct thickness of the seals to obtain from Vauxhall or Renault. To do this, place the bearing cap in position without any seals and secure it with the two retaining bolts. Locate a twist drill, dowel rod or any other suitable implement which will just fit in the side seal groove **(see illustration)**. Now measure the implement – this dimension is the side seal groove size. If the dimension is less than or equal to .5 mm, a 5.10 mm thick side seal is needed. If the dimension is more than 5 mm, a 5.4 mm thick side seal is required. If No 1 main bearing cap is to be fitted using sealant, a tube of Rhodorseal 5661 sealant, together

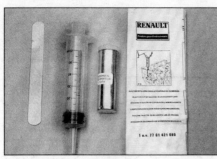

17.2b Sealing kit for No 1 main bearing cap grooves. Full instructions are provided in the kit

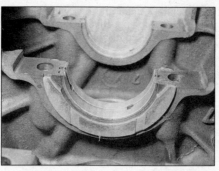

17.6 Position the thrustwashers with the oil grooves facing outwards

17.8 Tighten the bearing caps to the specified torque

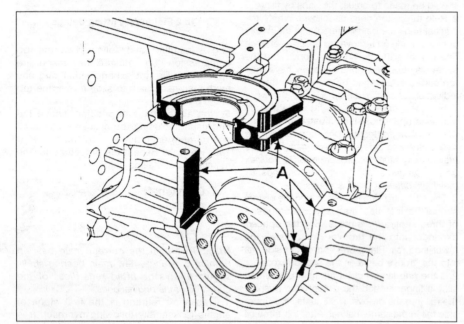

17.10 Thoroughly clean the cylinder block and No 1 main bearing cap faces (A)

with a hardening agent and application syringe, will be required. This is available as a kit from dealers **(see illustration)**.

3 Clean the backs of the bearing shells and the bearing locations in both the cylinder block and the main bearing caps. If new shells are being fitted, ensure that all traces

of the protective grease are cleaned off using paraffin. Wipe dry the shells, block and caps with a lint-free cloth.

4 Lay out the bearing shells ready for fitting, noting that the shells with the oil holes are fitted to the cylinder block. If the original bearing shells are being used they must be refitted in

their original locations and in their original fitted direction as noted during removal.

5 Press the bearing shells into their locations, ensuring that the tab on each shell engages in the notch in the cylinder block or main bearing cap.

6 Using a little grease, stick the thrustwashers to each side of the main bearing upper location; ensure that the oilway grooves on each thrustwasher face outwards (away from the cylinder block) **(see illustration)**.

7 Liberally lubricate each bearing shell in the cylinder block with clean engine oil then lower the crankshaft into position ensuring that the bearing shells and thrustwashers remain correctly seated.

8 Ensure that the cap locating dowels are in position and fit the main bearing caps numbers 2 to 5. Ensure that the caps are fitted in their correct locations and the correct way round. Insert the bearing cap bolts and tighten them to the specified torque setting **(see illustration)**.

9 Check that the crankshaft is free to turn without stiffness or tight spots, then check the crankshaft endfloat with reference to Section 13.

10 Thoroughly clean the contact surfaces of No 1 main bearing cap and its location in the cylinder block with methylated spirit and allow to dry thoroughly **(see illustration)**.

11 If fitting butyl seals to No 1 bearing cap, fit the seals with their grooves facing outwards.

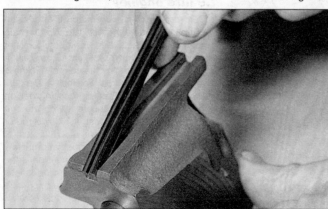

17.11a Fit the sealing strips to the No 1 bearing cap, so that its groove is facing away from the cap...

17.11b... then position the strip so that it protrudes above the cap mating surface by 0.2 mm approximately

Position the seals so that approximately 0.2 mm of seal protrudes at the bottom-facing side (the side towards the crankcase). Apply a thin coating of Rhodorseal 5661 sealant to the bearing cap lower mating surface in the cylinder block, and lubricate the seals with a little oil **(see illustrations)**. When the cap is being fitted, use the bolts as a guide by just starting them in their threads, then pressing the cap firmly into position. When the cap is almost fully home, check that the seals still protrude slightly at the cylinder block mating face.

12 Screw in the main bearing cap bolts and tighten them to the specified torque. Trim the protruding ends of the butyl seals flush with the surface of the cylinder block sump mating face.

13 If No 1 main bearing cap is to be fitted using sealant, apply a thin coating of Rhodorseal 5661 sealant to the bearing cap lower mating surface in the cylinder block, then fit the cap. Insert the main bearing cap bolts and tighten them to the specified torque.

14 Mix approximately half of the 100 g tube of Rhodorseal 5661 sealant together with half the hardener as described in the instructions supplied with the kit. Using the syringe supplied, inject the mixture into the grooves on each side of the bearing cap, until it can be seen to flow out slightly on both sides of the grooves. Using a clean cloth, wipe away any surplus mixture from the inside and outside of the cylinder block.

15 Allow the sealant to dry for a few minutes, then cut away any surplus sealant from the sump mating face.

16 Fit a new seal to the crankshaft timing belt end oil seal housing and refit the housing with reference to Chapter 2A.

17 Fit a new crankshaft flywheel end oil seal, with reference to Chapter 2A.

18 Where applicable, refit the timing belt lower inner cover.

19 Refit the piston/connecting rod assemblies as described in Section 18, then refit the oil pump, flywheel, cylinder head, timing belt sprockets and fit a new timing belt as described in Chapter 2A.

2.0 litre engines

20 Clean the backs of the bearing shells and the bearing locations in both the cylinder block and the main bearing caps. If new shells are being fitted, ensure that all traces of the protective grease are cleaned off using paraffin. Wipe dry the shells, block and caps with a lint-free cloth.

21 Lay out the bearing shells ready for fitting, noting that the shells with the oil holes are fitted to the cylinder block. If the original bearing shells are being used they must be refitted in their original locations and in their original fitted direction as noted during removal.

22 Press the new bearing shells into their positions in the cylinder block and main bearing caps..

23 If removed, refit the crankshaft position

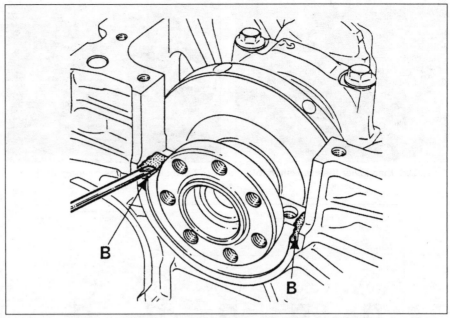

17.11c Apply sealant to the No 1 bearing cap lower mounting surface (B) in the cylinder block

ring and finger-tighten the bolts. Make sure the small centring pin locates correctly then tighten the 3 mounting bolts to the specified torque. Finally, tighten the centring pin securely.

24 If removed, fit a new spigot bearing. Use a suitable diameter tube or socket to drive the bearing fully into the end of the crankshaft **(see illustration)**.

25 Using a little grease, stick the thrust-washers

to each side of the main bearing upper location in the crankcase; ensure that the oilway grooves on each thrustwasher face outwards (away from the cylinder block) **(see illustrations)**.

26 Liberally lubricate each bearing shell in the cylinder block with clean engine oil then lower the crankshaft into position ensuring that the bearing shells and thrustwashers remain correctly seated **(see illustrations)**.

17.24 Drive the spigot bearing into the end of the crankshaft

17.25a Apply some grease to their inner contact face...

17.25b... then locate the thrustwashers in the crankcase

17.26a Lubricate the bearing shells...

17.26b... then lower the crankshaft into position

17.27a Lubricate the bearing shells...

17.27b... then refit them to their previously-noted locations

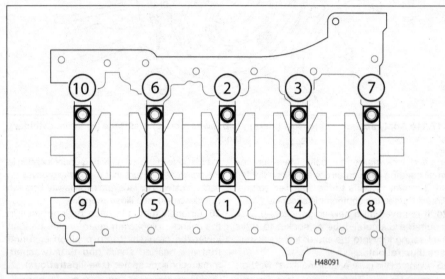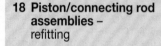

17.27c Crankshaft main bearing cap bolt tightening sequence

18 Piston/connecting rod assemblies – refitting

Note: *To obtain the correct big-end bearing running clearance, new bearing shells should always be fitted regardless of the condition of the original ones.*

1 Clean the backs of the big-end bearing shells and the recesses in the connecting rods and big-end caps. If new shells are being fitted, ensure that all traces of the protective grease are cleaned off using paraffin. Wipe the shells and connecting rods dry with a lint-free cloth.

2 On 1.9 litre engines, press the big-end bearing shells into the connecting rods and caps in their correct positions. Make sure that the location tabs are engaged with the cut-outs in the connecting rods.

3 On 2.0 litre engines, the big-end bearing shells must be accurately positioned centrally in the connecting rods and caps as follows, as there are no location tabs. Note that the connecting rod shell has a width of 19.3 mm, and the cap shell has a width of 18.3 mm. Fit the shells so that the distance from the outer face of the connecting rod or cap and the shell is 2.0 ± 0.1 mm measured with a micrometer at the centre and each end of the shell. Ensure that the ends of the shells are pressed down flush with the cap contact surfaces. If necessary, adjust the shell positions until correct **(see illustration)**.

27 Oil the bearing shells, then refit the main bearing caps to their previously-noted locations, insert the new bolts and initially finger-tight them. Tighten the bolts to the torque and angle given in the Specifications in the order shown **(see illustrations)**.

28 Check that the crankshaft is free to turn without stiffness or tight spots, then check the crankshaft endfloat with reference to Section 13.

29 Fit a new transmission end crankshaft oil seal, with reference to Chapter 2 then refit the crankcase oil deflector and tighten the retaining bolt securely.

30 Refit the piston/connecting rod assemblies as described in Section 18, then refit the timing chain, cylinder head, balancer shaft unit, oil pump and splash plate, cylinder block baseplate, timing cover and flywheel as described in Chapter 2B.

17.27d Insert the bolts...

17.27e... then torque and angle-tighten them

18.3 Check the bearing shell is central on the connecting rod

4 Lubricate the bores; the pistons and piston rings then lay out each piston/connecting rod assembly in its respective position.

5 Starting with assembly number 1, make sure that the piston rings are still spaced as described in Section 16, then clamp them in position with a piston ring compressor.

6 Insert the piston/connecting rod assembly into the top of cylinder No 1. On 1.9 litre engines, ensure that the combustion chamber recess on the piston crown is towards the front (oil filter side) of the cylinder block. On 2.0 litre engines, ensure the V marking on the piston crown points towards the transmission end of the engine **(see illustration)**. Using a block of wood or hammer handle against the piston crown, tap the assembly into the cylinder until the piston crown is flush with the top of the cylinder **(see illustration)**.

7 Taking care not to mark the cylinder bore, liberally lubricate the crankpin and both bearing shells, then pull the piston/connecting rod assembly down the bore and onto the crankpin. Refit the big-end bearing cap to the connecting rod.

8 On 1.9 litre engines, fit the new bearing cap bolts and tighten them evenly and progressively to the specified torque.

9 On 2.0 litre engines, fit the new bearing cap bolts and tighten them evenly and progressively to the Stage 1 torque setting. Once both bolts have been tightened to the Stage 1 setting, angle-tighten them through the specified Stage 2 angle, using a socket and extension bar. It is recommended that an angle-measuring gauge is used during this stage of the tightening, to ensure accuracy **(see illustrations)**.

10 Refit the remaining three piston and connecting rod assemblies in the same way.

11 Rotate the crankshaft, and check that it turns freely, with no signs of binding or tight spots.

12 Refit the oil pump, cylinder block baseplate (2.0 litre engine), sump and the cylinder head as described in Part A or B of this Chapter.

19 Engine – initial start-up after overhaul

1 With the engine refitted in the vehicle, double-check the engine oil and coolant

18.6a The V marking (arrowed) must point to the transmission end of the engine (2.0 litre engine)

18.6b Tap the piston into the bore using a hammer handle

18.9a Fit the new bearing cap bolts and tighten them first to the Stage 1 torque setting...

18.9b... then through the Stage 2 angle setting

levels. Make a final check that everything has been reconnected, and that there are no tools or rags left in the engine compartment.

2 Disconnect the wiring from the common rail pressure regulator on the front of the engine (see Chapter 4A). Turn the engine on the starter motor until the oil pressure warning light goes out, then reconnect the wiring.

3 Prime the fuel system (see Chapter 4A).

4 Fully depress the accelerator pedal, turn the ignition key and wait for the preheating warning light to go out.

5 Start the engine, noting that this may take a little longer than usual, due to the fuel system components having been disturbed.

6 While the engine is idling, check for fuel, water and oil leaks. Don't be alarmed if there are some odd smells and smoke from parts getting hot and burning off oil deposits.

7 Assuming all is well; keep the engine idling until hot water is felt circulating through the top hose, then switch off the engine.

8 After a few minutes recheck the oil and coolant levels as described in *Weekly checks*, and top-up as necessary.

9 If they were tightened as described, there is no need to retighten the cylinder head bolts once the engine has first run after reassembly.

10 If new pistons, rings or crankshaft bearings have been fitted, the engine must be treated as new, and run-in for the first 500 miles. *Do not* operate the engine at full-throttle, or allow it to labour at low engine speeds in any gear. It is recommended that the oil and filter be changed at the end of this period.

Chapter 3
Cooling, heating and air conditioning systems

Contents

Degrees of difficulty

Easy, suitable for novice with little experience 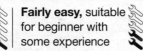	**Fairly easy,** suitable for beginner with some experience	**Fairly difficult,** suitable for competent DIY mechanic	**Difficult,** suitable for experienced DIY mechanic	**Very difficult,** suitable for expert DIY or professional

Specifications

General

Cooling system type	Pressurised sealed system, with front-mounted radiator and electric cooling fan
Cooling system pressure	1.2 bar

Thermostat

Opening temperatures:	
Starts to open	83°C
Fully open	95°C

Air conditioning

Oil quantity:	
Complete system	220 ml ± 15
Compressor	Supplied pre-filled
Condenser	30 ml
Evaporator	30 ml
Receiver/drier	15 ml
Any refrigerant pipe	10 ml
Refrigerant type	R 134a
Refrigerant quantity:	
1.9 litre engine:	
Without rear air conditioning	750g
With rear air conditioning	1150 g
2.0 litre engine:	
Without rear air conditioning	650 g
With rear air conditioning	950 g

Torque wrench settings

	Nm	lbf ft
Air conditioning compressor mounting bolts	25	18
Coolant pump:		
1.9 litre engines	10	7
2.0 litre engines	25	18
Coolant pump pulley (2.0 litre engines)	21	15
Thermostat housing:		
1.9 litre engines	8	6
2.0 litre engines	11	8
Refrigerant pipe bolts	8	6
Roadwheel bolts	140	103

1 General information and precautions

The cooling system is of pressurised type, comprising a coolant pump driven by the timing belt or the auxiliary drivebelt (depending on engine type), an aluminium crossflow radiator, expansion tank, electric cooling fan(s), a thermostat, heater matrix, and all associated hoses and switches.

The system functions as follows. Cold coolant in the bottom of the radiator passes through the bottom hose to the coolant pump, where it is pumped around the cylinder block and head passages, and through the oil cooler(s) (where fitted). After cooling the cylinder bores, combustion surfaces and valve seats, the coolant reaches the underside of the thermostat, which is initially closed. The coolant passes through the heater, and is returned via the cylinder block to the coolant pump.

When the engine is cold, the coolant circulates only through the cylinder block, cylinder head and heater. When the coolant reaches a predetermined temperature, the thermostat opens, and the coolant passes through the top hose to the radiator. As the coolant circulates through the radiator, it is cooled by the inrush of air when the vehicle is in forward motion. The airflow is supplemented by the action of the electric cooling fan(s) when necessary. Upon reaching the bottom of the radiator, the coolant has now cooled, and the cycle is repeated.

When the engine is at normal operating temperature, the coolant expands, and some of it is displaced into the expansion tank. Coolant collects in the tank, and is returned to the radiator when the system cools.

 Warning: Do not attempt to remove the expansion tank filler cap, or to disturb any part of the cooling system, while the engine is hot, as there is a high risk of scalding. If the expansion tank filler cap must be removed before the engine and radiator have fully cooled (even though this is not recommended), the pressure in the cooling system must first be relieved. Cover the cap with a thick layer of cloth, to avoid scalding, and slowly unscrew the filler cap until a hissing sound is heard. When the hissing has stopped, indicating that the pressure has reduced, slowly unscrew the filler cap until it can be removed; if more hissing sounds are heard, wait until they have stopped before unscrewing the cap completely. At all times, keep well away from the filler cap opening, and protect your hands.

Warning: Do not allow antifreeze to come into contact with your skin, or with the painted surfaces of the vehicle. Rinse off spills immediately, with plenty of water. Never leave antifreeze lying around in an open container, or in a puddle in the driveway or on the garage floor. Children and pets are attracted by its sweet smell, but antifreeze can be fatal if ingested.

 Warning: If the engine is hot, the electric cooling fan may start rotating even if the engine is not running. Be careful to keep your hands, hair and any loose clothing well clear when working in the engine compartment.

Warning: Refer to Section 10 for precautions to be observed when working on models equipped with air conditioning.

2 Cooling system hoses – disconnection and renewal

Note: Refer to the warnings given in Section 1 of this Chapter before proceeding. Hoses should only be disconnected once the engine has cooled sufficiently to avoid scalding.

1 If the checks described in Chapter 1 reveal a faulty hose, it must be renewed as follows.

2 The number, routing and pattern of hoses will vary according to model, but the same basic procedure applies. Before commencing work, make sure that the new hoses are to hand, along with new hose clips if needed. It is good practice to renew the hose clips at the same time as the hoses.

3 First drain the cooling system (see Chapter 1). If the coolant is not due for renewal, it may be re-used, providing it is collected in a clean container.

4 Release the hose clips from the hose concerned. Almost all the standard clips fitted at the factory are the spring type, released by squeezing its tangs together with pliers, at the same time working the clip away from the hose stub **(see illustration)**. These clips can be awkward to use, can pinch old hoses, and may become less effective with age, so may have been updated with Jubilee clips (released by turning the screw).

5 Unclip any wires, cables or other hoses that may be attached to the hose being removed. Make notes for reference when reassembling if necessary.

6 Note that the coolant unions are fragile (many are made of plastic); do not use excessive force when attempting to remove the hoses. If a hose proves to be difficult to

2.4 Use a pair of pliers to release the hose spring clip

remove, try to release it by rotating the hose ends before attempting to free it – if this fails, try gently prising up the end of the hose with a small screwdriver to 'break' the seal. Do not apply too much force, and take care not to damage the pipe stubs or hoses.

7 Before fitting the new hose, smear the stubs with washing-up liquid or a suitable rubber lubricant to aid fitting. **Do not** use oil or grease, which may attack the rubber.

8 Fit the hose clips over the ends of the hose, and then fit the hose over its stubs.

9 Work the hose into position, checking that it is correctly routed. When satisfied, slide each clip back along the hose until it passes over the flared end of the relevant intake/outlet, before tightening the clip securely.

10 Refill the cooling system as described in Chapter 1. Run the engine, and check that there are no leaks.

11 Recheck the tightness of the hose clips on any new hoses after a few hundred miles.

3 Radiator – removal, inspection and refitting

Removal – 1.9 litre models

1 Disconnect the battery negative lead as described in Chapter 5.

2 Remove the cooling fan and shroud as described in Section 5.

3 Remove the undertray (where fitted) from below the engine/transmission.

4 Drain the cooling system as described in Chapter 1.

5 Undo the screws and remove the splash shield from under the radiator.

6 Release the securing clips, and disconnect the top and bottom coolant hoses from the radiator. **Note:** *The bottom hose may have already been disconnected to drain the cooling system.*

7 On models with air conditioning, release the clip securing the condenser to the radiator.

8 Release the clips and remove the air deflector panels from each side of the radiator.

9 Pull out the clips securing the radiator to the support crossmember **(see illustration 3.15)**. Recover the washer above each clip.

10 Lift the radiator to release the lower locating lugs from the support crossmember, then withdraw the radiator downwards from the front of the vehicle.

Removal – 2.0 litre models

11 Disconnect the battery negative lead as described in Chapter 5.

12 Drain the cooling system as described in Chapter 1.

13 Raise the front of the vehicle and support it securely on axle stands (see *Jacking and vehicle support*). Remove the engine undertray (where fitted).

14 Undo the 3 screws and remove the splash shield under the radiator (where fitted).

3.15 Pull out the clip (arrowed) each side under the radiator crossmember

3.19a Undo the bolts (arrowed)...

3.19b... undo the nuts, drill out the rivets (arrowed)...

3.19c... and remove the impact absorber each side

3.23 Bonnet lock retaining bolts (arrowed)

3.24 Undo the bolt (arrowed) securing the ECM bracket to the front panel

15 Pull out the clips securing the radiator to the lower support crossmember (see illustration). Recover the washers above the clips.
16 Pull the rubber seal strip from the top edge of the bonnet slam panel.
17 Remove the bonnet, radiator grille and front bumper as described in Chapter 11.
18 Remove both headlights as described in Chapter 12.
19 Undo the bolts/drill out the rivets and remove the central impact absorber with air deflector, and the 2 outer impact absorbers (see illustrations).
20 Release the clip and slide the power steering fluid reservoir upwards from the mounting. Place it to one side. There's no need to disconnect the pipes.
21 Release the clamps and disconnect the air hoses from each side of the intercooler.
22 Undo the 2 bolts securing the air cleaner housing support frame to the bonnet slam panel.

23 Make alignment marks between the bonnet lock and the slam panel, then undo the bolts and manoeuvre the bonnet lock from place (see illustration). Unclip the release cable and wiring harness from the slam panel.
24 Undo the bolts and release the engine

management ECM bracket and bonnet switch bracket (where fitted) from the slam panel (see illustration).
25 Undo the 7 bolts and remove the front panel assembly from the vehicle (see illustrations).

3.25a The front panel is secured by 2 bolts (arrowed) at the right-hand edge...

3.25b... 3 bolts (arrowed) on the left-hand side...

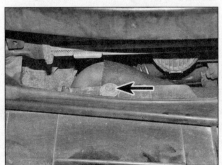

3.25c... 1 bolt (arrowed) to the right of centre...

3.25d... and 1 bolt (arrowed) at the base of the central bracket

3.25e Lift the entire front panel from place

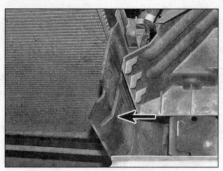

3.35 Unclip the air deflector panel (arrowed)

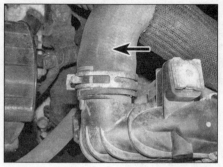

3.36a Disconnect the upper radiator hose (arrowed)...

3.36b... and expansion tank hose (arrowed)

M9R 630 engine

26 Remove the air cleaner assembly as described in Chapter 4A.
27 Pull the charge pressure sensor and bracket from the air filter support frame. Release the wiring harness from the frame as the sensor is withdrawn.
28 Unclip the fuel pipe, mass airflow sensor wiring harness, and coolant heater harness (where fitted) from the support frame.
29 Undo the bolt and detach the cooler heater assembly (where fitted) from the support frame.
30 Undo the 2 nuts and 2 bolts, and remove the support frame from the engine compartment.
31 Release the clips and remove the air deflector panel from the left-hand end of the radiator.
32 On models with air conditioning, unbolt the condenser from the radiator, and support it to prevent any strain on the refrigerant pipes.
33 Unclip the power steering hose, then lift the radiator upwards from the support crossmember.
34 If required, unbolt the cooling fan assembly from the radiator.

All except M9R 630 engine

35 Release the clips and remove the air deflector panel from the left-hand end of the radiator **(see illustration)**.
36 Release the clamps and disconnect the upper coolant hose and expansion tank hose from the radiator **(see illustrations)**.
37 Unclip the air deflector panels from each side of the lower radiator.

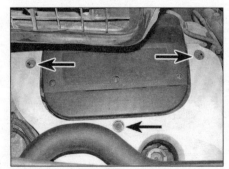

4.3 Prise out the caps, undo the nuts (arrowed) and remove the plastic cover

38 Release the clip each side, and slide the cooling fan shroud upwards, releasing it from the mountings on the radiator.
39 On models with air conditioning, carefully lift the condenser upwards from the mountings on the radiator, and support it in this position. Take care not to place any strain on the rigid refrigerant pipes.
40 Remove the radiator upwards from the support crossmember.

Inspection

41 If the radiator has been removed due to suspected blockage, reverse-flush it as described later in this Section. Clean dirt and debris from the radiator fins, using a low-pressure airline (in which case, wear eye protection) or a soft brush. Be careful, as the fins are sharp, and can be easily damaged.
42 If necessary, a radiator specialist can perform a 'flow test' on the radiator, to establish whether an internal blockage exists.
43 A leaking radiator must be referred to a specialist for permanent repair. Do not attempt to weld or solder a leaking radiator, as damage to the plastic components may result.
44 If the radiator is to be sent for repair or renewed, remove all hoses, and the cooling fan switch (where fitted).
45 Inspect the condition of the radiator mounting rubbers, and renew them if necessary.

Radiator flushing

46 Disconnect the top and bottom hoses and any other relevant hoses from the radiator, with reference to Chapter 3.

4.4 Depress the clip (arrowed) above and below the air intake ducting

47 Insert a garden hose into the radiator top intake. Direct a flow of clean water through the radiator, and continue flushing until clean water emerges from the radiator bottom outlet.
48 If after a reasonable period the water still does not run clear, the radiator can be flushed with a good proprietary cleaning agent. It is important that the manufacturer's instructions are followed carefully. If the contamination is particularly bad, insert the hose in the radiator bottom outlet, and reverse-flush the radiator.

Refitting

49 Refitting is a reversal of removal, bearing in mind the following points:
a) *Take care not to damage the radiator fins (nor the condenser/intercooler, where applicable) during refitting.*
b) *On completion, refill the cooling system as described in Chapter 1.*

4 Thermostat – removal, testing and refitting

Note: *On all engine types, the thermostat is part of the coolant housing and cannot be removed separately. The complete coolant housing/thermostat will need to be renewed as a unit.*

Removal

1 Disconnect the battery negative lead as described in Chapter 5, and drain the cooling system as described in Chapter 1.

1.9 litre engines

2 Unclip the oil filler funnel from the bonnet slam panel.
3 Prise up the caps, undo the 3 bolts and remove the plastic cover from the top of the engine **(see illustration)**.
4 Release the 2 clips and disconnect the air intake ducting from the air cleaner housing **(see illustration)**.
5 Release the clamp and disconnect the air outlet hose from the left-hand side of the intercooler.
6 Disconnect the engine breather hose from the oil separator, release it from the support clip and move it to one side.
7 Release the clamps, undo the bolt (models

4.10 Disconnect the coolant hoses (arrowed) from the thermostat housing

4.13 Pull the charge pressure sensor from the support frame

4.15 Undo the bolt (arrowed) securing the coolant heater bracket to the support frame

up to 2006 only) and remove the air hose from the intercooler to the intake manifold.

8 Disconnect the servo hose and vacuum hose from the vacuum pump at the left-hand end of the cylinder head

9 Disconnect the coolant temperature sensor wiring plug (located on the thermostat housing).

10 Note their fitted positions, then release the clamps and disconnect the coolant hoses from the thermostat housing **(see illustration)**.

11 Undo the 3 bolts and remove the thermostat housing. Recover the sealing ring.

2.0 litre engines

12 Remove the air cleaner assembly as described in Chapter 4A.

13 Pull the charge air pressure sensor from the bracket on the support frame, and release the wiring harness **(see illustration)**.

14 Unclip the fuel pipe and mass airflow sensor wiring harness from the support frame.

15 Undo the bolt securing the coolant heater assembly (where fitted) to the support frame, and unclip the wiring harness **(see illustration)**.

16 The support frame is secured by 2 nuts and 2 bolts. Undo the nuts/bolts and remove the frame from the engine compartment **(see illustrations)**.

17 Release the clamps, undo the bolt and remove the air duct from the turbocharger to the intercooler **(see illustration)**.

18 Undo the clips and remove the turbocharger intake hose. Release the heater hoses and vacuum pipe from the intake hose **(see illustrations)**.

19 Disconnect the coolant temperature sensor wiring plug (located on the thermostat housing).

20 Release the clip, disconnect the transmission breather hose and move it to one side.

21 Note their fitted positions, release the clamps, and disconnect the coolant hoses from the thermostat housing **(see illustration)**.

22 Undo the 3 bolts, and remove the thermostat housing. Recover the sealing ring.

Testing

23 A rough test of the thermostat may be made by suspending it with a piece of string in a container full of water. Heat the water to bring it to the boil – the thermostat must open by the time the water boils. If not, renew it.

24 If a thermometer is available, the precise opening temperature of the thermostat may be determined; compare with the figures given in the Specifications. The opening temperature is also marked on the thermostat.

25 A thermostat that fails to close as the cooling system gets cooler must also be renewed.

4.16a The support frame is secured by 2 bolts (arrowed) at the front...

4.16b... and 2 nuts (arrowed) at the engine compartment bulkhead

4.17 Remove the air duct from the turbocharger to the intercooler

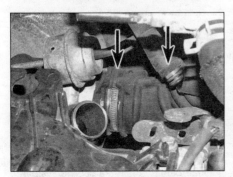

4.18a Slacken the clamp, disconnect the breather hose (arrowed)...

4.18b... and remove the turbocharger intake hose

4.21 Disconnect the hoses (arrowed) from the thermostat housing

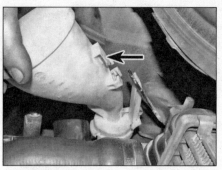

5.2 Release the clip (arrowed) and slide the oil filler funnel up from the bracket

5.4a Undo the radiator upper mounting bolt (arrowed) on the right-hand side...

5.4b... and on the left-hand side (arrowed)

5.9 Fan motor retaining bolts (arrowed)

Refitting

26 Refitting is a reversal of removal, bearing in mind the following points:

a) Renew the thermostat housing sealing ring.
b) On completion, refill the cooling system as described in Chapter 1, and reconnect the battery negative lead as described in Chapter 5.

5 Radiator cooling fan – removal and refitting

Removal – 1.9 litre models

1 Disconnect the battery negative lead as described in Chapter 5.
2 Unclip the oil filler funnel from the bonnet slam panel **(see illustration)**.

5.22 Press the clip each side rearwards a little and lift the cooling fan shroud upwards from the lower mountings

3 Remove the radiator grille as described in Chapter 11.
4 Undo the 2 upper radiator mounting bolts **(see illustrations)**.
5 Raise the front of the vehicle and support it securely on axle stands (see *Jacking and vehicle support*). Remove the engine undertray.
6 Disconnect the wiring plugs from the fan motor and resistor, then release the wiring harness from the fan shroud.
7 Unclip the radiator lower hose from the fan shroud.
8 Release the fan shroud retaining clip each side, lift it from the mounting, then lower it from place **(see illustration 5.22)**.
9 If required, undo the retaining bolts, detach the fan from the motor, then undo the 3 bolts and detach motor from the shroud **(see illustration)**.

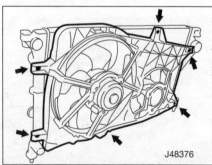

5.24 Undo the bolts (arrowed) and lift the cooling fan shroud from place – M9R 630 engine

Removal – 2.0 litre models

10 Disconnect the battery negative lead as described in Chapter 5.
11 Pull the rubber seal strip from the top edge of the bonnet slam panel. Remove the bonnet, radiator grille and front bumper as described in Chapter 11.
12 Remove both headlights as described in Chapter 12.
13 Undo the bolts/drill out the rivets and remove the central impact absorber with air deflector, and the 2 outer impact absorbers **(see illustrations 3.19a, 3.19b and 3.19c)**.
14 Unclip the power steering fluid reservoir and move it to one side. There's no need to disconnect the pipes.
15 Release the clamps and disconnect the air hoses from each side of the intercooler.
16 Undo the 2 bolts securing the air cleaner housing support frame to the bonnet slam panel.
17 Make alignment marks between the bonnet lock and the slam panel, then undo the bolts and manoeuvre the bonnet lock from place **(see illustration 3.23)**. Unclip the release cable and wiring harness from the slam panel.
18 Undo the bolts and release the engine management ECM bracket and bonnet switch bracket from the slam panel.
19 Undo the 7 bolts and remove the front panel assembly from the vehicle **(see illustrations 3.25a to 3.25e)**.
20 Disconnect the wiring plugs from the fan motor and resistor, then release the wiring harness from the fan shroud.

All except M9R 630 engine

21 Unclip the radiator lower hose from the fan shroud.
22 Release the fan shroud retaining clip each side, lift it from the mounting, then lower it from place **(see illustration)**.

M9R 630 engine

23 Unclip the air deflector panel from each side of the radiator.
24 Undo the 6 retaining bolts and lift the cooling fan and shroud from place **(see illustration)**.

All engines

25 If required, undo the 3 bolts and detach the motor from the shroud.

Refitting

26 Refit by reversing the removal operations.

6 Coolant temperature sensor – testing, removal and refitting

Testing

1 Testing of the sensor should be entrusted to a Vauxhall or Renault dealer.

Removal

2 Either partially drain the cooling system to just below the level of the sensor (as described in Chapter 1), or have ready a suitable plug

6.4 Depress the release button (arrowed) and disconnect the breather hose – engine removed for clarity

6.5 Slide out the clip (arrowed) and withdraw the sensor – 1.9 litre engines

6.8 Slide out the clip (arrowed) and withdraw the sensor – 2.0 litre engines

which can be used to plug the sensor aperture whilst it is removed. If a plug is used, take great care not to damage the sensor unit aperture, and do not use anything which will allow foreign matter to enter the cooling system.

1.9 litre engines

3 Prise up the caps, undo the 3 bolts and remove the plastic cover from the top of the engine **(see illustration 4.3)**.
4 Release the clip and disconnect the breather hose from the air intake hose **(see illustration)**.
5 Disconnect the wiring connector, then slide out the securing clip and withdraw the temperature sensor from the coolant housing **(see illustration)**. Recover the sealing ring.

2.0 litre models

6 Remove the air cleaner assembly as described in Chapter 4A.
7 On M9R 630 engines, release the clip and disconnect the turbocharger intake hose, unclip the wastegate vacuum hose, and release the wiring harness from the thermostat housing.
8 Disconnect the wiring connector, then slide out the securing clip and withdraw the temperature sensor from the coolant housing **(see illustration)**. Recover the sealing ring.

Refitting

9 Refit the temperature sensor with a new sealing ring into the coolant housing using a reversal of the removal procedure. Make sure it is securely held by the clip.
10 Top-up or refill the cooling system, with reference to *Weekly checks* or Chapter 1.

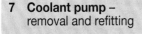

7 Coolant pump –
removal and refitting

1 The coolant pump on all models is mounted at the timing belt/chain end of the engine. Disconnect the battery negative lead as described in Chapter 5. Drain the cooling system as described in Chapter 1.

1.9 litre engine

2 Remove the timing belt as described in Chapter 2A.

3 Working in the **reverse** of the tightening sequence shown **(see illustration)**, unscrew the bolts securing the pump to the cylinder block, and withdraw the pump from the block. If the pump is stuck, tap it using a soft-faced mallet. Recover the gasket/seal and discard it; a new one must be used on refitting.
4 Commence refitting by thoroughly cleaning the mating faces of the pump and the cylinder block, then fitting a new gasket/seal.
5 Locate the pump in position and refit the retaining bolts to their correct locations. Note that a suitable thread sealant should be applied to the threads of bolts 1, 3 and 4 **(see illustration 7.3)**.
6 Working in the sequence shown in illustration 7.3 tighten all the bolts to the specified torque setting.
7 Refit the timing belt as described in Chapter 2A, it is recommended that a new belt is fitted

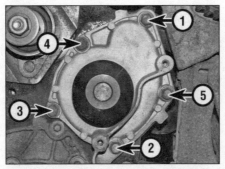

7.3 Coolant pump retaining bolts tightening sequence

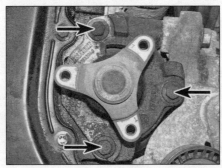

7.11a Undo the coolant pump bolts (arrowed)

8 On completion, refill the cooling system as described in Chapter 1.

2.0 litre engine

9 Remove the auxiliary drivebelt as described in Chapter 1. Slacken the coolant pump pulley bolts just prior to removing the drivebelt **(see illustration)**.
10 Completely unbolt and remove the coolant pump pulley.
11 Unscrew the mounting bolts and withdraw the pump from the cylinder block. Prise out the O-ring seal from the groove in the pump body **(see illustrations)**.
12 Commence refitting by thoroughly cleaning the mating faces of the pump and the cylinder block. Take care not to damage the O-ring seal contact face in the block.
13 Carefully fit the new O-ring seal to the groove in the pump body, then smear some soapy water on the seal.

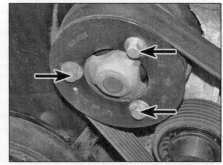

7.9 Slacken the coolant pump pulley bolts (arrowed) prior to belt removal

7.11b Renew the O-ring seal

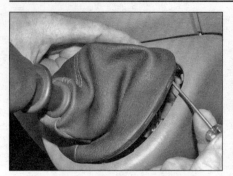

9.1 Prise up the gear lever gaiter

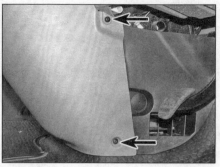

9.2a Undo the 2 screws (arrowed) each side...

9.2b... then pull the centre console rearwards a little to release the clips

14 Slide the coolant pump into the cylinder block, whilst twisting it back and forth to assist seal entry, then fit the mounting bolts finger-tight initially. Make sure the body of the pump is in contact with the cylinder block.

15 Tighten the coolant pump bolts to the specified torque.

16 The remainder of refitting is a reversal of removal.

8 Heating and ventilation system – general information

The heating/ventilation system consists of a four-speed blower motor (mounted on the engine compartment bulkhead), a control unit mounted in the facia, face level vents in the centre and at each end of the facia, and air ducts to the front and rear footwells.

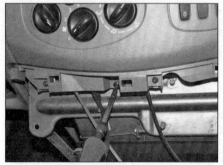

9.3a Undo the screw...

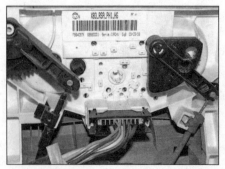

9.4 Disconnect the control cables and wiring plug from the control unit

The facia-mounted controls operate flap valves to deflect and mix the airflowing through the various parts of the heating/ventilation system. The flap valves are contained in the air distribution housing, which acts as a central distribution unit, passing air to the various ducts and vents.

Cold air enters the system through the grille at the top of the engine compartment scuttle. If required, the airflow is boosted by the blower motor, and then flows through the various ducts, according to the settings of the controls. Stale air is expelled via the vents in the rear of the vehicle. If warm air is required, the cold air is passed over the heater matrix, which is heated by the engine coolant. A recirculation position button on the blower motor switch enables the outside air supply to be closed off, while the air inside the vehicle is recirculated. This can be useful to prevent unpleasant odours entering from outside the

9.3b... and pull the control panel rearwards/downwards

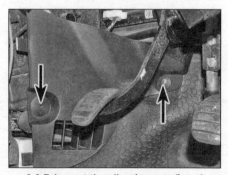

9.8 Prise out the clips (arrowed) and remove the panel

vehicle, but should only be used briefly, as the recirculated air inside the vehicle will soon become stale.

Models with manual air conditioning have a conventional heater/ventilation control unit, with a button that is used to switch on the air conditioning. Further details of the air conditioning system can be found in Section 10.

9 Heating and ventilation system components – removal and refitting

Control unit

1 Carefully unclip the gear lever gaiter from the centre console panel **(see illustration)**.

2 Undo the 4 screws, release the 3 clips, and remove the centre console panel **(see illustrations)**. Disconnect the hazard warning switch wiring plug as the panel is withdrawn.

3 The control unit and trim panel is secured by a single screw at its lower edge. Undo the screw and manoeuvre the panel rearwards **(see illustrations)**.

4 Disconnect the wiring plugs from the control unit, then carefully prise off the retaining clips and detach the control cables from the unit **(see illustration)**.

5 If required, undo the 2 screws, release the 2 clips and separate the control unit from the panel.

6 Refitting is a reversal of removal, check the operation of the heater controls before refitting the control unit securing screw.

Heater/ventilation control cables

7 Remove the heater/ventilation control unit as described previously in this Section.

8 Unclip the cover from the heater assembly **(see illustration)**.

9 Disconnect the end of the relevant cable from the lever on the air distribution unit, then withdraw the cable, noting its routing to aid refitting **(see illustration)**.

10 Refitting is a reversal of removal, bearing in mind the following points.

a) Route the cable(s) as noted before removal.

9.9 Disconnect the heater control cables (arrowed)

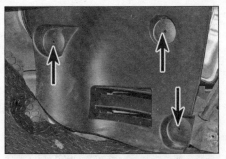

9.14 Prise out the clips (arrowed) and remove the panel in the passenger's side footwell

9.15 Undo the matrix pipe support bracket screw (arrowed) at the bulkhead

b) *Check the operation of the heater controls before refitting the control unit securing screws.*

Heater matrix

11 Drain the cooling system as described in Chapter 1.
12 Carefully unclip the gear lever gaiter from the centre console panel **(see illustration 9.1)**.
13 Undo the 4 screws, release the 3 clips, and remove the centre console panel **(see illustrations 9.2a and 9.2b)**. Disconnect the hazard warning switch wiring plug as the panel is withdrawn.
14 Prise out the clips and remove the passenger's side footwell inner panel **(see illustration)**.
15 Undo the matrix pipe support bracket screw at the bulkhead **(see illustration)**.
16 Release the clamps and pull the pipes from the heater matrix **(see illustrations)**. Be prepared for coolant spillage. Discard the seals – new ones must be fitted.
17 Undo the 2 retaining screws and pull the matrix from the housing, taking care not to spill any remaining coolant inside the vehicle **(see illustrations)**.
18 Refitting is a reversal of removal, noting the following points:
a) *Renew the matrix pipe seals.*
b) *On completion, refill the cooling system as described in Chapter 1.*

Heater blower motor

19 Disconnect the battery negative lead as described in Chapter 5.

2.0 litre models

20 Remove the air cleaner assembly as described in Chapter 4A.
21 Pull the charge air pressure sensor from the bracket on the support frame, and release the wiring harness **(see illustration 4.13)**.
22 Unclip the fuel pipe and mass airflow sensor wiring harness from the support frame.
23 Undo the bolt securing the coolant heater assembly (where fitted) to the support frame, and unclip the wiring harness **(see illustration 4.15)**.
24 The support frame is secured by 2 nuts, and 2 bolts. Undo the nuts/bolts and remove the frame from the engine compartment **(see illustration 4.16a and 4.16b)**.

9.16a Undo the pipe clamp bolts (arrowed)...

9.16b... and pull the pipes from the matrix

All models

25 Disconnect the wiring connector, then undo the 3 nuts/1 bolt and withdraw the

9.17a Undo the retaining screws (arrowed)...

9.17b... and pull the matrix from the heater

heater blower motor housing from the engine compartment bulkhead **(see illustrations)**.
26 Undo the 3 screws and remove the blower motor from the housing **(see illustrations)**.

9.25a The heater blower motor housing is secured by a nut (arrowed) on the right-hand side...

9.25b... a nut (arrowed) on the left-hand side...

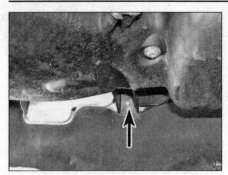

9.25c... a nut (arrowed) underneath...

9.25d... and a bolt (arrowed) at the top edge

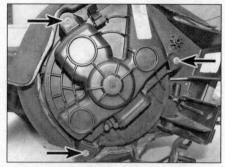

9.26a Undo the 3 screws (arrowed)...

9.26b... and withdraw the blower motor from the housing

9.30 Undo the screws (arrowed) and lower the insulation

9.31 Heater resistor retaining screw (arrowed)

Disconnect the wiring plug as the motor is withdrawn.

27 Refitting is a reversal of removal.

Heater blower motor resistor

28 On 2.0 litre models, remove the air cleaner assembly as described in Chapter 4A.
29 On all models, disconnect the resistor wiring plugs.
30 Undo the 3 screws and pull down the lower section of the blower motor insulation **(see illustration)**.
31 Undo the retaining screw and manoeuvre the resistor from place **(see illustration)**. Unclip the wiring harness from the housing, and disconnect the wiring plug from the blower motor.
32 Refitting is a reversal of removal.

10 Air conditioning system – general information and precautions

An air conditioning system is available on some models. It enables the temperature of incoming air to be lowered; it also dehumidifies the air, which makes for rapid demisting and increased comfort.

The cooling side of the system works in the same way as a domestic refrigerator. Refrigerant gas is drawn into a belt-driven compressor, and passes into a condenser in front of the radiator, where it loses heat and becomes liquid. The liquid passes through an expansion valve to an evaporator, where it changes from liquid under high pressure

to gas under low pressure. This change is accompanied by a drop in temperature, which cools the evaporator. The refrigerant returns to the compressor and the cycle begins again.

Air blown through the evaporator passes to the air distribution unit, where it is mixed with hot air blown through the heater matrix, to achieve the desired temperature in the passenger compartment. The heating side of the system works in the same way as on models without air conditioning.

⚠️ **Warning: The refrigerant is potentially dangerous, and should only be handled by qualified persons. If it is splashed onto the skin, it can cause frostbite. It is not itself poisonous, but in the presence of a naked flame (including a cigarette) it forms a poisonous gas.**

Uncontrolled discharging of the refrigerant is dangerous, and damaging to the environment. Have the refrigerant circuit

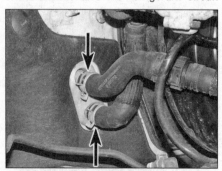

11.6 Release the clamps (arrowed) and disconnect the coolant hoses

evacuated by a dealer or suitably-equipped repairer, then recharged after the work has been carried out.

Do not operate the air conditioning system if it is known to be short of refrigerant; the compressor may be damaged.

11 Air conditioning system components – removal and refitting

Evaporator

1 Have the refrigerant circuit evacuated by a dealer or suitably-equipped repairer.
2 Drain the cooling system as described in Chapter 1.
3 Disconnect the battery negative lead as described in Chapter 5.
4 Remove the heater blower motor housing as described in Section 9.
5 Undo the retaining bolts and detach the refrigerant pipes from the connections at the engine compartment bulkhead. Plug the openings to prevent contamination. Discard the pipe seals – new ones must be fitted.
6 Release the clamps and disconnect the heater coolant pipes from the connections on the engine compartment bulkhead **(see illustration)**. Be prepared for fluid spillage.
7 Remove the complete facia as described in Chapter 11.
8 Remove the steering column as described in Chapter 10.
9 Undo the retaining nuts and move the gear lever assembly to one side – see Chapter 7.

10 Note their fitted positions, and routing, then disconnect the wiring plugs from the heater housing and release the wiring harnesses from the facia crossmember. Undo the screw, unclip the fusebox, and undo the screws securing the relay plate **(see illustrations)**. It's necessary to disconnect the wiring loom from the components at the right-hand side of the cabin (door, courtesy light switch, seat, handbrake warning light switch, etc), and fold the loom across to the left-hand side.
11 Undo the 4 bolts securing the heater housing to the facia crossmember **(see illustrations)**.
12 Prise out the clips and remove the trim panel from the driver's side footwell adjacent to the heater housing **(see illustration 9.8)**.
13 Undo the retaining bolts and, with the help of an assistant, pull the crossmember rearwards and manoeuvre it from the vehicle **(see illustrations)**. **Note:** *The edges of the crossmember are extremely sharp. Take care not to damage the cabin upholstery, or cause person injury.*
14 Disconnect the drain hose from the heater housing, and manoeuvre the housing from the cabin.
15 Undo the 7 screws and remove the lower cover from the housing.
16 Carefully remove the sponge seals from around the refrigerant pipes.
17 Undo the 5 screws and remove the side cover from the housing.
18 Withdraw the evaporator from the housing.
19 Refitting is a reversal of removal, noting the following points:
 a) *Ensure the heater housing drain hose is securing reconnected and routed when refitting.*
 b) *Renew the refrigerant pipe seals*
 c) *Refill the cooling system as described in Chapter 1.*
 d) *Reconnect the battery negative lead as described in Chapter 5.*
 e) *Upon completion, have the refrigerant circuit recharged by a dealer or suitably-equipped repairer.*

Compressor

20 If necessary, the compressor can be unbolted and moved aside, without dis-

11.10a Fusebox retaining screw (arrowed)

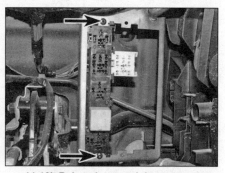

11.10b Relay plate retaining screws (arrowed)

11.11a The heater housing is secured by a bolt at the top corner each side (arrowed)...

11.11b... and a bolt at the lower corner each side (arrowed)

connecting its flexible hoses, after removing the drivebelt (see Chapter 1) and disconnecting the wiring plug.
21 To remove the compressor, first have the refrigerant circuit evacuated by a dealer or suitably-equipped repairer.
22 Remove the auxiliary drivebelt as described in Chapter 1.

2.0 litre models

23 Remove the radiator grille and front bumper as described in Chapter 11.
24 Undo the 4 bolts and remove the central impact absorber, along with the central air deflector and right-hand air deflector (adjacent to the radiator).

All models

25 Disconnect the compressor wiring plug, then undo the bolts and detach the refrigerant

pipes from the compressor. Discard the pipe seals, and plug the openings to prevent contamination.
26 Undo the 3 mounting bolts, and lower the compressor from position.
27 Position the compressor against the accessory bracket, install the mounting bolts and tighten them to the specified torque.
28 Fit new seals to the refrigerant pipes, lubricate them with clean refrigerant oil, then attach them to the compressor and tighten the retaining bolts to the specified torque.
29 The remainder of refitting is a reversal of removal. Have the refrigerant circuit recharged by a dealer or suitably-equipped repairer upon completion.

Condenser – 1.9 litre models

30 Have the refrigerant circuit evacuated by a dealer or suitably-equipped repairer.

11.13a The facia crossmember is secured by 2 bolts (arrowed) at each end...

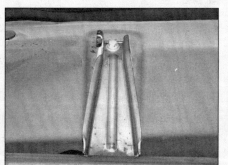

11.13b... a bolt (arrowed) in front of the steering column position...

11.13c... and a bolt (arrowed) each side in the lower/centre section

11.43 The radiator crossmember is secured by a bolt (arrowed) each end

31 Raise the front of the vehicle and support it securely on axle stands (see *Jacking and vehicle support*). Undo the fasteners and remove the engine/transmission undertray.

32 Undo the screws and remove the radiator undertray. Unclip the air deflector from the right-hand side of the radiator.

33 Undo the retaining bolts and detach the refrigerant pipes from the condenser. Discard the pipe seals. Plug the openings to prevent contamination. Release the retaining clip each side, then lower the condenser from place.

34 Refitting is a reversal of removal, noting the following points:

a) *Tighten all fasteners to their specified torque where given.*

b) *Renew the refrigerant pipe seals, and lubricate them with clean refrigerant oil prior to assembly.*

c) *Have the refrigerant circuit recharged by a dealer or suitably-equipped repairer upon completion.*

Condenser – 2.0 litre models

35 Have the refrigerant circuit evacuated by a dealer or suitably-equipped repairer.

36 Remove the radiator grille and front bumper as described in Chapter 11.

37 Undo the 4 bolts and remove the central impact absorber, along with the central air deflector and right-hand air deflector or drill out the rivets and remove impact absorber as applicable (adjacent to the radiator).

38 Raise the front of the vehicle and support it securely on axle stands (see *Jacking and vehicle support*). Undo the fasteners and remove the engine/transmission undertray.

39 Undo the screws and remove the radiator undertray.

All except M9R 630 engine

40 Undo the retaining bolts and detach the refrigerant pipes from the condenser. Discard the pipe seals. Plug the openings to prevent contamination.

41 Undo the 2 mounting bolts securing the condenser to the radiator. Use cable-ties, string, etc, to secure the radiator to the upper front panel.

42 Undo the bolt securing the power steering pipe bracket to the radiator support crossmember.

43 Undo the 2 retaining bolts and remove

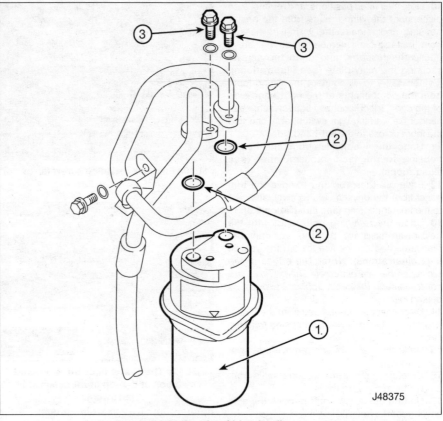

J48375

11.55 Receiver/drier details

1 *Receiver/drier*
2 *O-ring seals*

3 *Refrigerant pipe retaining bolts*

the radiator support crossmember **(see illustration)**.

44 Lower the radiator slightly, then slide the condenser upwards from the bracket each side and remove it.

M9R 630 engine

45 Unclip the air deflectors from each side of the radiator lower section.

46 Undo the retaining bolts and detach the refrigerant pipes from the condenser. Discard the pipe seals. Plug the openings to prevent contamination.

47 Undo the mounting bolts and remove the condenser.

All engines

48 Refitting is a reversal of removal, noting the following points:

a) *Tighten all fasteners to their specified torque where given.*

b) *Renew the refrigerant pipe seals, and lubricate them with clean refrigerant oil prior to assembly.*

c) *Have the refrigerant circuit recharged by a dealer or suitably-equipped repairer upon completion.*

Evaporator temperature sensor

49 Release the 2 retaining clips and remove the centre console right-hand trim panel from the driver's footwell area.

50 Rotate the temperature sensor anti-clockwise and pull it from the heater housing. Disconnect the wiring plug as the sensor is withdrawn.

51 Refitting is a reversal of removal.

Receiver/drier

52 Have the refrigerant circuit evacuated by a dealer or suitably-equipped repairer.

53 Remove the radiator grille as described in Chapter 11.

54 Remove the right-hand headlight as described in Chapter 12.

55 Undo the retaining bolts, and detach the refrigerant pipes from the receiver/drier **(see illustration)**. Discard the pipe seals. Plug the openings to prevent contamination.

56 Release the refrigerant pipes from any support brackets, and pull the receiver/drier from the rubber mounting.

57 Refitting is a reversal of removal, noting the following points:

a) *On 1.9 litre models, align the arrow on the receiver drier with the mark on the rubber mounting.*

b) *Renew the refrigerant pipe seals, and lubricate them with clean refrigerant oil prior to assembly.*

c) *Have the refrigerant circuit recharged by a dealer or suitably-equipped repairer upon completion.*

Chapter 4 Part A:
Fuel and exhaust systems

Contents

Degrees of difficulty

Easy, suitable for novice with little experience 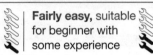	**Fairly easy,** suitable for beginner with some experience	**Fairly difficult,** suitable for competent DIY mechanic	**Difficult,** suitable for experienced DIY mechanic	**Very difficult,** suitable for expert DIY or professional

Specifications

General

System type . . . . Rear-mounted fuel tank, high-pressure pump with common rail, direct injection, turbocharger

Fuel system data

Idle speed:
  1.9 litre engines . . . . 800 ± 50 rpm
  2.0 litre engines . . . . 775 ± 50 rpm
Maximum with no load on engine:
  1.9 litre engines . . . . 4160 ± 150 rpm
  2.0 litre engines . . . . Not available
Maximum with load on engine:
  1.9 litre engines . . . . 3700 ± 100 rpm
  2.0 litre engines . . . . 4250 ± 150 rpm
High-pressure pump:
  Type . . . . Bosch
  Operating pressure. . . . . 250 to 1350 bar
  Direction of rotation . . . . Clockwise viewed from sprocket end
Injectors:
  Type . . . . Bosch solenoid injector
  Solenoid resistance . . . . 0.2 ohms
  Operating pressure. . . . . 1350 bar
  Maximum pressure . . . . 1600 bar
Glow plug:
  Type . . . . Beru or Champion
  Resistance (connector removed) . . . . 0.6 ohms
Thermoplungers resistance (at 20 degrees C) . . . . 0.45 ± 0.05 ohms

Torque wrench settings

	Nm	lbf ft
1.9 litre engines		
Catalytic converter-to-turbocharger nuts	21	15
EGR valve mounting bolts	21	15
Fuel pressure regulator bolts	6	4
Fuel rail mounting bolts	22	16
Fuel rail pressure sensor	35	26
High-pressure fuel pipe union nuts	25	18
Injection pump right-hand mounting bolts	30	22
Injection pump sprocket nut	70	52
Injector clamp bolts	25	18
Manifold nuts	28	21
Oil feed pipe-to-turbocharger union	25	18
Oil return pipe-to-turbocharger bolts	12	9
Throttle valve unit (damper unit) bolts	8	6
Turbocharger mounting nuts	24	18
2.0 litre engines		
Camshaft position sensor	10	7
Catalytic converter to turbocharger*	21	15
Crankshaft sensor	10	7
EGR valve to manifold	25	18
Exhaust elbow/injector housing*	25	18
Exhaust manifold:		
Studs	9	7
Mounting nuts:*		
Stage 1	18	13
Stage 2	30	22
Fuel rail mounting bolts	25	18
Fuel pipe mounting on valve cover	10	7
Fuel high-pressure pump pinion	90	66
Fuel high-pressure pump mounting	25	18
High-pressure pipe union nuts	32	24
Injector clamp bolt	35	26
Intake manifold	25	18
Throttle valve module:		
Mounting bracket to unit	12	9
Mounting bracket to intake manifold	12	9
Turbocharger to manifold*	28	21
Turbocharger bracket	25	18
Turbocharger oil return pipe bolts on turbocharger	10	7
Turbocharger oil feed pipe union bolts	16	12
Turbocharger temperature sensor	30	22

Do not re-use.

1 General information and precautions

The fuel system consists of a rear-mounted fuel tank, a fuel filter (with integral water separator on early models) and a high-pressure pump with common rail injection system, electronic injectors and associated components.

The main components of the system are:
a) Electronic control unit (ECU).
b) High-pressure pump.
c) Fuel filter.
d) Injector rail.
e) Four electronic solenoid injectors.
f) Airflow meter.
g) Fuel temperature sensor.
h) Coolant temperature sensor.
i) Cylinder reference sensor.
j) Engine speed sensor.
k) Turbocharger pressure sensor.
l) EGR valve.

The common rail injection system operates as follows. Fuel is drawn from the fuel tank to the high-pressure pump by a low-pressure transfer pump integrated in the high-pressure pump. Before reaching the high-pressure pump, the fuel passes through a fuel filter where foreign matter and water are removed. As the fuel passes through the filter, it is heated by an electric heater. On reaching the high-pressure pump, the fuel is pressurised according to demand, and accumulates in the injection common rail. The pressure in the rail is accurately maintained using a pressure sensor in the rail and a pressure regulator under the control of the engine management ECU. This arrangement keeps heat generation to a minimum, and improves engine output. The rail pressure is also maintained by the injectors themselves; short electrical pulses which are not long enough to open the injector allow fuel into the return (leak-off) circuit, and also the normal pulses which open the injectors cause a reduction in pressure. The ECU determines the exact timing and duration of the injection period according to engine operating conditions.

The four fuel injectors inject a homogeneous spray of fuel into the combustion chambers located in the cylinder head. The injectors operate sequentially according to the firing order of the cylinders, and each injector needle is lubricated by fuel which accumulates in the spring chamber. Each injector has its own unique flow characteristics, which are used by the system ECU to calculate the exact quantity of fuel to inject.

In terms of the sensors used by the ECU to control a modern common rail diesel system, these engines are very similar to their petrol equivalents. The ECU determines engine speed and position from a TDC sensor fitted to the transmission bellhousing/cylinder block which detects a reference tooth on the flywheel ring gear, and signals the ECU. A similar sensor is fitted to monitor the camshaft, to give a reference for No 1 cylinder. Further sensors are used to monitor airflow into the engine, air

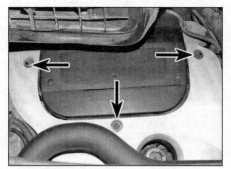

2.1 Prise out the caps, undo the nuts (arrowed) and remove the plastic cover

2.2 Depress the clip above (arrowed) and below the intake ducting

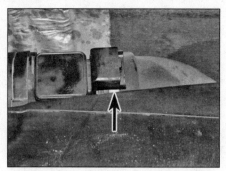

2.4 Release the clamp (arrowed) securing the hose to the mass airflow sensor

2.5a Undo the nut (arrowed) securing the air cleaner at the left-hand end...

2.5b... and right-hand end (arrowed)

temperature, and turbocharging pressure. On the fuel side, fuel pressure, temperature and flow rate are all monitored, according to model, via sensors on the high-pressure pump and/or the fuel rail. An 'electronic' throttle is fitted, with an accelerator position sensor instead of the mechanical cable previously used.

Provided that the specified maintenance is carried out, the fuel injection equipment will give long and trouble-free service. The main potential cause of damage to the high-pressure pump and injectors is dirt or water in the fuel. It is highly recommended that a set of fuel line plugs is obtained – these are available from motor accessory shops and better motor factors.

Servicing of the high-pressure pump, injectors, and electronic equipment and sensors is very limited for the home mechanic, and any dismantling or adjustment other than that described in this Chapter must be entrusted to a dealer or fuel injection specialist.

If a fault appears in the injection system, first ensure that all the system wiring connectors are securely connected and free of corrosion. Should the fault persist, the vehicle should be taken to a Vauxhall or Renault dealer or specialist who can test the system on a diagnostic tester. The tester will locate the fault quickly and simply, alleviating the need to test all the system components individually which is a time-consuming operation that carries a risk of damaging the ECU. It is advisable to have any faulty components renewed by the dealer as in many instances the tester is required to reprogramme the ECU in the event of component or sensor renewal.

⚠ **Warning: It is necessary to take certain precautions when working on the fuel system components, particularly the fuel injectors and high-pressure pump. Before carrying out any operations on the fuel system, refer to the precautions given in 'Safety first!' at the beginning of this manual. Allow the engine to cool for 5 to 10 minutes to ensure the fuel pressure and temperature are at a minimum.**

⚠ **Warning: Exercise extreme caution when working on the high-pressure fuel system. Do not attempt to test the fuel injectors or disconnect the high-pressure lines with the engine running. Never expose the hands or any part of the body to**

injector spray, as the high working pressure can cause the fuel to penetrate the skin, with possibly fatal results. You are strongly advised to have any work which involves testing the injectors under pressure carried out by a dealer or fuel injection specialist.

2 Air cleaner assembly and intake ducts – removal and refitting

Removal

1.9 litre models

1 Prise up the plastic caps, undo the 3 screws and remove the plastic cover from the top of the engine **(see illustration)**.
2 Release the 2 clips and disconnect the air intake ducting from the air cleaner **(see illustration)**.

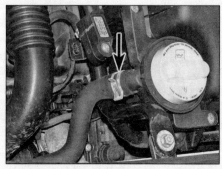

2.6 Disconnect the hose (arrowed) from the oil filler

3 Disconnect the mass airflow sensor wiring plug, and unclip the wiring harness.
4 Release the clamp and disconnect the air outlet hose from the mass airflow sensor **(see illustration)**. If necessary, cut the clip from place using a hacksaw, and renew it with a traditional worm-drive (Jubilee) clip.
5 Release any wiring harnesses/fuel pipes from the air cleaner housing, then undo the 2 retaining nuts and remove the air cleaner housing **(see illustrations)**.

2.0 litre models

6 Release the clip securing the hose to the base of the oil filler on the air cleaner housing, and move the pipe to one side **(see illustration)**.
7 Disconnect the mass airflow sensor wiring plug, and unclip the wiring harness.
8 Release the clamp and disconnect the air outlet hose from the mass airflow sensor **(see illustration)**.

2.8 Release the clamp (arrowed) and disconnect the outlet hose

2.9 Depress the button (arrowed) and disconnect the intake duct

9 Depress the release button, and disconnect the air intake duct from between the front panel and the air cleaner assembly **(see illustration)**.
10 Pull the air cleaner assembly upwards from the mounting pegs **(see illustration)**.

Refitting

11 Refitting is the reverse of removal, making sure all the hoses and ducts are securely reconnected.

3 Accelerator pedal – removal and refitting

Removal

1 Carefully prise the sensor link rod from the top of the accelerator pedal.
2 Undo the nut and remove the pedal **(see illustration)**.

3.2 Accelerator pedal retaining nut (arrowed)

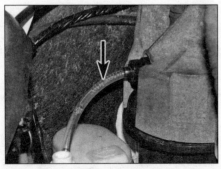

4.4 Note the bubbles (arrowed) in the clear, plastic hose

2.10 Pull the air cleaner housing upwards to release the mountings

3 Examine the pedal assembly for signs of wear and renew as necessary.

Refitting

4 Refitting is a reversal of the removal procedure, applying a little multipurpose grease to the pedal pivot point.

4 Fuel system – priming and bleeding

Note: *Refer to the precautions in Section 1 before proceeding.*

⚠ *Warning: Do not attempt to bleed the system by loosening any of the unions on the high-pressure circuit. Disconnecting any of the system sensors, or the fuel injectors, will result in a fault code being logged by the system ECU which must*

4.2 Hand-operated priming bulb (arrowed)

4.5 Disconnect the wiring plug from the glow plug control unit (arrowed)

then be cleared by a dealer or suitably-equipped repairer.

1 After disconnecting part of the fuel supply system or running out of fuel, it is necessary to prime the system and bleed off any air that may have entered the system components.
2 On most models, there is a pump to enable the system to be bled, this consists of a hand-operated priming bulb located next to the filter assembly on the right-hand inner wing panel **(see illustration)**. **Note:** *On models with no hand-operated priming pump, the ignition will need to be switched on and off (in 10 second bursts) several times for the pump to prime the filter.*
3 Attach a length of clear, plastic hose to the bleed nipple on the fuel filter, with the other end of the hose in a suitable container.

With hand-operated priming pump

4 Undo the bleed nipple approximately 1 turn, then squeeze the priming bulb several times to purge the low-pressure circuit of air, until bubble-free fuel can be seen emerging from the fuel filter bleed nipple **(see illustration)**. Close the nipple.

Without hand-operated priming pump

5 Disconnect the glow plug control unit wiring plug **(see illustration)**.
6 Undo the bleed nipple approximately 1 turn, then switch on the ignition between 3 to 7 times, for 10 seconds each time, with a 15 second pause. Bubble-free fuel should emerge from the nipple. Close the nipple.

All models

7 Attempt to start the engine normally. However, do not operate the starter motor for more than 5 seconds. If necessary, operate the starter motor in 4 to 5 second bursts followed by pauses of 8 to 10 seconds. As soon as the engine starts, let it run at fast idle speed until a regular idle speed is reached.

5 Fuel gauge sender unit – removal and refitting

Removal

1 Remove the fuel tank as described in Section 6.
2 Unscrew the fuel pump/level sensor unit locking ring and remove it from the tank. Although a Vauxhall tool (KM-6052) or Renault tool (MOT 1397) are available for this task, it can be accomplished using a large pair of grips to push on two opposite raised ribs on the locking ring. Alternatively, a home-made tool can be fabricated to engage with the raised ribs of the locking ring. Turn the ring anti-clockwise until it can be unscrewed by hand. Make an alignment mark between the locking ring and the tank to aid reassembly **(see illustrations)**.
3 Carefully manoeuvre the pump/sensor unit from the tank **(see illustration)**. Take great care not to bend/damage the float arm as the unit is withdrawn.

5.2a Commercial tools are available to unscrew the locking ring...

5.2b... or a homemade tool can be fabricated

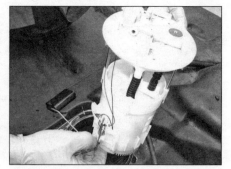

5.3 Carefully manoeuvre the pump/sensor unit from the tank

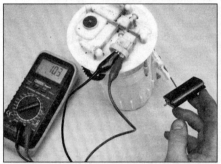

5.4a Check the resistance of the sender unit using a multimeter

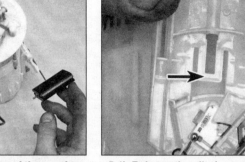
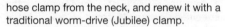
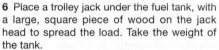

5.4b Release the clip (arrowed) and slide the sensor from the pump

5.5 Renew the sealing ring

4 If required, the level sensor can be unclipped from the pump assembly **(see illustrations)**. On full deflection the sensor resistance was approximately 10 Ω, and on zero deflection the resistance was 322 Ω.

Refitting

5 Refitting is a reversal of removal, noting the following points:

a) Use a new sealing ring **(see illustration)**.
b) To allow the unit to pass through the aperture in the fuel tank, press the float arm against the fuel pick-up body.
c) Align the marks made prior to removal.

6 Fuel tank –
removal and refitting

Removal

1 Before removing the fuel tank, all fuel should be drained from the tank. Since a fuel tank drain plug is not provided, it is preferable to carry out the removal operation when the tank is nearly empty.
2 Disconnect the battery negative lead as described in Chapter 5.
3 Raise the front and rear of the vehicle and support it securely on axle stands (see *Jacking and vehicle support*).
4 Release the clips and remove the protective plate around the filler neck **(see illustration)**.
5 Release the clips/clamps and disconnect the fuel filler hose and breather hose **(see illustration)**. If necessary, cut the original filler

hose clamp from the neck, and renew it with a traditional worm-drive (Jubilee) clamp.
6 Place a trolley jack under the fuel tank, with a large, square piece of wood on the jack head to spread the load. Take the weight of the tank.
7 Undo the tank strap retaining bolts, and with the help of an assistant, lower the tank a little to gain access to the connections on the top of the tank.
8 Note their fitted positions, then disconnect the wiring plug and fuel pipes from the tank sender/pump unit **(see illustration)**. Lower the tank to the ground and manoeuvre it from under the vehicle.

Refitting

9 Refitting is a reversal of removal, noting the following points:

a) When lifting the tank back into position, take care to ensure that none of the hoses

become trapped between the tank and vehicle body. Also ensure that the filler neck is correctly located as the tank is raised into position.
b) Ensure that all pipes and hoses are

6.4 Release the clips (arrowed) and remove the protective plate

6.5 Depress the release button (arrowed) to disconnect the breather hose, then release the filler hose clip (arrowed)

6.8 Depress the release buttons (arrowed) and disconnect the fuel hoses, then disconnect the wiring plug (arrowed)

7.3 Engine oil level dipstick guide tube retaining bolt (arrowed)

correctly routed. Make sure the sealing rings are in position in the quick-release fittings prior to fitting, and make sure they are securely clipped in position.
c) *Apply a little thread-locking compound to the retaining bolts prior to refitting.*
d) *On completion, refill the tank with a small amount of fuel, and check for signs of leakage prior to taking the vehicle out on the road.*

7 Throttle valve module – removal and refitting

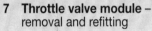

Note: *The throttle valve module is only fitted to 2.0 litre models.*

Removal

1 Remove the air cleaner assembly as described in Section 2.

8.2 Disconnect the pressure regulator wiring plug

8.12 Pull the charge pressure sensor upwards from the support frame

7.5 Undo the bolts (arrowed) securing the bracket the throttle valve module and cylinder head

2 Remove the intercooler as described in Section 16.
3 Undo the bolt and remove the engine oil level dipstick and guide tube assembly **(see illustration)**. Discard the tube O-ring seal, a new one must be fitted.
4 Disconnect the throttle valve module wiring plug.
5 Release the fuel pipe from the retaining clip, then undo the bolts and remove the bracket, then manoeuvre the module from place **(see illustration)**. Recover the gasket.

Refitting

6 Refitting is a reversal of removal, using a new gasket/seal and tightening to the specified torque. **Note:** *If a new throttle valve module has been fitted, it must be programmed using Vauxhall or Renault diagnostic equipment. Entrust this task to a dealer or suitably-equipped repairer.*

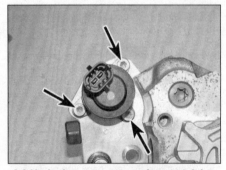

8.3 Undo the pressure regulator retaining bolts

8.14 Coolant heater assembly retaining bolt (arrowed)

8 Fuel system sensors and components – removal and refitting

Note: *Refer to the precautions in Section 1 before proceeding.*
1 Disconnect the battery negative lead as described in Chapter 5.

Pressure regulator

1.9 litre models

2 Disconnect the wiring plug from the fuel pressure regulator located on the rear of the high-pressure pump **(see illustration)**.
3 Clean the area around the base of the regulator, then remove the 3 regulator mounting bolts **(see illustration)**.
4 Ease the regulator out of position (any resistance is due to the O-ring seals) without using any tools. Once the regulator is free, recover any O-ring seals that were left behind – new seals should be obtained for refitting.
5 Fit the new seals, lubricated with clean diesel fuel, to the regulator.
6 Wash the regulator mating face and mounting aperture on the pump with clean diesel fuel, then wipe clean – it is most important that no dirt is introduced into the pump during refitting.
7 Offer up the regulator, and push it gently into position, twisting it slightly to help enter the O-rings. Once it is fully home, refit the bolts and tighten by hand initially.
8 Tighten the three bolts evenly to the specified torque.
9 Reconnect the regulator wiring plug and the battery negative lead.
10 On completion, start the engine and check for signs of leakage before refitting the engine covers.

2.0 litre models

11 Remove the air cleaner assembly as described in Section 2.
12 Pull the charge pressure sensor and bracket from the support frame **(see illustration)**. Release the wiring harness from the frame as the sensor is withdrawn.
13 Unclip the fuel pipe, mass airflow sensor wiring harness and coolant heater harness (where fitted) from the support frame.
14 Undo the bolt and detach the cooler heater assembly (where fitted) from the support frame **(see illustration)**.
15 Undo the 2 nuts and 2 bolts, and remove the support frame from the engine compartment **(see illustrations)**.
16 Release the clamp and remove the turbocharger intake hose. Unclip the breather hose and vacuum hose as the turbocharger hose is withdrawn.
17 Clean the area around the regulator, disconnect the wiring plug, undo the 3 bolts and remove the fuel pressure regulator. Renew the O-ring seals.
18 Refitting is a reversal of removal.

8.15a The support frame is secured by 2 nuts (arrowed) at the engine compartment bulkhead...

8.15b... and 2 bolts (arrowed) at the front

8.20 Disconnect the pressure sensor wiring plug – 1.9 litre engines

Fuel rail pressure sensor

1.9 litre models

19 Prise up the caps, undo the 3 screws and remove the plastic cover from the top of the engine **(see illustration 2.1)**.

20 Disconnect the wiring plug from the pressure sensor, then unscrew and remove it from the rail **(see illustration)**. Recover the sealing washer – a new one must be used when refitting. If the sensor is to be removed for a long period, cap the open connection on the fuel rail to prevent dirt entry.

21 Refitting is a reversal of removal. Use a new sealing washer, and tighten the sensor to the specified torque.

22 On completion, and before refitting the engine top cover, run the engine and check for signs of fuel leakage.

2.0 litre models

23 Remove the air cleaner assembly as described in Section 2.

24 Pull the charge pressure sensor and bracket from the support frame **(see illustration 8.12)**. Release the wiring harness from the frame as the sensor is withdrawn.

25 Unclip the fuel pipe, mass airflow sensor wiring harness, and coolant heater harness (where fitted) from the support frame.

26 Undo the bolt and detach the cooler heater assembly (where fitted) from the support frame **(see illustration 8.14)**.

27 Undo the 2 nuts and 2 bolts, and remove the support frame from the engine compartment **(see illustrations 8.15a and 8.15b)**.

28 Release the clamps and remove the intercooler outlet and intake pipes **(see illustrations 16.8a and 16.8b)**. Disconnect any wiring plugs as the pipes are withdrawn.

29 Undo the 6 retaining bolts and remove the cover from the top of the engine **(see illustration)**. Release the wiring harness as the cover is removed.

30 Clean the area around the sensor, disconnect the wiring plug, then unscrew the sensor from the common fuel rail **(see illustration)**. Plug the openings to prevent contamination. Be prepared for fuel spillage.

31 Refitting is a reversal of removal.

Fuel temperature sensor

1.9 litre models

32 Release the clamps, and remove the air pipe from the intercooler to the intake manifold. Remove any retaining bolts as necessary.

33 Remove the air cleaner assembly as described in Section 2.

34 Disconnect the connector on the top of the sensor **(see illustration)**.

35 The two remaining sensor pipes are heat-shrunk plastic, and may prove difficult to remove without causing damage. If suitable pieces of rubber joining sleeve can be found, the plastic could be cut off, providing the sensor stubs underneath are not damaged – the rubber sleeves can then be used when refitting, providing careful checks are made for signs of leaks. If the sensor is not being renewed, trace the pipes to the quick-release

connector on the pump, and to the rubber sleeve on the leak-off pipes, and disconnect there.

36 Unclip the sensor from the fuel rail, and remove it.

37 Refitting is a reversal of removal. Check for signs of leakage from any of the pipes that have been disturbed.

2.0 litre models

38 Remove the air cleaner assembly as described in Section 2.

39 Pull the charge pressure sensor and bracket from the support frame **(see illustration 8.12)**. Release the wiring harness from the frame as the sensor is withdrawn.

40 Unclip the fuel pipe, mass airflow sensor wiring harness, and coolant heater harness (where fitted) from the support frame.

41 Undo the bolt and detach the cooler heater assembly (where fitted) from the support frame **(see illustration 8.14)**.

42 Undo the 2 nuts and 2 bolts, and remove the support frame from the engine compartment **(see illustrations 8.15a and 8.15b)**.

43 Release the clamps and remove the intercooler outlet and intake pipes **(see illustrations 16.8a and 16.8b)**. Disconnect any wiring plugs as the pipes are withdrawn.

44 Undo the 6 retaining bolts and remove the cover from the top of the engine **(see illustration 8.29)**. Release the wiring harness as the cover is removed.

45 Disconnect the wiring plug from the fuel temperature sensor **(see illustration)**.

46 The fuel temperature sensor is supplied

8.29 Undo the bolts and remove the plastic cover from the top of the engine

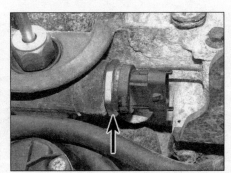

8.30 Fuel pressure sensor (arrowed) – 2.0 litre engines

8.34 Fuel temperature sensor (arrowed) – 1.9 litre engines

8.45 The fuel temperature sensor (arrowed) is located at the left-hand end of the cylinder head – 2.0 litre engines

8.54 Accelerator pedal position sensor wiring plug (arrowed)

8.52 Crankshaft speed/position sensor (arrowed) – 2.0 litre engines

8.56 Accelerator pedal position sensor retaining nuts (arrowed)

as an assembly complete with the fuel return hoses. Disconnect the fuel return hoses from the high-pressure fuel pump and the common rail, and withdrawn the assembly. Plug the openings to prevent contamination.

47 Refitting is a reversal of removal. Check for signs of leakage from any of the pipes that have been disturbed.

Crankshaft speed/ position sensor

1.9 litre engines

48 Raise the front of the vehicle and support it securely on axle stands (see *Jacking and vehicle support*). Undo the fasteners and remove the transmission/engine undertray.
49 The sensor is located on the front of the transmission bellhousing. Disconnect the wiring plug, then remove the sensor mounting bolt and withdraw it.
50 Check the sensor for signs of damage,

and clean it before refitting. Refitting is a reversal of removal.

2.0 engines

51 Raise the front of the vehicle and support it securely on axle stands (see *Jacking and vehicle support*). Undo the fasteners and remove the transmission/engine undertray.
52 The sensor is located on the rear of the engine cylinder block at the flywheel end. Disconnect the wiring plug, then release the retaining clip and remove the sensor **(see illustration)**.
53 Check the sensor for signs of damage, and clean it before refitting. Refitting is a reversal of removal.

Accelerator pedal position sensor

54 Working under the facia, disconnect the sensor wiring plug **(see illustration)**.
55 Carefully prise the link rod from the sensor arm.

56 Undo the 3 retaining nuts and remove the sensor assembly **(see illustration)**.
57 Refitting is a reversal of removal.

Camshaft position sensor

58 Remove the air cleaner assembly as described in Section 2.

1.9 litre engines

59 The sensor is located at the rear of the cylinder head, at the timing belt end. Disconnect the wiring plug from the position sensor, then unscrew the mounting bolt underneath, and withdraw it from the engine **(see illustration)**. Check the condition of the sensor seal and, if necessary, fit a new one.
60 Refitting is a reversal of removal.

2.0 litre engines

61 Release the 2 clamps, undo the support bracket bolt, and remove the air duct from the turbocharger to the intercooler.
62 The sensor is located on the top of the cylinder head, adjacent to the vacuum pump. Disconnect the wiring plug from the position sensor, then unscrew the mounting bolt, and withdraw it from the engine **(see illustration)**. Check the condition of the sensor seal, and if necessary, fit a new one.
63 Refitting is a reversal of removal.

Turbocharger pressure sensor

1.9 litre models

64 The turbocharger pressure sensor is fitted to the engine compartment bulkhead. Disconnect the sensor wiring plug, then release the clamp and disconnect the hose from the base of the sensor **(see illustration)**. Manoeuvre the sensor from the bracket.
65 Refitting is a reversal of removal.

2.0 litre models

66 The sensor is located on the air filter support frame. Disconnect the sensor wiring plug **(see illustration 8.12)**.
67 Pull the sensor upwards from the support frame.
68 Refitting is a reversal of removal.

Turbocharger pressure regulating solenoid

69 The pressure regulating solenoid valve is fitted to the left-hand side of the engine compartment bulkhead. Disconnect the

8.59 Camshaft position sensor retaining bolt (arrowed) – 1.9 litre engines

8.62 Camshaft position sensor (arrowed) – 2.0 litre engines

8.64 Turbocharger boost pressure sensor (arrowed) – 1.9 litre engines

8.69 Turbocharger pressure regulating solenoid (arrowed)

8.73 Disconnect the mass airflow sensor wiring plug (arrowed)

8.75 Mass airflow sensor mounting screws (arrowed)

solenoid wiring plug and the two vacuum hoses from the valve (noting the upper hose goes to the wastegate actuator), and remove the valve (see illustration).

70 Refitting is a reversal of removal.

Airflow and air temperature sensor

71 The hot film mass airflow sensor is fitted to the main air cleaner body has an integral air temperature sensor.

1.9 litre engines

72 Remove the air cleaner assembly as described in Section 2.

2.0 litre models

73 Disconnect the mass airflow sensor wiring plug, and release the wiring harness from the air cleaner housing (see illustration).

74 Release the clamp and disconnect the air hose from the sensor.

All models

75 Remove the two mounting screws, and withdraw the airflow meter from the air cleaner. Check the condition of the sealing ring, and renew if necessary (see illustration).

76 Refitting is a reversal of removal.

Electronic control unit (ECU)

Note: *The ECU is electronically-coded to match the engine immobiliser and certain other engine components. If the ECU is being removed in order to fit a new unit, it is highly recommended that a dealer or suitably-equipped repairer should carry out this work.*

Caution: The ECU wiring plugs should only be disconnected after the disconnecting battery. If the ECU is unplugged 'live', it could be damaged.

77 On 2.0 litre models, Release the clamp and disconnect the left-hand air hose from the intercooler – see Section 16.

78 Undo the bolt and move the coolant expansion tank to one side (see illustration).

79 Pull the boost pressure sensor from its mounting bracket (1.9 litre models), undo the nuts and move the turbocharger pressure regulating valve to one side (see illustration 8.64 and 8.69).

80 Undo the nut and move the preheater control unit to one side (see illustration).

81 On some models, a security shield is fitted over the ECU. Remove the bolts using a flat-bladed screwdriver, undo the nut, and pull shield upwards from the locating pin at its base (see illustration).

82 Undo the 4 retaining screws and remove the ECU (see illustration).

83 Fully lever over the locking catches, and disconnect the wiring plug connectors from the ECU (see illustrations).

84 Refitting is a reversal of removal. **Note:** *If a new ECU has been fitted, it must be*

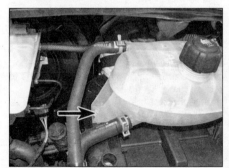

8.78 Remove the coolant expansion tank bolt (arrowed)

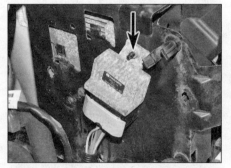

8.80 Preheater control unit retaining nut (arrowed)

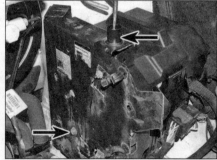

8.81 Use a large, flat-bladed screwdriver to undo the security bolts, and remove the cover

8.82 Undo the ECU screws (arrowed)...

8.83a... then manoeuvre the ECU from position...

8.83b... and disconnect the wiring plugs

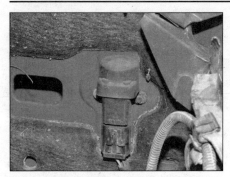

8.85 Inertia fuel cut-off switch

programmed using Vauxhall or Renault diagnostic equipment. Entrust this task to a dealer or suitably-equipped specialist.

Inertia fuel cut-off switch

85 In the event of a collision, this switch is designed to cut off the fuel supply. The switch is located on the left-hand inner wing in the engine compartment **(see illustration)**. Note that this switch is only fitted to 1.9 litre models.
86 To remove the switch, disconnect the wiring plug, undo the 2 retaining nuts and manoeuvre the switch from position.
87 Refitting is a reversal of removal.

9 Fuel injection pump – removal and refitting

Caution: Be careful not to allow dirt into the injection pump or injector pipes during this procedure. New sealing rings should be used on the fuel pipe banjo unions when refitting.
Note: *Refer to the precautions in Section 1 before proceeding.*

1.9 litre engines

Removal

1 Disconnect the battery negative lead as described in Chapter 5.
2 Remove the timing belt with reference to Chapter 2A.
3 Disconnect the crankcase breather hose that runs across the top of the engine, and move it to one side.

4 Disconnect the wiring plugs from the following fuel system components:
a) The fuel filter (see Chapter 1).
b) The glow plugs.
c) The fuel pressure regulator (back of the pump).
d) The fuel pressure sensor (at the pump end of the fuel rail).
5 Disconnect the fuel supply and return pipes from the injection pump **(see illustration)**. Unclip or undo the pipes as necessary, once disconnected. Cap or plug the open connections to reduce fuel loss, and to prevent the entry of dirt.
6 Loosen the fuel rail mounting bolts by a few turns, so that the rail is still fitted, but loose.
7 Unscrew the unions and remove the pump-to-rail high-pressure fuel pipe **(see illustration)**. Again, cap or plug the open connections, to reduce fuel loss, and to prevent the entry of dirt. **Note:** *A new high-pressure fuel pipe should be obtained for refitting.*
8 Remove the two mounting bolts from the rear of the pump **(see illustration)**, then the three from the front support (which forms the mounting point for the engine right-hand mounting), and carefully lift the pump out with the front support attached.
9 Separating the pump from the front support means removing the pump sprocket to access the support bolts. Removing the pump sprocket will require a suitable puller (the sprocket is located on a taper), and some means of holding the sprocket while the nut is loosened. Once the sprocket has been removed, three further bolts secure the front support. It may be preferable to entrust this part of the job to a dealer or well-equipped workshop.

Refitting

10 Refitting is a reversal of removal, noting the following points:
a) Fit a new high-pressure pipe as follows. Some pipes may be supplied with a sachet of lubricant, which should be used on the union nut threads before fitting – if no lubricant is provided, none should be applied. Finger-tighten the nuts before tightening them to the specified torque. Take care not to place the new

high-pressure pipe under any stress when the unions are tightened.
b) Tighten all nuts and bolts to the specified torque.
c) Fit a new timing belt as described in Chapter 2A.
d) On completion, prime and bleed the fuel system as described in Section 4. Run the engine, and check for fuel leaks.

2.0 litre engines

Removal

11 Disconnect the battery negative lead as described in Chapter 5.
12 Remove the air cleaner assembly as described in Section 2.
13 Pull the charge pressure sensor and bracket from the support frame **(see illustration 8.12)**. Release the wiring harness from the frame as the sensor is withdrawn.
14 Unclip the fuel pipe, mass airflow sensor wiring harness, and coolant heater harness (where fitted) from the support frame.
15 Undo the bolt and detach the cooler heater assembly (where fitted) from the support frame **(see illustration 8.14)**.
16 Undo the 2 nuts and 2 bolts, and remove the support frame from the engine compartment **(see illustrations 8.15a and 8.15b)**.
17 Release the clamps and remove the intercooler air hoses. Unclip any wiring harnesses as the hoses are withdrawn.
18 Release the clamp and remove the turbocharger intake hose. Unclip the breather hose and vacuum hose as the turbocharger hose is withdrawn.
19 Undo the 6 bolts and remove the fuel rail cover from the top of the engine **(see illustration 8.29)**.
20 Unscrew the union nuts and disconnect the high-pressure pipe from the fuel rail and pump. Cap or plug the open connections to reduce fuel spill and prevent dirt entry.
21 Disconnect the wiring plug from the fuel temperature sensor.
22 For improved access, disconnect the hose from the brake vacuum pump.
23 Disconnect the quick-release fuel supply and return hoses from the high-pressure pump and plug the openings **(see illustration)**.
24 Disconnect the wiring from the high-

9.5 Depress the release buttons (arrowed) and disconnect the fuel pipes from the pump

9.7 Undo the unions (arrowed) and remove the pipe from the pump to the fuel rail

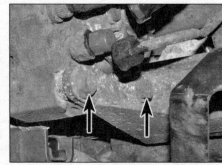

9.8 Pump rear mounting bracket bolts (arrowed)

9.23 Depress the button and disconnect the fuel pipes (arrowed)

9.24 Fuel pump pressure regulator

9.25a Undo the mounting bolts...

pressure pump pressure regulator (see illustration).

25 Progressively unscrew the mounting bolts then withdraw the high-pressure pump from the cylinder head. Remove the O-ring seal from the groove (see illustrations).

26 If necessary, the pinion may be removed from the high-pressure pump driveshaft. To do this, first lock the pinion in a soft-jawed vice and unscrew the retaining nut. A puller will now be required to remove the pinion from the driveshaft.

Refitting

27 Refitting is a reversal of removal, but note that the pump-to-fuel rail high-pressure pipe must always be renewed, together with new pump retaining bolts and a new O-ring. Before restarting the engine, it may be necessary to use a diagnostic tool to clear any faults that may be stored in the injection ECU.

10 Fuel injectors –
removal and refitting

Note: *Refer to the precautions in Section 1 before proceeding.*

Testing

1 Injectors deteriorate with prolonged use, and it is reasonable to expect them to need reconditioning or renewal after 60 000 miles or so. Accurate testing, overhaul and calibration of the injectors must be left to a specialist.

9.25b... withdraw the pump from the cylinder head...

Removal

Note: *Take care not to allow dirt into the injectors or fuel pipes during this procedure; clean around the area before commencing work. Note that all high-pressure pipes that are removed must be renewed as a matter of course. The injector flame shield washers must also be renewed.*

2 Disconnect the battery negative lead as described in Chapter 5.

1.9 litre engines

3 Remove the air cleaner assembly as described in Section 2.

4 Carefully clean around the injectors and injector pipe union nuts.

5 Disconnect the wiring connectors from the fuel injectors (see illustration).

6 Note the fitted position and disconnect the leak-off pipes from the injectors (see illustration).

9.25c... and remove the O-ring seal

7 Slacken the union nuts securing the injector pipes to the fuel rail whilst being prepared for some fuel spillage. Note carefully the locations of the pipe clamps, for use when refitting new pipes.

8 Unscrew the union nuts and disconnect the pipes from the injectors, then completely remove the pipes. Cover the ends of the injectors, to prevent dirt ingress (see illustration).

9 Unscrew the bolt securing each injector clamp plate, lift off the clamp plates and withdraw the injectors. Recover the flame shield washer between the injectors and the cylinder head. The injectors can be a tight fit in the cylinder head and may need to be withdrawn vertically with the aid of a puller or slide hammer. A releasing agent can be used around the injectors to aid removal.

2.0 litre engines

10 Remove the air cleaner assembly as described in Section 2.

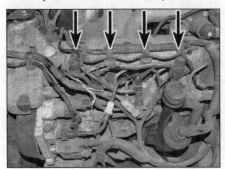

10.5 Disconnect the injector wiring plugs (arrowed)

10.6 Slide out the clip (arrowed) and disconnect the leak-off pipes from the injectors

10.8 Use plastic caps to cover the ends of the fuel pipes (arrowed)

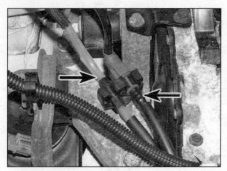

10.18 Unclip the fuel hoses (arrowed)

10.20 Release the clip (arrowed) and disconnect the breather hose

10.21 Squeeze together the clip each side (arrowed) and disconnect the wiring plugs from the injectors

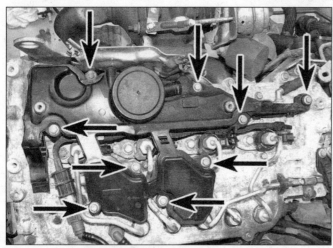

10.22a Undo the retaining bolts (arrowed)...

10.22b... and remove the oil separator assembly

11 Pull the charge pressure sensor and bracket from the support frame (see illustration 8.12). Release the wiring harness from the frame as the sensor is withdrawn.

12 Unclip the fuel pipe, mass airflow sensor wiring harness, and coolant heater harness (where fitted) from the support frame.

13 Undo the bolt and detach the coolant heater assembly (where fitted) from the support frame (see illustration 8.14).

14 Undo the 2 nuts and 2 bolts, and remove the support frame from the engine compartment (see illustrations 8.15a and 8.15b).

15 Release the clamps and remove inter-cooler air hoses, including the one from the turbocharger. Unclip any wiring harnesses as the hoses are withdrawn.

16 Undo the 6 bolts and remove the fuel rail cover from the top of the engine (see illustration 8.29).

17 Disconnect the wiring plugs from the fuel filter housing and release the wiring harness from the engine mounting bracket.

18 Unclip the fuel feed and return hoses from the bracket at the right-hand end of the engine (see illustration).

19 Disconnect the wiring plug from the fuel temperature sensor.

20 Release the retaining clip and move the breather hose from the oil separator on the top of the engine (see illustration).

21 Disconnect the wiring connectors from the fuel injectors, the camshaft position sensor, fuel pressure sensor, coolant temperature sensor, vacuum solenoid valve, fuel pressure regulator, throttle valve, EGR valve, and the glow plugs. Undo the bolt and detach the wiring harness from the engine lifting eye (see illustration).

22 Pull the breather hose from the turbocharger intake hose, then undo the bolts and remove the oil separator assembly from the cylinder head (see illustrations).

23 Note the fitted position of the leak-off pipes, disconnect them from the fuel injectors by sliding up the locking element, and pulling them upwards from the port on each injector (see illustration). Plug the openings to prevent contamination.

24 Undo the bolt securing the fuel return pipe to the cylinder head (see illustration).

25 Carefully clean around the fuel injectors and injector pipe union nuts.

26 Unscrew the union nuts securing the injector pipes to the fuel rail whilst being prepared for some fuel spillage, then unscrew the union nuts and disconnect the pipes from the injectors. Where necessary, undo the pipe support clamp bolts (see illustration).

10.23 Slide up the locking element and pull the leak-off pipes upwards from the injectors

10.24 Remove the fuel return pipe bolt (arrowed)

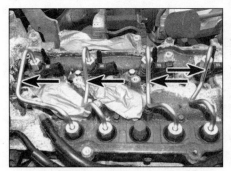

10.26 Undo the unions and remove the injector pipes (arrowed)

10.27 The 7-digit code is unique to each injector

10.28a Remove the injector clamp bolt (arrowed)...

10.28b... followed by the clamp plate

10.28c Withdraw the injector...

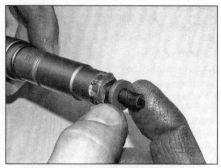

10.28d... and remove the flame shield washer

There is no need to remove the high-pressure pump-to-fuel rail pipe.

27 Using a felt-tipped pen, mark each injector for its position (No 1 cylinder at the timing chain end). This is important because the engine management ECU recognises each injector by the cylinder it is located in. If new injectors are obtained, the IMA code on each injector must be noted and programmed into the ECU. This is a 7-digit code, unique to each injector **(see illustration)**. To aid code identification, the IMA code does not contain the letter J and Q, or the numbers 0 and 9.

28 Unscrew the bolt securing each injector clamp plate, lift off the clamp plates and withdraw the injectors. Recover the flame shield washer between the injectors and the cylinder head **(see illustrations)**. **Note:** *If the injectors are seized in the cylinder head, apply plenty of penetrating oil/releasing agent, attach a slide hammer to the top of the injector and pull them out. A special Vauxhall (No EN-50143) or Renault (No MOT 1966) tool is available for this purpose.*

Refitting

29 Carefully clean the injector bores in the cylinder head, taking care not to allow any debris to fall into the cylinders.

30 Obtain new injector sealing washers and new high-pressure fuel pipes for refitting.

31 Take care not to drop the injectors, or allow the needles at their tips to become damaged. The injectors are precision-made to fine limits, and must not be handled roughly. In particular, never mount them in a bench vice.

32 Fit new flame shield washers between

the injectors and the cylinder head, insert the injectors then fit the mounting clamp plates. Tighten the clamp plate bolts to the specified torque.

33 Slacken the fuel rail mounting bolts before refitting the fuel pipes.

34 Fit new injector pipes, and tighten the union nuts on the injectors and the fuel rail by hand at first. Make sure the pipe clamps are in their previously-noted positions. Bearing in mind the high vibration levels with a diesel engine, if the clamps are wrongly positioned or missing, problems may be experienced with pipes breaking or splitting. With all the pipes in place tighten them to the specified torque setting **(see illustration)**.

35 With the fuel pipes all in position tighten the fuel rail mounting bolts to the specified torque.

36 The remainder of refitting is a reversal of removal. If new injectors have been fitted, have the IMA code programmed into the

engine management ECU by a dealer or suitably-equipped specialist.

37 Start the engine. If difficulty is experienced, bleed the fuel system as described in Section 4.

11 Fuel rail (common rail) – removal and refitting

Note: *Refer to precautions in Section 1 before proceeding. After switching off the engine, allow several minutes for the fuel pressure to subside before disconnecting any of the high-pressure fuel pipes. Take care not to allow dirt into the fuel pipes during this procedure; clean around the area before commencing work. Once disconnected, plug all openings to prevent contamination. Note that all high-pressure pipes removed must be renewed as a matter of course.*

10.28e We brazed an old pipe union to the end of a slide hammer, and pulled the seized injector from the cylinder head

10.34 Use a crow's foot adapter to tighten the pipe unions to the specified torque

11.9 Fuel rail mounting bolts (arrowed) – 1.9 litre engines

Removal

1 Disconnect the battery negative lead as described in Chapter 5.

1.9 litre engine

2 Remove the air cleaner assembly as described in Section 2.

3 While holding the injectors with one spanner, unscrew the high-pressure pipe union nuts with a further spanner. As a precaution against remaining pressure in the pipes, first wrap some cloth/rag around the union. Take care not to damage the leak-off stubs on the injectors. Similarly, unscrew the union nuts from the fuel rail, and then remove the pipes (new ones will be required for refitting).

4 Undo the unions, and remove the high-pressure fuel pipe between the fuel pump and the fuel rail.

5 Disconnect the wiring plug from the fuel pressure sensor, then unscrew it from the fuel rail.

6 Disconnect the wiring plug from the fuel temperature sensor, and unclip it from the support bracket.

7 Disconnect the fuel return pipe from the fuel temperature sensor, and the high-pressure fuel pump.

8 Disconnect the wiring plugs from the glow plugs, then remove the fuel return pipe assembly from the fuel injectors and the fuel rail.

9 Unbolt and remove the fuel rail **(see illustration)**.

2.0 litre models

10 The fuel rail is located on the side of

12.8 Depress the release button (arrowed) and disconnect the breather hose

11.12 Withdraw the fuel rail whilst guiding the outlets through the apertures – 2.0 litre engines

the camshaft housing, with the injector and pump connections emerging from inside the housing upper cavity. Proceed as described in Paragraphs 10 to 26 of the previous Section.

11 Unscrew the union nuts securing the pipes from the fuel rail to the injectors, and the fuel rail to the high-pressure pump, whilst being prepared for some fuel spillage. Where necessary, undo the pipe support clamp bolts **(see illustration 10.26)**.

12 Undo the bolts and remove the fuel rail **(see illustration)**.

Refitting

13 Refitting is a reversal of removal, noting the following points:

a) Tighten all nuts and bolts to the specified torque.

b) Fit a new high-pressure pipes, some may be supplied with a sachet of lubricant, which should be used on the union nut threads before fitting – if no lubricant is provided, none should be applied. Finger-tighten the nuts before tightening them to the specified torque. Take care not to place the new high-pressure pipes under any stress when the unions are tightened.

c) When tightening the pipe union nuts onto the injectors, counterhold the injectors with a further spanner.

d) Where applicable, refit the absorbent soundproofing material around the fuel rail, if it is contaminated with diesel it will need to be renewed.

e) On completion, prime and bleed the fuel system as described in Section 4. Run the engine, and check for fuel leaks.

12.10 EGR pipe-to-manifold clamp (arrowed)

12 Manifolds (1.9 litre engines) – removal and refitting

Removal

1 The intake and exhaust manifolds cannot be removed individually. Although the manifolds are separate, the same nuts retain them, since the stud holes are split between the manifold flanges.

2 Disconnect the battery negative lead as described in Chapter 5.

3 Remove the air cleaner assembly as described in Section 2.

4 Remove the turbocharger as described in Section 15.

5 Release the clamps, undo the support bracket bolt (where fitted) and remove the air hose from the intercooler to the intake manifold.

6 Release the clip and disconnect the charge pressure sensor hose from the intake manifold.

7 Disconnect the EGR valve wiring plug.

8 Depress the release buttons and remove the breather pipe from the engine oil separator to the air intake hose **(see illustration)**.

9 Undo the bolts securing the engine lifting eye to the right-hand end of the engine.

10 Release the clamp and disconnect the EGR pipe from the exhaust manifold **(see illustration)**.

11 Note the location of any wiring connectors or vacuum/breather hoses attached to the manifolds, and disconnect them.

12 Progressively unscrew the nuts securing the intake and exhaust manifolds and withdraw them from the cylinder head. Recover the manifold gasket. A new gasket will be required for refitting.

Refitting

13 Refitting is a reversal of removal, bearing in mind the following points.

a) Ensure that the cylinder head and manifold mating surfaces are clean and use a new gasket. Tighten all fixings to the specified torque.

b) Refit the turbocharger as described in Section 15.

c) Ensure that any vacuum/breather hoses are correctly reconnected as noted before removal.

d) Ensure that any wiring or hose brackets/clips are positioned as noted before removal.

13 Manifolds (2.0 litre engines) – removal and refitting

Intake manifold

1 Disconnect the battery negative lead as described in Chapter 5.

2 Remove the throttle valve housing as described in Section 7.

3 Unbolt the EGR cooler pipe from the cooler

and control valve, then recover the gaskets **(see illustrations)**.

4 Undo the bolts and remove the EGR valve.

5 Undo the 2 retaining bolts and remove the intercooler outlet hose support bracket from the intake manifold.

Models with air conditioning

6 Slacken the power steering pump pulley bolts, then remove the auxiliary drivebelt as described in Chapter 1.

7 Undo the bolts and remove auxiliary drivebelt tensioner assembly, then prise off the cover, undo the bolt beneath and remove the belt guide roller.

8 Completely unscrew the retaining bolts and remove the power steering pump pulley.

9 Disconnect the air conditioning pressure switch wiring plug.

10 Disconnect the wiring from the rear of the alternator, then undo the mounting bolts and position the alternator to one side. Refer to Chapter 5 if necessary.

11 Undo the mounting bolts and move the air conditioning compressor to one side. There's no need to disconnect the refrigerant pipes. Refer to Chapter 3 if necessary.

12 Undo the 4 retaining bolts and position the power steering pump to one side. There's no need to disconnect the fluid pipes. Refer to Chapter 10 if necessary.

13 Undo the 5 retaining bolts and remove the auxiliary support bracket from the right-hand front corner of the engine.

All models

14 Unscrew and remove the mounting bolts and withdraw the intake manifold from the cylinder head. Recover the gasket and discard it as a new gasket must be used on refitting **(see illustrations)**. Also obtain new gaskets for the EGR cooler pipe.

15 Refitting is the reverse of removal using new gaskets, and tightening the manifold retaining bolts to the specified torque.

Exhaust manifold

16 Remove the air cleaner assembly as described in Section 2.

17 Pull the charge pressure sensor and bracket from the support frame **(see illustration 8.12)**. Release the wiring harness from the frame as the sensor is withdrawn.

13.3a Remove the EGR cooler pipe...

13.14a Remove the intake manifold...

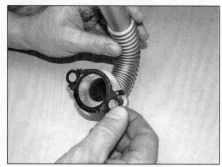

13.3b... and recover the gaskets

13.14b... and gasket

18 Unclip the fuel pipe, mass airflow sensor wiring harness, and coolant heater harness (where fitted) from the support frame.

19 Undo the bolt and detach the cooler heater assembly (where fitted) from the support frame **(see illustration 8.14)**.

20 Undo the 2 nuts and 2 bolts, and remove the support frame from the engine compartment **(see illustrations 8.15a and 8.15b)**.

21 Remove the turbocharger as described in Section 15.

22 Unbolt the heat shield, slide it along the EGR pipe, then unscrew the bolts securing the EGR rigid pipe to the exhaust manifold.

23 Unscrew and remove the nuts and spacers, then unscrew the 2 mounting studs at the left-hand end of the manifold. This is to ensure the EGR pipe is not damaged when removing the manifold.

24 Withdraw the exhaust manifold from the cylinder head. Recover the manifold gasket

and discard it as a new gasket must be used on refitting **(see illustrations)**. Also obtain new EGR rigid pipe seals. Vauxhall and Renault state that the manifold nuts must also be renewed.

25 Check the condition of the exhaust manifold studs and renew them if necessary. Tighten into the cylinder head to the specified torque.

26 Refitting is the reverse of removal using a new gasket and seals, and tightening the manifold retaining nuts to the specified torque. When positioning the gasket on the studs, the gasket end tab must be towards the flywheel end of the engine.

14 Turbocharger –
description and precautions

Description

A turbocharger increases engine efficiency by

13.24a Unscrew the nuts, remove the spacers...

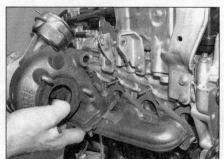

13.24b... then withdraw the exhaust manifold from the cylinder head...

13.24c... and renew the gasket

15.7a Turbocharger intake hose clamp (arrowed)...

15.7b... and outlet hose clamp (arrowed)

raising the pressure in the intake manifold above atmospheric pressure. Instead of the air simply being sucked into the cylinders, it is forced in. Additional fuel is supplied by the injection pump in proportion to the increased air intake.

Energy for the operation of the turbocharger comes from the exhaust gas. The gas flows through a specially-shaped housing (the turbine housing) and in so doing, spins the turbine wheel. The turbine wheel is attached to a shaft, at the end of which is another vaned wheel known as the compressor wheel. The compressor wheel spins in its own housing and compresses the inducted air on the way to the intake manifold.

Between the turbocharger and the intake manifold, the compressed air passes through an intercooler. This is an air-to-air heat exchanger, mounted in front of the radiator, and supplied with cooling air ducted through the front of the car. The purpose of the intercooler is to remove from the inducted air some of the heat gained in being compressed. Because cooler air is denser, removal of this heat further increases engine efficiency.

Boost pressure (the pressure in the intake manifold) is limited by a wastegate, which diverts the exhaust gas away from the turbine wheel in response to a pressure-sensitive actuator. Turbocharging pressure is controlled by a solenoid valve mounted on the engine compartment bulkhead.

The turbo shaft is pressure-lubricated by an oil feed pipe from the main oil gallery. The shaft 'floats' on a cushion of oil. A drain pipe returns the oil to the sump. Note that on 2.0 litre M9R 630 engines, a water-cooled turbocharger is fitted.

Precautions

The turbocharger operates at extremely high speeds and temperatures. Certain precautions must be observed to avoid premature failure of the turbo or injury to the operator.

• Do not race the engine immediately after start-up, especially if it is cold. Give the oil a few seconds to circulate.

• Always allow the engine to return to idle speed before switching it off – do not blip the throttle and switch off, as this will leave the turbo spinning without lubrication.

• Allow the engine to idle for several minutes before switching off after a high-speed run.

• Observe the recommended intervals for oil and filter changing, and use a reputable oil of the specified quality. Neglect of oil changing, or use of inferior oil, can cause carbon formation on the turbo shaft and subsequent failure.

⚠️ *Warning: Do not operate the turbo with any parts exposed. Foreign objects falling onto the rotating vanes could cause excessive damage and (if ejected) personal injury.*

15 Turbocharger – removal and refitting

Note: If the turbocharger is being renewed due to damage or wear, we recommend that an engine oil and filter change is performed at the same time, to eliminate the possibility of debris recirculating with the old oil, and causing further damage – See Chapter 1.

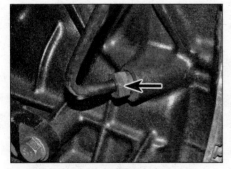

15.8a Undo the oil feed pipe union (arrowed)

15.8b Oil feed pipe support bracket bolt (arrowed)

Removal

1 Whilst the engine is still warm, spray the turbocharger mounting bolts with a penetrating oil to ease removal.

2 Ensure that the engine has cooled sufficiently to avoid burns.

3 Disconnect the battery negative lead as described in Chapter 5.

4 Apply the handbrake, then jack up the front of the vehicle, and support securely on axle stands (see *Jacking and vehicle support*). Where applicable, remove the engine undertray.

1.9 litre engines

5 Working under the vehicle, remove the exhaust front silencer and catalytic converter with reference to Section 17.

6 Undo the clamps and remove the air hose from the intercooler to the intake manifold.

7 Slacken the clamps and disconnect the air intake and outlet hoses from the turbocharger **(see illustrations)**.

8 Undo the union and disconnect the oil feed pipe from the cylinder block, then undo the bolt securing the oil feed pipe support bracket to the intake manifold **(see illustrations)**. Be prepared for oil spillage.

9 Undo the 2 retaining bolts and disconnect the oil return pipe on the underside of the turbocharger. Discard the gasket. Be prepared for some oil spillage.

10 Disconnect the rubber vacuum pipe from the wastegate pressure regulator valve.

11 Undo the 3 retaining nuts and manoeuvre the turbocharger from position.

2.0 litre engines except code M9R 630

12 Removal of the turbocharger is included within the catalytic converter renewal procedure, as described in Section 17.

2.0 litre engines with code M9R 630

13 These engines designed to emission level Euro IV, and are equipped with a particulate filter and a water-cooled turbocharger. On models with air conditioning, have the refrigerant circuit evacuated by a dealer or suitably-equipped repairer prior to commencing work, then have it recharged once the work is completed.

14 Remove the particulate filter as described in Section 17.

15 Remove the air cleaner assembly as described in Section 2.

16 Pull the charge pressure sensor and bracket from the support frame **(see illustration 8.12)**. Release the wiring harness from the frame as the sensor is withdrawn.

17 Unclip the fuel pipe, mass airflow sensor wiring harness, and coolant heater harness (where fitted) from the support frame.

18 Undo the bolt and detach the cooler heater assembly (where fitted) from the support frame **(see illustration 8.14)**.

19 Undo the 2 nuts and 2 bolts, and remove the support frame from the engine compartment **(see illustrations 8.15a and 8.15b)**.

20 Undo the retaining nuts/bolt and remove

15.20a The heater blower housing is secured by a nut (arrowed) on the right-hand side...

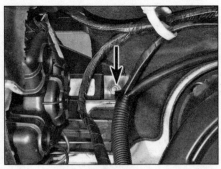

15.20b... and nut (arrowed) on the left-hand side...

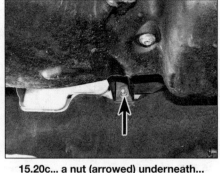

15.20c... a nut (arrowed) underneath...

the heater blower housing from the engine compartment bulkhead **(see illustrations)**. Disconnect any wiring plugs as the housing is withdrawn.

21 On models with air conditioning, undo the bolt securing the two pipes together, and disconnect the them. Plug the openings to prevent contamination. Discard the O-ring seals – new ones must be fitted.

22 Release the clamps/clips and disconnect the turbocharger outlet pipe.

23 Unclip the vacuum hose and wiring harness from the turbocharger intake pipe, and disconnect the vacuum hose from the wastegate actuator.

24 Undo the 2 retaining bolts and disconnect the intake pipe from the turbocharger **(see illustration)**.

25 Drain the coolant as described in Chapter 1.

26 Release the clip, undo the 2 bolts/nut, and remove the turbocharger-to-intercooler pipe. Release the wiring harness from the pipe as it's withdrawn. Renew the O-ring seals if they show signs of damage/deterioration.

27 Release the clip, and remove the hose from the turbocharger intake pipe. Unclip the vacuum pipe as the pipe is withdrawn.

28 Remove the support bracket bolt, disconnect the breather hose from the oil separator, unclip the vacuum hose and remove the turbocharger intake pipe from position.

29 Undo the 2 bolts, release the wiring harness, and remove the lifting eye from the cylinder head.

30 The crash protector is secured by 2 nuts above and a bolt below. Undo the 2 nuts, unscrew the studs from the cylinder head, and undo the nut below. Release the wiring harness and remove the crash protector **(see illustrations)**. **Note:** *Position the turbocharger wastegate pipe away from the crash protector to prevent damage.*

31 Undo the 3 nuts securing the turbocharger to the exhaust manifold.

32 Release the retaining clip and disconnect the exhaust manifold fuel injector fuel pipe and wiring plug. Plug the openings to prevent contamination.

33 Disconnect the turbocharger temperature sensor wiring plug.

34 Release the wiring harness from the

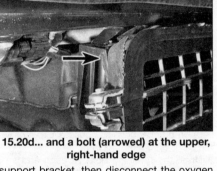

15.20d... and a bolt (arrowed) at the upper, right-hand edge

support bracket, then disconnect the oxygen sensor wiring plug.

35 Disconnect the primary temperature sensor wiring plug, and release it from the support bracket on the exhaust heat shield.

15.30a The crash protector is secured by a bolt (arrowed) beneath...

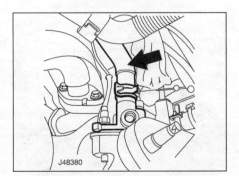

15.36a Disconnect the coolant hose (arrowed) from the exhaust manifold injector housing

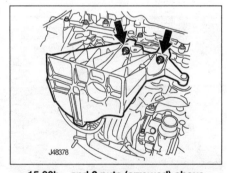

15.24 Undo the 2 bolts (arrowed) and disconnect the intake pipe

36 Release the clips and disconnect the coolant hoses from the exhaust manifold fuel injector housing and turbocharger **(see illustrations)**. Plug the openings to prevent contamination.

15.30b... and 2 nuts (arrowed) above

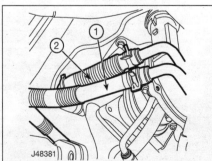

15.36b Disconnect the coolant hose from the turbocharger (1), and to the manifold injector housing (2)

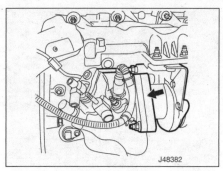

15.37 Remove the exhaust elbow/injector housing (arrowed)

37 Undo the 3 bolts and remove the support bracket from below the exhaust elbow, then undo the 4 retaining nuts and remove the exhaust elbow/injector housing from the turbocharger **(see illustration)**. Discard the gasket – a new one must be fitted.

38 Undo the union and remove the temperature sensor from the turbocharger.

39 Undo the bolts and remove the lower stabiliser arm from the rear of the engine.

40 Undo the bolts/release the clip and remove the turbocharger oil feed and return pipes. Plug the openings to prevent contamination.

41 Undo the remaining nuts and remove the turbocharger. Renew the gasket.

Refitting

42 Refitting is a reversal of removal, but renew any damaged hose clamps, and use new turbocharger-to-exhaust manifold nuts which should be tightened to the specified torque.

16.1a Disconnect the air pipe from the left-hand side...

16.2 Undo the bolt (arrowed) at each end of the intercooler

43 On completion, the following procedure must be observed before starting the engine.
a) To ensure an immediate oil supply to the turbo before the engine is started, Vauxhall and Renault specify that the engine first be prevented from firing by removing the engine immobiliser/instrument panel fuse from the passenger compartment fusebox, then crank the engine until the oil pressure warning light extinguishes, then continue for a further 2 seconds. Refit the fuse.
b) Run the engine at idle speed, and check the turbocharger oil unions for leakage. Rectify any problems without delay.
c) After the engine has been run, check the engine oil level, and top-up if necessary.

16 Intercooler – removal and refitting

Removal

1.9 litre engines

1 Release the clamps and disconnect the air pipes from the intercooler. Release any support bracket bolts as necessary to remove the pipes **(see illustrations)**.

2 Undo the retaining bolts at each end and manoeuvre the intercooler from place **(see illustration)**.

2.0 litre engines

3 Remove the air cleaner assembly as described in Section 2.

16.1b... and right-hand side of the intercooler – 1.9 litre engines

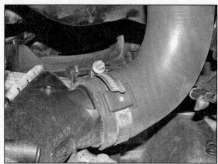

16.8a Disconnect the air pipe from the left-hand side...

4 Pull the charge pressure sensor and bracket from the support frame **(see illustration 8.12)**. Release the wiring harness from the frame as the sensor is withdrawn.

5 Unclip the fuel pipe, mass airflow sensor wiring harness, and coolant heater harness (where fitted) from the support frame.

6 Undo the bolt and detach the cooler heater assembly (where fitted) from the support frame **(see illustration 8.14)**.

7 Undo the 2 nuts and 2 bolts, and remove the support frame from the engine compartment **(see illustrations 8.15a and 8.15b)**.

8 Release the clamps and disconnect the intercooler air pipes **(see illustrations)**.

9 Undo the retaining bolts at each end and manoeuvre the intercooler from place **(see illustration 16.2)**.

Refitting

10 Refitting is a reversal of removal.

17 Exhaust system – general information, removal and refitting

General information

1 The Vivaro and Trafic was originally supplied with a one-piece exhaust system, but parts are available for the front pipe/silencer, intermediate pipe and tail pipe/silencer. The exhaust system consists of 4 sections:
1) Catalytic converter (or particulate filter on M9R 630 engines).
2) Front silencer (1.9 litre engines only) or pipe.
3) Rear silencer/tailpipe.
4) Intermediate pipe.

2 The catalytic converter and front pipe joints are secured by nuts and bolts. From the catalytic converter/particulate filter rearwards, the system is made of stainless steel. On models with a particulate filter, the front pipe incorporates a flexible pipe extension to allow for movement in the exhaust system. A clamping ring secures the joint between the front and rear sections.

3 Ensure that the exhaust has cooled sufficiently to avoid burns.

Removal

4 To remove the system or part of the system,

16.8b... and right-hand side of the intercooler – 2.0 litre engines

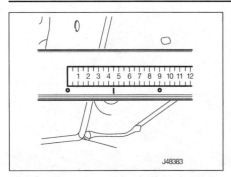

17.5 Cut the exhaust pipe halfway between the indentation marks

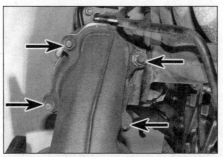

17.11 Undo the nuts (arrowed) securing the catalytic converter to the turbocharger – 1.9 litre engines

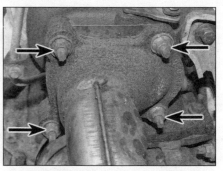

17.20 Catalytic converter-to-turbocharger nuts (arrowed) – 2.0 litre engines

first jack up the front or rear of the car, and support it on axle stands (see *Jacking and vehicle support*). Alternatively, position the vehicle over an inspection pit, or on ramps. Undo the fasteners and remove the engine undertray.

Front, intermediate pipe and rear silencer/tail pipe sections

5 Although the original system is supplied as a one-piece assembly, separate parts are available for the front, intermediate, and tail pipe/silencer. Indentation marks are provided and the pipe must be cut halfway between these marks, the new part is then offered into place, then joined to the original sections with a sleeve and clamps **(see illustration)**. Note that different lengths of new parts are available, depending on the wheelbase of the vehicle.

Front silencer – 1.9 litre engines only

6 Release the clamp securing the front silencer to the exhaust pipe, and undo the bolts securing the silencer to the catalytic converter. Remove the silencer.

Catalytic converter – 1.9 litre engines

7 Remove the front silencer as previously described.
8 Undo the retaining bolts and remove the inner wing splash shield from the wheel arch liner. Unclip the washer tube where applicable.
9 Undo the 2 bolts and remove the heat shield from below the catalytic converter.
10 Disconnect the earth lead from the mounting bracket, then undo the nuts/bolts and remove the catalytic converter support brackets.
11 Slacken and remove the nuts securing the catalytic converter to the turbo. Withdraw the converter from under the vehicle **(see illustration)**, recover the gasket – a new one will be needed for refitting.

Catalytic converter – 2.0 litre engines

12 Remove the air cleaner assembly as described in Section 2.
13 Pull the charge pressure sensor and bracket from the support frame **(see illustration 8.12)**. Release the wiring harness from the frame as the sensor is withdrawn.
14 Unclip the fuel pipe, mass airflow sensor wiring harness, and coolant heater harness (where fitted) from the support frame.

15 Undo the bolt and detach the cooler heater assembly (where fitted) from the support frame **(see illustration 8.14)**.
16 Undo the 2 nuts and 2 bolts, and remove the support frame from the engine compartment **(see illustrations 8.15a and 8.15b)**.
17 Undo the mounting nuts/bolt and remove the heater blower housing from the engine compartment bulkhead **(see illustrations 15.20a to 15.20d)**. Disconnect any wiring plugs as the housing is removed.
18 Release the clamps, undo the support bracket bolt, and remove the air pipe from the turbocharger to the intercooler.
19 Disconnect the breather hose, unclip the vacuum hose, then disconnect the turbocharger air intake pipe.
20 Undo the 4 retaining nuts securing the catalytic converter to the turbocharger **(see illustration)**.
21 Disconnect the turbocharger wastegate

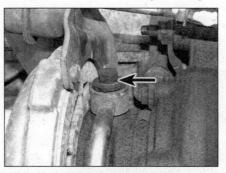

17.21 Undo the turbocharger oil feed pipe banjo bolt (arrowed)

17.24 The upper end of the straps located over hooks on the bracket

actuator hose, undo the banjo bolt and disconnect the oil feed pipe from the turbocharger. Remove the oil feed pipe support bracket bolt from the turbocharger **(see illustration)**.
22 Working underneath the vehicle, undo the nuts securing the front exhaust pipe to the catalytic converter, then slacken the clamp and remove the pipe.
23 Undo the nuts securing the support bracket to the base of the catalytic converter and the cylinder block **(see illustration)**.
24 Undo the retaining bolts, remove the straps, and move the catalytic converter to one side **(see illustration)**. Recover the support bracket beneath the converter.
25 Undo the retaining bolts and remove the turbocharger oil feed pipe, then undo the 2 bolts and disconnect the oil return pipe from the underside of the turbocharger **(see illustration)**. Renew the seals/gaskets, noting

17.23 Remove the support bracket from the base of the catalytic converter

17.25 Turbocharger oil return pipe retaining bolts (arrowed)

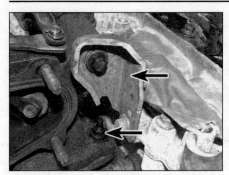

17.26a Remove the support bracket and front turbocharger retaining nut (arrowed)...

17.26b... then undo the remaining turbocharger retaining nuts (arrowed)

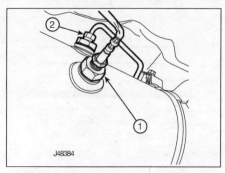

17.28 Particulate filter pressure differential sensor (2) and temperature sensor (1)

that the oil feed pipe sealing washers are not available separately from the pipe.

26 Remove the right-hand support bracket, then undo the nuts and manoeuvre the turbocharger from the engine **(see illustrations)**.

27 Remove the catalytic converter from place.

Particulate filter

28 Undo the union, remove the support bracket bolt, and disconnect the differential pressure sensor from the particulate filter **(see illustration)**. Counterhold the adapter as the union is slackened.

29 Undo the union, and disconnect the temperature sensor from the particulate filter **(see illustration 17.28)**. Counterhold the adapter as the union is slackened.

30 Slacken the clamp securing the particulate filter to the exhaust pipe, then undo the nuts securing it to the exhaust elbow.

31 Undo the retaining bolt and manoeuvre the particulate filter from position. Discard the gasket – a new one must be fitted.

Heat shield(s)

32 The heat shields are secured to the underside of the body by various nuts and bolts. Each shield can be removed once the relevant exhaust section has been removed. If a shield is being removed to gain access to a component located behind it, it may prove sufficient in some cases to remove the retaining nuts and/or bolts, and simply lower the shield, without disturbing the exhaust system.

Refitting

33 Each section is refitted by reversing the removal sequence, noting the following points:

 a) *Ensure that all traces of corrosion have*
 been removed from the flanges, and renew all necessary gaskets.
 b) *Inspect the rubber mountings for signs of damage or deterioration, and renew as necessary.*
 c) *When refitting the front flexible pipe to the catalytic converter, ensure that a new gasket is fitted.*
 d) *When reconnecting the intermediate pipe to rear silencer/tailpipe joint, apply a smear of exhaust system jointing paste to the flange joint, to ensure a gas-tight seal. Tighten the clamping ring nuts evenly and progressively so that the clearance between the clamp halves remains equal on either side.*
 e) *Prior to tightening the exhaust system fasteners, ensure that all rubber mountings are correctly located, and that there is adequate clearance between the exhaust system and vehicle underbody.*

Chapter 4 Part B:
Emission control systems

Contents

Degrees of difficulty

Easy, suitable for novice with little experience	Fairly easy, suitable for beginner with some experience	Fairly difficult, suitable for competent DIY mechanic	Difficult, suitable for experienced DIY mechanic	Very difficult, suitable for expert DIY or professional

Specifications

Torque wrench settings	Nm	lbf ft
EGR valve mounting bolts	21	15
EGR cooler	16	12
Oxygen (lambda) sensor	45	33

1 General information

All engines are designed to meet strict emission requirements and are equipped with a crankcase emission control system. In addition to this all models may also be fitted with a catalytic converter or particulate filter (M9R 630 engines) to reduce exhaust emissions. To further reduce emissions, they are also equipped with an exhaust gas recirculation (EGR) system.

The emission control systems function as follows.

Crankcase emission control

To reduce the emission of unburned hydrocarbons from the crankcase into the atmosphere, the engine is sealed and the blow-by gases and oil vapour are drawn from inside the crankcase, through a wire mesh oil separator, into the intake tract to be burned by the engine during normal combustion.

Under conditions of high manifold depression (idling, deceleration) the gases will be sucked positively out of the crankcase. Under conditions of low manifold depression (acceleration, full-throttle running) the gases are forced out of the crankcase by the (relatively) higher crankcase pressure; if the engine is worn, the raised crankcase pressure (due to increased blow-by) will cause some of the flow to return under all manifold conditions.

Exhaust emission control

To minimise the level of exhaust pollutants released into the atmosphere, a catalytic converter is fitted in the exhaust system on all models. The 2.0 litre M9R 630 engine is also fitted with a particulate filter. The catalytic converter consists of a canister containing a fine mesh impregnated with a catalyst material, over which the hot exhaust gases pass. The catalyst speeds up the oxidation of harmful carbon monoxide, unburnt hydrocarbons and soot, effectively reducing the quantity of harmful products released into the atmosphere via the exhaust gases.

The particulate filter is designed to trap carbon particulates produced by the combustion process. The particulate filter is combined with the catalytic converter. In order to prevent the filter blocking, pressure and temperature sensors are fitted to the filter. Under the normal, high-speed driving conditions, the soot particles are burnt off in the filter by the high temperature of the exhaust gases. However, where the driving conditions are such that the exhaust gases are not sufficiently high, the engine management system injects fuel into the exhaust manifold after the turbocharger to raise the gas temperature, causing the soot particles in the filter to be burnt off.

Exhaust gas recirculation system

This system is designed to recirculate small quantities of exhaust gas into the intake tract, and therefore into the combustion process. This process reduces the level of oxides of nitrogen present in the final exhaust gas which is released into the atmosphere.

The volume of exhaust gas recirculated is controlled by signals supplied to the injection computer. An electrically-operated EGR solenoid valve is fitted to the intake manifold/throttle body housing to regulate the quantity of exhaust gas recirculated.

The injection computer receives information from the following components:
a) Coolant temperature sensor.
b) Air temperature sensor.
c) Atmospheric pressure sensor.
d) Accelerator pedal position potentiometer.
e) Engine speed sensor.
f) Airflow meter.
g) Injection flow rate.
h) Turbocharger pressure sensor or solenoid valve.

If any faults develop in these components the supply to the EGR solenoid valve is stopped.

2 Engine emission control systems – testing and component renewal

Crankcase emission control

1 The components of this system require no attention other than to check that the hose(s) are clear and undamaged at regular intervals.
2 If the system is thought to be faulty, first check that the hoses are unobstructed and not damaged.
3 On high-mileage cars, particularly when regularly used for short journeys, a sludge-like deposit may be evident inside the system hoses and oil separators. If excessive deposits are present, the relevant component(s) should be removed and cleaned.
4 Periodically inspect the system components for security and damage, and renew them as necessary.

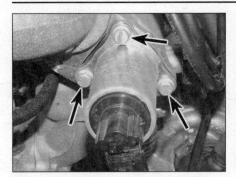

2.10 Undo the EGR valve mounting bolts (arrowed)

2.15 EGR valve retaining bolts (arrowed – one bolt hidden)

2.13 EGR pipe retaining bolts (arrowed)

2.20 EGR cooler coolant hoses (arrowed)

15 Undo the 3 bolts and remove the valve from place **(see illustration)**. Discard the gasket – a new one must be fitted.

16 Refitting is a reversal of removal, using a new gasket and ensuring that the valve and housing surfaces are clean and the bolts are securely tightened.

EGR cooler renewal – 2.0 litre engines

17 Remove the EGR valve as previously described in this Section.

18 Disconnect the oil pressure warning switch wiring plug.

19 Disconnect the wiring from the alternator and starter, unclip the wiring harness, and move it to one side.

20 Use hose clamps to prevent excess leakage, then release the clips and disconnect the coolant hoses from the EGR cooler. Plug the openings to prevent contamination/coolant loss **(see illustration)**.

21 Disconnect the vacuum hose from the bypass control valve on the cooler, then undo the 2 bolts and detach the EGR pipe from the control valve **(see illustration)**.

22 Undo the 4 retaining bolts and remove the cooler **(see illustration)**. Be prepared for coolant spillage.

23 Refitting is a reversal of removal, but tighten the bolts to the specified torque. Top up the coolant level as described in *Weekly checks*.

3 Catalytic converter – general information and precautions

The catalytic converter reduces harmful exhaust emissions by chemically converting the more poisonous gases to ones which (in theory at least) are less harmful. The chemical reaction is known as an 'oxidising' reaction, or one where oxygen is 'added'.

Inside the converter is a honeycomb structure, made of ceramic material and coated with the precious metals palladium, platinum and rhodium (the 'catalyst' which promotes the chemical reaction). The chemical reaction generates heat, which itself promotes the reaction – therefore, once the vehicle has been driven several miles, the body of the converter will be very hot.

The ceramic structure contained within the converter is understandably fragile, and will not withstand rough treatment. Since the converter runs at a high temperature, driving through deep standing water (in flood conditions, for example) is to be avoided, since the thermal stresses imposed when plunging the hot converter into cold water may well cause the ceramic internals to fracture, resulting in a 'blocked' converter – a common cause of failure. A converter that has been damaged in this way can be checked by shaking it (do not strike it) – if a rattling noise is heard, this indicates probable failure.

Exhaust emission control

Testing

5 The performance of the catalytic converter can be checked by measuring the exhaust gases using an exhaust gas analyser which is suitable for diesel engines.

Catalytic converter and particulate filter renewal

6 Refer to Chapter 4A, Section 17.

Exhaust gas recirculation system

Testing

7 Testing of the system should be entrusted to a dealer, who will have the specialist diagnostic equipment to carry out any tests.

EGR valve renewal – 1.9 litre engines

8 Remove the air cleaner assembly as described in Chapter 4A.

9 Release the clips and remove the air hose from the intercooler to the manifold.

10 Slacken and remove the retaining bolts and free the valve from the intake manifold **(see illustration)**. Recover the gasket and discard it; a new one must be used on refitting.

11 Refitting is the reverse of removal, using new gaskets and ensuring that the bolts are tighten to the specified torque.

EGR valve renewal – 2.0 litre engines

12 Remove the throttle valve module as described in Chapter 4A.

13 Undo the retaining bolts and remove the EGR pipe from the cooler and control valve **(see illustration)**. Discard the gaskets – new ones must be fitted.

14 Undo the 2 bolts and remove the intercooler outlet hose support bracket from the intake manifold.

2.21 Disconnect the vacuum hose from the bypass control valve (arrowed)

2.22 EGR cooler retaining bolts (arrowed)

Precautions

The catalytic converter fitted to diesel models is simpler than that fitted to petrol models, but it still needs to be treated with respect to avoid problems:

a) *DO NOT use fuel or engine oil additives – these may contain substances harmful to the catalytic converter.*

b) *DO NOT continue to use the vehicle if the engine burns (engine) oil to the extent of leaving a visible trail of blue smoke.*

c) *Remember that the catalytic converter operates at very high temperatures. DO NOT, therefore, park the vehicle in dry undergrowth, over long grass or piles of dead leaves after a long run.*

d) *As mentioned above, driving through deep water should be avoided if possible. The sudden cooling effect will fracture the ceramic honeycomb, damaging it beyond repair.*

e) *Remember that the catalytic converter is FRAGILE – do not strike it with tools during servicing work, and take care handling it when removing it from the vehicle for any reason.*

f) *If a substantial loss of power is experienced, remember that this could be due to the converter being blocked. This can occur simply as a result of high mileage, but may be due to the ceramic element having fractured and collapsed internally (see paragraph 3). A new converter is the only cure in this instance.*

g) *The catalytic converter, used on a well-maintained and well-driven car, should last at least 100 000 miles – if the converter is no longer effective, it must be renewed.*

Chapter 5
Starting and charging systems

Contents

Degrees of difficulty

| Easy, suitable for novice with little experience | 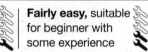 | Fairly easy, suitable for beginner with some experience | | Fairly difficult, suitable for competent DIY mechanic | | Difficult, suitable for experienced DIY mechanic | | Very difficult, suitable for expert DIY or professional | |

Specifications

Battery
Type . . . . Lead-acid, low-maintenance or 'maintenance-free'
Rating:
  Up to 2006 model year. . . . . 70 or 80 Ah
  From 2006 model year . . . . 85 or 95 Ah

Alternator
Type:
  1.9 litre engines . . . . Valeo SG12B 125A
  2.0 litre engines . . . . Valeo TG15 150A
Regulated voltage . . . . 13.5 to 14.8 volts

Starter motor
Type:
  1.9 litre engines . . . . Bosch 1106024
  2.0 litre engines:
    M9R 780 . . . . Mitsubishi MPM9R04 or Valeo TS22E5
    All others. . . . . Misubishi MPM9R04

Torque wrench settings	Nm	lbf ft
Alternator mounting bolts.	25	18
Auxiliary drivebelt guide roller	20	15
Auxiliary drivebelt tensioner roller	44	32
Glow plugs:		
1.9 litre engines	15	11
2.0 litre engines	18	13
Starter motor mounting bolts.	44	32

1 General information and precautions

General information

The engine electrical system consists mainly of the charging and starting systems. Because of their engine-related functions, these components are covered separately from the body electrical devices such as the lights, instruments, etc (which are covered in Chapter 12).

The electrical system is of the 12 volt negative earth type.

The battery is of the low-maintenance or 'maintenance-free' (sealed for life) type and is charged by the alternator, which is belt-driven from the crankshaft pulley.

The starter motor is of the pre-engaged type incorporating an integral solenoid. On starting, the solenoid moves the drive pinion into engagement with the flywheel ring gear before the starter motor is energised. Once the engine has started, a one-way clutch prevents the motor armature being driven by the engine until the pinion disengages from the flywheel.

Precautions

Further details of the various systems are given in the relevant Sections of this Chapter. While some repair procedures are given, the usual course of action is to renew the component concerned.

It is necessary to take extra care when working on the electrical system to avoid damage to semi-conductor devices (diodes and transistors), and to avoid the risk of personal injury. In addition to the precautions given in *Safety first!* at the beginning of this manual, observe the following when working on the system:

• *Always remove rings, watches, etc, before working on the electrical system*. Even with the battery disconnected, capacitive discharge could occur if a component's live terminal is earthed through a metal object. This could cause a shock or nasty burn.

• *Do not reverse the battery connections*. Components such as the alternator, electronic control units, or any other components having semi-conductor circuitry could be irreparably damaged.

• If the engine is being started using jump leads and a slave battery, connect the batteries *positive-to-positive* and *negative-to-negative* (see *Jump starting*). This also applies when connecting a battery charger.

• Never disconnect the battery terminals, the alternator, any electrical wiring or any test instruments when the engine is running.

• Do not allow the engine to turn the alternator when the alternator is not connected.

• Never test for alternator output by 'flashing' the output lead to earth.

• Never use an ohmmeter of the type incorporating a hand-cranked generator for circuit or continuity testing.

• Always ensure that the battery negative lead is disconnected when working on the electrical system.

• Before using electric-arc welding equipment on the car, disconnect the battery, alternator and components such as the fuel injection electronic control unit to protect them from the risk of damage.

• Several systems fitted to the vehicle require battery power to be available at all times, either to ensure their continued operation (such as the clock) or to maintain security codes which would be wiped if the battery were to be disconnected.

2 Electrical fault finding – general information

Refer to Chapter 12.

3 Battery – testing and charging

Testing

Standard and low-maintenance battery

1 If the vehicle covers a small annual mileage, it is worthwhile checking the specific gravity of the electrolyte every three months, to determine the state of charge of the battery. Use a hydrometer to make the check, and compare the results with the following table. The temperatures quoted in the table are ambient (air) temperatures. Note that the specific gravity readings assume an electrolyte temperature of 15°C; for every 10°C below 15°C, subtract 0.007. For every 10°C above 15°C, add 0.007.

	Above 25°C	Below 25°C
Fully-charged	1.210 to 1.230	1.270 to 1.290
70% charged	1.170 to 1.190	1.230 to 1.250
Discharged	1.050 to 1.070	1.110 to 1.130

2 If the battery condition is suspect, first check the specific gravity of electrolyte in each cell. A variation of 0.040 or more between any cells indicates loss of electrolyte or deterioration of the internal plates.

3 If the specific gravity variation is 0.040 or more, the battery should be renewed. If the cell variation is satisfactory but the battery is discharged, it should be charged as described later in this Section.

Maintenance-free battery

4 In cases where a 'sealed for life' maintenance-free battery is fitted, topping-up and testing of the electrolyte in each cell is not possible. The condition of the battery can therefore only be tested using a battery condition indicator or a voltmeter.

5 Certain models may be fitted with a Delco type maintenance-free battery, with a built-in charge condition indicator. The indicator is located in the top of the battery casing, and indicates the condition of the battery from its colour. If the indicator shows green, then the battery is in a good state of charge. If the indicator turns darker, eventually to black, then the battery requires charging, as described later in this Section. If the indicator shows clear/yellow, then the electrolyte level in the battery is too low to allow further use, and the battery should be renewed. **Do not** attempt to charge, load or jump start a battery when the indicator shows clear/yellow.

All battery types

6 If testing the battery using a voltmeter, connect the voltmeter across the battery. The test is only accurate if the battery has not been subjected to any kind of charge for the previous six hours. If this is not the case, switch on the headlights for 30 seconds, then wait four to five minutes before testing the battery after switching off the headlights. All other electrical circuits must be switched off, so check that the doors and tailgate are fully shut when making the test.

7 If the voltage reading is less than 12.0 volts, then the battery is discharged, whilst a reading of 12.2 to 12.4 volts indicates a partially-discharged condition.

8 If the battery is to be charged, remove it from the vehicle (Section 4) and charge it as described later in this Section.

Charging

Note: *The following is intended as a guide only. Always refer to the manufacturer's recommendations (often printed on a label attached to the battery) before charging a battery.*

Standard and low-maintenance battery

9 Charge the battery at a rate of 3.5 to 4 amps and continue to charge the battery at this rate until no further rise in specific gravity is noted over a four hour period.

10 Alternatively, a trickle charger charging at the rate of 1.5 amps can safely be used overnight.

11 Specially rapid 'boost' charges that are claimed to restore the power of the battery in 1 to 2 hours are not recommended, as they can cause serious damage to the battery plates through overheating.

12 While charging the battery, note that the temperature of the electrolyte should never exceed 38°C.

Maintenance-free battery

13 This battery type takes considerably longer to fully recharge than the standard type, the time taken being dependent on the extent of discharge, but it can take anything up to three days.

14 A constant voltage type charger is required, to be set to 13.9 to 14.9 volts with a charger current below 25 amps. Using this

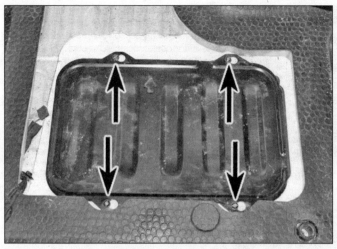

4.2a Undo the screws (arrowed)...

4.2b... and remove the battery cover

method, the battery should be usable within three hours, giving a voltage reading of 12.5 volts, but this is for a partially-discharged battery and, as mentioned, full charging can take considerably longer.

15 If the battery is to be charged from a fully-discharged state (condition reading less than 12 volts), have it recharged by your dealer or local automotive electrician, as the charge rate is higher and constant supervision during charging is necessary.

---

4 Battery –
disconnecting,
removal and refitting

Disconnecting

Several systems fitted to the vehicle require battery power to be available at all times, either to ensure their continued operation (such as the clock) or to maintain control unit memories which could be erased if the battery were to be disconnected. Whenever the battery is to be disconnected therefore, first note the following, to ensure that there are no unforeseen consequences of this action:

a) *First, on any vehicle with central locking, it is a wise precaution to remove the key, and to keep it with you, so that it does not get locked in, if the central locking should engage accidentally when the battery is reconnected.*

b) *The engine management system's ECU will lose the information stored in its memory when the battery is disconnected. This includes idling and operating values, and any fault codes detected – in the case of the fault codes, if it is thought likely that the system has developed a fault for which the corresponding code has been logged, the vehicle must be taken to a Vauxhall or Renault dealer or suitably-equipped repairer for the codes to be read, using the special diagnostic equipment necessary for this. Whenever the battery*

is disconnected, the information relating to idle speed control and other operating values will have to be reprogrammed into the unit's memory. The ECU does this by itself, but until then, there may be surging, hesitation, erratic idle and a generally inferior level of performance. To allow the ECU to relearn these values, start the engine and run it as close to idle speed as possible until it reaches its normal operating temperature, then run it for approximately two minutes at 1200 rpm. Next, drive the vehicle as far as necessary – approximately 5 miles of varied driving conditions is usually sufficient – to complete the relearning process.

c) *If the battery is disconnected while the alarm system is armed or activated, the alarm will remain in the same state when the battery is reconnected. The same applies to the engine immobiliser system.*

d) *If a Vauxhall or Renault audio unit is fitted, and the unit and/or the battery is disconnected, the unit may not function again on reconnection until the correct security code is entered. Details of this procedure, which varies according to the unit and model year, are given in the audio operating guide supplied with the vehicle when new. Ensure you have the correct code before you disconnect the battery. For obvious security reasons, the*

4.3 Slacken the nut (arrowed) and pull the negative terminal clamp from the battery

procedure is not given in this manual. If you do not have the code or details of the correct procedure, but can supply proof of ownership and a legitimate reason for wanting this information, the car's selling dealer may be able to help.

Devices known as 'memory-savers' (or 'code-savers') can be used to avoid some of the above problems. Precise details vary according to the device used. Typically, it is plugged into the cigarette lighter, and is connected by its own wires to a spare battery; the car's own battery is then disconnected from the electrical system, leaving the 'memory-saver' to pass sufficient current to maintain audio unit security codes and ECU memory values, and also to run permanently-live circuits such as the clock, all the while isolating the battery in the event of a short-circuit occurring while work is carried out.

⚠️ *Warning: Some of these devices allow a considerable amount of current to pass, which can mean that many of the vehicle's systems are still operational when the main battery is disconnected. If a 'memory saver' is used, ensure that the circuit concerned is actually 'dead' before carrying out any work on it!*

1 The battery is located under the passenger's side floor panel. Slide the passenger's seat fully rearwards, then remove the carpet/mat in front of the seat.

2 Slacken the 4 screws and remove the battery cover (see illustrations).

3 Slacken the clamp nut and disconnect the negative lead from the battery (see illustration). Position the lead away from the battery, or place a cover over the negative terminal to prevent accidental reconnection.

Removal

4 Disconnect the battery negative lead as described previously in this Section.

Up to 2006 model year

5 Slacken the clamp nut and disconnect the battery positive lead.

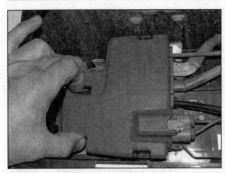

4.6 Unclip the plastic cover

4.7a Slacken the positive terminal clamp nut (arrowed)...

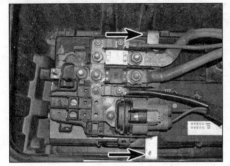

4.7b... and unclip the retaining strap (arrowed)

4.8 Undo the battery clamp bolt (arrowed)

From 2006 model year

6 Unclip the cover from the battery positive terminal **(see illustration)**.

7 Slacken the positive lead retaining nut, release the 2 clips and move the assembly away from the battery **(see illustrations)**.

All models

8 Unscrew the securing bolt and remove battery securing clamp **(see illustration)**.

9 The battery can then be lifted out of the engine compartment.

Refitting

10 Refitting is a reversal of removal. Smear petroleum jelly on the terminals after reconnecting the leads to reduce corrosion. Always reconnect the positive lead first, and the negative lead last.

6.6 Undo the drivebelt tensioner bolt (arrowed) – 1.9 litre engines

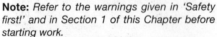

5 Charging system – testing

Note: *Refer to the warnings given in 'Safety first!' and in Section 1 of this Chapter before starting work.*

1 If the ignition warning light fails to illuminate when the ignition is on, first check the alternator wiring connections for security. If satisfactory, check that the warning light bulb has not blown, and that the bulbholder is secure in its location in the instrument panel. If the light still fails to illuminate, check the continuity of the warning light feed wire from the alternator to the bulbholder. If all is satisfactory, the alternator is at fault and should be renewed or taken to an auto-electrician for testing and repair.

2 If the ignition warning light illuminates when

6.9 Prise off the cap and undo the guide pulley bolt (arrowed) – 2.0 litre engines

the engine is running, stop the engine and check that the auxiliary drivebelt is correctly tensioned (see the relevant part of Chapter 1) and that the alternator connections are secure. If all is so far satisfactory, have the alternator checked by an auto-electrician for testing and repair.

3 If the alternator output is suspect even though the warning light functions correctly, the regulated voltage may be checked as follows.

4 Connect a voltmeter across the battery terminals and start the engine.

5 Increase the engine speed until the voltmeter reading remains steady; the reading should be approximately 13.2 to 14.8 volts, and no more than 14.8 volts.

6 Switch on as many electrical accessories (eg, the headlights, heated rear window and heater blower) as possible, and check that the alternator maintains the regulated voltage at around 13.2 to 14.8 volts.

7 If the regulated voltage is not as stated, the fault may be due to worn brushes, weak brush springs, a faulty voltage regulator, a faulty diode, a severed phase winding, or worn or damaged slip-rings. The alternator should be renewed or taken to an auto-electrician for testing and repair.

6 Alternator – testing, removal and refitting

Testing

1 If the alternator is thought to be suspect, it should be removed from the vehicle and taken to an auto-electrician for testing on specialist equipment. However, check on the cost of repairs before proceeding, as it may prove more economical to obtain a new or exchange alternator. If the brushes/regulator pack is at fault, it may be possible to renew it quite easily, see Section 7.

Removal

2 Disconnect the battery negative lead as described in Section 4.

3 Remove the auxiliary drivebelt as described in Chapter 1.

1.9 litre models

4 Remove the splash shield from beneath the radiator.

5 Unclip the air deflector from the right-hand side of the radiator.

6 Undo the bolt and remove the drivebelt tensioner **(see illustration)**.

2.0 litre models

7 Release the retaining clip and slide the power steering fluid reservoir upwards from the front panel and move it to one side. There's no need to disconnect the fluid pipes.

8 Release the clamps and remove the air pipe from the intercooler to the throttle valve module on the intake manifold.

9 Prise off the cap, undo the bolt and remove the drivebelt guide pulley **(see illustration)**.

All models

10 Disconnect the electrical wiring connectors from the rear of the alternator **(see illustration)**. Where applicable, disconnect the air conditioning compressor wiring plug.

11 Slacken and remove the lower and upper mounting bolts from the alternator. On some engines, the upper bolt does not need to be fully removed as the mounting bracket is slotted to allow the bolt to be removed with the alternator **(see illustration)**.

12 With spacers fitted to its mounting lugs, the alternator may prove difficult to remove from the mounting bracket. Take care when prising the alternator out from the mounting bracket to avoid damaging it, or any surrounding components. Support the alternator from underneath to prevent it falling, and then remove the alternator from the engine.

Refitting

13 Refitting is a reversal of removal. Refer to Chapter 1 for details of fitting (and tensioning, where necessary) the auxiliary drivebelt.

7 Alternator brushes/regulator – removal and refitting

Note: *Check the availability of parts before commencing work.*

Removal

1 Remove the alternator from the engine as described in previous Section.

2 Undo the retaining screws (where fitted) and carefully prise the rear plastic cover from the alternator **(see illustration)**.

3 Undo the retaining bolts/nuts and withdraw the brushes/regulator assembly from the alternator **(see illustration)**.

4 Check the carbon brushes and slip-rings for wear, make sure the brushes are able to slide freely in their guides without any sign of binding.

Refitting

5 Position the protective sleeve so it retains the brushes in the retracted position, and slide the brush/regulator assembly over the commutator **(see illustrations)**.

6 Tighten the retaining bolts, then press the sleeve downwards to release the brushes.

7 The remainder of refitting is a reversal of removal

8 Starting system – testing

Note: *Refer to the precautions given in 'Safety first!' and in Section 1 of this Chapter before starting work.*

1 If the starter motor fails to operate, the following possible causes may be to blame.

  a) The battery is faulty.

  b) The electrical connections between the

6.10 Disconnect the wiring from the rear of the alternator (arrowed)

  switch, solenoid, battery and starter motor are somewhere failing to pass the necessary current from the battery through the starter to earth.

  c) The solenoid is faulty.

  d) The starter motor is mechanically or electrically defective.

2 To check the battery, switch on the headlights. If they dim after a few seconds, this indicates that the battery is discharged – recharge (see Section 3) or renew the battery. If the headlights glow brightly, operate the ignition switch and observe the lights. If they dim, then this indicates that current is reaching the starter motor; therefore the fault must lie in the starter motor. If the lights continue to glow brightly (and no clicking sound can be heard from the starter motor solenoid), this indicates that there is a fault in the circuit or solenoid – see following paragraphs. If the starter motor turns slowly when operated, but the battery

7.2 Carefully prise up the plastic cover

7.5a Press in the brushes...

6.11 Alternator mounting bolts (arrowed)

is in good condition, then this indicates that either the starter motor is faulty, or there is considerable resistance somewhere in the circuit.

3 If a fault in the circuit is suspected, disconnect the battery leads (including the earth connection to the body), the starter/solenoid wiring and the engine/transmission earth strap. Thoroughly clean the connections, and reconnect the leads and wiring, then use a voltmeter or test lamp to check that full battery voltage is available at the battery positive lead connection to the solenoid, and that the earth is sound. Smear petroleum jelly around the battery terminals to prevent corrosion – corroded connections are amongst the most frequent causes of electrical system faults.

4 If the battery and all connections are in good condition, check the circuit by disconnecting the wire from the solenoid blade terminal.

7.3 Undo the bolts (arrowed) and remove the brush/regulator assembly

7.5b... and slide the sleeve so that it holds the brushes in the retracted position

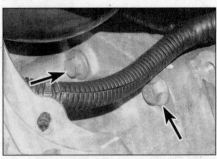

9.5 Remove the starter motor upper mounting bolts from the transmission side (arrowed)

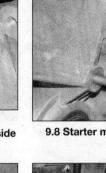

9.8 Starter motor lower mounting bolt (arrowed)

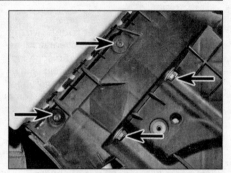

9.12a Drill out the rivets, undo the bolts (arrowed) at the side...

9.12b... and front of the impact absorber (arrowed)

9.15 Undo the bolts (arrowed) securing the support frame to the slam panel

Connect a voltmeter or test lamp between the wire end and a good earth (such as the battery negative terminal), and check that the wire is live when the key is turned. If it is, then the circuit is sound – if not the circuit wiring can be checked as described in Chapter 12.
5 The solenoid contacts can be checked by connecting a voltmeter or test lamp between the battery positive feed connection on the starter side of the solenoid, and earth. When the key is turned, there should be a reading or lighted bulb, as applicable. If there is no reading or lighted bulb, the solenoid is faulty and should be renewed.
6 If the circuit and solenoid are proved sound, the fault must lie in the starter motor. In this event, it may be possible to have the starter motor overhauled by a specialist, but check on the cost of spares before proceeding, as it may prove more economical to obtain a new or exchange motor.

9 Starter motor – removal and refitting

Removal – 1.9 litre models

1 Disconnect the battery negative lead as described in Section 4.
2 Raise the front of the vehicle and support it securely on axle stands (see *Jacking and vehicle support*). Undo the fasteners, remove the engine undertray and the right-hand wheel arch liner inner splash panel. Where necessary, unclip the washer hose.
3 Release the clips and disconnect the air intake and outlet hoses from the turbocharger.
4 Working above the transmission, undo the bolt securing the engine wiring harness bracket to the transmission.

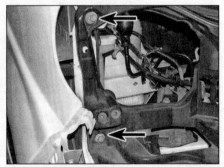

5 Remove the starter motor upper mounting bolts (see illustration).
6 Working underneath the vehicle, disconnect the wiring from the starter motor.
7 Disconnect the earth lead from the catalytic converter bracket, then undo the 3 bolts and remove the bracket.
8 Undo the remaining retaining bolt and manoeuvre the starter from place (see illustration).

Removal – 2.0 litre models

9 Disconnect the battery negative lead as described in Section 4.
10 Remove the front bumper, bonnet and radiator grille as described in Chapter 11. Pull the rubber seal from the top edge of the bonnet slam panel.
11 Remove both front headlights as described in Chapter 12.
12 Undo the bolts, drill out the rivets and remove the front impact absorbers/air deflector assembly (see illustrations).
13 Release the retaining clip and move the power steering fluid reservoir to one side. There's no need to disconnect the pipes.
14 Release the clamps and remove the intercooler hoses.
15 Undo the bolts securing the air cleaner support frame to the bonnet slam panel (see illustration).
16 Make alignment marks between the bonnet lock and the slam panel, then undo the bolts, and manoeuvre the lock from place. Release the cable/wiring loom from the retaining clips on the slam panel.
17 Undo the bolts and release the engine management ECM bracket and bonnet alarm contact switch bracket from the slam panel (see illustration).
18 Release the clips, undo the bolts, and remove the complete front/slam panel from the vehicle (see illustrations).

All except M9R 630 engines

19 Undo the 2 bolts and move the engine wiring harness trunking at the left-hand side of the engine to one side. Unclip the clutch fluid pressure pipe from the trunking.
20 Pull out the R-clips securing the radiator (and condenser where applicable) to the underside of the lower support crossmember,

9.17 Undo the bolt (arrowed) securing the ECM bracket

9.18a The front panel is secured by 2 bolts (arrowed) at the right-hand edge...

then secure the radiator and condenser to the front upper crossmember with cable-ties, etc. Recover the washers.

M9R 630 engines

21 Working underneath the vehicle, release the high-pressure power steering hose from the retaining clip, then undo the bolt securing the pipe to the oil cooler housing.
22 Undo the 2 retaining bolts, release the clips and remove the air deflector panel from above the alternator.
23 Disconnect the wiring from the alternator and oil pressure warning switch.

All engines

24 Disconnect the wiring from the starter motor, and the earth lead from the starter motor mounting flange **(see illustration)**.
25 Undo the retaining bolts and remove the starter motor.

Refitting

26 Refitting is a reversal of removal. There is a locating dowel, either fitted to the transmission bellhousing or the starter motor bolt hole, to ensure that the starter motor is centralised. Make sure this is correctly positioned before refitting the starter motor.

10 Starter motor – testing and overhaul

If the starter motor is thought to be suspect, it should be removed from the vehicle and taken to an auto-electrician for testing. Most auto-electricians will be able to supply and fit brushes at a reasonable cost. However, check on the cost of repairs before proceeding, as it may prove more economical to obtain a new or exchange motor.

11 Preheater system – testing, removal and refitting

Description

1 To assist cold starting, diesel engines are fitted with a preheating system, which consists of four of glow plugs (one per cylinder), a glow plug relay unit, a facia-mounted warning lamp, the engine management ECM, and the associated electrical wiring.
2 The glow plugs are miniature electric heating elements, encapsulated in a metal case with a probe at one end and electrical connection at the other. Each combustion chamber has one glow plug threaded into it, with the tip of the glow plug probe positioned directly in line with incoming spray of fuel from the injectors. When the glow plug is energised, it heats up rapidly, causing the fuel passing over the glow plug probe to be heated to its optimum combustion temperature, ready for combustion. In

9.18b... 3 bolts (arrowed) on the left-hand side...

9.18d... and 1 bolt (arrowed) at the base of the central bracket

addition, some of the fuel passing over the glow plugs is ignited and this helps to trigger the combustion process.
3 The preheating system begins to operate as soon as the ignition key is switched to the second position, but only if the engine coolant temperature is below 20ºC and the engine is turned at more than 70 rpm for 0.2 seconds. A facia-mounted warning lamp informs the driver that preheating is taking place. The lamp extinguishes when sufficient preheating has taken place to allow the engine to be started, but power will still be supplied to the glow plugs for a further period until the engine is started. If no attempt is made to start the engine, the power supply to the glow plugs is switched off after 10 seconds, to prevent battery drain and glow plug burn-out.
4 With the electronically-controlled diesel injection systems fitted to models in this manual, the glow plug relay unit is controlled by the engine management system ECM, which determines the necessary preheating time based on inputs from the various system sensors. The system monitors the temperature of the intake air, then alters the preheating time (the length for which the glow plugs are supplied with current) to suit the conditions.
5 Post-heating takes place after the ignition key has been released from the 'Start' position, but only if the engine coolant temperature is below 20ºC, the injected fuel flow is less than a certain rate, and the engine speed is less than 2000 rpm. The glow plugs continue to operate for a maximum of 60 sec-

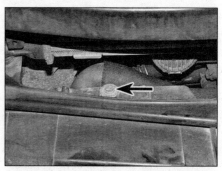

9.18c... 1 bolt (arrowed) to the right of centre...

9.18e Lift the entire front panel from place

onds, helping to improve fuel combustion whilst the engine is warming-up, resulting in quieter, smoother running and reduced exhaust emissions.

Testing

6 If the system malfunctions, testing is ultimately by substitution of known good units, but some preliminary checks may be made as follows. Note that the preheating system is included in the vehicle's self-diagnosis system. Consequently, have the system interrogated using a fault code reader or scanner, via the vehicle's diagnostic socket.
7 Remove the glow plugs as described in this Section, then connect an ohmmeter between the threaded body of the plug and the insulated terminal. Renew the glow plug if the resistance is infinite.
8 Have an assistant switch on the ignition,

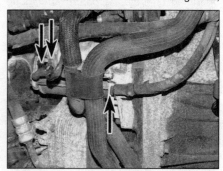

9.24 Disconnect the starter motor wiring and the earth lead from the mounting flange (arrowed)

11.12 Slacken the clamp (arrowed) and disconnect the hose from the right-hand end of the intercooler

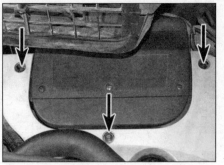

11.13 Prise out the caps, undo the bolts (arrowed) and remove the engine cover

11.14 Pull the connector from the glow plug – 1.9 litre engines

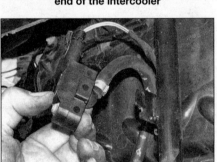

11.16 Pull the charge pressure sensor upwards from the support frame

11.18 Undo the bolt (arrowed) securing the coolant heater assembly

and check that voltage is applied to the glow plugs. Note that glow plugs with a white ring on some 2.0 litre engines, are supplied with a voltage of 7V, not 12V (black ring). These plugs are not interchangeable. Note the time for which the warning light is lit, and the total time for which voltage is applied before the system cuts out. Switch off the ignition.

9 Warning light time will increase with lower temperatures and decrease with higher temperatures.

10 If there is no supply at all, the control unit or associated wiring is at fault.

11 To gain access to the glow plugs for further testing, refer to Chapter 4A, where necessary, and remove the intake manifold.

Glow plugs

Note: *Ideally, the engine should be at operating temperature before attempting*

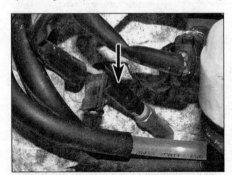

11.22 Pull the connector from the glow plug (arrowed) – 2.0 litre engines

to unscrew the glow plugs. If the plugs are removed from a cold engine, the threads in the cylinder head may be damaged.

1.9 litre engines

12 Release the clamps and remove the air hose from the right-hand side of the intercooler. Undo the support bracket bolt where applicable **(see illustration)**.

13 Prise out the caps, undo the 3 bolts and remove the plastic cover from the top of the engine **(see illustration)**.

14 Squeeze together the sides to release the clips, then pull the electrical connector from each glow plug **(see illustration)**.

2.0 litre engines

15 Remove the air cleaner assembly as described in Section 2.

16 Pull the charge pressure sensor and bracket from the air cleaner support frame

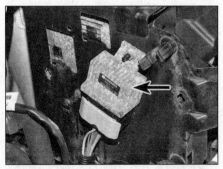

11.28 Pre/post-heating system control/relay unit (arrowed)

(see illustration). Release the wiring harness from the frame as the sensor is withdrawn.

17 Unclip the fuel pipe, mass airflow sensor wiring harness, and coolant heater harness (where fitted) from the support frame.

18 Undo the bolt and detach the cooler heater assembly (where fitted) from the support frame **(see illustration)**.

19 Undo the 2 nuts, 2 bolts and remove the support frame from the engine compartment **(see illustration 9.15)**.

20 Release the clip and slide the power steering fluid reservoir upwards from the front panel. There's no need to disconnect the fluid pipes.

21 Release the clamps/bolt and remove the air pipe from the intercooler to the intake manifold.

22 Pull the wiring connector from the top of the glow plugs **(see illustration)**.

All engines

23 Spray the area around each glow plug with releasing agent/penetrating spray, and leave it for a few minutes to soak in. Unscrew the glow plug(s) and remove from the cylinder head **(see illustration)**.

24 Inspect each glow plug for physical damage. Burnt or eroded glow plug tips can be caused by a bad injector spray pattern. Have the injectors checked if this sort of damage is found.

25 Refit by reversing the removal operations. Apply a smear of copper-based anti-seize compound to the plug threads and tighten the glow plugs to the specified torque. Do not overtighten, as this can damage the glow plug element.

26 Refit any components removed for access.

Pre/post-heating system control/relay unit

27 The preheating control unit is located at the left-hand side of the engine compartment. On 1.9 litre engines, disconnect the wiring plug from the charger pressure sensor.

28 On all engines, undo the retaining nut and remove the preheating control unit **(see illustration)**. Disconnect the wiring plug as the unit is withdrawn.

29 Refitting is a reversal of removal, ensuring that the wiring connectors are correctly connected.

Chapter 6
Clutch

Contents

Degrees of difficulty

Easy, suitable for novice with little experience	**Fairly easy,** suitable for beginner with some experience	**Fairly difficult,** suitable for competent DIY mechanic	**Difficult,** suitable for experienced DIY mechanic	**Very difficult,** suitable for expert DIY or professional

Specifications

General
Type . . . .   Single dry friction plate, with diaphragm spring pressure plate, hydraulically-operated release bearing

Torque wrench settings

	Nm	lbf ft
Pressure plate to flywheel*	20	15
Slave cylinder/release bearing bolts	11	8

* Do not re-use

1 General information

The clutch consists of a friction plate, a pressure plate assembly and a release bearing; all of these components are contained in the large cast-aluminium alloy bellhousing, sandwiched between the engine and the transmission. The release mechanism is hydraulic, operated by a master cylinder and a slave cylinder, which is part of the release bearing. The hydraulic master cylinder is located in the pedal bracket on the bulkhead, and the clutch fluid reservoir is shared with the brake fluid reservoir on the top of the brake master cylinder. Inside the reservoir each circuit has its own compartment, so that in the event of fluid loss in the clutch circuit, the brake circuit remains fully operational.

The friction plate is fitted between the engine flywheel and the clutch pressure plate, and is allowed to slide on the transmission input shaft splines.

The pressure plate assembly is bolted to the engine flywheel. When the engine is running, drive is transmitted from the crankshaft, via the flywheel, to the friction plate (these components being clamped securely together by the pressure plate assembly) and from the friction plate to the transmission input shaft.

To interrupt the drive, the spring pressure must be relaxed by the hydraulically-operated release mechanism. Depressing the clutch pedal operates the master cylinder, which in turn operates the slave cylinder and presses the release bearing against the pressure plate spring fingers. This causes the springs to deform and releases the clamping force on the pressure plate.

When the pedal is released, the diaphragm spring forces the pressure plate into contact with the friction linings on the friction plate. The disc is now firmly sandwiched between the pressure plate and the flywheel, thus transmitting engine power to transmission.

Wear of the friction material on the friction plate is automatically compensated for by the operation of the hydraulic system. As the friction material on the friction plate wears, the pressure plate moves towards the flywheel causing the clutch diaphragm spring inner fingers to move outwards. When the clutch pedal is released, excess fluid is expelled through the master cylinder into the fluid reservoir.

 Warning: Hydraulic fluid is poisonous; wash off immediately and thoroughly in the case of skin contact, and seek immediate medical advice if any fluid is swallowed or gets into the eyes. Certain types of hydraulic fluid are flammable, and may ignite when allowed into contact with hot components; when servicing any hydraulic system, it is safest to assume that the fluid is flammable, and to take precautions against the risk of fire as though it is petrol that is being handled. Hydraulic fluid is also an effective paint stripper, and will attack plastics; if any is spilt, it should be washed off immediately, using copious quantities of fresh water. Finally, it is hygroscopic (it absorbs moisture from the air) – old fluid may be contaminated and unfit for further use. When topping-up or renewing the fluid, always use the recommended type, and ensure that it comes from a freshly-opened sealed container.

2.1 Apply a clamp to the fluid supply hose – facia removed for clarity

2.2 Prise out the clip (arrowed) and pull the pipe from the base of the master cylinder

2.3 Release the clips (arrowed) and pull the pushrod from the clutch pedal

2 Clutch master cylinder – removal and refitting

Note: *Refer to the warning in Section 1 before proceeding.*

Removal

1 Working inside the vehicle in the driver's side footwell, place a hose clamp around the fluid supply hose to the master cylinder, then pull the hose from the cylinder **(see illustration)**. Be prepared for fluid spillage. Plug the openings to prevent contamination.
2 Prise out the clip a little, and disconnect the pressure pipe from the master cylinder **(see illustration)**. Plug the openings to prevent contamination.
3 Release the retaining clip and disconnect the pushrod from the clutch pedal **(see illustration)**.

4 Rotate the master cylinder anti-clockwise and detach it from the support bracket.

Refitting

5 Refitting is a reversal of removal, noting the following points:
a) *Check the condition of the pipe seals, and renew if necessary.*
b) *Ensure that all fluid hose connections are clean, and are securely made.*
c) *Fill and bleed the clutch system on completion, as described in Section 4.*
d) *Check the clutch system is operating correctly with no leaks.*

3 Clutch slave cylinder – removal and refitting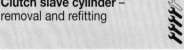

Note: *Refer to the warning in Section 1 before proceeding.*

Removal

1 Remove the transmission (see Chapter 7).
2 Pull out the retaining clip to split the slave cylinder from the connecting pipe in the transmission housing **(see illustration)**.
3 Inside the bellhousing, unscrew and remove the 3 mounting bolts, then withdraw the slave cylinder/release bearing over the transmission input shaft **(see illustration)**.

Refitting

4 Refitting is a reversal of removal, noting the following points:
a) *Renew the slave cylinder/release bearing seal.*
b) *Make sure the retaining clip is located securely.*
c) *Tighten the release bearing mounting bolts to the specified torque.*
d) *Refit the transmission (Chapter 7).*
e) *On completion, bleed the clutch as described in Section 4.*

4 Clutch hydraulic system – bleeding

Note: *Refer to the warning in Section 1 before proceeding.*

1 The correct operation of any hydraulic system is only possible after removing all air from the components and circuit; this is achieved by bleeding the system.
2 During the bleeding procedure, add only clean, unused hydraulic fluid of the recommended type; never re-use fluid that has already been bled from the system. Ensure that sufficient fluid is available before starting work.
3 If there is any possibility of incorrect fluid being already in the system, the hydraulic circuit must be flushed completely with uncontaminated, correct fluid.
4 If hydraulic fluid has been lost from the system, or air has entered because of a leak, ensure that the fault is cured before continuing further.
5 The bleed nipple is fitted to the slave cylinder at the front of the transmission bellhousing **(see illustration)**.

2.0 litre engines

6 Remove the air cleaner assembly as described in Section 2.

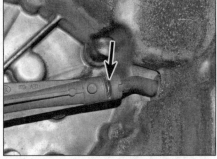

3.2 Release the retaining clip (arrowed)

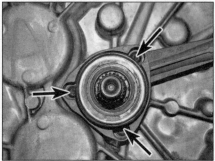

3.3 Slave cylinder mounting bolts (arrowed)

4.5 Cultch slave cylinder bleed nipple (arrowed)

4.7 Pull the charge pressure sensor upwards from the support frame

7 Pull the charge pressure sensor and bracket from the support frame **(see illustration)**. Release the wiring harness from the frame as the sensor is withdrawn.

8 Unclip the fuel pipe, mass airflow sensor wiring harness, and coolant heater harness (where fitted) from the support frame.

9 Undo the bolt and detach the cooler heater assembly (where fitted) from the support frame **(see illustration)**.

10 Undo the 2 nuts and 2 bolts, and remove the support frame from the engine compartment.

11 Release the clip, disconnect the outlet pipe from the turbocharger, undo the bolts and move the pipe to one side.

All engines

12 Unscrew the brake fluid reservoir cap, and top-up the fluid level to the MAX mark. Keep an eye on the fluid level as bleeding progresses, and keep it topped-up above the MIN mark throughout.

13 Connect a piece of tube to the bleed nipple, and open the circuit as described – bleeding and filling the system is done by gravity **(see illustration)**.

14 If the system is known to be empty (or if new parts have been fitted), have an assistant hold the clutch pedal depressed until the flow of bubbles seen in the pipe ceases. Depress and release the clutch pedal a few times, to purge the air from the master cylinder and pipes. Top-up the fluid level as necessary.

15 When no more bubbles are seen in the fluid, release the clutch pedal, and then press the slave cylinder pipe firmly back into place.

16 Top-up the fluid level to the MAX mark, and refit the reservoir cap.

17 Check the operation of the clutch – lack of response indicates the need for further bleeding.

18 If the clutch system was emptied, check the brakes for any sign of 'sponginess' in the pedal, which would mean the brakes also require bleeding, as described in Chapter 9.

19 Discard any hydraulic fluid that has been bled from the system; it will not be fit for re-use.

20 If the clutch is not operating correctly after repeated bleeding, the master cylinder or slave cylinder may be faulty. If new parts are fitted, it may be that there is an airlock in the system; disconnect the hoses from each component in turn to check there is fluid at that point. Place some absorbent cloth below the pipe connections as they are removed, to soak up the fluid that escapes. The system will then need further bleeding. **Note:** *If any fluid is spilt, it should be washed off immediately, using copious quantities of fresh water.*

5 Clutch pedal assembly – removal and refitting

Removal

1 Carefully prise the switch panel from the facia to release the retaining clips **(see illustration)**.

4.9 Coolant heater assembly retaining bolt (arrowed)

2 Working through the switch panel aperture, disconnect the wiring plug, then rotate the pedal switch anti-clockwise and pull it from place **(see illustration 6.2)**.

3 Release the clip and disconnect the master cylinder pushrod from the pedal **(see illustration 2.3)**.

4 Undo the retaining bolt/nut and remove the pedal from the bracket **(see illustrations)**. Recover the over-centre spring as the pedal is withdrawn.

5 If required, remove the pivot shaft and nylon bushes from the pedal **(see illustration)**.

Refitting

6 Refitting is a reversal of removal, noting the following points:

  a) *Ensure the switch is located correctly and the wiring connectors are secure.*

  b) *Check the clutch pedal is operating*

5.1 Starting at the top, prise the switch panel from the facia

5.4b Clutch pedal over-centre spring

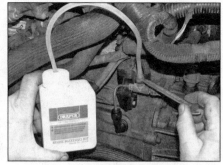

4.13 Attach a plastic hose to the bleed nipple

correctly and not fouling any other components and wiring.

6 Clutch pedal switch – removal, adjustment and refitting

Removal

1 Carefully prise the switch panel from the facia to release the retaining clips **(see illustration 5.1)**.

2 Working through the switch panel aperture, disconnect the wiring plug, then rotate the pedal switch anti-clockwise and pull it from place **(see illustration)**.

3 The manufacturers state that the switch must be renewed if the plunger is separated from the switch.

5.4a Clutch pedal pivot bolt/nut (arrowed)

5.5 Clutch pedal pivot shaft and bushes

6.2 Rotate the clutch pedal switch anti-clockwise to remove it

Adjustment

4 Measure the protrusion of the plunger from the switch. If it is less that 17 mm or greater than 18 mm, push/pull the plunger until this dimension is achieved (see illustration). Note: *The manufacturers insist that the switch must be renewed if the plunger position is adjusted more than 3 times.*

Refitting

5 Refitting is a reversal of removal.

7	Clutch assembly – removal, inspection and refitting	

⚠ Warning: *Dust created by clutch wear and deposited on the clutch components may contain*

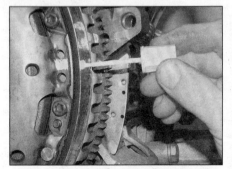

7.2 Mark the relationship of the pressure plate to the flywheel

7.5a Withdraw the pressure plate assembly...

6.4 The distance from the underside of the plunger head to the end of the switch body should be 17 to 18 mm

asbestos, which is a health hazard. DO NOT blow it out with compressed air, or inhale any of it. DO NOT use petrol or petroleum-based solvents to clean off the dust. Brake system cleaner or methylated spirit should be used to flush the dust into a suitable receptacle. After the clutch components are wiped clean with rags, dispose of the contaminated rags and cleaner in a sealed, marked container.

Removal

1 Remove the transmission as described in Chapter 7.
2 Before disturbing the clutch, use paint or a marker pen to mark the relationship of the pressure plate assembly to the flywheel (see illustration).
3 To prevent the flywheel from turning, position a screwdriver over the dowel on the

7.3 Use a large screwdriver to prevent the flywheel from rotating

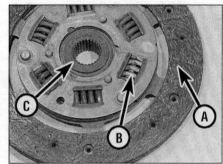

7.5b... and the friction plate, noting which way around it is fitted

cylinder block and engage it with one of the teeth on the starter ring gear (see illustration).
4 Working in a diagonal sequence, slacken the pressure plate bolts by half a turn at a time, until spring pressure is released and the bolts can be unscrewed by hand. Discard the bolts – new ones must be fitted.
5 Carefully prise the pressure plate assembly off its locating dowels, and collect the friction plate, noting which way round the friction plate is fitted (see illustrations). Note: *Be prepared to catch the friction plate, which may drop out when the pressure plate assembly is removed.*

Inspection

Note: *Due to the amount of work necessary to remove and refit clutch components, it is usually considered good practice to renew the clutch friction plate, pressure plate assembly and release bearing as a matched set, even if only one of these is actually worn enough to require renewal. It is also worth considering the renewal of the clutch components on a preventive basis if the engine and/or transmission have been removed for some other reason.*

6 With the clutch assembly removed, clean off all traces of dust using a dry cloth, working in a well-ventilated atmosphere. When cleaning clutch components, read first the warning at the beginning of this Section.
7 Examine the friction plate linings for signs of wear, damage or oil contamination. If the friction material is cracked, burnt, scored or damaged, or if it is contaminated with oil or grease (shown by shiny black patches), the friction plate must be renewed (see illustration). Check the depth of the rivets below the friction material surface. If any are at or near the surface of the friction material, then the friction plate must be renewed.
8 If the friction material is still serviceable, check that the centre boss splines are unworn, that the torsion springs are in good condition and securely fastened, and that all the rivets are tight. If any wear or damage is found, the friction plate must be renewed.
9 If the friction material is fouled with oil, this must be due to an oil leak from the crankshaft oil seal, from the sump-to-cylinder block joint, or from the transmission input shaft. Renew

7.7 Inspect the friction disc linings (A), springs (B), and splines (C)

7.10 Check the diaphragm spring fingers for wear, especially at the tips (arrowed)

7.11 Check the machined face (arrowed) of the pressure plate

7.18 Use a clutch aligning tool to centralise the friction plate

the seal or repair the joint, as appropriate, as described in the relevant parts of Chapters 2 or 7, before installing the new friction plate.
10 Check the pressure plate assembly for obvious signs of wear or damage; shake it to check for loose rivets or worn or damaged fulcrum rings, and check that the drive straps securing the pressure plate to the cover do not show signs of overheating (such as a deep yellow or blue discoloration). If the diaphragm spring is worn or damaged, or if its pressure is in any way suspect, the pressure plate assembly should be renewed **(see illustration)**.
11 Examine the machined bearing surfaces of the pressure plate and of the flywheel; they should be clean, completely flat, and free from scratches or scoring **(see illustration)**. If either is discoloured from excessive heat, or shows signs of cracks, it should be renewed – although minor damage of this nature can sometimes be polished away using emery paper.
12 Check that the release bearing contact surface rotates smoothly and easily, with no sign of noise or roughness. Also check that the surface itself is smooth and unworn, with no signs of cracks, pitting or scoring. If there is any doubt about its condition, the bearing must be renewed.

Refitting

13 On reassembly, ensure that the disc contact surfaces of the flywheel and pressure plate are completely clean, smooth, and free from oil or grease. Use solvent to remove any protective grease from new components.
14 Fit the friction plate so that its spring hub assembly faces away from the flywheel. There may also be a marking showing which way round the plate is to be refitted. Depending on the type of centralising tool being used, the friction plate may be held in position at this stage.
15 Refit the pressure plate assembly, aligning the marks made on dismantling (if the original pressure plate is re-used), and locating the pressure plate on its locating dowels. Fit the new pressure plate bolts, but tighten them only finger-tight, so that the friction plate can still be moved.
16 The friction plate must now be centralised, so that when the transmission is refitted its

input shaft will pass through the splines at the centre of the friction plate.
17 Centralisation can be achieved by passing a screwdriver or other long bar through the friction plate and into the hole in the crankshaft; the friction plate can then be moved around until it is centred on the crankshaft hole.
18 Alternatively, a clutch-aligning tool can be used to eliminate the guesswork; these can be obtained from most accessory shops. The normal type consists of a spigot bar with several different adapters, but a home-made aligning tool can be fabricated from a length of metal rod or wooden dowel which fits closely inside the crankshaft hole, and has insulating tape wound around it to match the diameter of the friction plate splined hole **(see illustration)**.
19 A more recent type of aligning tool works by clamping the friction plate to the pressure plate before locating the two items on the flywheel **(see illustrations)**.

7.19a Centralise the pressure plate on the disc...

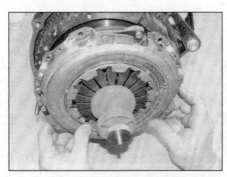

7.19c... then locate the assembly on the flywheel

20 When the friction plate is centralised, tighten the pressure plate bolts evenly and in a diagonal sequence to the specified torque setting **(see illustration)**.
21 Ensure that the clutch friction plate and transmission input shaft splines are clean and dry. Do not apply grease to the splines as they have a special low-friction nickel coating.
22 Refit the transmission as described in Chapter 7.

8 Clutch release bearing – removal, inspection and refitting

Removal

1 For access to the clutch release bearing, the transmission must be removed as described in Chapter 7.
2 The clutch release bearing is part of

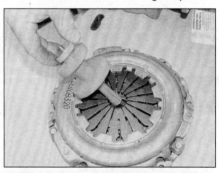

7.19b... fit the tool and tighten it to clamp the friction plate to the pressure plate...

7.20 Hold the flywheel stationary whilst tightening the clutch cover bolts

the slave cylinder assembly and cannot be renewed separately. Remove the slave cylinder as described in Section 3.

Inspection

3 Note that it is often considered worthwhile to renew the release bearing as a matter of course regardless of its condition, considering the amount of work necessary to access it. Check that the contact surface rotates smoothly and easily, with no sign of noise or roughness, and that the surface itself is smooth and unworn, with no signs of cracks, pitting or scoring. If there is any doubt about its condition, the bearing (and slave cylinder) must be renewed.

Refitting

4 Refit the slave cylinder as described in Section 3.
5 Refit the transmission with reference to Chapter 7.

Chapter 7
Manual transmission

Contents

Degrees of difficulty

Easy, suitable for novice with little experience	Fairly easy, suitable for beginner with some experience	Fairly difficult, suitable for competent DIY mechanic	Difficult, suitable for experienced DIY mechanic	Very difficult, suitable for expert DIY or professional

Specifications

General

Type	Manual, five or six forward gears and reverse. Synchromesh on all gears

Designation:
1.9 litre engines:	
F9Q 762	PK5
F9Q 760	PK6
2.0 litre engines	PF6

Note: *Transmission code is stamped on a plate attached to the transmission (see Section 1).*

Lubrication

Type	See *Lubricants and fluids* on page 0•17
Capacity	See Chapter 1

Torque wrench settings

	Nm	lbf ft
Engine-to-transmission bolts/nuts	44	32
Engine/transmission mountings	See the relevant part of Chapter 2	
Roadwheels bolts	140	103
Transmission drain plug:		
PK5 and PK6	24	18
PF6	18	13
Transmission filler plug	2	1.5
Transmission mounting:		
Mounting bracket-to-transmission bolts	85	63
Mounting stud nut	60	44
Rubber mounting bracket-to-body bolts	85	63

1 General information

The transmission is contained in a cast-aluminium alloy casing bolted to the engine's left-hand end, and consists of the gearbox and final drive differential – often called a transaxle. Throughout this Chapter, the operations often differ depending on which type of transmission is fitted. The transmission type is stamped on an identification plate which is attached to the transmission, either on the top of the casing or on the underside.

Drive is transmitted from the crankshaft via the clutch to the input shaft, which has a splined extension to accept the clutch friction plate, and rotates in sealed ball-bearings. From the input shaft, drive is transmitted to the output shaft, which rotates in a roller bearing at its right-hand end, and a sealed ball-bearing at its left-hand end. From the output shaft, the drive is transmitted to the differential crownwheel, which rotates with the differential case and planetary gears, thus driving the sun gears and driveshafts. The rotation of the planetary gears on their shaft allows the inner roadwheel to rotate at a slower speed than the outer roadwheel when the vehicle is cornering.

The input and output shafts are arranged side-by-side, parallel to the crankshaft and driveshafts, so that their gear pinion teeth are in constant mesh. In the neutral position, the output shaft gear pinions rotate freely, so that drive cannot be transmitted to the crownwheel.

The gear selection is via a floor-mounted lever and dual cable arrangement. The transmission selector rod(s) causes the appropriate selector fork to move its respective synchro-sleeve along the shaft to lock the gear pinion to the synchro-hub. Since the synchro-hubs are splined to the output shaft, this locks the pinion to the shaft

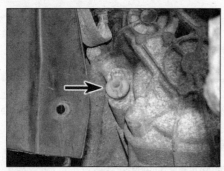

2.3a The oil filler plug (arrowed) is located at the left-hand end of the transmission casing

2.3b Oil drain plug and sealing washer

so that drive can be transmitted. To ensure that gearchanging can be made quickly and quietly, a synchromesh system is fitted to all forward gears, consisting of baulk rings and spring-loaded fingers, as well as the gear pinions and synchro-hubs. The synchromesh cones are formed on the mating faces of the baulk rings and gear pinions.

2 Transmission – draining and refilling

Note: *See Chapter 1 for checking the oil level in the transmission.*

1 This operation is much quicker and more efficient if the vehicle is first taken on a journey of sufficient length to warm the engine/transmission up to operating temperature.
2 Park the vehicle on level ground, switch off

3.1 Prise up the gearchange lever gaiter

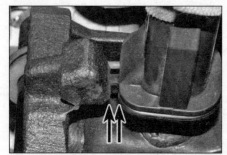

3.2 The clearance between the gear lever and the reverse gear blocker (arrowed) should be 3.3 to 4.3 mm

the ignition and apply the handbrake firmly. For improved access, jack up the front of the vehicle and support it on axle stands (see *Jacking and vehicle support*). The vehicle must be lowered to the ground and level, to ensure accuracy, when refilling and checking the oil level.
3 Undo the retaining screws and remove the undertray from beneath the engine/transmission. Remove all dirt from around the drain and filler/level plugs then unscrew from the left-hand end of the transmission. Renew the sealing washer **(see illustrations)**.
4 Position a suitable container under the drain plug situated on the base of the transmission housing.
5 Unscrew the drain plug and allow the oil to drain completely into the container. If the oil is hot, take precautions against scalding. Clean both the filler/level and the drain plugs, being especially careful to wipe any metallic particles off the magnetic inserts. Discard the original sealing washers; they should be renewed whenever they are disturbed.
6 When the oil has finished draining, clean the drain plug threads and those of the transmission casing, fit a new sealing washer and refit the drain plug, tightening it to the specified torque. It the vehicle was raised for the draining operation, now lower it to the ground. Where necessary, refit the undertray to the vehicle.
7 Refilling the transmission is an extremely awkward operation. Above all, allow plenty of time for the oil level to settle properly before checking it. Note that the vehicle must be parked on flat level ground when checking the oil level.

3.5 Prise up the securing clip (arrowed) from the end of the cable

8 Refill the transmission with the exact amount of the specified type of oil (see *Weekly checks*) then check the oil level as described in Chapter 1. When the level is correct, refit the filler or filler level plug with a new sealing washer and tighten securely.
Note: *If the correct amount was poured into the transmission and a large amount flows out on checking the level, refit the filler or filler/level plug and take the vehicle on a short journey so that the new oil is distributed fully around the transmission components, then check the level again on your return.*

3 Gearchange mechanism – adjustment

Gear control adjustment

1 If a stiff, sloppy or imprecise gearchange leads you to suspect that a fault exists within the mechanism, first unclip the gear lever gaiter and pull it upwards to release it from the centre console **(see illustration)**.
2 With the gear lever at rest in the neutral position, a spacer (strip of metal or similar) will be required to check the clearance between the gear lever and the reverse gear blocker **(see illustration)**.
3 The clearance should be between 3.3 mm and 4.3 mm. If the clearance is not correct, adjust the gear control cable at the transmission end.

Gear control cable adjustment

4 Open the bonnet and locate the gear control cable linkage on the top of the transmission.
5 Release the securing clip from the end of the cable **(see illustration)**, then insert a 4.0 mm thickness spacer (strip of metal or similar) in between the gear lever and the reverse gear blocker inside the vehicle.
6 Making sure the gear lever and gear linkage on the transmission are still both in the neutral position, refit the clip back into the transmission end of the gear control cable.
7 Remove the thickness gauge, then move the gear lever through all the gears to check that they can all be selected.
8 Use the thickness gauge to check that the clearance is within the tolerance specified.
9 If clearance is correct, refit the gear lever gaiter back in place in the centre console.
10 If this does not cure the fault, check the selector cables and lever for any wear or damage.

4 Gearchange cables – removal and refitting

Removal

1 Working inside the vehicle, remove the centre console as described in Chapter 11.
2 Remove the foam soundproofing (where fitted)

4.4a To disconnect the left-hand cable, depress the release button

4.4b The right-hand cable simply prises up from the lever stud

4.5 Slide up the retaining clips (arrowed)

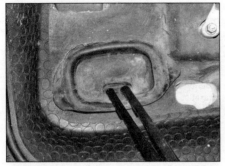

4.6a Working under the centre console, peel up the edges of the cable grommet...

4.6b... and undo the retaining nuts (arrowed)

4.7 Undo the nuts (arrowed) securing the gearchange assembly

from around the gear lever, and then ensure that the gear lever is in the neutral position.

3 To improve access to the top of the transmission on 2.0 litre models, remove the air cleaner housing and intake ducts as described in Chapter 4A. Remove the cover

from the top of the transmission (where fitted).
4 To release the cables from their operating levers on top of the transmission, depress the release button (where applicable), then carefully prise the cable balljoints from the studs on the levers (see illustrations).

5 Work back along the cables to the clips that secure them into the mounting bracket on the transmission. Release the retaining clips and lift the cables from the bracket (see illustration).
6 Undo the 2 nuts securing the cable grommet assembly to the floor (see illustrations).
7 Undo the nuts securing the gearchange lever assembly to the facia (see illustration).
8 Undo the fasteners securing the 'shield' around the gearchange lever assembly (see illustration).
9 Carefully prise the cable balljoints from the studs on the levers, slide out the clips and detach the outer cables from the brackets (see illustrations).

Refitting

10 Refitting is a reversal of removal, noting that an assistant will be required to feed the cables into the engine compartment. If necessary, check the cable adjustment as described in Section 3.

4.8 Undo the fasteners securing the 'shield'

4.9a Slide up the outer cable retaining clips...

5 Oil seals – renewal

Right-hand driveshaft oil seal

1 Apply the handbrake, then jack up the front of the vehicle and support it on axle stands (see *Jacking and vehicle support*). Remove the roadwheel.
2 Drain the transmission oil (see Section 2).
3 Referring to Chapter 8, remove the drive-shaft.

4.9b... prise the end of the cables from the ball studs...

4.9c... and disconnect them from the gearchange assembly

5.6 Carefully lever the oil seal from the casing

4 Wipe clean the area around the differential oil seal.
5 Measure the seal's fitted depth below the casing edge. This is necessary to determine the correct fitted position of the new oil seal if the special Vauxhall or Renault fitting tool is not being used.
6 Free the old oil seal, either by levering it out, or, using a small drift to tap the outer edge of the seal inwards so that the opposite edge of the seal tilts out of the casing **(see illustration)**. A pair of pliers or grips can then be used to pull out the oil seal. Take care not to damage the splines of the differential side gear.
7 Wipe clean the oil seal seating in the casing. Press the new seal squarely into the transmission; making sure its sealing lip is facing inwards, until it is positioned at the same depth as the original was prior to removal **(see illustration)**. If necessary the seal can be tapped into position using a piece of metal tube or a socket, which bears only on the hard outer edge of the seal. **Note:** *The new seal may have a protective sleeve fitted; leave this in place until the driveshaft is fitted.*
8 Carefully refit the driveshaft assembly as described in Chapter 8. With the driveshaft in place slide the protective sleeve from inside the oil seal and clip it into position in the groove in the driveshaft. **Note:** *If there is no groove in the driveshaft for the protective sleeve to locate, then the protective sleeve will need to be cut from the shaft.*
9 Refill the transmission with oil as described in Section 2.

6.1 The reversing light switch (arrowed) is located on the top of the transmission casing

5.7 Drive the seal in using a socket that bears only on the hard, outer edge

10 Refit the roadwheel and lower the vehicle to the ground and tighten the roadwheel bolts to the specified torque.

Left-hand driveshaft oil seal

PK5 and PK6 transmissions

11 On the left-hand side of the transmission there is no oil seal. The driveshaft gaiter forms the seal. If oil is leaking from the left-hand driveshaft to the transmission joint, renew the gaiter as described in Chapter 8.

PF6 transmission

12 Refer to paragraphs 1 to 10.

Input shaft oil seal

13 Remove the transmission as described in Section 7.
14 Slacken and remove the retaining bolts and remove the clutch slave cylinder/release bearing as described in Chapter 6.
15 Note the correct fitted position of the seal then carefully punch or drill two small holes opposite each other in the oil seal. Screw a self-tapping screw into each, and pull on the screws with pliers to extract the seal.

 Warning: Take care not to damage or scratch the shaft or seal surface on removal.

16 Clean the seal housing, and polish off any burrs or raised edges, which may have caused the seal to fail in the first place.
17 Wrap tape around the end of the input shaft and slide the new seal into position, making sure its sealing lip is facing inwards. Press the seal squarely into the transmission

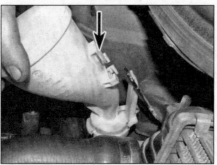

7.3 Release the clip (arrowed) and slide the oil filler funnel upwards from the bracket

housing, if necessary, using a suitable tubular drift which bears only on the hard outer edge of the seal.
18 Remove the tape from the input shaft then refit the slave cylinder/release bearing assembly as described in Chapter 6.
19 Refit the transmission (see Section 7).

6 Reversing light switch – testing, removal and refitting

Testing

1 The reversing light circuit is controlled by a plunger-type switch, screwed into the top of the transmission casing **(see illustration)**. If a fault develops in the circuit, first ensure that the circuit fuse has not blown.
2 To test the switch, disconnect the wiring connector, and use a multimeter (set to the resistance function) or a battery-and-bulb test circuit to check that there is continuity between the switch terminals only when reverse gear is selected. If this is not the case, and there are no obvious breaks or other damage to the wires, the switch is faulty, and must be renewed.

Removal

3 To improve access to the top of the transmission on 2.0 litre models, remove the air cleaner and intake ducts as described in Chapter 4A, as necessary.
4 Disconnect the wiring connector **(see illustration 6.1)**, and then unscrew it from the transmission casing along with its sealing washer.

Refitting

5 Fit a new sealing washer to the switch, then screw it back into the transmission housing and tighten it securely.
6 Reconnect the wiring connector, and test the operation of the circuit.

7 Transmission – removal and refitting

Note: *This Section describes the removal of the transmission leaving the engine in position in the car. Alternatively, the engine and transmission can be removed together, as described in Chapter 2C, and then separated on the bench.*

Removal

1 Disconnect the battery negative lead as described in Chapter 5.

1.9 litre models

2 Release the clips and remove the air hose from the intercooler to the intake manifold.
3 Release the clip and remove the engine oil filler funnel **(see illustration)**.
4 Release the clip, disconnect the intercooler intake air hose, and move it to one side.

5 Unclip the upper insulation cover from the transmission (where fitted).

2.0 litre models

6 Remove the air cleaner assembly as described in Section 2.

7 Pull the charge pressure sensor and bracket from the support frame (see illustration). Release the wiring harness from the frame as the sensor is withdrawn.

8 Unclip the fuel pipe, mass airflow sensor wiring harness, and coolant heater harness (where fitted) from the support frame.

9 Undo the bolt and detach the cooler heater assembly (where fitted) from the support frame (see illustration).

10 Undo the 2 nuts and 2 bolts, and remove the support frame from the engine compartment (see illustrations).

11 Release the clamp and remove the turbocharger intake hose. Unclip the breather hose and vacuum hose as the turbocharger hose is withdrawn.

12 Undo the bolt/nuts and remove the heater blower housing from the engine compartment bulkhead. Disconnect any wiring plugs as the housing is removed (see illustrations).

13 Release the clips, undo the support bracket bolts and remove the outlet and intake pipes from the turbocharger to the intercooler.

All models

14 Disconnect the reversing light switch (see illustration 6.1).

15 Where applicable, disconnect the speed sensor wiring plug from the transmission casing.

16 Release the clip and disconnect the breather hose from the transmission casing.

17 Unclip the wiring harness, then undo the bolts and remove the harness bracket from top of the transmission.

18 Prise out the clip a little, then disconnect the clutch pressure pipe from the connection on the transmission. Plug the openings to prevent contamination. Be prepared for fluid spillage.

19 Disconnect the gearchange cables as described in Section 4.

20 Undo the bolts securing the power steering pipe support brackets to the transmission.

21 With reference to Chapter 8, slacken the driveshaft retaining nuts at each wheel hub.

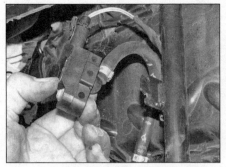
7.7 Pull the charge pressure sensor upwards from the support frame

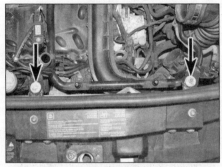
7.10a The support frame is secured by 2 bolts (arrowed) at the front edge...

22 On 1.9 litre models, disconnect the wiring plug, then undo the bolt and remove the crankshaft position sensor from the casing (see illustration).

23 Remove front subframe as described in Chapter 10.

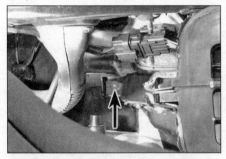
7.12a The heater blower housing is secured by a nut (arrowed) on the right-hand side...

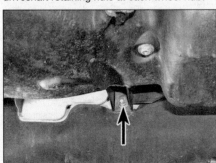
7.12c... a nut (arrowed) underneath...

7.12d... and a bolt (arrowed) at the right-hand, upper edge

7.9 Undo the bolt (arrowed) securing the coolant heater assembly

7.10b... and 2 nuts (arrowed) at the engine compartment bulkhead

24 On 1.9 litre models, disconnect the earth lead from the catalytic converter bracket, then undo the nut/bolt securing the starter and transmission to the bracket, undo the remaining bolts and move the starter to the side away from the transmission.

7.12b... a nut (arrowed) on the left-hand side...

7.22 On 1.9 litre models, the crankshaft position sensor is located on the front face of the transmission casing (arrowed)

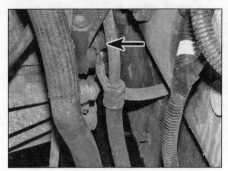

7.28 Undo the bolt (arrowed) and detach the earth strap from the end of the transmission

25 Drain the transmission oil as described in Section 2.
26 Remove both driveshafts as described in Chapter 8.
27 Undo the retaining bolt securing the power steering pipes to the end of the transmission. Position the pipes clear of the transmission so they will not hinder removal.
28 Where applicable, unscrew the bolt securing the wiring harness earth lead to the transmission casing **(see illustration)**.
29 Place a jack with a block of wood beneath the engine, to take the weight of the engine. Alternatively, attach a hoist or support bar to the engine lifting eyes to take the engine weight. Also place a trolley jack and block of wood beneath the transmission, and raise the jack to take the weight of the transmission.
30 With the weight of the transmission now supported, the engine/transmission left-hand mounting must be unscrewed and removed **(see illustration)**.
31 Unscrew the bolts and detach the left-hand mounting bracket from the transmission casing.
32 With the jack positioned beneath the transmission taking the weight, slacken and remove the remaining nuts and bolts securing the transmission housing to the engine. Note that on 2.0 litre models, the upper mounting studs must be unscrewed from the engine block. Work your way around the circumference of the transmission housing, noting the correct fitted positions of each nut/bolt, and the necessary brackets, as they are removed (this will be useful as a reference on refitting). Make a final check that all components have been disconnected, and are positioned clear of the transmission so that they will not hinder the removal procedure.
33 With the nuts/bolts removed, move the

7.30 Undo the bolts/nut (arrowed) and remove the left-hand engine/ transmission mounting

trolley jack and transmission to the left, to free it from its locating dowels. Once the transmission is free, lower the jack and manoeuvre the unit out from under the car. Remove the locating dowels from the transmission or engine if they are loose, and keep them in a safe place.

Refitting

34 The transmission is refitted by a reversal of the removal procedure, bearing in mind the following points:
a) Ensure that the clutch friction plate and transmission input shaft splines are clean and dry. Do not apply grease to the splines as they have a special low-friction nickel coating.
b) Ensure that the locating dowels are correctly positioned prior to installation and make sure the clutch release mechanism components are correctly fitted (see Chapter 6).
c) Tighten all nuts and bolts to the specified torque (where given).
d) Refit the driveshafts as described in Chapter 8.
e) Bleed the clutch system as described in Chapter 6.
f) Check the gearchange and where applicable adjust the mechanism as described in Section 3.
g) On completion, refill the transmission with the specified type and quantity of lubricant, as described in Section 2.

8 Transmission overhaul – general information

Overhauling a manual transmission is a

difficult and involved job for the DIY home mechanic. In addition to dismantling and reassembling many small parts, clearances must be precisely measured and, if necessary, changed by selecting shims and spacers. Internal transmission components are also often difficult to obtain, and in many instances, extremely expensive. Because of this, if the transmission develops a fault or becomes noisy, the best course of action is to have the unit overhauled by a specialist repairer, or to obtain an exchange reconditioned unit.

Nevertheless, it is not impossible for the more experienced mechanic to overhaul the transmission, provided the special tools are available, and the job is done in a deliberate step-by-step manner, so that nothing is overlooked.

The tools necessary for an overhaul include internal and external circlip pliers, bearing pullers, a slide hammer, a set of pin punches, a dial test indicator, and possibly a hydraulic press. In addition, a large, sturdy workbench and a vice will be required.

During dismantling of the transmission, make careful notes of how each component is fitted, to make reassembly easier and more accurate.

Before dismantling the transmission, it will help if you have some idea what area is malfunctioning. Certain problems can be closely related to specific areas in the transmission, which can make component examination and renewal easier. Refer to the *Fault finding* Section at the end of this manual for more information.

9 Vehicle speed sensor – removal and refitting

Note: *A vehicle speed sensor is only fitted to non-ABS models.*
1 Raise the front of the vehicle and support it securely on axle stands (see *Jacking and vehicle support*). Undo the fasteners and remove the engine/transmission undertray (where fitted).
2 The sensor is located at the top of the differential housing at the rear of the transmission. Disconnect the sensor wiring plug.
3 Undo the bolt and pull the sensor from the differential housing.
4 Refitting is a reversal of removal. Tighten the sensor securely.

Chapter 8
Driveshafts

Contents

Degrees of difficulty

Easy, suitable for novice with little experience	Fairly easy, suitable for beginner with some experience	Fairly difficult, suitable for competent DIY mechanic	Difficult, suitable for experienced DIY mechanic	Very difficult, suitable for expert DIY or professional

Specifications

General
Type . . . . Steel shafts with constant velocity (CV) joint at each end
Lubrication . . . . Special grease supplied in sachets with gaiter kits – joints are otherwise prepacked with grease, and sealed

Torque wrench settings

	Nm	lbf ft
Driveshaft nut*	280	207
Driveshaft support bearing bolts (right-hand side)	30	22
Left-hand driveshaft inner gaiter retaining plate bolts (1.9 litre models)	25	18
Roadwheel bolts	140	103
Suspension strut-to-hub carrier nuts*	180	133
Track rod end balljoint nut*	37	27

* Use new nuts.

1 General information

1 Drive is transmitted from the differential to the front wheels by means of two driveshafts of unequal length. Constant velocity (CV) joints are fitted to each end of the driveshafts, to ensure the smooth and efficient transmission of power at all suspension and steering angles.
2 Both driveshafts are fitted with ball-and-cage-type constant velocity (CV) joints at their outer ends **(see illustration)**. Each joint has an outer member, which is splined at its outer end to accept the wheel hub, and is threaded so that the hub can be fastened by a large nut. The inner joint of the driveshafts are of the spider and yoke-type CV joint.
3 The right-hand driveshaft is a two-piece

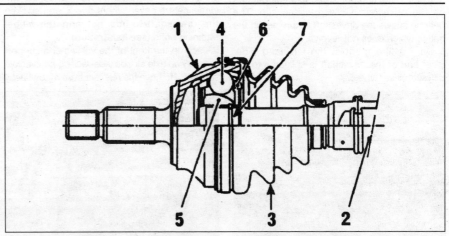

1.2 Section view of the ball-and-cage type constant velocity joint

1 Outer member
2 Driveshaft
3 Gaiter
4 Ball-bearing
5 Inner member
6 Ball cage
7 Circlip

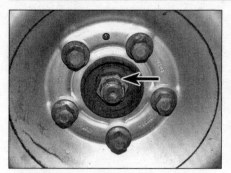

2.1 Slacken the driveshaft nut (arrowed) and the wheel bolts

2.7a Counterhold the track rod end balljoint nut with a Torx key/bit

shaft, which is supported by an intermediate bearing, located at the rear of the cylinder block. The inner section of the right-hand driveshaft is a connecting shaft, which is splined into the differential sunwheel. The inner and outer sections are joined together at the intermediate support bearing by a spider-and-yoke-type CV joint.

4 On 1.9 litre models, the left-hand side, inner end of the driveshaft also engages with a spider-type joint, but the yoke in which the tripod is free to slide is an integral part of the differential sunwheel. The inner gaiter is secured to the transmission casing via a retaining plate and bolts, and to a ball-bearing on the driveshaft via a retaining clip. The bearing allows the driveshaft to turn within the gaiter, which does not revolve.

5 On 2.0 litre models, the left-hand side, inner end of the driveshaft is splined into the differential sunwheel.

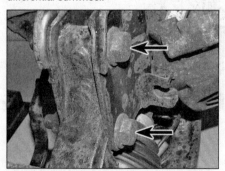

2.8 Note that the hub carrier-to-strut bolts (arrowed) are inserted from the front

2.3 Undo the fasteners (arrowed) and remove the splash shield

2.7b Use a balljoint separator

2 Right-hand driveshaft – removal and refitting

Note: The driveshaft can be removed as a complete assembly, as described in the following paragraphs, or the driveshaft outer section can be removed independently, as described later in this Section.

Complete driveshaft

Removal

1 Apply the handbrake, then prise off the wheel centre cover (where fitted), and slacken the driveshaft-to-hub nut and the wheel retaining bolts **(see illustration)**.

2 Jack up the front of the vehicle and support securely on axle stands (see *Jacking and vehicle support*). Remove the relevant front roadwheel.

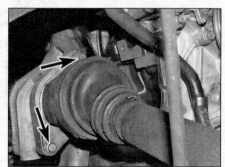

2.9 Undo the intermediate bracket plate bolts (arrowed)

3 Undo the fasteners and remove the engine undertray (where fitted), then undo the bolts and remove the inner splash panel from the wheel arch liner **(see illustration)**. Unclip the washer hose (where applicable).

4 Undo the drain plug and allow the transmission oil to drain into a container – refer to Chapter 7 if necessary. Refit the drain plug with a new washer and tighten it to the specified torque.

5 Completely undo the driveshaft retaining nut from the hub. Recover the washer (where fitted). Discard the nut – a new one must be fitted.

6 Unbolt the brake caliper mounting bracket from the hub carrier as described in Chapter 9. Note that there is no need to disconnect the fluid hose – suspend the caliper from the suspension strut using wire or string, ensuring that the hose is not strained. Unclip the hose from any securing brackets.

7 Slacken and partially unscrew the track rod end balljoint nut (unscrew the nut as far as the end of the threads on the balljoint to prevent damage to the threads as the joint is released), then release the balljoint using a balljoint separator tool **(see illustrations)**. Remove the nut, and discard it – a new nut must be used on refitting. If necessary, use a Torx bit in the balljoint shank to prevent rotation.

8 Undo the nuts, and remove the 2 bolts securing the hub carrier to the suspension strut. Temporarily screw the nut onto the end of the bolts to protect the bolt threads, and then tap the bolts from the hub carrier, using a soft-faced hammer **(see illustration)**. Noting the direction the bolts are fitted (from the front), withdraw the bolts.

9 Working at the inner end of the driveshaft, unscrew the two bolts securing the driveshaft inner section retaining plate to the engine intermediate mounting bracket/bearing carrier **(see illustration)**.

10 The driveshaft must now be released from the hub carrier. It should be possible to release the driveshaft by tapping the end of the driveshaft using a soft-faced hammer, or a hammer and a soft metal drift – **do not** strike the end of the driveshaft hard, as this may cause damage to the joints. If the driveshaft is stuck, use a suitable puller to pull the hub from the shaft **(see illustration)**. Note that

2.10 If necessary, use a puller to force the driveshaft coupling from the hub

Vauxhall/Renault special tool No KM-6218 may be available for this purpose.

11 Pivot the hub carrier downwards as necessary until the end of the driveshaft can be withdrawn from the hub **(see illustration).**

12 Place a container beneath the transmission end of the driveshaft to catch escaping oil/fluid, which may be released as the end of the driveshaft, is withdrawn.

13 Pull the driveshaft from the transmission and the engine mounting bracket/bearing carrier. If necessary, lever between the inner shaft, outer coupling housing and the intermediate bearing housing.

Refitting

14 Before refitting, thoroughly clean the mating faces of the driveshaft bearing and bearing carrier, making sure it is well-greased. Check the condition of the oil seal contact face on the driveshaft – if the driveshaft surface is excessively worn or deeply grooved, the driveshaft inner section should be renewed (as described later in this Section).

15 It is recommended that the oil seal is renewed before refitting the driveshaft (see Chapter 7).

16 Thoroughly clean the driveshaft splines, and the apertures in the transmission and hub assembly. Apply some Molykote BR2 type of grease to the driveshaft inner splines and shoulders. Check that all gaiter clips are securely fastened.

17 Slide the inner end of the driveshaft into position in the transmission, and engage the intermediate bearing with the engine mounting bracket/bearing carrier, then secure with the retaining plate, and securely tighten the bolts.

18 Engage the outer end of the driveshaft with the hub assembly.

19 Refit the lower suspension strut-to-hub carrier bolt (noting that the bolts fits from the front of the vehicle), and screw a new nut onto the bolt. Do not screw the nut fully onto the bolt at this stage.

20 Screw the new driveshaft nut onto the end of the driveshaft as far as possible by hand, and then tighten the nut until the end of the driveshaft is fully engaged with the hub. Do not fully tighten the nut at this stage.

21 Refit the upper suspension strut-to-hub carrier bolt (noting that the bolts fits from the front of the vehicle), and screw a new nut onto the bolt. Tap the bolts into position in the hub carrier (until the splines are engaged and the underside of the bolt head touches the suspension strut, then tighten the upper and lower suspension strut-to-hub carrier nuts to the specified torque.

22 Reconnect the track rod end to the hub carrier, and tighten a new balljoint nut to the specified torque.

23 Refit the brake caliper, with reference to Chapter 9.

24 Refit the roadwheel, but do not fully tighten the bolts at this stage.

25 Refit the inner splash panel and engine/transmission undertray.

2.11 Withdraw the end of the driveshaft from the hub

26 Lower the vehicle to the ground and tighten the roadwheel bolts to the specified torque.

27 Tighten the driveshaft retaining nut to the specified torque, and refit the wheel cover (where applicable).

28 On completion, check the transmission oil/fluid level using the information in Chapter 1 or Chapter 7.

Driveshaft outer section

Note: *A sachet of the appropriate grease and new retaining clip (available from a Vauxhall or Renault dealer) will be required to pack the driveshaft joint on refitting. Check parts availability before commencing work.*

Removal

29 Remove the driveshaft as previously described in this Section.

30 Cut the clips securing the rubber gaiter to the centre joint housing, and slide the housing from the end of the outer driveshaft. Carefully withdraw the driveshaft outer section spider joint from the driveshaft yoke inner section. Be prepared to hold the rollers in place, otherwise they may fall off the tripod ends as the driveshaft outer section is withdrawn. If necessary, secure the rollers in place using tape. The rollers are matched to the tripod stems, and it is important that they are not interchanged. Remove the grease from the housing and gaiter.

31 Use circlip pliers to remove the retaining circlip, and use a puller to remove the spider and bearings from the end of the driveshaft.

32 Pull the rubber gaiter from the outer shaft.

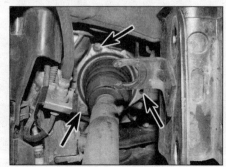

3.2 Undo the gaiter retaining plate bolts (arrowed)

Refitting

33 Place the inner retaining clip onto the small diameter of the new gaiter, then slide the gaiter to the driveshaft, ensuring its smaller diameter locates correctly.

34 Slide the spider/bearing assembly on the end of the driveshaft, ensuring the chamfered inner edge of the spider is facing towards the driveshaft (towards the roadwheel). If necessary, tap it into place using a suitable tubular drift and hammer. Secure it in place with a new circlip.

35 Wipe clean the driveshaft inner section and the joint spider, then pack about half of the sachet of new grease into the inner yoke/housing and around the joint spider. Insert the driveshaft outer section joint spider into the driveshaft inner section yoke, keeping the driveshaft horizontal as far as possible.

36 Pack the remainder of the grease evenly into the joint gaiter. Slide the gaiter over the end of the driveshaft inner section, and then secure the gaiter with a new retaining clip.

37 Refit the driveshaft as previously described.

3 Left-hand driveshaft – removal and refitting

Removal

1 Proceed as described in Section 2, paragraphs 1 to 8 and paragraphs 10 to 12.

1.9 litre models

2 Working at the transmission end of the driveshaft, unscrew the three bolts securing the gaiter retaining plate to the transmission casing **(see illustration)**.

3 Pull the driveshaft from the transmission, and then withdraw the assembly from under the vehicle.

2.0 litre models

4 Using a suitable lever/bar, carefully prise the driveshaft from the transmission. Be prepared for fluid spillage.

Refitting

Note: *If a new driveshaft is being fitted, it may be supplied with a protective cardboard cover fitted over the outer driveshaft gaiter. In this case, do not remove the cover until the completion of the refitting procedure.*

1.9 litre models

5 Wipe clean the side of the transmission. Insert the driveshaft joint spider into the sunwheel yoke, keeping the driveshaft horizontal as far as possible.

6 Align the gaiter retaining plate with its bolt holes in the transmission casing, then refit the retaining plate bolts, and tighten them to the specified torque. Ensure the gaiter is not twisted.

2.0 litre models

7 It is recommended that the oil seal is

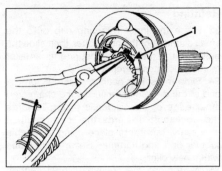

4.4 Open the circlip (1) and tap the exposed face of the ball hub (2) to free the joint

renewed before refitting the driveshaft (see Chapter 7).

8 Thoroughly clean the driveshaft splines, and the apertures in the transmission and hub assembly. Apply some Molykote BR2 type of grease to the driveshaft inner splines and shoulders. Check that all gaiter clips are securely fastened.

9 Slide the inner end of the driveshaft into position in the transmission, taking great care not to damage the driveshaft seals.

All models

10 Engage the outer end of the driveshaft with the hub assembly.

11 Proceed as described in Section 2, paragraphs 18 to 28.

4 Driveshaft rubber gaiters – renewal

Note: *Check with your local dealer or motor factors, to ensure that the appropriate gaiter repair kit is available before starting work.*

Outer joint

1 Remove the driveshaft as described in Section 2 or 3, as applicable.

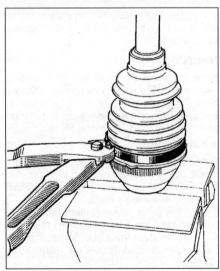

4.9 Securing the gaiter retaining clip using crimping pliers

2 Cut through the gaiter retaining clips, then slide the gaiter down the shaft to expose the outer constant velocity joint.

3 Scoop out as much grease as possible from the joint.

4 Using circlip pliers, expand the joint internal circlip **(see illustration)**. At the same time, tap the exposed face of the ball hub with a mallet to separate the joint from the driveshaft. Slide off the gaiter.

5 With the constant velocity joint removed from the driveshaft, clean the joint using paraffin, or a suitable solvent, and dry it thoroughly. Carry out a visual inspection of the joint.

6 Move the inner splined driving member from side-to-side, to expose each ball in turn at the top of its track. Examine the balls for cracks, flat spots or signs of surface pitting.

7 Inspect the ball tracks on the inner and outer members. If the tracks have widened, the balls will no longer be a tight fit. At the same time, check the ball cage windows for wear or cracking between the windows.

8 If any of the constant velocity joint components are found to be worn or damaged, it will be necessary to renew the joint (check on the availability of components with a Vauxhall or Renault dealer). If the joint is in satisfactory condition, obtain a repair kit from your dealer consisting of a new gaiter, rubber collar, clips, and the correct type and quantity of grease.

9 Tape over the splines on the end of the driveshaft, then slide the smaller retaining clip and the gaiter onto the shaft. Locate the inner end of the gaiter in the groove on the driveshaft, and secure it in position with the retaining clip. A special tool is available to compress the retaining clip, but a satisfactory result can be achieved by carefully using a pair of side-cutters – take care not to cut the clip **(see illustration)**.

10 Remove the tape, then slide the constant velocity joint coupling onto the driveshaft until the internal circlip locates in the driveshaft groove.

11 Check that the circlip holds the joint securely on the driveshaft, then pack the joint with the grease supplied. Work the grease well into the ball tracks, and fill the gaiter with any excess.

12 Locate the outer lip of the gaiter in the

groove on the joint outer member. With the coupling aligned with the driveshaft, lift the lip of the gaiter to equalise the air pressure. Secure the gaiter in position with the large retaining clip.

13 Check that the constant velocity joint moves freely in all directions, then refit the driveshaft to the vehicle as described in Section 2 or 3, as applicable.

Right-hand inner joint

14 Remove the right-hand driveshaft as described in Section 2.

15 Using a pair of snips, cut through the gaiter securing clips (note that it may be necessary to saw through the larger clip).

16 Slide back the gaiter, and wipe out as much grease as possible from the joint.

17 Slide the outer member off the end of the spider-tripod joint. Be prepared to hold the rollers in place, otherwise they may fall off the tripod ends as the outer member is withdrawn. If necessary, secure the rollers in place using tape after removal of the outer member. The rollers are matched to the tripod stems, and it is important that they are not interchanged.

18 The tripod joint can now be removed. Remove the circlip securing the tripod to the end of the driveshaft **(see illustrations)**. Make alignment marks between the tripod and the shaft for use when refitting.

19 If the tripod is tight, draw the tripod off the driveshaft end using a puller. Ensure that the legs of the puller are located behind the tripod inner member and do not contact the joint rollers. Alternatively, support the tripod inner member, and press the shaft out using a hydraulic press, again ensuring that no load is applied to the joint rollers.

20 With the joint spider removed, slide the gaiter and inner retaining collar off the end of the driveshaft.

21 Wipe clean the joint components, taking care not to remove the alignment marks made on dismantling. **Do not** use paraffin or other solvents to clean this type of joint.

22 Examine the tripod joint, rollers and outer member for any signs of scoring or wear. Check that the rollers move smoothly on the tripod stems. If wear is evident, the tripod joint and roller assembly can be renewed, but it is

4.18a Remove the circlip...

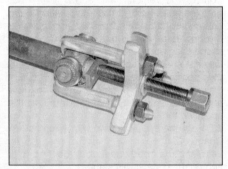

4.18b ... and withdraw the tripod, using a puller

4.23 Align the small diameter of the gaiter with the locating groove in the driveshaft (arrowed)

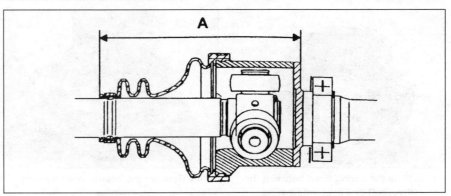

4.29 Slide the gaiter until the dimension is as shown

A = 156 ± 1.0 mm

not possible to obtain a new outer member (check with a dealer on the availability of spares). Obtain a repair kit consisting of a gaiter, retaining clip, circlip, and the correct type and amount of special grease.

23 Tape over the driveshaft splines, and slide the gaiter (complete with the retaining clips) onto the driveshaft **(see illustration)**.

24 Remove the tape, then, aligning the marks made on dismantling, engage the tripod joint with the driveshaft splines. Use a hammer and soft metal drift to tap the joint onto the shaft, taking great care not to damage the driveshaft splines or joint rollers. Alternatively, support the driveshaft, and press the joint into position using a hydraulic press and suitable tubular spacer which bears only on the joint inner member.

25 Secure the tripod joint in position with the circlip, ensuring that it is correctly located in the driveshaft groove.

26 Evenly distribute the special grease contained in the repair kit around the tripod joint and inside the outer member. Pack the gaiter with the remainder of the grease.

27 Slide the outer member into position over the tripod joint.

28 Engage the inside of the gaiter with the groove in the outer member. Using a blunt rod, carefully lift the inner lip of the gaiter to equalise the air pressure.

29 With the rod in position, slide the outer end of the gaiter on the driveshaft until the dimension from the inner machined face of the outer member to the outer end of the driveshaft gaiter is as shown **(see illustration)**. Hold the gaiter in this position and withdraw the rod.

30 Fit the small retaining clip to the outer end of the gaiter. Remove any slack in the gaiter retaining clip by carefully compressing the raised section of the clip. In the absence of the special tool, a pair of side-cutters may be used – take care not to cut the clip.

31 Similarly fit the larger retaining clip to the gaiter and secure the gaiter in position in the outer member groove, as described previously.

32 Check that the constant velocity joint moves freely in all directions, then refit the driveshaft as described in Section 2.

Left-hand inner joint

33 Remove the left-hand driveshaft as described in Section 3.

1.9 litre models

Note: *This procedure can only be carried out using the Vauxhall/Renault special tool (KM-6250). At the time of writing, no measurement was available. Before removing the bearing and gaiter, make a note of the measurement as a guide for refitting.*

34 Using circlip pliers, extract the circlip securing the tripod joint to the driveshaft. Note that on some models, the joint may be staked in position; if so, relieve the stakings using a file.

35 Using a dab of paint or a hammer and punch, mark the tripod joint in relation to the driveshaft, to use as a guide to refitting.

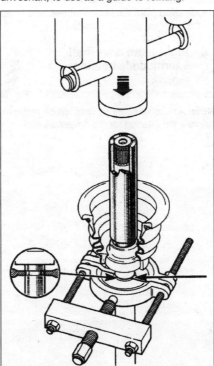

4.41a Press the inner bearing/gaiter onto the driveshaft – inset shows clamp located in driveshaft groove

36 The tripod joint can now be removed. If it is tight, draw the joint off the driveshaft end using a puller. Ensure that the legs of the puller are located behind the joint inner member and do not contact the joint rollers. Alternatively, support the inner member of the tripod joint and press the shaft out of the joint, again ensuring that no load is applied to the joint rollers.

37 The gaiter and bearing assembly is removed in the same way, either by drawing the bearing off the driveshaft, or by pressing the driveshaft out of the bearing. Remove the retaining plate; noting which way round it is fitted. Check the measurement of the fitted position of the bearing as a guide for refitting.

38 Obtain a new gaiter, which is supplied complete with the small bearing.

39 Owing to the lip-type seal used in the bearing, the bearing and gaiter must be pressed into position. If a hammer and tubular drift are used to drive the assembly onto the driveshaft, there is a risk of distorting the seal.

40 Refit the retaining plate to the driveshaft, ensuring that it is fitted the correct way round.

41 Support the driveshaft, and press the gaiter bearing onto the shaft, using the manufacturers' special tool (see note above), which bears only on the bearing inner race. Position the bearing so that the end of the tool is level with the end of the shaft **(see illustrations)**. If no tool is available

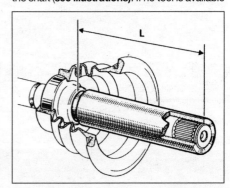

4.41b Fitting dimension for the driveshaft inner bearing/gaiter

L   Length obtained using special tool KM-6250

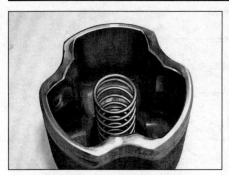

4.45 Note the spring fitted between the driveshaft and the joint housing

6.4 Remove the intermediate bearing circlip

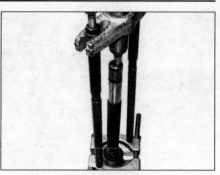

6.5 Extract the intermediate bearing using and long-reach puller

fit the bearing and gaiter to the measurement noted on removal.

42 Align the marks made on dismantling, and engage the tripod joint with the driveshaft splines. Use a hammer and soft metal drift to tap the joint onto the shaft, taking care not to damage the driveshaft splines or joint rollers. Alternatively, support the driveshaft, and press the joint into position using a tubular spacer that bears only on the joint inner member.

43 Secure the tripod joint in position with the circlip, ensuring that it is correctly located in the driveshaft groove.

44 Refit the driveshaft to the vehicle as described in Section 3.

2.0 litre models

45 Proceed as described for the right-hand inner joint in paragraphs 14 to 32 of this Section, noting that there is a spring fitted between the end of the driveshaft and the joint housing **(see illustration)**.

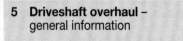

5 Driveshaft overhaul – general information

1 If any of the checks described in the relevant part of Chapter 1 reveal wear in a driveshaft joint, first remove the roadwheel trim or centre cap (as appropriate) and check that the driveshaft retaining nut is still correctly tightened; if in doubt, use a torque wrench to check it. Refit the centre cap or trim, and repeat the check on the other driveshaft.

2 Road test the vehicle, and listen for a metallic clicking from the front as the vehicle is driven slowly in a circle on full-lock. If a clicking noise is heard, this indicates wear in the outer constant velocity joint.

3 If vibration, consistent with roadspeed, is felt through the vehicle when accelerating, there is a possibility of wear in the inner constant velocity joints.

4 Constant velocity joints can be dismantled and inspected for wear as described in Section 4. Check on the availability of components before dismantling a joint.

5 On models with ABS, the sensor ring should be removed from the old driveshaft and fitted to the new one. See Chapter 9.

6 Right-hand driveshaft intermediate bearing – renewal

Note: *A suitable bearing puller will be required to draw the bearing off the driveshaft end.*

1 Remove the right-hand driveshaft as described in Section 2.

2 Check that the bearing outer race rotates smoothly and easily, without any signs of roughness or undue free play between the inner and outer races. If necessary, renew the bearing as follows.

3 If desired, remove the driveshaft inner section, with reference to Section 2.

4 Where applicable, remove the bearing retaining circlip **(see illustration)**.

5 Using a long-reach universal bearing puller, carefully draw the bearing off the inner end of the driveshaft **(see illustration)**.

6 Thoroughly clean the contact faces of the driveshaft and the new bearing.

7 Apply a smear of grease to the inner race of the new bearing, then fit the bearing over the end of the driveshaft.

8 Using hammer and a suitable piece of tubing, which bears only on the bearing inner race, tap the new bearing into position on the driveshaft until it contacts the locating shoulder on the shaft.

9 Where applicable, fit the bearing retaining circlip.

10 Check that the bearing rotates freely, then refit the driveshaft as described in Section 2.

Chapter 9
Braking system

Contents

Degrees of difficulty

Easy, suitable for novice with little experience 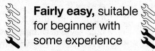	**Fairly easy,** suitable for beginner with some experience	**Fairly difficult,** suitable for competent DIY mechanic	**Difficult,** suitable for experienced DIY mechanic	**Very difficult,** suitable for expert DIY or professional

Specifications

Front brakes
Disc thickness:
  New . . . . 28.0 mm
  Minimum. . . . . 24.0 mm
Disc diameter . . . . 305 mm
Maximum disc run-out . . . . 0.7 mm
Brake pad minimum thickness (including backing plate). . . . . 9.0 mm

Rear disc brakes
Disc thickness:
  New . . . . 12.0 mm
  Minimum. . . . . 10.0 mm
Disc diameter . . . . 280 mm
Maximum disc run-out . . . . 0.7 mm
Brake pad minimum thickness (including backing plate). . . . . 9.0 mm

Torque wrench settings

	Nm	lbf ft
ABS wheel sensor retaining bolts.	8	6
Brake hose unions:		
M10 thread	17	13
M12 thread	19	14
Front brake caliper:		
Guide pin bolts*	35	26
Mounting bracket bolts	107	79
Front brake disc retaining screw	21	15
Handbrake lever mounting bolts	44	32
Master cylinder mounting nuts*	26	19
Rear brake caliper:		
Guide pin bolts*	35	26
Mounting bracket bolts	100	74
Rear brake disc/hub retaining nut*	280	207
Roadwheel bolts.	140	103
Servo unit mounting nuts	22	16

* Do not re-use

1 General information

The braking system is of the servo-assisted, dual-circuit hydraulic type. Under normal circumstances, both circuits operate in unison. However, if there is hydraulic failure in one circuit, full braking force will still be available at two wheels.

All models are fitted with front and rear disc brakes. ABS is available as an option on all models (refer to Section 19 for further information on ABS operation). **Note:** *On models also equipped with Dynamic Stability Control (DSC), the ABS system also operates the traction control side of the system.*

The front ventilated disc brakes are actuated by twin-piston sliding type calipers, which ensure that equal pressure is applied to each disc pad.

All models are fitted with rear solid disc brakes, actuated by single-piston sliding calipers, which incorporate mechanical handbrake mechanisms.

Note: *When servicing any part of the system, work carefully and methodically; also observe scrupulous cleanliness when overhauling any part of the hydraulic system. Always renew components (in axle sets, where applicable) if in doubt about their condition, and use only genuine Vauxhall or Renault parts, or at least those of known good quality. Note the warnings given in 'Safety first!' and at relevant points in this Chapter concerning the dangers of asbestos dust and hydraulic fluid.*

2 Hydraulic system – bleeding

⚠️ **Warning:** *Hydraulic fluid is poisonous; wash off immediately and thoroughly in the case of skin contact, and seek immediate medical advice if any fluid is swallowed or gets into the eyes. Certain types of hydraulic fluid are flammable, and may ignite when allowed into contact with hot components; when servicing any hydraulic system, it is safest to assume that the fluid is flammable, and to take precautions against the risk of fire as though it is petrol that is being handled. Hydraulic fluid is also an effective paint stripper, and will attack plastics; if any is spilt, it should be washed off immediately, using copious quantities of fresh water. Finally, it is hygroscopic (it absorbs moisture from the air) – old fluid may be contaminated and unfit for further use. When topping-up or renewing the fluid, always use the recommended type, and ensure that it comes from a freshly-opened sealed container.*

General

1 The correct operation of any hydraulic system is only possible after removing all air from the components and circuit; this is achieved by bleeding the system.

2 During the bleeding procedure, add only clean, unused hydraulic fluid of the recommended type; never re-use fluid that has already been bled from the system. Ensure that sufficient fluid is available before starting work.

3 If there is any possibility of incorrect fluid being already in the system, the brake components and circuit must be flushed completely with uncontaminated, correct fluid, and new seals should be fitted to the various components.

4 If hydraulic fluid has been lost from the system, or air has entered because of a leak, ensure that the fault is cured before continuing further.

5 Park the vehicle on level ground, switch off the engine and select first or reverse gear, then chock the wheels and release the handbrake.

6 Check that all pipes and hoses are secure, unions tight and bleed screws closed. Clean any dirt from around the bleed screws.

7 Unscrew the master cylinder reservoir cap, and top the master cylinder reservoir up to the MAX level line; refit the cap loosely, and remember to maintain the fluid level at least above the MIN level line throughout the procedure, or there is a risk of further air entering the system.

8 There are a number of one-man, do-it-yourself brake bleeding kits currently available from motor accessory shops. It is recommended that one of these kits is used whenever possible, as they greatly simplify the bleeding operation, and reduce the risk of expelled air and fluid being drawn back into the system. If such a kit is not available, the basic (two-man) method must be used, which is described in detail below.

9 If a kit is to be used, prepare the vehicle as described previously, and follow the kit manufacturer's instructions, as the procedure may vary slightly according to the type being used; generally, they are as outlined below in the relevant sub-section.

10 Whichever method is used, the same sequence must be followed (paragraphs 11 and 12) to ensure the removal of all air from the system.

2.21 Attach the kit to the bleed screw on the caliper

Bleeding sequence

11 If the system has been only partially disconnected, and suitable precautions were taken to minimise fluid loss, it should be necessary only to bleed that part of the system.

12 If the complete system is to be bled, then it should be done working in the following sequence:
  a) Right-hand rear brake.
  b) Left-hand front brake.
  c) Left-hand rear brake.
  d) Right-hand front brake.

Bleeding

Basic (two-man) method

13 Collect a clean glass jar, a suitable length of plastic or rubber tubing which is a tight fit over the bleed screw, and a ring spanner to fit the screw. The help of an assistant will also be required.

14 Remove the dust cap from the first screw in the sequence. Fit the spanner and tube to the screw, place the other end of the tube in the jar, and pour in sufficient fluid to cover the end of the tube.

15 Ensure that the master cylinder reservoir fluid level is maintained at least above the MIN level line throughout the procedure.

16 Have the assistant fully depress the brake pedal several times to build-up pressure, then maintain it on the final downstroke.

17 While pedal pressure is maintained, unscrew the bleed screw (approximately one turn) and allow the compressed fluid and air to flow into the jar. The assistant should maintain pedal pressure, following it down to the floor if necessary, and should not release it until instructed to do so. When the flow stops, tighten the bleed screw again, have the assistant release the pedal slowly, and recheck the reservoir fluid level.

18 Repeat the steps in paragraphs 16 and 17 until the fluid emerging from the bleed screw is free from air bubbles. If the master cylinder has been drained and refilled, and air is being bled from the first screw in the sequence, allow about 5 seconds between cycles for the master cylinder passages to refill.

19 When no more air bubbles appear, tighten the bleed screw securely, remove the tube and spanner, and refit the dust cap. Do not overtighten the bleed screw.

20 Repeat the procedure on the remaining screws in the sequence until all air is removed from the system and the brake pedal feels firm again.

Using a one-way valve kit

21 As their name implies, these kits consist of a length of tubing with a one-way valve fitted, to prevent expelled air and fluid being drawn back into the system; some kits include a translucent container, which can be positioned so that the air bubbles can be more easily seen flowing from the end of the tube **(see illustration)**.

22 The kit is connected to the bleed screw, which is then opened. The user returns to the driver's seat, depresses the brake pedal with a smooth, steady stroke, and slowly releases it; this is repeated until the expelled fluid is clear of air bubbles.

23 Note that these kits simplify work so much that it is easy to forget the master cylinder reservoir fluid level; ensure that this is maintained at least above the MIN level line at all times.

Using a pressure-bleeding kit

24 These kits are usually operated by the reservoir of pressurised air contained in the spare tyre. However, note that it will probably be necessary to reduce the pressure to a lower level than normal; refer to the instructions supplied with the kit. **Note:** *Vauxhall and Renault specify that a pressure of 1 bar (14 psi) on models without ESP, or 2 bar (29 psi) on models with ESP, should not be exceeded.*

25 By connecting a pressurised, fluid-filled container to the master cylinder reservoir, bleeding can be carried out simply by opening each screw in turn (in the specified sequence), and allowing the fluid to flow out until no more air bubbles can be seen in the expelled fluid.

26 This method has the advantage that the large reservoir of fluid provides an additional safeguard against air being drawn into the system during bleeding.

27 Pressure-bleeding is particularly effective when bleeding 'difficult' systems, or when bleeding the complete system at the time of routine fluid renewal.

All methods

28 When bleeding is complete, and firm pedal feel is restored, wash off any spilt fluid, tighten the bleed screws securely, and refit their dust caps.

29 Check the hydraulic fluid level in the master cylinder reservoir, and top-up if necessary (*Weekly checks*).

30 Discard any hydraulic fluid that has been bled from the system; it will not be fit for re-use.

31 Check the feel of the brake pedal. If it feels at all spongy, air must still be present in the system, and further bleeding is required. Failure to bleed satisfactorily after a reasonable repetition of the bleeding procedure may be due to worn master cylinder seals.

3 Hydraulic pipes and hoses – renewal

Note: *Before starting work, refer to the warnings at the beginning of Section 2.*

1 If any pipe or hose is to be renewed, minimise fluid loss by first removing the master cylinder reservoir cap, then tightening it down onto a piece of polythene to obtain an airtight seal. Alternatively, flexible hoses can be sealed, if required, using a proprietary brake hose clamp; metal brake pipe unions can be plugged (if care is taken not to allow dirt into the system) or capped immediately they are disconnected. Place a wad of rag under any union that is to be disconnected, to catch any spilt fluid.

2 If a flexible hose is to be disconnected, unscrew the brake pipe union nut before removing the spring clip which secures the hose to its mounting bracket.

3 To unscrew the union nuts, it is preferable to obtain a brake pipe spanner of the correct size; these are available from most large motor accessory shops. Failing this, a close-fitting open-ended spanner will be required, though if the nuts are tight or corroded, their flats may be rounded-off if the spanner slips. In such a case, using self-locking pliers is often the only way to unscrew a stubborn union, but it follows that the pipe and the damaged nuts must be renewed on reassembly. Always clean a union and surrounding area before disconnecting it. If disconnecting a component with more than one union, make a careful note of the connections before disturbing any of them.

4 If a brake pipe is to be renewed, it can be obtained, cut to length and with the union nuts and end flares in place, from Vauxhall and Renault dealers. All that is then necessary is to bend it to shape, following the line of the original, before fitting it to the car. Alternatively, most motor accessory shops can make up brake pipes from kits, but this requires very careful measurement of the original, to ensure that the new one is of the correct length. The safest answer is usually to take the original to the shop as a pattern.

5 On refitting, do not overtighten the union nuts. It is not necessary to exercise brute force to obtain a sound joint.

6 Ensure that the pipes and hoses are correctly routed, with no kinks, and that they are secured in the clips or brackets provided. After fitting, remove the polythene from the reservoir, and bleed the hydraulic system as described in Section 2. Wash off any spilt fluid, and check carefully for fluid leaks.

4 Front brake pads – renewal

⚠ *Warning: Renew both sets of front brake pads at the same time – never renew the pads on only one wheel, as uneven braking may result. Note that the dust created by wear of the pads may contain asbestos, which is a health hazard. Never blow it out with compressed air, and don't inhale any of it. An approved filtering mask should be worn when working on the brakes. DO NOT use petrol or petroleum-based solvents to clean brake parts; use brake cleaner or methylated spirit only.*

1 Apply the handbrake, then slacken the front roadwheel bolts. Jack up the front of the vehicle and support it on axle stands (see *Jacking and vehicle support*). Remove both front roadwheels.

2 Follow the relevant accompanying photos **(illustrations 4.2a to 4.2q)** for the pad renewal procedure. Be sure to stay in order and read the caption under each illustration, and note the following points:

a) *New pads may have an adhesive foil on the backplates. Remove this prior to installation.*
b) *Gently clean the caliper guide surfaces, and apply a little brake assembly grease.*
c) *When pushing the caliper piston back to accommodate new pads, keep a close eye on the fluid level in the reservoir.*

3 Depress the brake pedal repeatedly, until the pads are pressed into firm contact with the brake disc, and normal (non-assisted) pedal pressure is restored.

4 Repeat the above procedure on the remaining front brake caliper.

5 Apply the little anti-seize grease to the hub surface, then refit the roadwheels, lower the vehicle to the ground and tighten the roadwheel bolts to the specified torque.

6 Check the hydraulic fluid level as described in *Weekly checks*.

Caution: New pads will not give full braking efficiency until they have bedded-in. Be prepared for this, and avoid hard braking as far as possible for the first hundred miles or so after pad renewal.

4.2a If there's a wear/rust lip around the disc, use a screwdriver to force the inner pad away from the disc a little

4.2b Undo the caliper lower guide pin bolt...

4.2c... unclip the flexible brake hose from the bracket...

4.2d... and pivot the caliper upwards

4.2e Remove the outer pad...

4.2f... and the inner pad

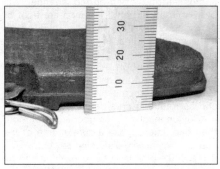

4.2g Measure the thickness of the pad (including the backing plate) – if it's less than 9.0 mm, renew all 4 pads

4.2h Use brake cleaner and a soft brush to clean the caliper/bracket mounting surfaces

4.2i If new pads are to be fitted, push the pistons back into the caliper body, using a retraction tool, and a block of wood to prevent the other piston from being ejected. Keep an eye on the fluid level whilst pushing the pistons back!

4.2j Apply a little high-temperature anti-seize grease to the pad backing plate...

4.2k... and mounting edges. Take care not to get any on the friction material

4.2l Fit the inner pad to the bracket. Ensure the friction material is against the disc surface

4.2m Fit the outer pad to the bracket

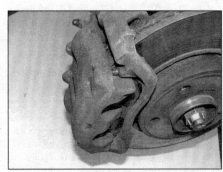

4.2n Pivot the caliper down into place...

4.2o... fit the new guide pin bolt...

4.2p... and tighten it to the specified torque

4.2q Press the brake hose back into the bracket

5 Rear brake pads – renewal

⚠️ *Warning: Renew both sets of rear brake pads at the same time – never renew the pads on only one wheel, as uneven braking may result. Note that the dust created by wear of the pads may contain asbestos, which is a health hazard. Never blow it out with compressed air, and do not inhale any of it. An approved filtering mask should be worn when working on the brakes. DO NOT use petrol or petroleum-based solvents to clean brake parts; use brake cleaner or methylated spirit only.*

1 Apply the handbrake, then slacken the rear roadwheel bolts. Jack up the rear of the vehicle and support it on axle stands (see *Jacking and vehicle support*). Remove both roadwheels.
2 Follow the accompanying photos **(illustrations 5.2a to 5.2p)** for the pad renewal procedure. Be sure to stay in order and read the caption under each illustration, and note the following points:
 a) *New pads may have an adhesive foil on the backplates. Remove this prior to installation.*
 b) *Thoroughly clean the caliper guide surfaces using brake cleaner, and apply a little brake assembly grease.*
 c) *When pushing the caliper piston back to accommodate new pads, keep a close eye on the fluid level in the reservoir.*

3 Depress the brake pedal repeatedly, until the pads are pressed into firm contact with the brake disc, and normal (non-assisted) pedal pressure is restored.
4 Repeat the above procedure on the remaining front brake caliper.
5 Refit the roadwheels (see Section 4), then lower the vehicle to the ground and tighten the roadwheel bolts to the specified torque.
6 Check the hydraulic fluid level as described in *Weekly checks*.
Caution: New pads will not give full braking efficiency until they have bedded-in. Be prepared for this, and avoid hard braking as far as possible for the first hundred miles or so after pad renewal.

5.2a Undo and remove the caliper guide pin bolts (arrowed)...

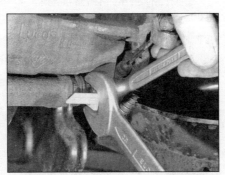

5.2b... using an open-ended spanner to counterhold the pin

5.2c Slide the caliper from place...

5.2d... and suspend it from the coil spring to prevent straining the brake hose

5.2e Remove the outer brake pad...

5.2f... and the inner brake pad

5.2g Use brake cleaner and a soft brush to clean the caliper/bracket mounting surface

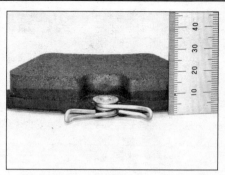

5.2h Measure the thickness of the pad (including the backing plate) – if it's less than 9.0 mm, renew all 4 pads

5.2i If new pads are to be fitted, push the piston back using a retraction tool that rotates the piston clockwise, at the same time as pressing it into the caliper body. Keep an eye on the fluid level whilst pushing the pistons back!

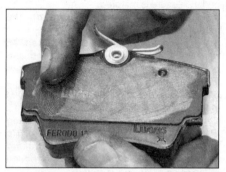

5.2j Apply a little high-temperature anti-seize grease to the pad backing plate...

5.2k... and mounting edges. Take care not to get any on the friction material

5.2l Fit the inner pad to the bracket. Ensure the friction material is against the disc surface

5.2m Fit the outer pad to the bracket

5.2n Slide the caliper into place

5.2o Fit the new guide pin bolts...

5.2p... and tighten them to the specified torque

6 Front brake disc –
inspection, removal and refitting

Note: *Before starting work, refer to the note at the beginning of Section 4 concerning the dangers of asbestos dust.*

Inspection

Note: *If either disc requires renewal, BOTH should be renewed at the same time, to ensure even and consistent braking. New brake pads should also be fitted.*

1 Apply the handbrake, then jack up the front of the vehicle and support it on axle stands. Remove the appropriate front roadwheel.
2 Slowly rotate the brake disc so that the full area of both sides can be checked; remove the brake pads if better access is required to the inboard surface (see Section 4). Light scoring is normal in the area swept by the brake pads, but if heavy scoring or cracks are found, the disc must be renewed.
3 It is normal to find a lip of rust and brake dust around the disc's perimeter; this can be scraped off if required. If, however, a lip has formed due to excessive wear of the brake pad swept area, then the disc's thickness must be measured using a micrometer **(see illustration)**. Take measurements at several

6.3 Use a micrometer to measure the thickness of the disc

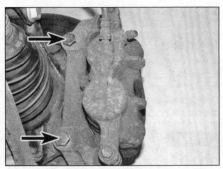

6.6 Undo the bolts (arrowed) and slide the caliper and mounting bracket from the disc

6.7 Disc retaining screw (arrowed)

places around the disc, at the inside and outside of the pad swept area; if the disc has worn at any point to the specified minimum thickness or less, the disc must be renewed.

4 If the disc is thought to be warped, it can be checked for run-out. Either use a dial gauge mounted on any convenient fixed point, while the disc is slowly rotated, or use feeler blades to measure (at several points all around the disc) the clearance between the disc and a fixed point, such as the caliper mounting bracket. If the measurements obtained are at the specified maximum or beyond, the disc is excessively warped, and must be renewed; however, it is worth checking first that the hub bearing is in good condition (Chapters 1 and/or 10). If the run-out is excessive, the disc must be renewed.

5 Check the disc for cracks, especially around the wheel bolt holes, and any other wear or damage, and renew if necessary.

Removal

6 Unscrew the two bolts securing the brake caliper mounting bracket to the hub carrier, then slide the caliper assembly off the disc **(see illustration)**. Using a piece of wire or string, tie the caliper to the front suspension coil spring, to avoid placing any strain on the hydraulic brake hose.

7 Use chalk or paint to mark the relationship of the disc to the hub, then remove the screw securing the brake disc to the hub, and remove the disc **(see illustration)**. If it is tight, lightly tap its rear face with a hide or plastic mallet.

Refitting

8 Refitting is the reverse of the removal procedure, noting the following points:
  a) *Ensure that the mating surfaces of the disc and hub are clean and flat.*
  b) *Align (if applicable) the marks made on removal, and tighten the disc retaining screw to the specified torque.*
  c) *If a new disc has been fitted, use a suitable solvent to wipe any preservative coating from the disc, before refitting the caliper.*
  d) *Slide the caliper into position over the disc, making sure the pads pass either side of the disc. Apply a little thread-locking compound, then tighten the caliper mounting bolts to the specified torque setting.*
  e) *Refit the roadwheel, then lower the vehicle to the ground and tighten the*

roadwheel bolts to the specified torque. On completion, repeatedly depress the brake pedal until normal (non-assisted) pedal pressure returns.

7 Rear brake disc – inspection, removal and refitting

Note: *Before starting work, refer to the note at the beginning of Section 5 concerning the dangers of asbestos dust.*

Inspection

Note: *If either disc requires renewal, BOTH should be renewed at the same time, to ensure even and consistent braking. New brake pads should also be fitted.*

1 Firmly chock the front wheels, then jack up the rear of the vehicle and support it on axle stands. Remove the appropriate rear roadwheel. Release the handbrake

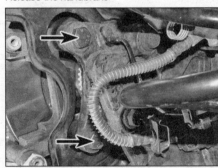

7.4 Rear caliper mounting bracket bolts (arrowed)

7.5b... then undo the hub retaining nut

2 Inspect the disc as described in Section 6.

Removal

3 Remove the brake pads as described in Section 5.

4 Undo the 2 bolts and remove the caliper mounting bracket **(see illustration)**.

5 Carefully prise away the dust cover, and undo the retaining nut **(see illustrations)**. Discard the nut – a new one is required.

6 It should now be possible to withdraw the brake disc from the stub axle by hand. If it is tight, lightly tap its rear face with a hide or plastic mallet.

Refitting

7 Where necessary, fit a new rear hub bearing as described in Chapter 10.

8 If a new disc is been fitted, use a suitable solvent to wipe any preservative coating from the disc. Ensure the disc mounting surface on the hub is free from dirt and corrosion.

9 Position the new disc/hub, fit the new

7.5a Use a chisel to carefully prise away the cap...

7.9 The rear disc is integral with the hub

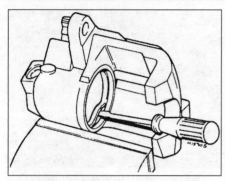

8.8 Take care not to scratch the piston bore whilst extracting the seal

retaining nut and tighten it to the specified torque **(see illustration)**.

10 Refit the caliper mounting bracket, apply a little thread-locking compound, then tighten the bolts to the specified torque.

11 Fit the new brake pads as described in Section 5.

12 Refit the roadwheel, then lower the vehicle to the ground, and tighten the roadwheel bolts to the specified torque. On completion, repeatedly depress the brake pedal until normal (non-assisted) pedal pressure returns. Recheck the handbrake adjustment.

---

8 Front brake caliper – removal, overhaul and refitting

Note: *Before starting work, refer to the note at the beginning of Section 2 concerning the dangers of hydraulic fluid, and to the warning at the beginning of Section 4 concerning the dangers of asbestos dust.*

Removal

1 Apply the handbrake, then jack up the front of the vehicle and support it on axle stands. Remove the appropriate roadwheel.

2 Minimise fluid loss by using a brake hose clamp, a G-clamp or a similar tool to clamp the flexible hose.

3 Clean the area around the union, then slacken the brake hose union nut.

4 Remove the brake pads (see Section 4).

5 Remove the remaining guide pin bolt,

9.4a Working underneath the vehicle, slacken the handbrake cable adjuster nut to the end of the thread

---

unscrew the caliper from the end of the brake hose and remove it from the vehicle.

Overhaul

6 With the caliper on the bench, wipe away all traces of dust and dirt, but *avoid inhaling the dust, as it is a health hazard.*

7 Withdraw the partially-ejected pistons from the caliper body, and remove the dust seals.

 If the piston cannot be withdrawn by hand, it can be pushed out by applying compressed air to the brake hose union hole. Only low pressure should be required, such as is generated by a foot pump. As the piston is expelled, take great care not to trap your fingers between the piston and caliper.

8 Using a small screwdriver, extract the piston hydraulic seals, taking great care not to damage the caliper bore **(see illustration)**.

9 Thoroughly clean all components, using only methylated spirit, isopropyl alcohol or clean hydraulic fluid as a cleaning medium. Never use mineral-based solvents such as petrol or paraffin, as they will attack the hydraulic system's rubber components. Dry the components immediately, using compressed air or a clean, lint-free cloth. Use compressed air to blow clear the fluid passages.

10 Check all components, and renew any that are worn or damaged. Check particularly the cylinder bore and piston; these should be renewed (note that this means the renewal of the complete body assembly) if they are scratched, worn or corroded in any way. Similarly check the condition of the guide pins and their bushes; both pins should be undamaged and (when cleaned) a reasonably tight sliding fit in the bushes. If there is any doubt about the condition of any component, renew it.

11 If the assembly is fit for further use, obtain the appropriate repair kit; the components are available from Vauxhall and Renault dealers in various combinations. All rubber seals should be renewed as a matter of course; these should never be re-used.

12 On reassembly, ensure that all components are clean and dry.

9.4b Disengage the end of the handbrake cable...

---

13 Soak the piston and the new piston (fluid) seals in clean hydraulic fluid. Smear clean fluid on the cylinder bore surface.

14 Fit the new piston (fluid) seal, using only your fingers (no tools) to manipulate it into the cylinder bore groove.

15 Fit the new dust seal to the piston. Locate the rear of the seal in the recess in the caliper body, and refit the piston to the cylinder bore using a twisting motion. Ensure that the piston enters squarely into the bore, and press it fully into the bore.

Refitting

16 Screw the caliper fully onto the flexible hose union.

17 Refit the brake pads (see Section 4).

18 Securely tighten the brake pipe union nut.

19 Remove the brake hose clamp, and bleed the hydraulic system as described in Section 2. Note that, providing the precautions described were taken to minimise brake fluid loss, it should only be necessary to bleed the relevant front brake.

20 Refit the roadwheel, then lower the vehicle to the ground and tighten the roadwheel bolts to the specified torque. On completion, check the hydraulic fluid level as described in *Weekly checks.*

---

9 Rear brake caliper – removal, overhaul and refitting

Note: *Before starting work, refer to the note at the beginning of Section 2 concerning the dangers of hydraulic fluid, and to the warning at the beginning of Section 5 concerning the dangers of asbestos dust.*

Removal

1 Chock the front wheels, then jack up the rear of the vehicle and support on axle stands. Remove the relevant rear wheel.

2 Minimise fluid loss by using a brake hose clamp, a G-clamp or a similar tool to clamp the flexible hose.

3 Clean the area around the union, then loosen the brake hose union nut.

4 Disconnect the handbrake cable from the caliper lever **(see illustrations)**.

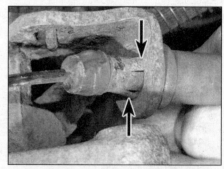

9.4c... then compress the clips (arrowed) and pull the outer cable from the bracket

5 Remove the brake pads as described in Section 5.

6 Unscrew the caliper from the end of the flexible hose, and remove it from the vehicle.

Overhaul

7 At the time of writing, it would appear that no caliper overhaul kits are available. Check with your local Vauxhall or Renault dealer or parts specialist.

Refitting

8 Screw the caliper fully onto the flexible hose union.

9 Refit the brake pads (refer to Section 5).

10 Reconnect the handbrake cable.

11 Securely tighten the brake pipe union nut, then tighten the guide pin bolts to the specified torque.

12 Remove the brake hose clamp, and bleed the hydraulic system as described in Section 2. Note that, providing the precautions described were taken to minimise brake fluid loss, it should only be necessary to bleed the relevant rear brake.

13 Refit the roadwheel, then lower the vehicle to the ground and tighten the roadwheel bolts to the specified torque. On completion, check the hydraulic fluid level as described in *Weekly checks*. Adjust the handbrake as described in Section 14.

10 Master cylinder – removal, overhaul and refitting

Removal

1 Disconnect the wiring plug from the level sensor on the top of the fluid reservoir **(see illustration)**.

2 Remove the master cylinder reservoir cap, and siphon the hydraulic fluid from the reservoir. **Note:** *Do not siphon the fluid by mouth, as it is poisonous; use a syringe or a hand-held vacuum pump.* Alternatively, open any convenient bleed screw in the system, and gently pump the brake pedal to expel the fluid through a plastic tube connected to the screw until the level of fluid drops below that of the reservoir (see Section 2).

3 Disconnect the fluid hose(s) from the side of the reservoir, and plug the hose end(s) to minimise fluid loss **(see illustration)**.

4 Unscrew and pull out the master cylinder reservoir locking pin **(see illustration)**.

5 Carefully ease the fluid reservoir out from the top of the master cylinder. Recover the reservoir seals, and plug the cylinder ports to prevent dirt entry.

6 Wipe clean the area around the brake pipe unions on the on the pipes from the master cylinder to the ABS modulator/hydraulic unit, and place absorbent rags beneath the pipe unions to catch any surplus fluid. Make a note of the correct fitted positions of the unions, then unscrew the union nuts and

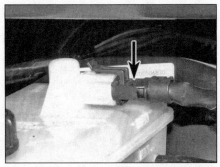

10.1 Disconnect the brake master cylinder fluid warning sensor wiring plug (arrowed)

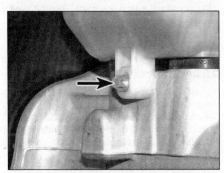

10.4 Unscrew the reservoir locking pin (arrowed)

carefully withdraw the pipes. The pipes must not be bent. Plug or tape over the pipe ends and master cylinder orifices, to minimise the loss of brake fluid, and to prevent the entry of dirt into the system. Wash off any spilt fluid immediately with cold water.

7 Slacken and remove the two nuts and washers securing the master cylinder to the vacuum servo unit, then withdraw the unit from the engine compartment **(see illustration)**. Remove the O-ring from the rear of the master cylinder. Discard the retaining nuts, new ones should be used on refitting.

Overhaul

8 If the master cylinder is faulty, it must be renewed. Repair kits are not available from dealers so the cylinder must be treated as a sealed unit. Renew the master cylinder O-ring seal and reservoir seals regardless of their apparent condition.

11.1 Undo the nut (arrowed) securing the cross-shaft link to the pedal – facia removed for clarity

10.3 Disconnect the hose (arrowed) from the side of the fluid reservoir

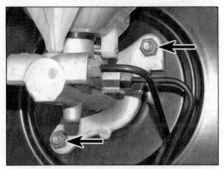

10.7 Master cylinder retaining nuts (arrowed)

Refitting

9 Remove all traces of dirt from the master cylinder and servo unit mating surfaces, and fit a new O-ring to the groove on the master cylinder body.

10 Fit the master cylinder to the servo unit, ensuring that the servo unit pushrod enters the master cylinder bore centrally. Fit the new master cylinder retaining nuts and washers, and tighten them to the specified torque.

11 Wipe clean the brake pipe unions, then refit them to the master cylinder/hydraulic unit ports and tighten them securely.

12 Press the new reservoir seals firmly into the master cylinder ports, then ease the reservoir into position. Refit the reservoir locking pin securely. Reconnect the fluid hose(s) to the reservoir, and reconnect the wiring connector(s).

13 The remainder of refitting is a reversal of removal, noting the following points:

a) Tighten all fasteners to their specified torque where given.

b) Refill the master cylinder reservoir with new fluid, and bleed the complete hydraulic system as described in Section 2.

11 Brake pedal – removal and refitting

Removal

1 Working under the driver's side of the facia, undo the nut securing the brake pedal to the cross-shaft link **(see illustration)**.

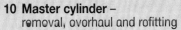

2 Position the steering wheel in the 'straight-ahead' position, then remove the ignition key to set the steering lock.

3 Undo the 2 bolts and slide the lower coupling down from the steering column shaft **(see illustration)**.

4 Undo the nut and pull the pivot bolt from the pedal/bracket. Depress the cross-shaft lever a little to facilitate the removal of the bolt. Remove the pedal downwards **(see illustration)**.

Refitting

5 Refitting is the reverse of removal. Refit the brake light switch as described in Section 18.

12 Vacuum servo unit – testing, removal and refitting

Testing

1 To test the operation of the servo unit, depress the footbrake several times to exhaust the vacuum, then start the engine whilst keeping the pedal firmly depressed. As the engine starts, there should be a noticeable 'give' in the brake pedal as the vacuum builds-up. Allow the engine to run for at least two minutes, then switch it off. If the brake pedal is now depressed it should feel normal, but further applications should result in the pedal feeling firmer, with the pedal stroke decreasing with each application.

2 If the servo does not operate as described, first inspect the servo unit check valve as described in Section 13.

3 If the servo unit still fails to operate

11.3 Undo the bolts (arrowed) and slide the coupling downwards

satisfactorily, the fault lies within the unit itself. Repairs to the unit are not possible – if faulty, the servo unit must be renewed.

Removal

2.0 litre models

4 Remove the air cleaner assembly as described in Chapter 4A.

5 Pull the charge pressure sensor and bracket from the support frame **(see illustration)**. Release the wiring harness from the frame as the sensor is withdrawn.

6 Unclip the fuel pipe, mass airflow sensor wiring harness, and coolant heater harness (where fitted) from the support frame.

7 Undo the bolt and detach the cooler heater assembly (where fitted) from the support frame **(see illustration)**.

8 Undo the 2 nuts and 2 bolts, and remove the support frame from the engine compartment **(see illustrations)**.

11.4 Brake pedal pivot bolt

All models

9 Remove the master cylinder as described in Section 10.

10 Undo the screw, and remove the cover from the bulkhead on the passenger's side under the facia **(see illustration)**.

11 Slide off the retaining clip and remove the clevis pin securing the brake pedal cross-shaft to the servo unit pushrod **(see illustration)**.

12 Undo the 2 diagonally-opposite nuts securing the brake pedal bracket to the bulkhead.

13 Prise the servo unit check valve from place **(see illustration 13.1)**.

14 Manoeuvre the servo unit from place. Renew the seal between the servo and the bulkhead.

Refitting

15 Refitting is a reversal of removal.

12.5 Pull the charge pressure sensor from the support frame

12.7 Undo the bolt (arrowed) securing coolant heater bracket to the support frame

12.8a The support frame is secured by 2 bolts (arrowed) at the front...

12.8b ...and 2 nuts (arrowed) at the engine compartment bulkhead

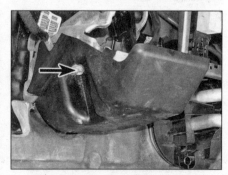

12.10 Undo the screw (arrowed) and remove the cover

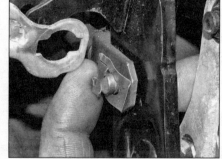

12.11 Slide off the retaining clip from the clevis pin on the cross-shaft

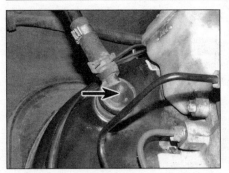

13.1 Prise the check valve (arrowed) from the servo

14.3 Measure the gap (arrowed) between the handbrake operating lever and the stop on the caliper body using a feeler gauge

15.4 Prise up the handbrake lever gaiter

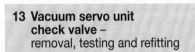

13 Vacuum servo unit check valve –
removal, testing and refitting

Removal

1 Prise the check valve from the servo, and disconnect the hose **(see illustration)**.

Testing

2 Examine the valve for signs of damage and renew if necessary.
3 Test the valve by blowing through it in both directions; air should only flow through the valve in one direction only – when blown through from the servo end of the valve. Renew the valve if this is not the case.

Refitting

4 Refitting is a reversal of removal.

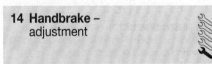

14 Handbrake –
adjustment

1 Chock the front wheels, then fully release the handbrake.
2 Jack up the rear of the vehicle and support it on axle stands (see *Jacking and vehicle support*).
3 Rotate the adjusting nut **(see illustration 9.4a)** as necessary to obtain a clearance of 0.1 to 0.5 mm between the operating lever and the stop on the caliper body **(see illustration)**.

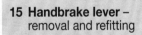

15 Handbrake lever –
removal and refitting

Removal

1 Raise the rear of the vehicle and support it securely on axle stands (see *Jacking and vehicle support*). Chock the front wheels.
2 Release the handbrake, then slacken the cable adjustment nut anti-clockwise until all tension in the cable is released **(see illustration 9.4a)**.
3 Remove both front seats as described in Chapter 11.

15.7 Disengage the front section of the cable from the handbrake lever

4 Carefully prise up the handbrake lever gaiter **(see illustration)**.
5 Disconnect the handbrake warning switch wiring plug.
6 Fold the floor covering forwards around the handbrake lever.
7 Release the front section of the cable from the lever **(see illustration)**.
8 Undo the 2 retaining bolts and remove the lever from the vehicle **(see illustration)**.

Refitting

9 Refitting is a reversal of the removal. Prior to refitting the centre console, adjust the handbrake as described in Section 14.

16 Handbrake cables –
removal and refitting

Removal

Front section

1 Detach the front end of the cable from the lever as described in Section 15.
2 Remove the retaining clips and detach the handbrake cables from the levers on the calipers **(see illustration 9.4b and 9.4c)**.
3 On models with an additional fuel-powered heater, remove the fuel tank as described in Chapter 4A.
4 Disconnect the front cable from the centre cable **(see illustration)**.
5 Free the cable grommet from the floor panel, and remove the front section of the cable.

15.8 Handbrake lever retaining bolts (arrowed)

Centre section

6 Raise the rear of the vehicle and support it securely on axle stands (see *Jacking and vehicle support*). Chock the front wheels.
7 On models with an additional fuel-powered heater, remove the fuel tank as described in Chapter 4A, then undo the bolts and remove the heat shield.
8 Release the handbrake, then slacken the cable adjustment nut anti-clockwise until all tension in the cable is released **(see illustration 9.4a)**.
9 Remove the retaining clips and detach the handbrake cables from the levers on the calipers **(see illustration 9.4b and 9.4c)**.
10 Disconnect the left- and right-hand handbrake cables from the equaliser arm and bracket **(see illustration)**.

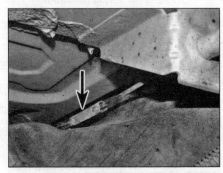

16.4 Disconnect the front section of the cable at the coupling (arrowed) above the fuel tank

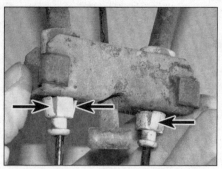

16.10 Compress the clips (arrowed) and detach the left- and right-hand sections of the cable from the bracket

11 Disconnect the centre section of the cable from the front section, and remove it.

Left- and right-hand sections

12 Raise the rear of the vehicle and support it securely on axle stands (see *Jacking and vehicle support*). Chock the front wheels.
13 Release the handbrake, then slacken the cable adjustment nut anti-clockwise until all tension in the cable is released.
14 Release the left- and right-hand cables from the equaliser arm **(see illustration)**.
15 Remove the retaining clips and detach the handbrake cables from the levers on the calipers **(see illustration 9.4b and 9.4c)**.
16 Release the cables from the any retaining clips on the axle, note the cable routing, and remove it from under the vehicle.

Refitting

17 Refitting is a reversal of the removal pro-

17.2 Note the distance from the end of the rod and the spring (arrowed)

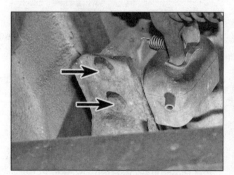

17.4a Load-sensing valve mounting bolts (arrowed)

16.14 Disconnect the end of the cables from the equaliser arm

cedure. Prior to refitting the centre console, adjust the handbrake as described in Section 14.

---

17 Load-sensing valve – removed and refitting

Removal

1 Raise the rear of the vehicle and support it securely on axle stands (see *Jacking and vehicle support*). The valve is located just in front of the spare wheel.
2 Measure the distance between the end of the spring and the end of the fixed linkage rod **(see illustration)**. Make a note of this dimension.
3 Note their fitted positions, then undo the unions and disconnect the brake pipes from

17.3 Disconnect the pipes from the load-sensing valve

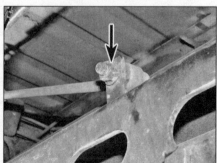

17.4b Remove the fixed linkage rod retaining nut (arrowed)

the valve **(see illustration)**. Plug the openings to prevent fluid leakage/contamination.
4 Undo the valve mounting bolts, remove the fixed linkage rod retaining nut and manoeuvre the assembly from under the vehicle **(see illustrations)**. Note that testing of the valve is only possible with access to Vauxhall or Renault diagnostic equipment.

Refitting

5 Refit the valve and fixed linkage rod into position, and tighten the retaining bolts/nuts securely.
6 Measure the distance between the end of the spring and then of the fixed linkage rod **(see illustration 17.2)**. If this measurement differs from the dimension noted earlier, slacken the adjustment screw on the fixed linkage rod, and move the inner rod as necessary to achieve the required measurement. Note that the only other way of setting up the linkage rod dimension is with access to Vauxhall or Renault diagnostic equipment. If the original dimension is lost, entrust this task to a dealer or suitably-equipped repairer.
7 Bleed the brakes as described in Section 2.

---

18 Brake light switch – removal, adjustment and refitting

Removal

1 The brake light switch is located on the pedal bracket behind the facia.
2 Working under the facia on the passenger's side, undo the bolt, release the clip and remove the cover from the cross-shaft linkage **(see illustration 12.10)**.
3 Reach up behind the facia and disconnect the wiring connector from the switch
4 Rotate the switch anti-clockwise and remove it from the bracket **(see illustration)**.

Adjustment

5 Measure the protrusion of the plunger from the switch. If it is less that 13 mm or greater than 14 mm, push/pull the plunger until this dimension is achieved **(see illustration)**.
Note: *Vauxhall and Renault insist that the switch must be renewed if the plunger position is adjusted more than 3 times.*

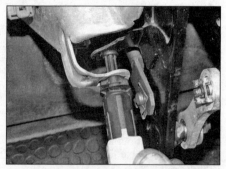

18.4 Rotate the brake light switch anti-clockwise and remove it

Refitting

6 Fully depress the brake pedal and hold it down, then manoeuvre the switch into position, and twist it clockwise to lock it in place. **Slowly** release the brake pedal and allow it to return to its stop. This will automatically adjust the brake light switch. **Note:** *If the pedal is released too quickly, the switch will be incorrectly adjusted.*

7 Reconnect the wiring connector, and check the operation of the brake lights. If the switch is not functioning correctly, it is faulty and may need to be renewed; no other adjustment is possible.

8 Refit the linkage cover.

19 Anti-lock Braking System (ABS) – general information

Note: *On all models the ABS unit is a dual function unit, and works both the anti-lock braking system (ABS) and traction control function of the Dynamic Stability Control (DSC) system.*

1 ABS is available to all models as an option. The system comprises a hydraulic block which contains the hydraulic solenoid valves and the electrically-driven return pump, the four roadwheel sensors (one fitted to each wheel), and the electronic control unit (ECU). The purpose of the system is to prevent the wheel(s) locking during heavy braking. This is achieved by automatic release of the brake on the relevant wheel, followed by re-application of the brake.

2 The solenoids are controlled by the ECU, which itself receives signals from the four wheel sensors (one fitted on each hub), which monitor the speed of rotation of each wheel. By comparing these signals, the ECU can determine the speed at which the vehicle is travelling. It can then use this speed to determine when a wheel is decelerating at an abnormal rate, compared to the speed of the vehicle, and therefore predicts when a wheel is about to lock. During normal operation, the system functions in the same way as a non-ABS braking system. In addition to this, the brake pedal position sensor (which is fitted to the vacuum servo unit) also informs the ECU of how hard the brake pedal is being depressed.

3 If the ECU senses that a wheel is about to lock, it operates the relevant solenoid valve in the hydraulic unit, which then isolates the brake caliper on the wheel which is about to lock from the master cylinder, effectively sealing-in the hydraulic pressure.

4 If the speed of rotation of the wheel continues to decrease at an abnormal rate, the ECU switches on the electrically-driven return pump operates, and pumps the hydraulic fluid back into the master cylinder, releasing pressure on the brake caliper so that the brake is released. Once the speed of rotation of the wheel returns to an acceptable rate, the pump

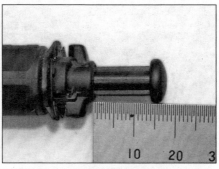

18.5 There should be 13 to 14 mm between the underside of the plunger head and the end of the switch casing

stops and the solenoid valve opens, allowing the hydraulic master cylinder pressure to return to the caliper, which then re-applies the brake. This cycle can be carried out at up to 10 times a second.

5 The action of the solenoid valves and return pump creates pulses in the hydraulic circuit. When the ABS system is functioning, these pulses can be felt through the brake pedal.

6 The operation of the ABS system is entirely dependent on electrical signals. To prevent the system responding to any inaccurate signals, a built-in safety circuit monitors all signals received by the ECU. If an inaccurate signal or low battery voltage is detected, the ABS system is automatically shut down, and the warning light on the instrument panel is illuminated, to inform the driver that the ABS system is not operational. Normal braking should still be available, however.

7 If a fault does develop in the ABS system, the vehicle must be taken to a dealer or suitably-equipped specialist for fault diagnosis and repair.

8 An accumulator is also incorporated into the hydraulic system. As well as performing the ABS function as described above, the hydraulic unit also works the traction/stability control side of the DSC system. If the ECU senses that the wheels are about to lose traction under acceleration, the hydraulic unit momentarily applies the rear brakes to prevent the wheel(s) spinning. If the system senses that the lateral acceleration/yaw rate of the vehicle is about to exceed a pre-determined threshold – resulting in oversteer

20.3 The front ABS wheel speed sensor connector is clipped to the subframe strut (arrowed)

or understeer, the system can apply the brake of each individual wheel to maintain stability and prevent/control a skid.

9 Should a fault develop with the ABS/DSC system, the vehicle must be taken to a Vauxhall or Renault dealer or suitably-equipped specialist who will be able to interrogate the system's self-diagnosis capacity, and pin-point the fault.

20 Anti-lock braking system (ABS) components – removal and refitting

Hydraulic/modulator/accumulator unit

1 Although it is possible for the home mechanic to remove the hydraulic unit, the unit's self-diagnosis system must be interrogated by dedicated test equipment before and after removal, and the unit must be bled by Vauxhall or Renault service test equipment. Consequently, we recommend that removal and refitting the hydraulic unit should be entrusted to a dealer or suitably-equipped specialist.

Electronic control unit (ECU)

2 In order to remove the ECU, the hydraulic unit must first be removed, as the ECU is screwed to the side of the hydraulic unit. Consequently, we recommend that removal and refitting of the ECU is entrusted to a dealer or suitably-equipped specialist.

Front wheel sensor

Removal

3 Chock the rear wheels, then firmly apply the handbrake, jack up the front of the vehicle and support on axle stands. Remove the appropriate front roadwheel. Trace the wiring back from the sensor to the connector, disconnect it and release the harness from any retaining clips **(see illustration)**.

4 Release the clip securing the sensor to the hub carrier, and remove the sensor and lead assembly from the vehicle **(see illustration)**.

Refitting

5 Ensure that the sensor and hub carrier sealing faces are clean, then fit the sensor to

20.4 Lift the edge of the clip and slide out the ABS wheel speed sensor

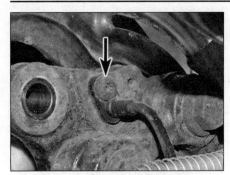

20.9 Rear ABS wheel speed sensor retaining bolt (arrowed)

20.10 Rear ABS wheel speed sensor wiring connector (arrowed)

the hub, ensuring it engages the retaining clip correctly.

6 Ensure that the sensor wiring is correctly routed and retained by all the necessary clips, and reconnect it to its wiring connector.

7 Refit the roadwheel, then lower the vehicle to the ground and tighten the roadwheel bolts to the specified torque.

Rear wheel sensor

Removal

8 Chock the front wheels, then jack up the rear of the vehicle and support it on axle stands. Remove the appropriate roadwheel.

9 Undo the retaining bolt and carefully extract the sensor from the hub carrier (see illustration).

10 Trace the wiring back from the sensor to the connector, disconnect it and release

the harness from any retaining clips (see illustration).

Refitting

11 Install the sensor into the hub carrier, and tighten the retaining bolt to the specified torque.

12 Refit the harness into the retaining clips and reconnect the wiring plug. Lower the vehicle to the ground.

21 Vacuum pump – testing, removal and refitting

Testing

Note: *A vacuum gauge will be required.*

1 The operation of the braking system

vacuum pump can be checked using a vacuum gauge.

2 Disconnect the vacuum pipe from the pump, and connect the gauge to the pump union using a suitable length of hose.

3 Start the engine and allow it to idle, and then measure the vacuum created by the pump. As a guide, after one minute, a minimum of approximately 500 mm Hg should be recorded. If the vacuum registered is significantly less than this, it is likely that the pump is faulty. However, seek the advice of a Vauxhall or Renault dealer before condemning the pump.

Removal

4 Unclip and remove the engine cover.

5 If required, to give better access to the vacuum pump, remove the air intake hoses and intercooler hoses as described in Chapter 4A.

6 Squeeze together the tabs on the hose end fitting, and disconnect the vacuum hose from the pump (see illustrations).

7 Slacken and remove the two mounting bolts securing the pump to the end of the cylinder head (see illustrations), then remove the pump. Recover the pump gasket/O-ring seal and discard it; a new one should be used on refitting.

Refitting

8 Ensure that the pump and cylinder head mating surfaces are clean and dry, and fit the new gasket/O-ring seal to the head (see illustration).

9 Manoeuvre the pump into position aligning the drive dog with the slot in the end of the camshaft. Refit the pump to the cylinder head, ensuring that the gasket/O-ring remains correctly seated, then refit the pump mounting bolts and tighten them securely.

10 Reconnect the vacuum hose to the pump, making sure that it is securely clipped into position.

11 If removed, refit the air intake hose and intercooler hoses, as described in Chapter 4A. Refit the engine cover.

12 On completion, check the operation of the brakes.

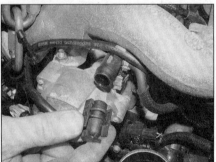

21.6a Disconnect the vacuum hose from the pump – 1.9 litre models

21.6b Squeeze together the sides (arrowed) and disconnect the vacuum hose from the pump – 2.0 litre models

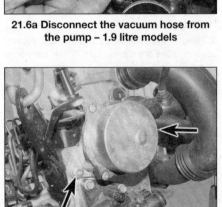

21.7a Remove the pump mounting bolts (arrowed) – 1.9 litre engines...

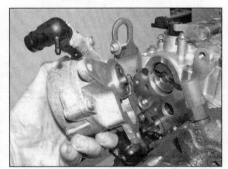

21.7b... and 2.0 litre engines

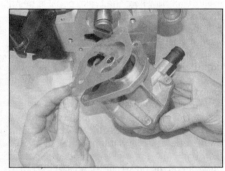

21.8 Fit a new gasket to the vacuum pump – 1.9 litre engine shown

Chapter 10
Suspension and steering

Contents

Degrees of difficulty

Easy, suitable for novice with little experience	Fairly easy, suitable for beginner with some experience	Fairly difficult, suitable for competent DIY mechanic	Difficult, suitable for experienced DIY mechanic	Very difficult, suitable for expert DIY or professional

Specifications

Wheel alignment and steering angles

Front wheel:
Toe setting (unladen)	-0° 10' ± 10'
Camber (depending on vehicle load)	-0° 20' ± 30' (nominal)
Castor (unladen)	3° 10' ± 30' (nominal)
King pin inclination (depending on vehicle load)	11° 33' ± 20'

Rear wheel:
Toe setting	0° 30' ± 20'
Camber	-0° 45' ± 20'

Roadwheels

Tyre pressures	See end of *Weekly checks* on page 0•17

Torque wrench settings

	Nm	lbf ft
Front suspension		
Anti-roll bar:		
Connecting link nuts*	44	32
Mounting clamp bolts	21	15
Control arm-to-subframe nuts	180	133
Driveshaft retaining nut*	280	207
Hub carrier-to-strut nuts*	180	133
Lower balljoint:		
Balljoint-to-control arm nuts/bolts*	110	81
Balljoint-to-hub carrier nut*	100	74
Subframe mounting bolts:		
Front bolts	60	44
Rear bolts	120	89
Reaction links	100	74
Rear stabiliser link arm:		
Front bolt	280	207
Rear bolt	100	74
Suspension strut piston nuts*	60	44

Torque wrench settings (continued)

	Nm	lbf ft
Rear suspension		
Hub nut*	280	207
Lateral control rod nuts	105	77
Rear axle-to-mounting bracket nuts*	105	77
Shock absorber mounting bolts/nuts	180	133
Stub axle bolts	100	74
Steering		
Column-to-steering rack pinch-bolt nut*	22	16
Power steering pump mounting bolts	25	18
Steering column coupling nuts*	22	16
Steering column mounting bolts	22	16
Steering rack mounting nuts*	180	133
Steering wheel bolt*	44	32
Track rod:		
Balljoint-to-hub carrier nut*	37	27
Balljoint locknut	53	39
Inner balljoint to steering rack	80	59
Roadwheels		
Wheel bolts	140	103

* Do not re-use

1 General information

The independent front suspension is of the MacPherson strut type, incorporating coil springs and integral telescopic shock absorbers. The MacPherson struts are located by transverse control arms, which utilise vertically-mounted rubber inner mounting bushes. The front hub carriers, which carry the wheel bearings, brake calipers and the hub/disc assemblies and lower balljoints, are bolted to the MacPherson struts, and connected to the lower arms via the balljoints. A front anti-roll bar is fitted to all models. The anti-roll bar is rubber-mounted onto the subframe, and is connected to the front suspension struts by link rods (see illustration).

The rear suspension has separate telescopic shock absorbers and coil springs fitted between the beam axle and the vehicle body. The rear beam axle has integral trailing arms, attached to the vehicle body by rubber bushes. A lateral rod above the axle controls side-to-side movements (see illustration).

The steering column has a universal joint fitted to its upper and lower ends, which is connected to the steering rack pinion and upper column by means of a clamp bolt. A collapsible coupling is fitted to the steering column, and is designed to collapse in the case of the frontal accident.

The steering rack is mounted onto the front subframe, and is connected by two track rods, with balljoints at their outer ends, to the steering arms projecting rearwards from the hub carriers. The track rod ends are threaded, to facilitate adjustment. The hydraulic steering system is powered by an engine-driven pump.

2 Front hub carrier assembly – removal and refitting

Removal

1 Remove the wheel trim/hub cap then slacken the driveshaft nut with the vehicle resting on its wheels (see illustration). Also slacken the wheel bolts.
2 Chock the rear wheels of the car, firmly apply the handbrake, then jack up the front of the vehicle and support it on axle stands (see *Jacking and vehicle support*). Remove the appropriate front roadwheel.
3 Unclip the ABS wheel sensor (where fitted) and harness then position it clear of the hub assembly (see Chapter 9).
4 Slacken and remove the driveshaft retaining nut. If the nut was not slackened with the

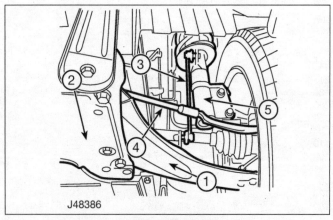

1.1 Front axle detail

1	Control arm	3	Anti-roll bar link	5	Shock absorber
2	Subframe	4	Track rod		

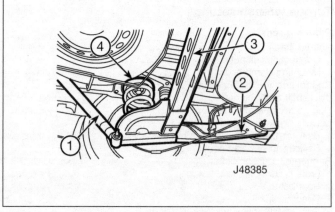

1.2 Rear axle detail

1	Shock absorber	3	Rear axle
2	Trailing link	4	Coil spring

wheels on the ground (see paragraph 1), refit at least two roadwheel bolts to the front hub, tightening them securely, then have an assistant firmly depress the brake pedal to prevent the front hub from rotating, whilst you slacken and remove the driveshaft retaining nut. Alternatively, a tool can be fabricated to hold the hub stationary.

5 Slacken and remove the nut securing the steering rack track rod to the hub carrier then free the balljoint from the hub. If the balljoint is tight, use a universal balljoint separator to free it. Discard the nut, a new one should be used on refitting.

6 If the hub bearings are to be disturbed, remove the brake disc as described in Chapter 9. If not, unscrew the two bolts securing the brake caliper mounting bracket assembly to the hub carrier, and slide the caliper assembly off the disc **(see illustration)**. Using a piece of wire or string, tie the caliper to the front suspension coil spring, to avoid placing any strain on the hydraulic brake hose.

7 Slacken and remove the lower balljoint nut and free the balljoint shank from the hub carrier, if necessary, using a universal balljoint separator **(see illustrations)**. Use an Allen key/bit in the balljoint end to counterhold the nut. Discard the nut – a new one must be fitted. Withdraw the protective plate from between the hub carrier and balljoint.

8 Undo the nut and withdraw the hub carrier-to-suspension strut bolts, noting that the bolts are inserted from the front of the vehicle. Again, new nuts must be fitted.

9 Free the hub carrier assembly from the end of the strut, then release it from the outer constant velocity joint splines, and remove it from the vehicle. If necessary, use a puller to force the driveshaft from the hub **(see illustration)**. Vauxhall and Renault technicians use tool No KM-6218 for this task. Suspend the driveshaft with string from the suspension strut to prevent and damage to the constant velocity joints.

Refitting

10 Ensure that the driveshaft outer constant velocity joint and hub splines are clean, then slide the hub fully onto the driveshaft splines.

11 Fit the protective plate over the balljoint, then align the balljoint with the hub carrier and fit the new retaining nut **(see illustration)**. Only finger-tighten it at this stage.

12 Slide the hub assembly fully into the suspension strut bracket. Inset the bolts from the front using new nuts, and tighten them to the specified torque.

13 Tighten the lower balljoint nut to the specified torque.

14 Engage the track rod balljoint in the hub carrier, then fit the new retaining nut and tighten it to the specified torque.

15 Where necessary, refit the brake disc to the hub, referring to Chapter 9 for further

2.1 Slacken the driveshaft nut (arrowed) whilst the wheel is on the ground

2.7a Undo the lower balljoint nut, using an Allen key/bit in the end of the shank to counterhold

information. Slide the caliper into position, making sure the pads pass either side of the disc, and tighten the new caliper bracket bolts to the specified torque setting (see Chapter 9).

16 Refit the wheel sensor as described in Chapter 9.

17 Fit the new driveshaft nut to the end of the driveshaft. Use the method employed on removal to prevent the hub from rotating (see paragraph 4), and tighten the driveshaft retaining nut to the specified torque. Check that the hub rotates freely. Alternatively, lightly tighten (50 Nm/37 lbf ft) the nut at this stage and tighten it to the specified torque once the vehicle is resting on its wheels again.

18 Refit the roadwheel, then lower the vehicle to the ground and tighten the roadwheel bolts to the specified torque. If not already having done so, tighten the driveshaft retaining nut to the specified torque.

2.9 Pull the driveshaft from the hub splines

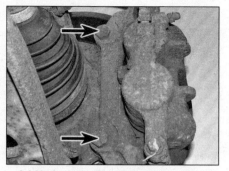

2.6 Undo the caliper mounting bracket bolts (arrowed)

2.7b Separate the balljoint from the hub carrier using a balljoint separator

3 Front hub bearings – renewal

Note: *The bearing is a sealed, pre-adjusted and pre-lubricated, double-row roller type, and is intended to last the car's entire service life without maintenance or attention. Never overtighten the driveshaft nut beyond the specified torque wrench setting in an attempt to 'adjust' the bearing.*

Note: *A press will be required to dismantle and rebuild the assembly; if such a tool is not available, a large bench vice and spacers (such as large sockets) will serve as an adequate substitute. The bearing's inner races are an interference fit on the hub; if the inner race remains on the hub when it is pressed out of the hub carrier, a knife-edged bearing puller will be required to remove it.*

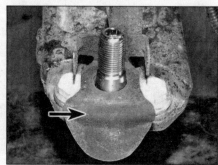

2.11 Fit the protective plate (arrowed) over the balljoint

3.2a Press the hub flange from the bearing

3.2b Use a knife-edge bearing puller to remove the inner bearing race from the flange

3.6a Fit the ABS sensor ring to the hub carrier...

3.6b... ensuring it's correctly located

3.6c The magnetic signal ring (arrowed) must face inwards...

3.6d... and the metal seal (arrowed) must face outwards

1 Remove the hub carrier assembly as described in Section 2.

2 Support the hub carrier securely on blocks or in a vice. Using a tubular spacer which bears only on the inner end of the hub flange, press the hub flange out of the bearing **(see illustrations)**. If the bearing's outboard inner race remains on the hub, remove it using a bearing puller (see note above).

3 Securely support the outer face of the hub carrier. Using a tubular spacer which bears only on the inner race, press the complete bearing assembly out of the hub carrier.

4 Note its fitted position, and remove the ABS wheel speed sensor ring (if fitted) from the carrier.

5 Thoroughly clean the hub and hub carrier, removing all traces of dirt and grease, and polish away any burrs or raised edges which might hinder reassembly. Check both for cracks or any other signs of wear or damage, and renew them if necessary.

6 Where applicable, fit the new ABS wheel speed sensor ring (supplied with genuine bearing kits) to the wheel bearing, ensuring it's correctly located. Securely support the hub carrier, and locate the bearing in the hub, with the magnetic ABS sensor signal ring facing inwards. Press the bearing fully into position, ensuring that it enters the hub squarely, using a tubular spacer which bears only on the bearing outer race **(see illustrations)**.

7 Securely support the outer face of the hub flange, and locate the hub carrier bearing inner race over the end of the hub flange. Press the bearing onto the hub, using a tubular spacer which bears only on the inner race of the hub bearing, until it seats against the hub shoulder. Check that the hub flange rotates freely, and wipe off any excess oil or grease.

8 Refit the hub carrier assembly as described in Section 2.

4 Front strut – removal and refitting

Note: *Always renew any self-locking nuts when working on the suspension/steering components.*

Removal

1 If removing a left-hand suspension strut, Undo the bolt, and move the coolant reservoir to one side **(see illustration)**.

2 Remove the plastic cover, undo the nut from the top of the strut and recover the large mounting washer. Prevent the strut rod from rotating by inserting an Allen key/bit into the end of the rod **(see illustrations)**.

3 Chock the rear wheels, apply the handbrake, slacken the appropriate front roadwheel bolts, then jack up the front of the vehicle and

4.1 Undo the bolt (arrowed) and move the coolant expansion tank to one side

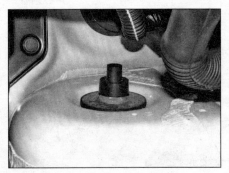

4.2a Pull off the plastic cover...

4.2b... then undo the upper nut, using an Allen key/bit to counterhold

4.5 Remove the strut-to-hub carrier bolts (arrowed)

support on axle stands (see *Jacking and vehicle support*). Remove the appropriate roadwheel.

4 Unscrew the nut securing the anti-roll bar connecting link to the strut, and position the link clear of the strut; if necessary, retain the balljoint shank with a Allen key/bit to prevent rotation whilst the nut is slackened. Discard the nut, a new one should be used on refitting.

5 Remove the bolts and pull the hub carrier from the lower end of the strut, noting that the bolts fit from the front of the strut **(see illustration)**. To prevent the hub carrier assembly dropping whilst the strut is removed support the lower control arm. Unclip the brake hose. Take care not to strain the brake hose and the wiring attached to the brake caliper and the hub carrier.

Caution: As soon as the strut-to-hub carrier bolts are removed, the strut will be unsupported.

6 With the help of an assistant, withdraw the strut from under the wheel arch.

Refitting

7 Manoeuvre the strut assembly into position, ensuring that the end of the strut rod is correctly located in the corresponding hole in the inner wing. Fit the upper mounting nut, but only finger-tighten at this stage.

8 Engage the lower end of the strut with the hub carrier, insert the bolts from the front and tighten them to the specified torque. Refit the brake hose to the retaining clip.

9 Reconnect the anti-roll bar connecting link to the strut. Tighten the nut to the specified torque.

10 Tighten the upper mounting nut to the specified torque, then refit the plastic cover.

11 Where applicable, refit the coolant reservoir and tighten the retaining bolt securely.

12 Refit the roadwheel, then lower the vehicle to the ground and tighten the roadwheel bolts to the specified torque.

5 Front strut – overhaul

⚠️ *Warning: Before attempting to dismantle the front suspension strut, a suitable tool to hold the coil spring in compression must be obtained. Adjustable coil spring compressors are readily available, and are recommended for this operation. Any attempt to dismantle*

5.1 Compress the spring until all tension is relieved from the seats

the strut without such a tool is likely to result in damage or personal injury.

Note: *Always renew any self-locking nuts when working on the suspension/steering components.*

1 With the strut removed from the vehicle (as described in Section 4), clean away all external dirt. Fit the spring compressor and compress the coil spring until tension is relieved from the spring seats **(see illustration)**.

2 Slacken and remove the upper spring seat nut whilst retaining the shock absorber piston with a suitable Allen key **(see illustration)**.

3 Remove the nut, then lift off the spacer, followed by the thrust bearing and upper spring seat **(see illustrations)**.

4 Lift off the bump stop/gaiter, then remove the compressed spring **(see illustrations)**.

5 Examine the shock absorber for signs of fluid leakage. Check the piston for signs of pitting along its entire length, and check

5.2 Slacken the piston nut using an Allen key/bit to counterhold

5.3a Remove the nut...

5.3b... spacer...

5.3c... thrust bearing...

5.3d... upper spring seat...

5.4a... bump stop...

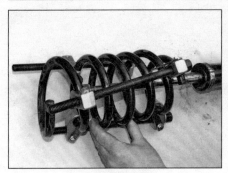

5.4b... and spring

5.8a Ensure the ends of the springs are correctly located against the lower seat stop...

5.8b... and upper seat stop

the shock body for signs of damage. While holding it in an upright position, test the operation of the shock absorber by moving the piston through a full stroke, and then through short strokes of 50 to 100 mm. In both cases, the resistance felt should be smooth and continuous. If the resistance is jerky, or uneven, or if there is any visible sign of wear or damage to the shock absorber, renewal is necessary.

6 Inspect all other components for signs of damage or deterioration, and renew any that are suspect.

7 Slide the rubber bump stop/gaiter onto the piston, making sure the lower end of gaiter is correctly positioned over the shock absorber end.

8 Refit the coil spring, making sure its lower end is correctly seated against the spring seat stop. Fit the upper spring seat, aligning its stop with the spring end, then the thrust bearing and spacer **(see illustrations)**.

9 Fit the new nut. Retain the shock absorber piston and tighten the spring seat nut to the specified torque.

6 Front control arm – removal, overhaul and refitting

Note: *Always renew any self-locking nuts when working on the suspension/steering components.*

Removal

1 Slacken the roadwheel bolts, then raise the

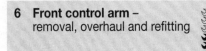

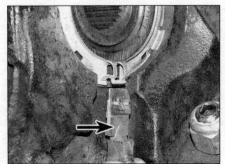

6.3 Unclip the ABS wheel speed sensor (arrowed)

vehicle and support it securely on axle stands (see *Jacking and vehicle support*). Remove the relevant roadwheel.

2 Undo the fasteners and remove the engine undertray (where fitted).

3 Unclip the ABS wheel speed sensor (where fitted) from the hub carrier, then unclip its harness from the control arm **(see illustration)**. Place it to one side.

4 Slacken and remove the nut, then free the lower balljoint shank from the hub carrier, if necessary, using a universal balljoint separator. Discard the nut and lift off the protector plate (if loose). Use an Allen key/bit in the end of the balljoint shank to counterhold the nut.

5 Slacken and remove the control arm pivot bolts and nuts **(see illustration)**.

6 Manoeuvre the lower arm assembly out from underneath the vehicle.

Overhaul

7 Thoroughly clean the lower arm and the area around the arm mountings, removing all traces of dirt and underseal if necessary, then check carefully for cracks, distortion or any other signs of wear or damage, paying particular attention to the pivot bushes, and renew components as necessary.

8 It would appear, at the time of writing, that the bushes are not available separately from the control arm. Check with your local dealer or parts specialist.

Refitting

9 Manoeuvre the control arm assembly into position, and refit the pivot bolts and nuts, then tighten them to the specified torque.

6.5 Lower control arm front and rear pivot bolts/nuts (arrowed)

10 Refit the protector plate (where removed) to the lower balljoint, then locate the balljoint shank in the hub carrier. Fit the new retaining nut and tighten it to the specified torque.

11 Refit the ABS sensor (where applicable), and clip the wiring harness into place.

12 Refit the engine undertray and tighten the fasteners securely.

13 Refit the roadwheel, then lower the vehicle and tighten the roadwheel bolts to the specified torque.

14 Check and, if necessary, adjust the front wheel alignment as described in Section 27.

7 Front lower balljoint – removal and refitting

Removal

1 Slacken the roadwheel bolts, then raise the vehicle and support it securely on axle stands (see *Jacking and vehicle support*). Remove the relevant roadwheel.

2 Unclip the ABS wheel speed sensor (where fitted) from the hub carrier, then unclip its harness from the control arm. Place it to one side.

3 Slacken and remove the nut, then free the lower balljoint shank from the hub carrier, if necessary, using a universal balljoint separator **(see illustrations 2.7a and 2.7b)**. Discard the nut and lift off the protector plate. Use an Allen key/bit in the end of the balljoint shank to counterhold the nut.

4 The lower balljoint may be riveted or bolted to the control arm – proceed as applicable.

Riveted type – early models

5 Centre punch each of the 3 rivets securing the balljoint to the control arm, then drill them out. Start off with a 4 mm drill bit, ending with an 11 mm drill bit. Take care not to damage the control arm **(see illustration)**. Remove the balljoint from the control arm.

Bolted type – late models

6 Undo the nuts, withdrawn the bolts and remove the balljoint from the end of the control arm **(see illustration)**. Discard the bolts and nuts – new ones must be fitted.

Refitting

Note: *The new balljoint should be positioned*

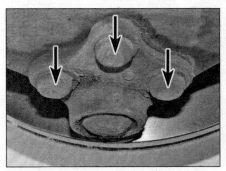

7.5 Drill out the rivets (arrowed) securing the balljoint to the control arm

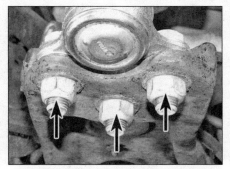

7.6 Balljoint retaining nuts (arrowed)

7.7 Insert the balljoint bolts from above – ensure that the new balljoint is positioned below the control arm if that is where the original was fitted

below the control arm if that is where the original was fitted.

7 New balljoints are always bolted to the control arm. Position the new balljoint, and insert the new bolts from above. Fit the new nuts and tighten them to the specified torque (see illustration).

8 Refit the protector plate (where removed) to the lower balljoint, then locate the balljoint shank in the hub carrier. Fit the new retaining nut and tighten it to the specified torque.

9 Refit the ABS sensor (where applicable), and clip the wiring harness into place.

10 Refit the roadwheel, then lower the vehicle and tighten the roadwheel bolts to the specified torque.

11 Check and, if necessary, adjust the front wheel alignment as described in Section 27.

8 Front anti-roll bar – removal and refitting

Note: *Always renew any self-locking nuts when working on the suspension/steering components.*

Removal

1 Chock the rear wheels, firmly apply the handbrake, slacken the front roadwheel bolts, then jack up the front of the vehicle and support on axle stands (see *Jacking and vehicle support*). Remove both front roadwheels.

2 Slacken and remove the nuts securing the left- and right-hand connecting links to the anti-roll bar, and position the links clear of

the bar; if necessary, retain the balljoint shank with a Torx bit or Allen key (as applicable) to prevent rotation whilst the nut is slackened (see illustration). Discard the nuts, new ones should be used on refitting.

3 Slacken the two anti-roll bar mounting clamp retaining bolts, and remove both clamps from the top of the subframe (see illustration).

1.9 litre models

4 Slacken and remove the nut securing the right-hand steering rack track rod to the hub carrier then free the balljoint from the hub. If the balljoint is tight, use a universal balljoint separator to free it. Discard the nut, a new one should be used on refitting.

5 Undo the 2 bolts and remove the heat shield from the subframe.

6 Undo the bolt and detach the wiring harness support bracket from the steering rack.

7 Undo the nuts securing the front silencer to the front exhaust pipe, slacken the clamp at the rear of the silencer, then manoeuvre the silencer from place.

2.0 litre models

8 Undo the 2 nuts securing the steering rack to the front subframe. Discard the nuts – new ones must be fitted. Secure the rack to the vehicle body using cable-ties, etc.

9 Undo the 2 retaining bolts and move the heat shield above the subframe to one side.

10 Undo the bolts and remove the rear lower stabiliser arms from between the subframe and the vehicle body (see illustration).

11 Place a workshop jack under the subframe, then undo the mounting bolts and lower the subframe sufficiently to manoeuvre the anti-roll

bar from the right-hand side of the engine compartment (see illustrations 10.13a, 10.13b and 10.13c). Unclip the brake pipes and any wiring harnesses as necessary.

All models

12 With the help of an assistant, manoeuvre the anti-roll bar out from the right-hand side of the vehicle, and remove the mounting bushes from the bar.

13 Carefully examine the anti-roll bar components for signs of wear, damage or deterioration, paying particular attention to the mounting bushes. Renew worn components as necessary.

Refitting

14 Offer up the anti-roll bar, and manoeuvre it into position on the subframe. Refit the mounting clamps, and refit the retaining bolts and nuts. Engage the connecting links with the ends of the bar then tighten the mounting clamp retaining bolts to the specified torque.

15 The remainder of refitting is a reversal of removal. Where applicable, apply a little thread-locking compound to the subframe mounting bolts.

9 Front anti-roll bar connecting link – removal and refitting

Removal

1 Chock the rear wheels, firmly apply the

8.2 Undo the anti-roll bar-to-link nut (arrowed)

8.3 Anti-roll bar clamp bolts (arrowed)

8.10 Undo the bolts (arrowed) and remove the stabiliser bar each side

handbrake, slacken the relevant roadwheel bolts, then jack up the front of the vehicle and support on axle stands (see *Jacking and vehicle support*). Remove the relevant roadwheel.

2 Slacken and remove the nuts securing the connecting link to the anti-roll bar and suspension strut and remove the link from the vehicle; if necessary, retain the balljoint shanks with a Torx bit or Allen key (as applicable) to prevent rotation whilst each nut is slackened **(see illustration)**. Discard the nuts, new ones should be used on refitting.

3 Inspect the link for signs of wear or damage and renew if necessary.

Refitting

4 Refitting is the reverse of removal, using new nuts and tightening them to the specified torque setting.

10 Front subframe – removal and refitting

Note: *Always renew any self-locking nuts when working on the suspension/steering components.*

Removal

1 Chock the rear wheels, firmly apply the handbrake, slacken the front roadwheel bolts, and then jack up the front of the vehicle and support it on axle stands (see *Jacking and vehicle support*). Remove both front roadwheels.

2 Undo the fasteners and remove the engine/transmission undertray.

9.2 Undo the nuts securing the anti-roll bar links to the suspension strut

3 Undo the bolts and remove the heat shield from the above the subframe.

4 Undo the nuts/bolts securing the steering rack to the subframe. Discard the nuts – new ones must be fitted. Secure the rack to the vehicle body using cable-ties, etc.

5 Slacken the two anti-roll bar mounting clamp retaining bolts, and remove both clamps from the top of the subframe **(see illustration 8.3)**.

6 Release the brake pipes each side from the retaining clips on the subframe.

7 Undo the bolts and remove the rear stabiliser arms from between the subframe and vehicle body **(see illustration 8.10)**.

8 Undo the bolts securing the lower rear mounting link from between the engine and subframe **(see illustration)**.

9 Slacken and remove the left-hand lower balljoint nut and free the balljoint shank from the hub carrier, if necessary, using a universal

balljoint separator. Discard the nut. Repeat the procedure on the right-hand side.

10 Unclip the ABS wheel speed sensor wiring harnesses (where fitted) from the control arm each side.

11 Make a final check that all control cables/hoses that are attached to the subframe have been released and positioned clear so that they will not hinder the removal procedure.

12 Place a jack and a suitable block of wood under the subframe to support the subframe as it is lowered.

13 Slacken and remove the subframe mounting bolts then carefully lower the subframe assembly out of position and remove it from underneath the vehicle, taking great care to ensure that the subframe assembly does not catch the power steering pipes as it is lowered out of position **(see illustrations)**.

Refitting

14 Refitting is a reversal of the removal procedure, noting the following points:

a) *Apply a little thread-locking compound to the subrame mounting bolts.*

b) *Use new stabiliser arm nuts, lower balljoint nuts, and steering rack nuts.*

c) *Tighten all nuts and bolts to the specified torque settings (where given).*

d) *On completion check and, if necessary, adjust the front wheel alignment as described in Section 27.*

11 Rear hub assembly – removal and refitting

The rear hub is integral with the rear brake disc. Removal of the disc is described in Chapter 9.

12 Rear hub bearings – renewal

Removal

1 Remove the rear brake disc as described in Chapter 9.

2 Remove the retaining circlip **(see illustration)**.

10.8 Remove the lower rear mounting link (arrowed)

10.13a Undo the remaining subframe mounting bolt (arrowed) each side

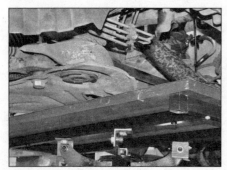

10.13b Support the subframe and gently lower it

10.13c Note the dowels at the rear mounting points (arrowed)

12.2 Remove the bearing circlip

3 Using a hydraulic press and a suitable tubular spacer, press the bearing from the disc/hub **(see illustration)**.

Refitting

4 Position the new bearing in the hub, then using a tubular spacer that acts only on the hard outer edge of the bearing, press the bearing into place.

5 Fit the new circlip.

6 Refit the brake disc/hub as described in Chapter 9.

12.3 Press the bearing from the hub/disc

13 Rear shock absorber – removal, testing and refitting

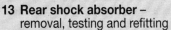
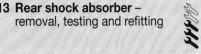

Note: *Always renew any self-locking nuts when working on the suspension/steering components.*

Removal

1 Slacken the roadwheel bolts, raise the rear of the vehicle and support it securely on axle stands (see *Jacking and vehicle support*). Remove the rear roadwheels.

2 Position a trolley jack under the rear axle on the relevant side, and raise the axle to relieve any tension on the shock absorber **(see illustration)**.

3 If removing the left-hand side shock absorber, undo the bolts, lower the carrier and remove the spare wheel.

4 Working underneath the vehicle, undo the bolt, release the clips and remove the plastic panel beneath the shock absorber upper mounting bolt **(see illustration)**.

5 Slacken and remove the mounting bolts/nuts and nut then manoeuvre the shock absorber out of position **(see illustrations)**. Recover the deflector plate from the lower mounting bolts.

Testing

6 Examine the shock absorber for signs of fluid leakage or damage. Test the operation of the shock absorber, while holding it in an upright position, by moving the piston through a full stroke and then through short strokes of 50 to 100 mm. In both cases, the resistance felt should be smooth and continuous. If the resistance is jerky, or

uneven, or if there is any visible sign of wear or damage, renewal is necessary. Also check the rubber mountings for damage and deterioration. Renew worn components as necessary. Inspect the shank of the mounting bolt for signs of wear or damage, and renew as necessary. The self-locking nuts should be renewed as a matter of course.

Refitting

7 Measure the distance between the centres of the shock absorber upper and lower mounting bolts, and adjust the height of the axle with the trolley jacks until the distance is 400 mm ± 10 mm.

8 Manoeuvre the shock absorber into position. Refit the upper mounting bolt/nut, and tighten them to the specified torque.

9 Align the shock absorber lower mounting with the rear axle and refit the mounting bolt.

13.2 Place a trolley jack under the rear axle

Fit the nut, tightening it lightly only at this stage. Do not omit the deflector plate from the lower mounting bolts.

10 Refit the plastic panel beneath the upper mounting.

11 Where applicable refit the spare wheel.

12 Refit the rear roadwheel then lower the vehicle to the ground and tighten the wheel bolts to the specified torque. Rock the vehicle to settle the shock absorber in position then tighten the shock absorber lower mounting to the specified torque setting.

14 Rear coil spring – removal and refitting

Removal

1 Chock the front wheels, slacken the rear roadwheel bolts, then jack up the rear of the vehicle and support it on axle stands (see *Jacking and vehicle support*). Remove the rear roadwheels.

2 Place a trolley jack under the axle each side. Raise the jacks to relieve any tension on the shock absorbers, then undo the nuts and pull out the shock absorber lower mounting bolts each side **(see illustrations 13.2 and 13.5b)**.

3 Lower the trolley jack each side, just enough to uncompress the coil springs and manoeuvre them from place. Do not lower the axle too far, or the brake flexible hoses will be damaged **(see illustration)**.

4 If required, undo the bolts and remove the

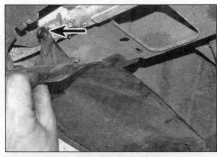

13.4 Undo the bolt (arrowed) and remove the plastic panel beneath the shock absorber upper mounting

13.5a Remove the upper mounting bolt/nut (arrowed)

13.5b Remove the lower mounting bolt/nut (arrowed)...

13.5c... and the deflector plate

14.3 Lower the axle and manoeuvre the coil spring from place

14.4 Undo the bolts (arrowed) and remove the spring seat

spring upper mounting from the vehicle body **(see illustration)**.

5 Inspect the coil spring and its seats for signs of wear or damage and renew if necessary.

Refitting

6 If removed, locate the upper spring seat on the vehicle body, fit the bolts and tighten them securely.

7 Manoeuvre the spring into place, ensuring it locates correctly with the upper, and lower seats.

8 Gradually raise the trolley jack each side, until the shock absorber lower mounting bolts can be inserted. Tighten the nuts to the specified torque.

9 Refit the rear roadwheel then lower the vehicle to the ground and tighten the wheel bolts to the specified torque.

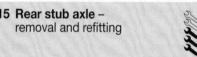

15 Rear stub axle –
removal and refitting

Removal

1 Chock the front wheels, slacken the relevant rear roadwheel bolts, then jack up the rear of the vehicle and support it on axle stands (see *Jacking and vehicle support*). Remove the relevant roadwheel.

2 Unbolt the wheel sensor and position it clear of the stub axle (see Chapter 9). Note that there is no need to disconnect the wiring.

3 Remove the brake disc as described in Chapter 9.

4 Undo the retaining bolts and remove the disc backplate **(see illustration)**.

5 Undo the four bolts securing the stub axle to the axle and remove it **(see illustration)**.

6 Inspect the stub axle for signs of wear or damage. If the stub axle shaft is worn or damaged then the assembly must be renewed

Refitting

7 Clean the contact faces of the stub axle and rear axle, then use a suitable tap to clean out the threads.

8 Apply a little thread-locking fluid to the bolts, then position the stub axle, and tighten the bolts to the specified torque.

9 The remainder of refitting is a reversal of removal.

16 Rear beam axle –
removal, overhaul and refitting

Note: *Always renew any self-locking nuts when working on the suspension/steering components.*

Removal

1 Remove the coil springs as described in Section 14, and the shock absorbers as described in Section 13.

2 Undo the nut and detach the load-sensing valve fixed rod (where fitted) from the axle **(see illustration)**.

3 Undo the bolt securing the lateral control rod to the axle **(see illustration 17.2)**.

4 Slacken the handbrake adjustment nut, and detach the ends of the cables from the calipers – refer to Chapter 9.

5 Trace the ABS wheel speed sensor (where fitted) wiring back to its connector, and unplug it. Free the sensor harness from any retaining clips on the axle.

6 Clamp the flexible brake hose, and undo the hose union where the flexible hose connects to the rigid hose **(see illustration)**. Plug the end of the hose/pipe to prevent dirt ingress. Repeat this procedure on the remaining side.

7 Undo the bolt/nut each side securing the axle to the vehicle body, and with the help of an assistant, lower the axle to the floor **(see illustration)**. If the axle is to be renewed, remove the brake caliper and disc (Chapter 9), and the stub axle (Section 15).

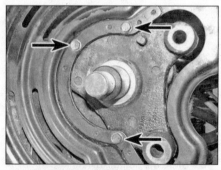

15.4 Disc backplate retaining bolts (arrowed)

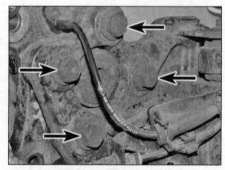

15.5 Undo the bolts (arrowed) securing the stub axle

16.2 Load-sensing valve link-rod retaining nut (arrowed)

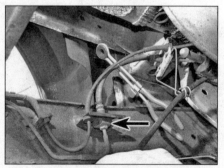

16.6 Clamp the hose, and disconnect the brake pipe union (arrowed)

16.7 Undo the bolt (arrowed) each side securing the axle to the vehicle body

Overhaul

8 Thoroughly clean the axle and the area around the axle mountings, removing all traces of dirt and underseal if necessary, then check carefully for cracks, distortion or any other signs of wear or damage, paying particular attention to the pivot bushes.
9 Renewal of the pivot bushes is possible without completely removing the axle – see Section 18.

Refitting

10 With the help of an assistant, offer up the axle, and insert the retaining bolts. Only finger-tighten the new nuts at this stage.
11 Refit the shock absorbers as described in Section 13, then tighten the axle retaining bolts to the specified torque.
12 Reconnect the brake pipes/hoses, remove the hose clamps.
13 Refit the handbrake cables to their retaining clips on the axle, and reconnect the cable ends to the caliper levers (see Chapter 9).
14 Reconnect the lateral control rod to the axle, refit the bolt and tighten it to the specified torque.
15 Re-attach the load-sensing valve fixed rod, and tighten the retaining nut securely.
16 The remainder of refitting is a reversal of removal. On completion bleed the brakes and adjust the handbrake as described in Chapter 9.

17 Lateral control rod – removal and refitting

Removal

1 Chock the front wheels, slacken the rear roadwheel bolts, then jack up the rear of the vehicle and support it on axle stands (see *Jacking and vehicle support*). Remove the roadwheels.
2 Undo the nut, and remove the bolt securing the lateral control rod to the axle **(see illustration)**.
3 Undo the nut, and remove the bolt securing the lateral control rod to the vehicle body **(see illustration)**. Manoeuvre the lateral control rod from under the vehicle.

17.2 Lateral control rod-to-axle bolt (arrowed)

Refitting

4 Manoeuvre the lateral control rod into position, install the bolts and tighten the retaining nuts to the specified torque.
5 Refit the roadwheels, lower the vehicle to the ground, then tighten the wheel bolts to the specified torque.

18 Rear axle bushes – removal and refitting

Removal

1 Chock the front wheels, slacken the rear roadwheel bolts, then jack up the rear of the vehicle and support it on axle stands (see *Jacking and vehicle support*). Remove the roadwheels.
2 Unclip the handbrake cable and ABS sensor wires (where fitted) each side from the retaining clips/brackets on the axle.
3 Clamp the flexible brake hose, and undo the hose union where the flexible hose connects to the rigid hose **(see illustration 16.6)**. Plug the end of the hose/pipe to prevent dirt ingress. Repeat this procedure on the other side.
4 Place a trolley jack under the axle arms on each side, then undo the nuts and withdraw the bolts securing the front of the axle to the vehicle body **(see illustration 16.7)**. Take care as the axle will try to move rearwards a little.
5 Lower the axle arms a little to access the rubber bushes.

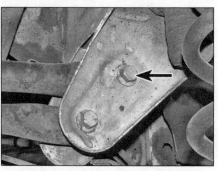
17.3 Lateral control rod-to-body bolt (arrowed)

6 The bushes must now be pressed from the axle. Vauxhall and Renault technicians use tool No KM-6229 to draw the bushes out. Similar tools may be available from specialist automotive tools suppliers.
7 In the absence of special tools, use 2 suitably-sized spacers and a length of threaded rod, with washers and nuts. Remove the bushes as shown in the accompanying illustrations **(see illustrations)**. As the diameter of the bush is 70 mm, one spacer needs to have an internal diameter of approximately 72 mm so the bush can pass through it, whilst the other spacer needs to have an external diameter of approximately 69 mm so that it bears only on the hard outer surface of the bush. Note the fitted depth of the bushes prior to removal.

Refitting

8 There are two types of bushes fitted: Solid type – where there is no particular orientation of the bush, and Void type. Position the void type bushes so the larger V-shaped holes are horizontal.
9 The bushes are fitted into the holes in the axle arms from the outside, using a combination of suitable-sized spacers, washers, threaded rod and nuts. Vauxhall and Renault technicians use tool No KM-6229 to draw the bushes into place. Similar tools may be available from specialist automotive tools suppliers **(see illustrations)**.
10 Lift the axle arms, insert the bolts, but do not tighten the new retaining nuts at this stage. Note that an assistant will be required

18.7a Position a spacer of approximately 72 mm diameter on one side of the bush...

18.7b... and a spacer of approximately 69 mm on the other side...

18.7c... then tighten the nut on the threaded rod, and draw out the bush

18.9a Position the new bush in the axle arm...

18.11 Set the distance between the upper and lower shock absorber mountings to 400 ± 10 mm

to help stabilise the axle as it's manoeuvred into place.

11 Measure the distance between the centres of the shock absorber upper and lower mounting bolts, and adjust the height of

19.3 Undo the steering wheel retaining bolt (arrowed)

20.2b ...remove the upper steering column shroud...

18.9b ...and draw into place, so the fitted depth is 11.5 mm on the inside edge

the axle with the trolley jacks until the distance is 400 mm ± 10 mm **(see illustration)**. Now tighten the front axle mounting bolts to the specified torque.

12 Reconnect the brake pipes/hoses, remove the hose clamps, and bleed the brakes as described in Chapter 9.

13 Refit the handbrake cables to their retaining clips on the axle.

14 Refit the roadwheels, lower the vehicle to the ground, then tighten the wheel bolts to the specified torque.

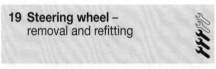

19 Steering wheel –
removal and refitting

> ⚠️ **Warning: Refer to the precautions given in Chapter 12, Section 23 before proceeding.**

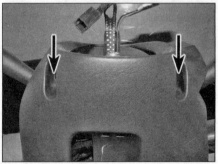

20.2a Undo the 2 screws (arrowed)...

20.2c ...and the lower shroud

Removal

1 Remove the airbag unit as described in Chapter 12.

2 Position the front wheels in the straight-ahead position and engage the steering lock.

3 Slacken and remove the steering wheel retaining bolt then mark the steering wheel and steering column shaft in relation to each other **(see illustration)**. Discard the bolt – a new one must be fitted.

4 Lift the steering wheel off the column splines, feeding the airbag wires through the aperture in the steering wheel as it is withdrawn.

> **HAYNES HiNT** *If the wheel is tight, tap it up near the centre, using the palm of your hand, or twist it from side-to-side, whilst carefully pulling it upwards to release it from the shaft splines.*

Refitting

5 Prior to refitting the steering wheel, ensure that the front wheels are still in the straight-ahead.

6 Refitting is a reversal of removal, noting the following points:

a) On refitting, align the marks made on removal, taking great care not to damage the airbag unit wiring, then tighten the new retaining bolt to the specified torque.

b) On completion, refit the airbag unit as described in Chapter 12.

20 Steering column –
removal, inspection and refitting

Removal

1 Raise the steering wheel to its highest position, then remove the steering wheel as described in Section 19.

2 Undo the 2 screws and remove the upper and lower steering column shrouds **(see illustrations)**.

3 On models with ESP, release the 4 clips, disconnect the wiring plug and remove the steering angle sensor.

4 Remove the steering column combination switches as described in Chapter 12.

5 Note their fitted locations, then disconnect the various wiring plugs from the column, and release the wiring harnesses from the retaining clips.

6 Pull the instrument cluster panel rearwards to release the 4 retaining clips **(see illustration)**.

7 Working in the driver's footwell, undo the bolts/nuts and slide the column shaft coupling downwards **(see illustration)**. Discard the nuts – new ones must be fitted.

8 Remove the combination switches from the top of the steering column as described in Chapter 12.

9 Slacken and remove the 2 mounting bolts

from the top of the column **(see illustration)**. Slide the column assembly upwards, and remove it from the vehicle.

Inspection

10 Before refitting the steering column, examine the column and mountings for signs of damage and deformation, and renew as necessary. Check the steering shaft for signs of free play in the column bushes, and check the universal joints for signs of damage or roughness in the joint bearings.

Refitting

11 Align the master splines, and engage the column shafts with the coupling **(see illustration)**.
12 Slide the column assembly into position making sure its mounting bracket is correctly engaged with the facia bracket. Refit the column mounting bolts and tighten them to the specified torque setting.
13 Refit the coupling bolt and new nut, tighten them to the specified torque setting.
14 The remainder of refitting is a direct reversal of the removal procedure, noting the following.
 a) Ensure that all wiring is correctly routed and retained by all the necessary clips and ties.
 b) Refit the steering wheel as described in Section 19.

21 Ignition switch lock cylinder – removal and refitting

Removal

1 Raise the steering wheel to its highest position, then remove the steering wheel as described in Section 19.
2 Undo the 2 screws and remove the upper and lower steering column shrouds **(see illustrations 20.2a, 20.2b and 20.2c)**.
3 Release the clip and remove the immobiliser antenna from the ignition switch **(see illustration)**.
4 Insert the ignition key, then undo the lock cylinder retaining screw **(see illustration)**.
5 Turn the ignition key to align it with the 'non-lettered' position, depress the clips on the underside, and pull the lock cylinder from

20.6 Pull the instrument cluster panel rearwards

20.9 Steering column mounting bolts (arrowed)

place **(see illustrations)**. Trace the wiring back to the connectors and unplug them.

Refitting

6 With the key inserted, align the cylinder as described in paragraph 5.

21.3 Lift up the clip (arrowed) and slide the immobiliser antenna from the ignition switch

21.5a Align the key with the 'non-lettered' position (arrowed)...

21.5b... depress the clips (arrowed) and pull the switch from place

20.7 Steering column coupling retaining nuts (arrowed)

20.11 Align the master spline (arrowed) on the column shaft with the groove in the coupling

7 Insert the lock cylinder into place until the retaining clips audibly engage.
8 Refit the retaining screw, and tighten it securely.
9 The remainder of refitting is a reversal of removal.

21.4 Undo the ignition switch retaining screw (arrowed)

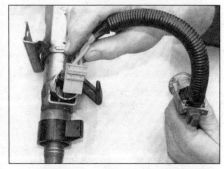
21.5c Feed the wiring loom through the bracket

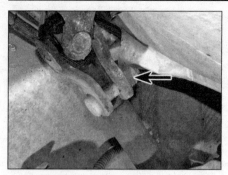

22.8 Undo the steering column lower universal joint pinch-bolt (arrowed)

22 Steering rack assembly – removal, overhaul and refitting

Note: *Always renew any self-locking nuts when working on the suspension/steering components.*

Removal

1 Set the front wheels in the 'straight-ahead' position, and engage the steering lock.
2 Slacken and remove the nuts securing the steering rack track rod balljoints to the hub carriers. Release the balljoint tapered shanks using a universal balljoint separator. Discard the nuts, new ones will be needed on refitting.
3 Remove the front subframe as described in Section 10.
4 Release the clips and remove the inner splash panel from the right-hand inner wheel arch liner.
5 Undo the 2 bolts and remove the heat shield from the steering rack pinion housing.
6 Clean the area around the rack pinion housing, then undo the nuts securing the fluid pipes to the rack pinion housing, release the pipes from the retaining clamp, and drain the fluid into a container. Discard the pipes O-ring seals, new ones must be fitted. Plug the ends of the pipes to prevent dirt ingress.
7 Undo the bolt securing the power steering fluid pipe bracket to the steering rack.
8 Make alignment marks between the universal joint and the steering rack pinion, then remove the pinch-bolt from the lower steering column universal joint **(see illustration)**.

23.2a Steering rack gaiter outer clip (arrowed)...

9 With the help of as assistant, manoeuvre the steering rack from position.

Overhaul

10 Examine the steering rack assembly for signs of wear or damage, and check that the rack moves freely throughout the full length of its travel, with no signs of roughness or excessive free play between the steering rack pinion and rack. Inspect all the steering rack fluid unions for signs of leakage, and check that all union nuts are securely tightened.
11 It is possible to overhaul the steering rack assembly housing components, but this task should be entrusted to a dealer or specialist. The only components which can be renewed easily by the home mechanic are the steering rack gaiters, the track rod balljoints and the track rods which are covered elsewhere in this Chapter.

Refitting

12 Manoeuvre the steering rack into position and engage it with the column universal joint, aligning the marks made prior to removal.
13 Refit the universal joint pinch-bolt, but tighten the new nut to the specified torque.
14 The remainder of refitting is a reversal of removal, noting the following points:
   a) Refit the steering rack using new mounting nuts.
   b) Top-up the fluid reservoir and bleed the hydraulic system as described in Section 24.
   c) On completion check and, if necessary, adjust the front wheel alignment as described in Section 27.

23 Steering rack rubber gaiters – renewal

1 Remove the track rod balljoint as described in Section 26.
2 Mark the correct fitted position of the gaiter on the track rod, then release the retaining clips and slide the gaiter off the steering rack housing and track rod end **(see illustrations)**.
3 Thoroughly clean the track rod and the steering rack housing, using fine abrasive paper to polish off any corrosion, burrs or sharp edges which might damage the new gaiter's sealing lips on installation. Scrape off

23.2b... and inner clip (arrowed)

all the grease from the old gaiter, and apply it to the track rod inner balljoint. (This assumes that grease has not been lost or contaminated as a result of damage to the old gaiter. Use fresh grease if in doubt.)
4 Carefully slide the new gaiter onto the track rod end, and locate it on the steering rack housing. Align the outer edge of the gaiter with the mark made on the track rod prior to removal, then secure it in position with new retaining clips (where fitted).
5 Refit the track rod balljoint as described in Section 26.

24 Power steering system – bleeding

1 This procedure will only be necessary when any of the hydraulic system has been disconnected.
2 Referring to *Weekly checks*, remove the fluid reservoir filler cap, and top-up with the new specified fluid to the upper level mark. Allow the fluid level to settle for at least 2 minutes.
3 Without starting the engine, slowly turn the steering wheel from lock-to-lock. Check the fluid level again.
4 Start the engine, and slowly move the steering from lock-to-lock several times to purge out the trapped air.
5 Turn the engine off and allow the system to cool. Once cool, check that fluid level is up to the upper mark on the power steering fluid reservoir, topping-up if necessary. If the fluid is aerated (foamy), allow the system to settle for a few minutes, and check again.

25 Power steering pump – removal and refitting

Removal – 1.9 litre models

1 Remove the auxiliary drivebelt as described in Chapter 1.
2 Undo the retaining bolt and remove the auxiliary drivebelt tensioner assembly.
3 Undo the pipe securing the power steering fluid pipe support bracket to the engine block.

Models with air conditioning

4 Disconnect the battery negative lead as described in Chapter 5.
5 Prise out the plastic caps, undo the bolts and remove the plastic cover from the top of the engine.
6 Release the clips, undo the support bracket bolt (where fitted), and remove the air hose between the intercooler and the intake manifold.
7 Unclip the power steering fluid reservoir from the bonnet slam panel **(see illustration)**.
8 Release the clip, disconnect the hose, and drain the power steering fluid reservoir into a container. Be prepared for fluid spillage.

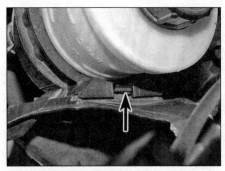

25.7 Push the clip (arrowed) rearwards and slide the reservoir upwards

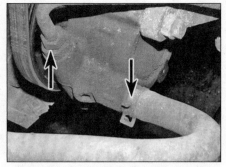

25.9 Power steering pump fluid feed and return pipes (arrowed) – 1.9 litre engines

25.13 Power steering pump pulley (arrowed) – 2.0 litre engines

25.16 Remove the intercooler outlet hose (arrowed)

25.17 Oil level dipstick guide tube retaining bolt (arrowed)

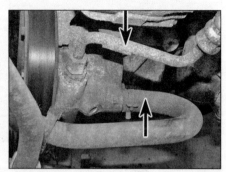

25.19 Power steering pump fluid feed and return hoses (arrowed) – 2.0 litre engines

All models

9 Undo the union and disconnect the fluid pipe from the power steering pump **(see illustration)**. Be prepared for fluid spillage, and plug the pump and pipe openings to prevent dirt ingress.
Caution: Do not bend the rigid power steering pump fluid pipe.
10 Undo the upper and lower pump mounting bolt/nuts and remove the pump from position.
11 Release the clip and disconnect the fluid return hose from the pump **(see illustration 25.9)**. Be prepared for fluid spillage.
12 If the power steering pump is faulty it must be renewed. The pump is a sealed unit and cannot be overhauled.

Removal – 2.0 litre models

13 Remove the auxiliary drivebelt as described in Chapter 1. **Note:** *Before removing the drivebelt, slacken the power steering pump pulley bolts (see illustration).*

Models with air conditioning

14 Disconnect the battery negative lead as described in Chapter 5.
15 Unclip the hose from the oil filler funnel on the air cleaner assembly and move it to one side.
16 Release the clips and remove the intercooler outlet hose from the engine compartment **(see illustration)**. Disconnect any wiring plugs as the hose is withdrawn.
17 Undo the retaining bolt and remove the engine oil level dipstick guide tube **(see illustration)**. Renew the tube O-ring seal.

All models

18 Completely undo the retaining bolts and remove the power steering pump pulley.
19 Release the clip, undo the union nut, and disconnect the power steering fluid return and feed pipes from the pump **(see illustration)**. Be prepared for fluid spillage. Plug the openings to prevent contamination.
20 Undo the mounting bolts and remove the pump from the auxiliary support bracket.

Refitting

21 Reconnect the fluid return hose to the pump, and secure it with the retaining clip.
22 Manoeuvre the pump into position, then refit its mounting bolts and tighten them to the specified torque.
23 Reconnect the feed pipe to the pump and securely tighten the union nut.
24 The remainder of refitting is a reversal of removal, noting the following points:
  a) *Tighten all fasteners to their specified torque where given.*
  b) *Refit the auxiliary drivebelt as described in Chapter 1.*
  c) *On completion, bleed the hydraulic system as described in Section 24.*

26 Track rod balljoint – removal and refitting

Removal

1 Apply the handbrake, slacken the appropriate front roadwheel bolts, then jack up the front of the vehicle and support it on axle stands (see *Jacking and vehicle support*). Remove the appropriate front roadwheel.
2 If the balljoint is to be re-used, use a straight-edge and a scriber, or similar, to mark its relationship to the track rod.
3 Hold the track rod, and unscrew the balljoint locknut by a quarter of a turn. Do not move the locknut from this position, as it will serve as a handy reference mark on refitting.
4 Slacken and remove the nut securing the track rod balljoint to the hub carrier; discard the nut, a new one will be needed on refitting. Release the balljoint tapered shank using a universal balljoint separator **(see illustration)**.
5 Counting the **exact** number of turns necessary to do so, unscrew the balljoint from the track rod end.
6 Count the number of exposed threads

26.4 Undo the nut securing the track rod end balljoint to the hub carrier, using a Torx bit/key to counterhold

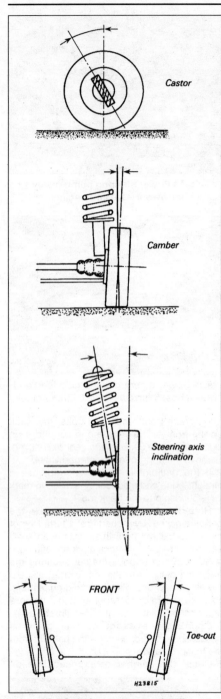

27.1 Steering geometry details

between the end of the balljoint and the locknut, and record this figure. If a new balljoint is to be fitted, unscrew the locknut from the old balljoint.

7 Carefully clean the balljoint and the threads. Renew the balljoint if its movement is sloppy or too stiff, if excessively worn, or if damaged in any way; carefully check the stud taper and threads. If the balljoint gaiter is damaged, the complete balljoint assembly must be renewed; it is not possible to obtain the gaiter separately.

Refitting

8 If a new balljoint is to be fitted, screw the locknut onto its threads, and position it so that the same number of exposed threads are visible, as was noted prior to removal.

9 Screw the balljoint into the track rod by the number of turns noted on removal. This should bring the balljoint locknut to within a quarter of a turn from the track rod, with the alignment marks that were made on removal (if applicable) lined up.

10 Ensure that the protector plate is in position then locate the balljoint shank in the hub carrier. Fit a new retaining nut and tighten it to the specified torque.

11 Refit the roadwheel, then lower the vehicle to the ground and tighten the roadwheel bolts to the specified torque.

12 Check and, if necessary, adjust the front wheel alignment as described in Section 27, then securely tighten the balljoint locknut.

27 Wheel alignment and steering angles – information, checking and adjustment

Definitions

1 A car's steering and suspension geometry is defined in four basic settings (**see illustration**) – all angles are expressed in degrees (toe settings are also expressed as a measurement); the steering axis is defined as an imaginary line drawn through the axis of the suspension strut, extended where necessary to contact the ground.

2 **Camber** is the angle between each roadwheel and a vertical line drawn through its centre and tyre contact patch, when viewed from the front or rear of the car. Positive camber is when the roadwheels are tilted outwards from the vertical at the top; negative camber is when they are tilted inwards. The camber angle is not adjustable

3 **Castor** is the angle between the steering axis and a vertical line drawn through each roadwheel's centre and tyre contact patch, when viewed from the side of the car. Positive castor is when the steering axis is tilted so that it contacts the ground ahead of the vertical; negative castor is when it contacts the ground behind the vertical. The castor angle is not adjustable.

4 **Toe** is the difference, viewed from above, between lines drawn through the roadwheel centres and the car's centre-line. 'Toe-in' is when the roadwheels point inwards, towards each other at the front, while 'toe-out' is when they splay outwards from each other at the front.

5 The front wheel toe setting is adjusted by screwing the track rod in or out of its balljoints, to alter the effective length of the track rod assembly.

6 Rear wheel toe setting is not adjustable.

Checking and adjustment

7 Due to the special measuring equipment necessary to check the wheel alignment and steering angles, and the skill required to use it properly, the checking and adjustment of these settings is best left to a dealer or similar expert. Note that most tyre-fitting shops now possess sophisticated checking equipment. The following is provided as a guide, should the owner decide to carry out a DIY check.

Front wheel toe setting

8 The front wheel toe setting is checked by measuring the angle of the wheels in relation to the longitudinal axis of the vehicle. Proprietary toe measurement gauges are available from motor accessory shops. Adjustment is made by screwing the balljoints in or out of their track rods, to alter the effective length of the track rod assemblies.

9 Before starting work, check first that the tyre sizes and types are as specified, then check the tyre pressures and tread wear, the roadwheel run-out, the condition of the hub bearings, the steering wheel free play, and the condition of the front suspension components (see *Weekly checks* and Chapter 1). Correct any faults found.

10 Park the vehicle on level ground, check that the front roadwheels are in the straight-ahead position, then rock the rear and front ends to settle the suspension. Release the handbrake, and roll the vehicle backwards 1 metre, then forwards again, to relieve any stresses in the steering and suspension components.

11 Follow the tracking gauge manufacturers instructions and measure the toe setting.

12 If adjustment is necessary, apply the handbrake, then jack up the front of the vehicle and support it securely on axle stands. Turn the steering wheel onto full-left lock, and record the number of exposed threads on the right-hand track rod end. Now turn the steering onto full-right lock, and record the number of threads on the left-hand side. If there are the same number of threads visible on both sides, then subsequent adjustment should be made equally on both sides. If there are more threads visible on one side than the other, it will be necessary to compensate for this during adjustment. **Note:** *It is most important that after adjustment, the same number of threads are visible on each track rod end.*

13 First clean the track rod threads; if they are corroded, apply penetrating fluid before starting adjustment. Release the rubber gaiter outboard clips (where necessary), and peel back the gaiters; apply a smear of grease to the inside of the gaiters, so that both are free, and will not be twisted or strained as their respective track rods are rotated.

14 Use a straight-edge and a scriber or similar to mark the relationship of each track rod to its balljoint then, holding each track rod in turn, unscrew its locknut fully.

15 Alter the length of the track rods, bearing in mind the note made in paragraph 12. **Note:** *One complete rotation of the track rod equals approximately 2 mm of adjustment.* Screw them onto or off the balljoints, rotating the track rod using an open-ended spanner fitted to the flats provided on the track rod. Shortening the track rods (screwing them into their balljoints) will reduce toe-in/increase toe-out.

16 When the setting is correct, hold the track rods and tighten the balljoint locknuts to the specified torque setting. Check that the balljoints are seated correctly in their sockets, and count the exposed threads to check the length of both track rods. If they are not the same, then the adjustment has not been made equally, and problems will be encountered with tyre scrubbing in turns; also, the steering wheel spokes will no longer be horizontal when the wheels are in the straight-ahead position.

17 If the track rod lengths are the same, lower the vehicle to the ground and recheck the toe setting; re-adjust if necessary. When the setting is correct, tighten the track rod balljoint locknuts to the specified torque. Ensure that the rubber gaiters are seated correctly, and are not twisted or strained, and secure them in position with new retaining clips (where necessary).

Chapter 11
Bodywork and fittings

Contents

Degrees of difficulty

Easy, suitable for novice with little experience	Fairly easy, suitable for beginner with some experience	Fairly difficult, suitable for competent DIY mechanic 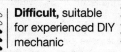	Difficult, suitable for experienced DIY mechanic 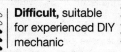	Very difficult, suitable for expert DIY or professional

Specifications

Torque wrench settings	Nm	lbf ft
Front seat retaining bolts	44	32
Seat belt mounting bolts:		
Inertia reel:		
Except centre belt.	37	27
Centre belt	19	14
Upper anchorage	25	18
Lower anchorage	37	27
Stalk/pretensioner	37	27

1 General information

The body and chassis on all versions of the Vivaro and Trafic are of all-steel construction, with galvanised panels. Two basic chassis types are available: short-wheelbase and long-wheelbase.

Twin opening rear doors or a tailgate are fitted and, on some models, side opening door(s) are available. The bodyshell is as aerodynamic in shape as possible, to promote economy and reduce wind noise levels.

Extensive use is made of plastic materials, mainly on the interior, but also in exterior components. The front and rear bumpers are injection-moulded from a synthetic material which is very strong and yet light. Plastic components such as wheel arch liners are fitted to the underside of the vehicle, to improve the body's resistance to corrosion.

Due to the large number of specialist applications of this vehicle range, information contained in this Chapter is given on parts found to be common on the popular factory-produced versions. No information is provided on special body versions.

2 Maintenance – bodywork and underframe

The general condition of a vehicle's bodywork is the one thing that significantly affects its value. Maintenance is easy, but needs to be regular. Neglect, particularly after minor damage, can lead quickly to further deterioration and costly repair bills. It is important also to keep watch on those parts of the vehicle not immediately visible, for instance the underside, inside all the wheel arches, and the lower part of the engine compartment.

The basic maintenance routine for the bodywork is washing – preferably with a lot of water, from a hose. This will remove all the loose solids which may have stuck to the vehicle. It is important to flush these off in such a way as to prevent grit from scratching the finish. The wheel arches and underframe need washing in the same way, to remove any accumulated mud, which will retain moisture and tend to encourage rust. Paradoxically enough, the best time to clean the underframe and wheel arches is in wet weather, when the mud is thoroughly wet and soft. In very wet weather, the underframe is usually cleaned of large accumulations automatically, and this is a good time for inspection.

Periodically, except on vehicles with a wax-based underbody protective coating, it is a good idea to have the whole of the underframe of the vehicle steam-cleaned, engine compartment included, so that a thorough inspection can be carried out to see what minor repairs and renovations are necessary. Steam-cleaning is available at many garages, and is necessary for the removal of the accumulation of oily grime, which sometimes is allowed to become thick in certain areas. If steam-cleaning facilities are not available, there are some excellent grease solvents available which can be brush-applied; the dirt can then be simply hosed off. Note that these methods should not be used on vehicles with wax-based underbody protective coating, or the coating will be removed. Such vehicles should be inspected annually, preferably just prior to Winter, when the underbody should be washed down, and any damage to the wax coating repaired. Ideally, a completely fresh coat should be applied. It would also be worth considering the use of such wax-based protection for injection into door panels, sills, box sections, etc, as an additional safeguard against rust damage, where such protection is not provided by the vehicle manufacturer.

After washing paintwork, wipe off with a chamois leather to give an unspotted clear finish. A coat of clear protective wax polish will give added protection against chemical pollutants in the air. If the paintwork sheen has dulled or oxidised, use a cleaner/polisher combination to restore the brilliance of the shine. This requires a little effort, but such dulling is usually caused because regular washing has been neglected. Care needs to be taken with metallic paintwork, as special non-abrasive cleaner/polisher is required to avoid damage to the finish. Always check that the door and ventilator opening drain holes and pipes are completely clear, so that water can be drained out. Brightwork should be treated in the same way as paintwork. Windscreens and windows can be kept clear of the smeary film which often appears, by the use of proprietary glass cleaner. Never use any form of wax or other body or chromium polish on glass.

3 Maintenance – upholstery and carpets

Mats and carpets should be brushed or vacuum-cleaned regularly, to keep them free of grit. If they are badly stained, remove them from the vehicle for scrubbing or sponging, and make quite sure they are dry before refitting. Seats and interior trim panels can be kept clean by wiping with a damp cloth. If they do become stained (which can be more apparent on light-coloured upholstery), use a little liquid detergent and a soft nail brush to scour the grime out of the grain of the material. Do not forget to keep the headlining clean in the same way as the upholstery. When using liquid cleaners inside the vehicle, do not over-wet the surfaces being cleaned. Excessive damp could get into the seams and padded interior, causing stains, offensive odours or even rot.

4 Minor body damage – repair

Minor scratches

If the scratch is very superficial, and does not penetrate to the metal of the bodywork, repair is very simple. Lightly rub the area of the scratch with a paintwork renovator, or a very fine cutting paste, to remove loose paint from the scratch, and to clear the surrounding bodywork of wax polish. Rinse the area with clean water.

Apply touch-up paint to the scratch using a fine paint brush; continue to apply fine layers of paint until the surface of the paint in the scratch is level with the surrounding paintwork. Allow the new paint at least two weeks to harden, then blend it into the surrounding paintwork by rubbing the scratch area with a paintwork renovator or a very fine cutting paste. Finally, apply wax polish.

Where the scratch has penetrated right through to the metal of the bodywork, causing the metal to rust, a different repair technique is required. Remove any loose rust from the bottom of the scratch with a penknife, then apply rust-inhibiting paint to prevent the formation of rust in the future. Using a rubber or nylon applicator, fill the scratch with bodystopper paste. If required, this paste can be mixed with cellulose thinners to provide a very thin paste which is ideal for filling narrow scratches. Before the stopper-paste in the scratch hardens, wrap a piece of smooth cotton rag around the top of a finger. Dip the finger in cellulose thinners, and quickly sweep it across the surface of the stopper-paste in the scratch; this will ensure that the surface of the stopper-paste is slightly hollowed. The scratch can now be painted over as described earlier in this Section.

Dents

When deep denting of the vehicle's bodywork has taken place, the first task is to pull the dent out, until the affected bodywork almost attains its original shape. There is little point in trying to restore the original shape completely, as the metal in the damaged area will have stretched on impact, and cannot be reshaped fully to its original contour. It is better to bring the level of the dent up to a point which is about 3 mm below the level of the surrounding bodywork. In cases where the dent is very shallow anyway, it is not worth trying to pull it out at all. If the underside of the dent is accessible, it can be hammered out gently from behind, using a mallet with a wooden or plastic head. Whilst doing this, hold a suitable block of wood firmly against the outside of the panel, to absorb the impact from the hammer blows and thus prevent a large area of the bodywork from being 'belled-out'.

Should the dent be in a section of the

bodywork which has a double skin, or some other factor making it inaccessible from behind, a different technique is called for. Drill several small holes through the metal inside the area – particularly in the deeper section. Then screw long self-tapping screws into the holes, just sufficiently for them to gain a good purchase in the metal. Now the dent can be pulled out by pulling on the protruding heads of the screws with a pair of pliers.

The next stage of the repair is the removal of the paint from the damaged area, and from an inch or so of the surrounding 'sound' bodywork. This is accomplished most easily by using a wire brush or abrasive pad on a power drill, although it can be done just as effectively by hand, using sheets of abrasive paper. To complete the preparation for filling, score the surface of the bare metal with a screwdriver or the tang of a file, or alternatively, drill small holes in the affected area. This will provide a really good 'key' for the filler paste.

To complete the repair, see the Section on filling and respraying.

Rust holes or gashes

Remove all paint from the affected area, and from an inch or so of the surrounding 'sound' bodywork, using an abrasive pad or a wire brush on a power drill. If these are not available, a few sheets of abrasive paper will do the job most effectively. With the paint removed, you will be able to judge the severity of the corrosion, and therefore decide whether to renew the whole panel (if this is possible) or to repair the affected area. New body panels are not as expensive as most people think, and it is often quicker and more satisfactory to fit a new panel than to attempt to repair large areas of corrosion.

Remove all fittings from the affected area, except those which will act as a guide to the original shape of the damaged bodywork (eg headlight shells etc). Then, using tin snips or a hacksaw blade, remove all loose metal and any other metal badly affected by corrosion. Hammer the edges of the hole inwards, in order to create a slight depression for the filler paste.

Wire-brush the affected area to remove the powdery rust from the surface of the remaining metal. Paint the affected area with rust-inhibiting paint, if the back of the rusted area is accessible, treat this also.

Before filling can take place, it will be necessary to block the hole in some way. This can be achieved by the use of aluminium or plastic mesh, or aluminium tape.

Aluminium or plastic mesh, or glass-fibre matting, is probably the best material to use for a large hole. Cut a piece to the approximate size and shape of the hole to be filled, then position it in the hole so that its edges are below the level of the surrounding bodywork. It can be retained in position by several blobs of filler paste around its periphery.

Aluminium tape should be used for small or very narrow holes. Pull a piece off the roll,

trim it to the approximate size and shape required, then pull off the backing paper (if used) and stick the tape over the hole; it can be overlapped if the thickness of one piece is insufficient. Burnish down the edges of the tape with the handle of a screwdriver or similar, to ensure that the tape is securely attached to the metal underneath.

Filling and respraying

Before using this Section, see the Sections on dent, deep scratch, rust holes and gash repairs.

Many types of bodyfiller are available, but generally speaking, those proprietary kits which contain a tin of filler paste and a tube of resin hardener are best for this type of repair. A wide, flexible plastic or nylon applicator will be found invaluable for imparting a smooth and well-contoured finish to the surface of the filler.

Mix up a little filler on a clean piece of card or board – measure the hardener carefully (follow the maker's instructions on the pack), otherwise the filler will set too rapidly or too slowly. Using the applicator, apply the filler paste to the prepared area; draw the applicator across the surface of the filler to achieve the correct contour and to level the surface. As soon as a contour that approximates to the correct one is achieved, stop working the paste – if you carry on too long, the paste will become sticky and begin to 'pick-up' on the applicator. Continue to add thin layers of filler paste at 20-minute intervals, until the level of the filler is just proud of the surrounding bodywork.

Once the filler has hardened, the excess can be removed using a metal plane or file. From then on, progressively-finer grades of abrasive paper should be used, starting with a 40-grade production paper, and finishing with a 400-grade wet-and-dry paper. Always wrap the abrasive paper around a flat rubber, cork, or wooden block – otherwise the surface of the filler will not be completely flat. During the smoothing of the filler surface, the wet-and-dry paper should be periodically rinsed in water. This will ensure that a very smooth finish is imparted to the filler at the final stage.

At this stage, the 'dent' should be surrounded by a ring of bare metal, which in turn should be encircled by the finely 'feathered' edge of the good paintwork. Rinse the repair area with clean water, until all of the dust produced by the rubbing-down operation has gone.

Spray the whole area with a light coat of primer – this will show up any imperfections in the surface of the filler. Repair these imperfections with fresh filler paste or bodystopper, and once more smooth the surface with abrasive paper. Repeat this spray-and-repair procedure until you are satisfied that the surface of the filler, and the feathered edge of the paintwork, are perfect. Clean the repair area with clean water, and allow to dry fully.

The repair area is now ready for final spraying. Paint spraying must be carried out in a warm, dry, windless and dust-free atmosphere. This condition can be created artificially if you have access to a large indoor working area, but if you are forced to work in the open, you will have to pick your day very carefully. If you are working indoors, dousing the floor in the work area with water will help to settle the dust which would otherwise be in the atmosphere. If the repair area is confined to one body panel, mask off the surrounding panels; this will help to minimise the effects of a slight mis-match in paint colours. Bodywork fittings (eg chrome strips, door handles etc) will also need to be masked off. Use genuine masking tape, and several thicknesses of newspaper, for the masking operations.

Before commencing to spray, agitate the aerosol can thoroughly, then spray a test area (an old tin, or similar) until the technique is mastered. Cover the repair area with a thick coat of primer; the thickness should be built up using several thin layers of paint, rather than one thick one. Using 400-grade wet-and-dry paper, rub down the surface of the primer until it is really smooth. While doing this, the work area should be thoroughly doused with water, and the wet-and-dry paper periodically rinsed in water. Allow to dry before spraying on more paint.

Spray on the top coat, again building up the thickness by using several thin layers of paint. Start spraying at one edge of the repair area, and then, using a side-to-side motion, work until the whole repair area and about 2 inches of the surrounding original paintwork is covered. Remove all masking material 10 to 15 minutes after spraying on the final coat of paint.

Allow the new paint at least two weeks to harden, then, using a paintwork renovator, or a very fine cutting paste, blend the edges of the paint into the existing paintwork. Finally, apply wax polish.

Plastic components

With the use of more and more plastic body components by the vehicle manufacturers (eg bumpers. spoilers, and in some cases major body panels), rectification of more serious damage to such items has become a matter of either entrusting repair work to a specialist in this field, or renewing complete components. Repair of such damage by the DIY owner is not really feasible, owing to the cost of the equipment and materials required for effecting such repairs. The basic technique involves making a groove along the line of the crack in the plastic, using a rotary burr in a power drill. The damaged part is then welded back together, using a hot-air gun to heat up and fuse a plastic filler rod into the groove. Any excess plastic is then removed, and the area rubbed down to a smooth finish. It is important that a filler rod of the correct plastic is used, as body

7.2 Make alignment marks and undo the bonnet lock bolts

7.3a Slide out the plate...

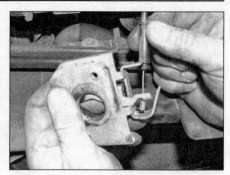

7.3b... and disconnect the release cable

components can be made of a variety of different types (eg polycarbonate, ABS, polypropylene).

Damage of a less serious nature (abrasions, minor cracks etc) can be repaired by the DIY owner using a two-part epoxy filler repair material. Once mixed in equal proportions, this is used in similar fashion to the bodywork filler used on metal panels. The filler is usually cured in twenty to thirty minutes, ready for sanding and painting.

If the owner is renewing a complete component himself, or if he has repaired it with epoxy filler, he will be left with the problem of finding a suitable paint for finishing which is compatible with the type of plastic used. At one time, the use of a universal paint was not possible, owing to the complex range of plastics encountered in body component applications. Standard paints, generally speaking, will not bond to plastic or rubber satisfactorily. However, it is now possible to obtain a plastic body parts finishing kit which consists of a pre-primer treatment, a primer and coloured top coat. Full instructions are normally supplied with a kit, but basically, the method of use is to first apply the pre-primer to the component concerned, and allow it to dry for up to 30 minutes. Then the primer is applied, and left to dry for about an hour before finally applying the special-coloured top coat. The result is a correctly-coloured component, where the paint will flex with the plastic or rubber, a property that standard paint does not normally possess.

7.6a Prise out the centre pin beneath the release handle

5 Major body damage – repair

With the exception of Chassis Cab versions, the chassis members are spot-welded to the underbody, and in this respect can be termed of being monocoque or unit construction. Major damage repairs to this type of body combination must of necessity be carried out by body shops with welding and hydraulic straightening facilities.

Extensive damage to the body may distort the chassis, and result in unstable and dangerous handling, as well as excessive wear to tyres and suspension or steering components. It is recommended that checking of the chassis alignment be entrusted to a dealer or accident repair specialist with special checking jigs.

6 Bonnet – removal, refitting and adjustment

Removal

1 Open the bonnet, and support it with its stay rod.
2 Mark around the bonnet hinges, to show the outline of their fitted positions for correct realignment on assembly.
3 Have an assistant support the bonnet whilst you unscrew and remove the hinge retaining

7.6b Note the lug (arrowed)

bolts, then lift the bonnet clear. Note that 2 of the bolts may be 'security' bolts, that require a special socket to undo them.

Refitting

4 Refitting is a reversal of removal. Tighten the hinge bolts fully when bonnet alignment is satisfactory.

Adjustment

5 Adjustment of the bonnet fit is available by loosening the bonnet hinge bolts. The bonnet can now be adjusted to give an even clearance between its outer edges and the surrounding panels. Adjust the front bump stops to align the edges of the bonnet with the front wing panels, then retighten the hinge bolts.

7 Bonnet lock and release cable – removal and refitting

Removal

Bonnet lock

1 Make alignment marks between the bonnet lock and the slam panel.
2 Undo the 2 retaining bolts and remove the bonnet lock from the slam panel **(see illustration)**.
3 Disconnect the release cable from the underside of the lock **(see illustrations)**.

Bonnet release cable

4 Remove the bonnet lock as previously described.
5 Trace along the route of the release cable and free it from the retaining clips.
6 Working under the facia, prise out the centre pin underneath, pull the release handle from the bracket, noting the lug at the top **(see illustrations)**.
7 Prise the rubber grommet from the bulkhead, and remove the cable from the vehicle. Note that the cable is integral with the release handle.

Refitting

8 Refitting is a reversal of removal. Check the operation of the lock before closing the bonnet.

8.1 Pull the window regulator handle from the shaft

8.2a Undo the interior handle surround screw (arrowed)...

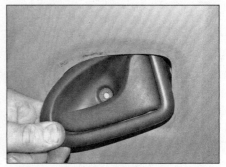

8.2b... and push the surround back through the door trim

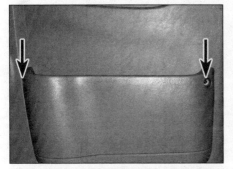

8.3a Undo the screws each side of the door pocket (arrowed)...

8.3b... and the screw in the pull handle recess

8.4 Prise the trim panel from the door

8 Door trim panels – removal and refitting

Front doors

Removal

1 On models with manual window regulators, note the position of the regulator handle, then carefully pull the handle from the regulator shaft **(see illustration)**.

2 Undo the retaining screw securing the interior release handle surround **(see illustrations)**. Do not disconnect the release cable – feed the handle and surround through the aperture as the door trim is removed.

3 Undo the 3 screws securing the trim panel to the door **(see illustrations)**.

4 Carefully prise free the door trim panel with a suitable tool between the panel around its outer and lower edges, and remove the panel **(see illustration)**. Where applicable, lift the panels over the buttons.

5 On models with electric window regulators, disconnect the wiring connector at the electric window switch as the panel is removed.

6 If the panel has been removed for access to the door internal components, the plastic insulation sheet will have to be removed for access. To do this, cut through the adhesive securing the plastic sheet to the door using a sharp knife, undo the screws and remove the main door speaker. Now carefully peel back the insulation sheet as necessary **(see illustration)**. Do not attempt to peel back the sheet without first cutting through the adhesive, and take care not to touch the adhesive after the sheet has been removed. If care is taken, the existing adhesive will re-bond the sheet on completion.

Refitting

7 Refitting is a reversal of removal. On models with manual window regulators, push the handle onto the regulator shaft in the position noted on removal, then tighten the retaining screw securely.

Rear doors and tailgate

Removal

8 Remove the interior handle (where applicable) by undoing the screw, pulling the handle from the door and disconnecting the linkage **(see illustrations)**.

9 The rear door and tailgate trim panels are secured by plastic retaining clips, the removal of which requires the use of a suitable forked tool **(see illustration)**. These clips are easily broken, so take care when prising them free. Remove the trim panel.

10 If necessary, remove the plastic insulation

8.6 Use a sharp blade to cut through the sealant between the plastic sheet and the door frame

8.8a Undo the interior handle retaining screw

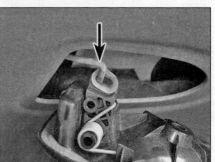

8.8b Pull the handle from the door trim and disconnect the linkage (arrowed)

8.9 Carefully prise between the trim panel and the door frame to release the clips

8.12 Prise out the cover and undo the sliding door interior handle retaining screw (arrowed)

13 Pull the lock lever cover from place **(see illustration)**.
14 Remove the 5 clips from the upper edge of the panel, then carefully prise free the trim panel, prising with a suitable tool between the panel around its outer and lower edges, and remove the panel **(see illustration)**.
15 If necessary, remove the plastic insulation sheet with reference to paragraph 6.

Refitting

16 Refitting is a reversal of removal.

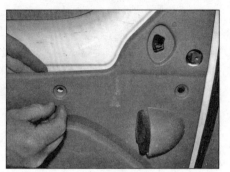

8.13 Pull the lock lever cover from place

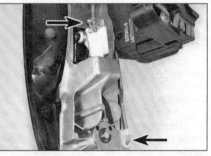

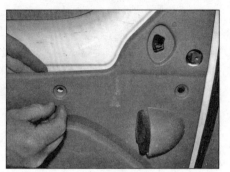

8.14 Pull out the clips at the top of the door trim panel

Sliding side door

Removal

12 Unclip the cover, remove the inner door handle retaining screw **(see illustration)**.

sheet (where fitted) with reference to paragraph 6.

Refitting

11 Refitting is a reversal of removal. Align the panel, and press the clips into position.

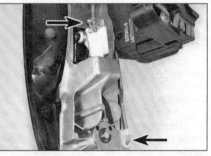

9.3 Disconnect the control rods from the lock (arrowed) – shown with the assembly removed for clarity

9.4 Undo the lock retaining screws (arrowed)

9 Front door fittings – removal and refitting

Exterior handle

Removal

1 Remove the front door trim panel and weatherproof membrane as described in Section 8.
2 Undo the 2 screws and remove the protective shield behind the handle (where fitted).
3 Release the clips and disconnect the control rods from the lock cylinder and exterior handle **(see illustration)**.
4 Undo the 3 retaining screws and remove the door lock assembly **(see illustration)**. Disconnect the wiring plug as the lock is withdrawn.
5 Prise out the 2 grommets, undo the retaining nuts and remove the exterior handle from the door, followed by the mounting plate **(see illustrations)**.

Refitting

6 Refitting is a reversal of removal.

Door lock cylinder

Removal

7 Remove the exterior handle and mounting plate as previously described.
8 Extract the lock cylinder retaining clip, and withdraw the lock cylinder from the handle **(see illustrations)**.

Refitting

9 Refitting is a reversal of removal.

9.5a Prise out the rubber grommets (arrowed), undo the retaining nuts and remove the exterior handle...

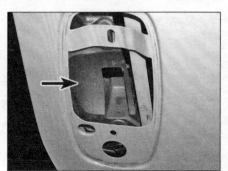

9.5b... then manoeuvre the mounting plate (arrowed) with lock cylinder...

9.5c... through the aperture on the inside of the door

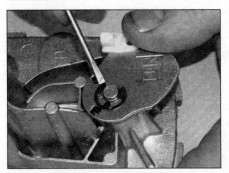

9.8a Slide off the circlip...

9.8b... and withdraw the lock cylinder from the mounting plate

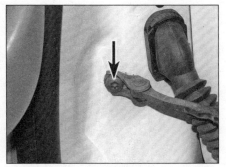

10.3 Door check strap retaining bolt (arrowed)

Door lock unit

10 Front door lock unit renewal is described within the exterior handle procedure previously described in this Section.

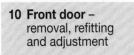

10 Front door –
removal, refitting and adjustment

Removal

1 Disconnect the battery negative lead as described in Chapter 5.
2 Open the door, and position a suitably padded jack or support blocks underneath it; don't lift the door, just take its weight.
3 Undo the screw and remove the door check strap bracket from the body pillar **(see illustration)**.
4 Disconnect the door wiring harness connector **(see illustration)**.
5 Have an assistant support the door, then undo the hinge retaining bolts and remove the door **(see illustration)**.

Refitting and adjustment

6 Refitting is a reversal of removal. Open and shut the door to ensure that it does not bind with the body aperture at any point. Adjust the door striker plate if necessary.

11 Sliding side door fittings –
removal and refitting

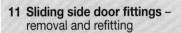

Exterior handle

Removal

1 Remove the door inner trim panel as described in Section 8.
2 Undo the 3 retaining screws and remove the interior handle mechanism **(see illustrations)**.
3 Undo the exterior handle retaining nuts, then withdraw the handle from the door **(see illustration)**.
4 Disconnect the operating cable as the handle is withdrawn **(see illustration)**.

Refitting

5 Refitting is a reversal of removal.

10.4 Slide up the catch (arrowed) and disconnect the wiring plug

Door lock cylinder

Removal

6 Remove the exterior handle as described previously in this Section.

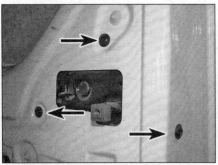

11.2a Undo the 3 screws (arrowed)...

11.2c If required, turn the mechanism over and disconnect the operating cables

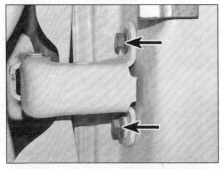

10.5 Door hinge retaining bolts (arrowed)

7 Extract the circlip securing the lock cylinder to the handle, and withdraw it.

Refitting

8 Refitting is a reversal of removal.

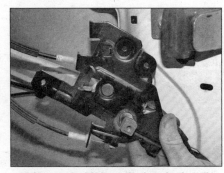

11.2b... and withdraw the interior handle mechanism

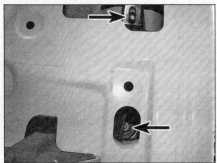

11.3 Exterior handle retaining nuts (arrowed)

11.4 Disconnect the handle operating cable

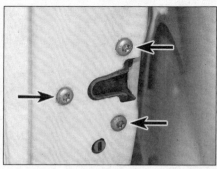

11.10 Undo the lock unit retaining screws (arrowed)

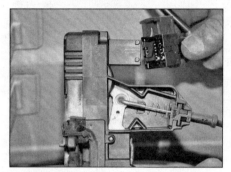

11.11 Slide up the locking catch and disconnect the wiring plug

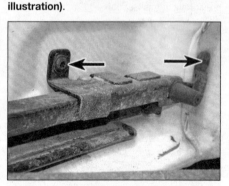

11.12 Disconnect the cables (arrowed) from the lock unit

Door lock unit

Removal

9 Remove the door inner trim panel as described in Section 8.

10 Undo the 3 screws securing the lock to the door (see illustration).
11 Withdraw the lock unit from its location and disconnect the wiring connector (see illustration).
12 Note their fitted locations, release the clips and disconnect the control cables from the lock (see illustration).

Refitting

13 Refitting is a reversal of removal.

Interior release handle

14 Removal of the interior release handle is described within the exterior handle procedure previously described in this Section.

12 Sliding side door –
removal, refitting and adjustment

Note: *Before slackening any retaining bolts, make alignment marks on the guide supports to aid alignment when refitting.*

Removal

1 Disconnect the battery negative lead as described in Chapter 5.
2 Remove the relevant rear light assembly as described in Chapter 12.
3 Undo the bolt and remove the door stop from the centre guide rail (see illustration).
4 Open the side door, undo the 2 retaining bolts, and remove the door stop from the lower guide rail (see illustration). Have an assistant support the door.
5 Undo the 2 retaining bolts securing the upper guide roller to the door, and slide the door from position (see illustration).

Refitting

6 Refitting is a reversal of removal. Align the door and engage it onto the centre and lower tracks, then reconnect the fittings.

Adjustment

7 Check the door for satisfactory flush-fitting adjustment. Adjust if necessary by carefully prising away the outer, lower trim from the door, loosening off the lower support bolts to reposition the door as required, then tighten them and recheck the fitting.
8 When fitted, and in the closed position, the door should be aligned flush to the surrounding body, and should close securely. If required, adjust the striker plate position to suit.

13 Rear door fittings –
removal and refitting

Exterior handle

Removal

1 Remove the rear door trim panel as described in Section 8.
2 Using a small screwdriver, open the retaining clip and detach the control rod from the exterior handle (see illustration).
3 Undo the 2 retaining nuts and remove the exterior handle (see illustration).

12.3 Sliding door centre rail door stop bolt (arrowed)

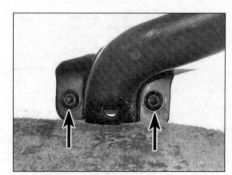

12.5 Upper guide roller retaining bolts (arrowed)

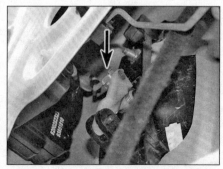

13.2 Disconnect the control rod (arrowed) from the rear door exterior handle

12.4 Lower guide rail door stop bolts (arrowed)

Refitting

4 Refitting is a reversal of removal.

Door lock cylinder

Removal

5 Remove the exterior handle as described previously in this Section. Note that not all models are fitted with rear door lock cylinders.
6 Extract the circlip securing the lock cylinder to the handle, and withdraw it.

Refitting

7 Refitting is a reversal of removal.

Door lock unit

Removal

8 Remove the exterior handle assembly as previously described in this Section.
9 Undo the 3 retaining screws and remove the lock unit (see illustration). Disconnect the wiring plug as the unit is withdrawn.

Refitting

10 Refitting is a reversal of removal.

Lock upper or lower latch

Removal

11 Remove the door inner trim panel as described in Section 8.
12 Detach the latch operating cable from the release handle unit (see illustration).
13 Undo the 3 bolts and remove the latch from the door. Disconnect the operating cable as the latch is withdrawn (see illustration).

Refitting

14 Refitting is a reversal of removal.

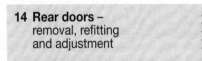

14 Rear doors –
removal, refitting and adjustment

Removal

1 Disconnect the battery negative lead as described in Chapter 5.
2 Unclip and remove the upper air vent from the D-pillar (where fitted).
3 Prise out the grommet, and disconnect the door wiring harness wiring plug from the D-pillar (see illustration).
4 Mark around the periphery of each door hinge with a suitable marker pen, to show the fitted position of the hinges when refitting the door. Have an assistant support the door, undo the retaining bolts from each hinge, and withdraw the door (see illustration).

Refitting and adjustment

5 Refitting is a reversal of removal. Align the hinges with the previously-made marks, then tighten the bolts.
6 Open and shut the doors, and ensure that they don't bind with the body aperture at any point. Adjust the door hinges and striker plate if necessary to provide an even clearance all round.

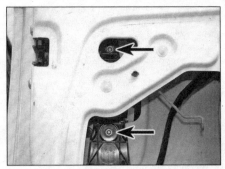

13.3 Rear door exterior handle retaining nuts (arrowed)

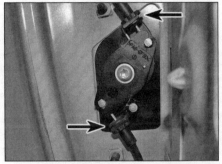

13.12 Disconnect the cable(s) from the release handle unit (arrowed)

15 Tailgate fittings –
removal and refitting
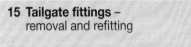

Exterior handle

Removal

1 Remove the tailgate inner trim panel as described in Section 8.
2 Undo the 2 nuts and 2 bolts securing the exterior handle to the tailgate.

Refitting

3 Refitting is a reversal of removal.

Tailgate lock cylinder

4 It would appear that at the time of writing, the lock cylinder is not available as a separate part. Check with your Vauxhall or Renault dealer or parts specialist.

14.3 Disconnect the wiring plug in the D-pillar

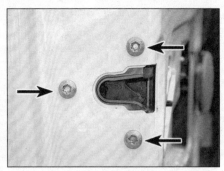

13.9 Rear door lock retaining screws (arrowed)

13.13 Undo the bolts (arrowed) and remove the upper or lower latch

Tailgate lock unit

Removal

5 Remove the tailgate inner trim panel as described in Section 8.
6 Undo the 4 retaining screws, unclip the control linkage, and remove the lock unit.

Refitting

7 Refitting is a reversal of removal.

16 Tailgate –
removal, refitting and adjustment

Removal

1 The aid of two assistants will be required to support the tailgate as it is removed. First open the tailgate, then support it in the open position.

14.4 Rear door hinge bolts

17.2a Prise up the inner...

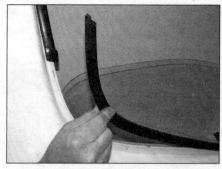

17.2b... and outer lower weatherstrips

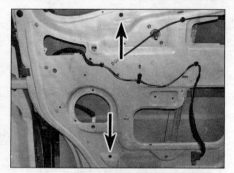

17.3a Undo the window guide channel screws (arrowed)...

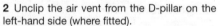

17.3b... lower the guide channel (note the lug at the top – arrowed)...

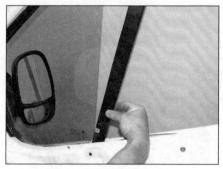

17.3c... and lift it from place

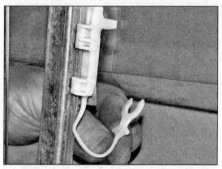

17.4 Slide the retaining clip down from the window clamp

2 Unclip the air vent from the D-pillar on the left-hand side (where fitted).

3 Prise out the grommet, and detach the wiring harness at the connector in the D-pillar. Pull the wiring loom through the body, and leave it attached to the tailgate.

4 Loosen the tailgate hinge bolts, and have the two assistants support the weight of the tailgate.

5 Prise up the retaining clips securing the tailgate strut balljoints, and detach the balljoint from the stud each side. Take care not to lift the clips by more than 4 mm.

6 Unscrew the hinge bolts and remove the tailgate.

Refitting

7 Refit the tailgate in the reverse order of removal. Press the strut balljoints onto their studs, using hand pressure only. Note that the struts are gas-filled, and therefore cannot be repaired. If renewing them, be sure to obtain the correct replacements.

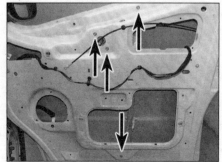

18.3a Undo the regulator retaining nuts (arrowed)...

18.3b... and manoeuvre it from the door

Adjustment

8 When the tailgate is refitted, check its adjustment and if necessary re-adjust as follows.

Height adjustment

9 Loosen the hinge retaining bolts, and reset the tailgate at the required height to suit the latch/striker engagement and the body aperture, then fully retighten the bolts.

Side clearance adjustment

10 Loosen off the tailgate side bump guides, the striker plate and the hinge bolts. Centralise the tailgate in its aperture, then retighten the hinge bolts. If required, re-adjust the position of the striker plate so that the tailgate closes securely. Now adjust the position of the side bump guides so that they only just contact the D-pillar bumpers when the tailgate is set at the safety catch position, and only make full contact when the tailgate is closed.

17 Front door window glass – removal and refitting

Removal

1 Lower the window completely, then remove the door inner trim panel and weatherproof membrane as described in Section 8.

2 Using a blunt, flat-bladed tool, carefully prise up and remove the inner, and outer weather-strips from the door frame **(see illustrations)**.

3 Undo the 2 screws, lower the window front guide channel a little, then remove it from the door **(see illustrations)**.

4 Release the window regulator clamp, and carefully manoeuvre the glass from the door **(see illustration)**.

Refitting

5 Refitting is a reversal of removal. Before refitting the door trim panel, raise and lower the window to ensure that it operates in a satisfactory manner.

18 Front door window regulator – removal and refitting

Removal

1 Remove the front door window glass as described in Section 17.

2 On models with electric front windows, disconnect the regulator motor wiring plug.

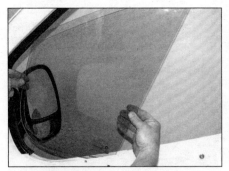

19.2 Pull the quarter glass rearwards

21.1 Prise the top edge of the mirror rearwards

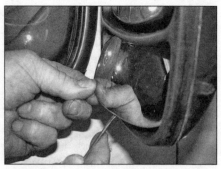

21.2 Prise the lower edge of the glass rearwards

3 The regulator assembly is secured by 4 nuts. Undo the nuts, and manipulate the regulator assembly out through the door aperture **(see illustrations)**.

Refitting
4 Refitting is a reversal of removal.

19 Front door quarter glass – removal and refitting

Removal
1 Remove the door window glass as described in Section 17.
2 Pull the quarter glass rearwards, and manoeuvre it from the door **(see illustration)**.

Refitting
3 Refitting is a reversal of removal.

20 Windscreen/tailgate and fixed/sliding windows – removal and refitting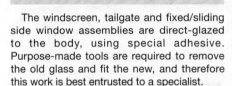

The windscreen, tailgate and fixed/sliding side window assemblies are direct-glazed to the body, using special adhesive. Purpose-made tools are required to remove the old glass and fit the new, and therefore this work is best entrusted to a specialist.

21 Exterior mirrors – removal and refitting

Removal
Upper glass
1 Push in the lower edge of the glass, insert a blunt, flat-bladed tool between the upper edge of the glass and the housing, then carefully prise the glass from the retaining clips **(see illustration)**. Disconnect any wiring plugs as the glass is removed.
Lower glass
2 Starting at the lower edge, carefully prise

the lens from place using a blunt, flat-bladed tool **(see illustration)**.
Complete mirror assembly
3 On manually-adjustable mirrors, open the relevant front door, prise out the cover at the front edge, and undo the mirror retaining nut exposed **(see illustration)**.
4 On electrically-adjustable mirrors, prise the internal trim cover from the door, and disconnect the mirror wiring plug.
5 Prise up the cover from the top of the mirror mounting bracket, support the mirror assembly, undo the bolt and remove the mirror **(see illustrations)**.
Mirror motor
6 Remove the mirror glass as describe previously in this Section.
7 Undo the 3 retaining screws and remove the motor. Disconnect the wiring plug as the motor is withdrawn.

21.3 Prise out the cover and undo the mirror lower mounting nut

21.5b... and undo the mirror upper mounting bolt

Refitting
8 Refitting is a reversal of removal.

22 Front bumper – removal and refitting

Removal
1 Remove the radiator grille as described in Section 24.
Models up to 09/2006
2 Remove the front indicators and front foglights (where applicable) as described in Chapter 12.
3 The front bumper is secured by 14 Torx screws. Undo the screws, and with the help of an assistant, manoeuvre the bumper from place **(see illustrations)**.

21.5a Prise up the cover...

22.3a Undo the screws (arrowed) on the left-hand side...

22.3b... 3 screws in the centre (arrowed)...

22.3c... one screw in the centre (arrowed)...

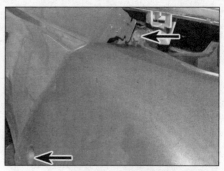

22.3d... 2 screws (arrowed) at each end of the bumper...

22.3e... and 2 screws (arrowed) in each wheel arch

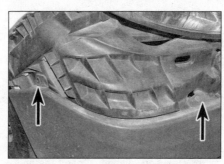

22.4a On post-facelift models, the front bumper is secured by 2 screws each side (arrowed)...

22.4b... 3 screws in the centre (arrowed)...

Models from 09/2006

4 The front bumper is secured by 11 Torx screws. Undo the screws, pull the bumper forwards a little, disconnect any wiring plugs,

and with the help of an assistant, remove the bumper **(see illustrations)**.

Refitting

5 Refitting is a reversal of removal. Align the

bumper correctly before fully-tightening the retaining bolts.

23 Rear bumper –
removal and refitting

Removal

1 Raise the rear of the vehicle and support it securely on axle stands (see *Jacking and vehicle support*).
2 Working underneath, disconnect the parking distance sensors wiring plug (where fitted).
3 Undo the 3 screws, release the 6 retaining clips, and pull the bumper centre section rearwards to remove **(see illustrations)**.
4 Remove the reversing lights, and upper rear lights as described in Chapter 12.

22.4c... and 2 screws (arrowed) securing the bumper to the wheel arch liner each side

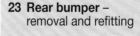

22.4d Pull the bumper forwards

23.3a Undo the screw in each corner (arrowed)...

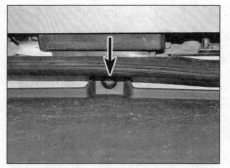

23.3b... the screw in the centre (arrowed)...

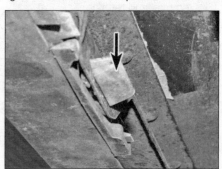

23.3c... then release the clips underneath (arrowed)...

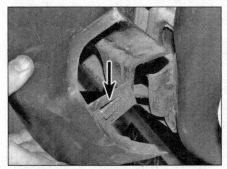

23.3d... and the ones at the outer edges (arrowed)

23.5a The bumper outer sections are secured by a screw at the upper, inner edge (arrowed)...

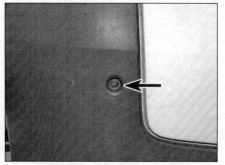

23.5b... a screw at the outer edge (arrowed)...

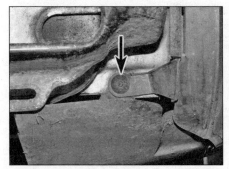

23.5c... a screw at the lower, inner edge (arrowed)...

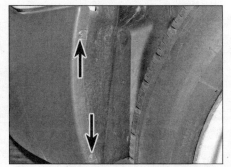

23.5d... 2 screws securing the bumper to the wheel arch liner (arrowed)...

23.5e... and a clip at the upper edge

5 The outer sections of the bumper are secured by 4 screws (models from 09/2006) or 5 screws (models up to 09/2006) and 1 retaining clip each. Undo the screws, prise out the clip, and remove the outer sections of the bumper **(see illustrations)**.

Refitting

6 Refitting is a reversal of removal.

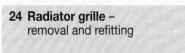

24 Radiator grille –
removal and refitting

Models up to 09/2006

1 Open the bonnet, undo the 5 screws, release the 2 clips and remove the radiator grille **(see illustrations)**.
2 Refitting is a reversal of removal. Check the

alignment of the front wings with the bonnet and surrounding panels when tightening the retaining bolts.

Models from 09/2006

3 Open the bonnet, undo the 5 screws,

24.1a The pre-facelift radiator grille is secured by 3 screws along the top edge (arrowed)...

release the 10 clips and remove the radiator grille **(see illustrations)**.
4 Refitting is a reversal of removal. Check the alignment of the front wings with the bonnet and surrounding panels when tightening the retaining bolts.

24.1b... a screw beside the headlight each side (arrowed)...

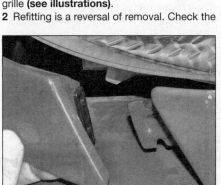

24.1c... then unclips at each end

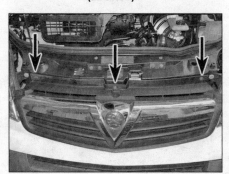

24.3a Undo the 3 screws at the top of the grille (arrowed)...

24.3b... and the 2 screws at the lower edge (arrowed)

24.3c Pull the outer edges of the radiator grille outwards to release the clips...

24.3d... and manoeuvre it forwards

25 Body exterior fittings –
removal and refitting

Wheel arch liners and body under-panels

1 The various plastic covers fitted to the underside of the vehicle are secured in position by a mixture of screws, nuts and retaining clips and removal will be fairly obvious on inspection. Work methodically around, removing its retaining screws and releasing its retaining clips until the panel is free and can be removed from the underside of the vehicle. Most clips used on the vehicle are simply prised out of position. Other clips can be released by unscrewing/prising out the centre pins and then removing the clip.

2 On refitting, renew any retaining clips that may have been broken on removal, and ensure that the panel is securely retained by all the relevant clips and screws.

Body trim strips and badges

3 The various body trim strips and badges are held in position with a special adhesive tape, or plastic clips. Removal often requires the trim/badge to be heated, to soften the adhesive, and then cut away from the surface. Due to the high risk of damage to the vehicle's paintwork during this operation, it is recommended that this task should be entrusted to a dealer or suitably-equipped specialist.

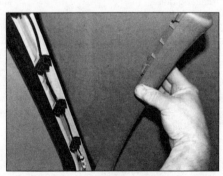

26.3 Pull the A-pillar trim panel inwards to disengage the clips

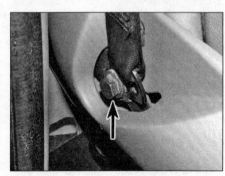

26.5 Undo the bolt (arrowed) securing the seat belt to the front seat

26 Interior trim –
removal and refitting

Door trim panels

1 Refer to the procedures contained in Section 8.

A-pillar trim

2 Pull the rubber weather strip from the pillar adjacent to the trim.
3 Pull the upper edge of the trim away from the pillar to disengage the retaining clips (see illustration).
4 Refitting is a reversal of removal.

B-pillar trim

5 Prise off the cap (where fitted), undo the bolt and detach the seat belt from the front seat (see illustration).
6 Pull the rubber weatherstrip from the pillar adjacent to the trim.
7 Pull the upper B-pillar trim inwards to release the clips, and lower it from the top locating lugs (see illustrations). Feed the seat belt through the trim as it's withdrawn.
8 Pull the lower B-pillar trim inwards to release the clips (see illustration).
9 Refitting is a reversal of removal, ensuring that the seat belt mountings are tightened to the specified torque.

Loadspace trim

10 The loadspace trim panels are secured by a combination of screws and plastic retaining clips, the removal of which requires the use of a suitable forked tool. These clips are easily broken, so take care when prising them free.
11 Remove the rear seats, where applicable, for access to the panel attachments.
12 Release the panel retaining clips and screws, and withdraw the panel.
13 Refitting is a reversal of removal.

Grab handles

Roof mounted

14 Prise out the handle retaining pins (see illustration). Remove the grab handles.
15 Refitting is a reversal of removal.

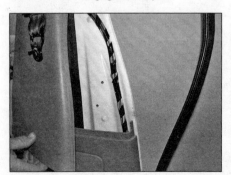

26.7a Pull the upper B-pillar trim panel inwards...

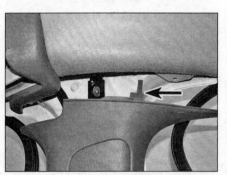

26.7b... then downwards to release the upper lug (arrowed)

26.8 Pull the lower B-pillar trim panel inwards to release the clips

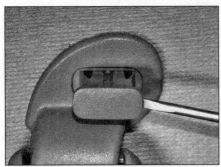

26.14 Prise out the grab handle retaining pins

B-pillar mounted

16 Prise up the 2 covers, undo the 2 screws and remove the handle from the pillar.
17 Refitting is a reversal of removal.

Sunvisor

18 Undo the mounting screw and remove the sunvisor **(see illustration)**.
19 Refitting is a reversal of removal.

27 Seats –
removal and refitting

Driver's seat

1 Disconnect the battery negative lead as described in Chapter 5.
2 Undo the seat belt lower mounting bolt from the base of the seat **(see illustration 26.5)**.

27.4 Driver's seat front mounting bolts (arrowed)

28.3a Outer seat belt upper anchorage retaining bolt (arrowed)

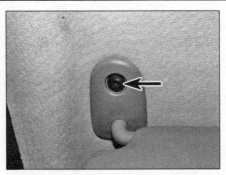

26.18 Sunvisor mounting screw (arrowed)

3 Prise out the yellow locking catch, and disconnect any wiring plugs from under the front of the seat.
4 Position the seat as necessary, then undo the 3 Torx mounting bolts (there's no need to undo the rear, innermost bolt) and slide the seat sideways from the cabin **(see illustration)**.
5 Refitting is a reversal of removal.

Front passenger's seat

6 Disconnect the battery negative lead as described in Chapter 5.
7 Prise out the yellow locking catch, then disconnect the wiring plugs under the bench seat, and release the wiring harness from any retaining clips **(see illustration)**.
8 Prise off the cap (where fitted), undo the bolt and detach the seat belt lower mounting from the seat **(see illustration 26.5)**.
9 Undo the inner and outer bolts securing the seat frame to the floor (there's no need

27.7 Prise out the yellow locking tab (arrowed) and disconnect the wiring plug

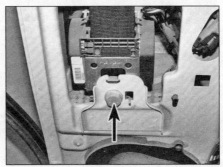

28.3b Outer seat belt inertia reel retaining bolt (arrowed)

to remove the rear, innermost bolt) and slide the seat sideways from the vehicle **(see illustration)**.
10 Refitting is a reversal of removal.

Rear seats

11 Various combinations of rear seats may be fitted, according to vehicle type and specification. The removal and refitting procedures are essentially the same as those described previously for the front seats.

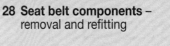

28 Seat belt components –
removal and refitting

Removal

1 Disconnect the battery negative lead as described in Chapter 5.

Outer seat belts

2 Remove the B-pillar trim as described in Section 26.
3 Undo the retaining bolts and remove the inertia reel and upper anchorage from the B-pillar **(see illustrations)**.
4 Refitting is a reversal of removal, ensuring that the tag on the inertia reel engages correctly in the B-pillar. Tighten the retaining bolts to the specified torque.

Centre seat belts

5 Remove the passenger's/bench seat assembly as described in Section 27.
6 Undo the 2 screws and remove the belt trim from the backrest **(see illustration)**.

27.9 Passenger's seat outer mounting bolts (arrowed)

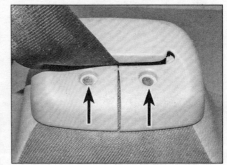

28.6 Undo the screws (arrowed) and remove the belt trim

28.8 Undo the seat belt lower mounting bolt (arrowed)

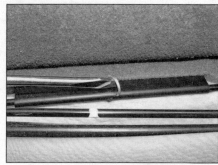

28.9a Open the clasps, unhook the seat covering from the front...

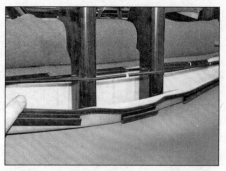

28.9b... and rear of the seat, then slide it upwards

28.10a Inertia reel mounting bolt (arrowed)

28.10b Note the locating lug (arrowed) at the rear of the inertia reel

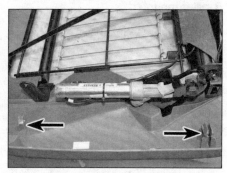

28.12 Seat base trim panel retaining clips (arrowed)

7 Depress the release buttons and remove both headrests from the backrest.

8 Undo the retaining bolt and detach the seat belt from the lower mounting on the underside of the seat frame **(see illustration)**.

9 Carefully unclip the seat covering from the base of the backrest frame and slide it upwards **(see illustrations)**. Note that the covering remains attached to the frame due to the headrest guide tubes.

10 Undo the inertia reel retaining bolt, and remove the assembly from the seat frame **(see illustrations)**.

Seat belt stalks

11 Remove the relevant seat as described in Section 27.

12 Carefully pull the trim panel from the side of the seat base to release the retaining clips. Note that the clips are easily damaged **(see illustration)**.

13 Disconnect the heated seat wiring plugs (where fitted).

14 Release the wiring and cable-tie, then undo the bolt and remove the pretensioner/stalk from the seat base **(see illustration)**.

Refitting

15 Refitting is a reversal of removal, remembering to tighten the fasteners to their specified torque where given.

28.14 Seat belt pretensioner retaining bolt (arrowed)

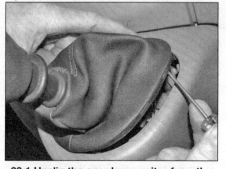

29.1 Unclip the gear lever gaiter from the centre console

29 Facia panel components – removal and refitting

Centre console

1 Carefully prise the gear lever gaiter from the centre console **(see illustration)**.

2 Undo the 4 retaining screws, and unclip the centre console **(see illustrations)**. Disconnect the hazard warning light switch wiring plug as the console is withdrawn.

3 Refitting is a reversal of removal.

29.2a Undo the 2 screws (arrowed) each side...

29.2b... and pull the centre console rearwards to release the clips

Steering column shrouds

4 Fully extend the steering column, then remove the steering wheel as described in Chapter 10.
5 Undo the 2 retaining screws and unclip the shrouds **(see illustrations)**.
6 Refitting is a reversal of removal.

Driver's side switch panel

7 Disconnect the battery negative lead as described in Chapter 5.
8 Starting at the top, using a blunt, flat-bladed tool, carefully prise the switch panel rearwards **(see illustration)**. Disconnect the wiring plugs as the panel is withdrawn.
9 Refitting is a reversal of removal.

Complete facia assembly

10 Disconnect the battery negative lead as described in Chapter 5.
11 Remove the steering column combination switch as described in Chapter 12.
12 Unclip the immobiliser antenna from the ignition switch, and disconnect the wiring plug **(see illustration)**.
13 Note their fitted positions and harness routing, then disconnect any wiring plugs from the steering column.
14 Remove the instrument cluster, information display unit (where fitted), facia-mounted speakers and facia-mounted audio unit as described in Chapter 12. On models without an information display unit, prise the trim panel above the radio upwards from place **(see illustration)**.
15 Undo the retaining screw, unclip and remove the radio mounting bracket **(see illustrations)**.

29.5a Undo the screws (arrowed) on the underside of the steering column shrouds...

29.5b... and carefully prise apart the shrouds

29.8 Prise the top edge of the driver's switch panel rearwards

29.12 Lift the clip (arrowed) and slide the immobiliser antenna from the switch

16 Remove the driver's side switch panel and centre console as described in this Section.
17 Undo the 3 retaining nuts, and detach the gearchange lever assembly from the support bracket and move it to one side (see

illustrations). Remove the earth connection from the mounting stud.
18 Remove the heating/ventilation control panel as described in Chapter 3.
19 Unclip the upper storage unit from the facia **(see illustration)**

29.14 Prise the panel from above the radio location

29.15a Undo the screw (arrowed), release the clips...

29.15b... and pull the support bracket from the facia

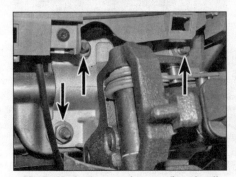
29.17a Undo the nuts (arrowed) and pull the gearchange lever assembly rearwards

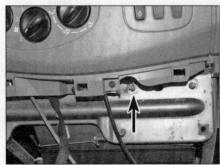
29.17b Pull the earth connection (arrowed) from the mounting stud

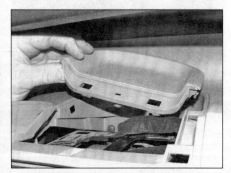
29.19 Unclip the upper storage unit

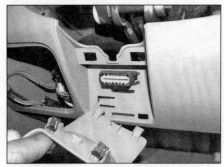

29.20 Unclip the diagnostic plug cover

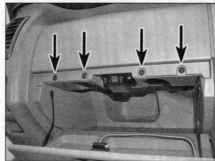

29.24a Undo the screws (arrowed)...

20 Unclip the cover, then release the retaining clip and detach the diagnostic plug from the facia panel **(see illustration)**.
21 Disconnect the wiring plugs from the cigarette lighter and unclip the harness from the facia.
22 Unclip the body control module from the facia adjacent to the steering column. Move the module to one side, and feed it through the aperture as the facia with withdrawn.
23 Remove the passenger's side airbag (where fitted) as described in Chapter 12.
24 On models without a passenger's airbag, open the glovebox, undo the 4 screws, and remove the upper trim panel above the glovebox **(see illustrations)**. Disconnect the glovebox light wiring plug.
25 Carefully prise the ashtray housing from each end of the facia **(see illustration)**.
26 Remove the A-pillar trim panels on both sides as described in Section 26, then unplug the radio antenna lead at the left-hand A-pillar.
27 The facia is now secured by 11 bolts **(see illustrations)**. Undo the bolts, make a final check to ensure all necessary wiring plugs have been disconnected, then with the help of an assistant, pull the facia rearwards a little, release the cooling ducts from the heater housing, and manoeuvre the facia from the cabin.
28 Refitting is a reversal of removal ensuring that all wiring is correctly reconnected and all mountings securely tightened.

29.24b... and remove the trim above the glovebox

29.25 Pull the trim from each end of the facia

29.27a The facia is secured by bolts at the left-hand end (arrowed)...

29.27b... each side of the steering column (arrowed)...

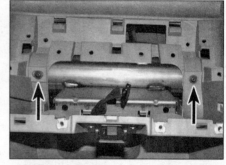

29.27c... above the glovebox (arrowed)...

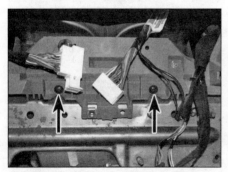

29.27d... in the centre (arrowed)...

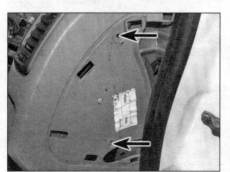

29.27e... at the right-hand end (arrowed)...

29.27f... and in the radio aperture (arrowed)

Chapter 12
Body electrical system

Contents

Degrees of difficulty

Easy, suitable for novice with little experience	**Fairly easy,** suitable for beginner with some experience	**Fairly difficult,** suitable for competent DIY mechanic	**Difficult,** suitable for experienced DIY mechanic	**Very difficult,** suitable for expert DIY or professional

Specifications

System type... 12 volt negative earth

Fuses.. See inside fusebox lid

Bulbs — Wattage

Exterior lights

	Wattage
Brake/tail light	21/5
Direction indicator	21 PY
Direction indicator side repeater	5
Foglight:	
Front	55 (H1 type)
Rear	21
Headlight	55/60 (H4 type)
High-level brake light	21
Number plate light	5
Reversing light	21
Sidelight	5 capless

Interior lights

	Wattage
Roof lights	10 festoon
Heater control panel	1.3

Torque wrench settings	Nm	lbf ft
Wiper arm-to-wiper spindle nut:		
Front	26	19
Rear	12	9

1 General information and precautions

⚠️ **Warning: Before carrying out any work on the electrical system, read through the precautions given in 'Safety First!' at the beginning of this manual and Chapter 5.**

The electrical system is of the 12 volt negative earth type. Power for the lights and all electrical accessories is supplied by a lead-acid type battery which is charged by the alternator.

This Chapter covers repair and service procedures for the various electrical components not associated with the engine. Information on the battery, alternator and starter motor can be found in Chapter 5.

It should be noted that prior to working on any component in the electrical system, the battery negative terminal should first be disconnected to prevent the possibility of electrical short circuits and/or fires (see Chapter 5).

2 Electrical fault finding – general information

Note: *Refer to the precautions given in 'Safety first!' and in Section 1 of this Chapter before starting work. The following tests relate to testing of the main electrical circuits, and should not be used to test delicate electronic circuits (such as anti-lock braking systems), particularly where an electronic control module/unit (ECM/ECU) is used.*
Caution: *The Vauxhall Vivaro/Renault Trafic electrical system is extremely complex. Many of the ECMs are connected via a 'Databus' system, where they are able to share information from the various sensors, and communicate with each other. Due to the design of the Databus system, it is not advisable to backprobe the ECMs with a multimeter in the traditional manner. Instead, the electrical systems are equipped with a sophisticated self-diagnosis system, which can interrogate the various ECMs to reveal stored fault codes, and help pin-point faults. In order to access the self-diagnosis system, specialist test equipment (fault code reader/scanner) is required.*

General

1 A typical electrical circuit consists of an electrical component, any switches, relays, motors, fuses, fusible links or circuit breakers related to that component, and the wiring and connectors which link the component to both the battery and the chassis. To help to pin-point a problem in an electrical circuit, wiring diagrams are included at the end of this Chapter.

2 Before attempting to diagnose an electrical fault, first study the appropriate wiring diagram to obtain a complete understanding of the components included in the particular circuit concerned. The possible sources of a fault can be narrowed down by noting if other components related to the circuit are operating properly. If several components or circuits fail at one time, the problem is likely to be related to a shared fuse or earth connection.

3 Electrical problems usually stem from simple causes, such as loose or corroded connections, a faulty earth connection, a blown fuse, a melted fusible link, or a faulty relay (refer to Section 3 for details of testing relays). Visually inspect the condition of all fuses, wires and connections in a problem circuit before testing the components. Use the wiring diagrams to determine which terminal connections will need to be checked in order to pin-point the trouble spot.

4 The basic tools required for electrical fault finding include a circuit tester or voltmeter (a 12 volt bulb with a set of test leads can also be used for certain tests); a self-powered test light (sometimes known as a continuity tester); an ohmmeter (to measure resistance); a battery and set of test leads; and a jumper wire, preferably with a circuit breaker or fuse incorporated, which can be used to bypass suspect wires or electrical components. Before attempting to locate a problem with test instruments, use the wiring diagram to determine where to make the connections.

5 To find the source of an intermittent wiring fault (usually due to a poor or dirty connection, or damaged wiring insulation), a 'wiggle' test can be performed on the wiring. This involves wiggling the wiring by hand to see if the fault occurs as the wiring is moved. It should be possible to narrow down the source of the fault to a particular section of wiring. This method of testing can be used in conjunction with any of the tests described in the following sub-Sections.

6 Apart from problems due to poor connections, two basic types of fault can occur in an electrical circuit – open circuit, or short circuit.

7 Open circuit faults are caused by a break somewhere in the circuit, which prevents current from flowing. An open circuit fault will prevent a component from working, but will not cause the relevant circuit fuse to blow.

8 Short circuit faults are caused by a 'short' somewhere in the circuit, which allows the current flowing in the circuit to 'escape' along an alternative route, usually to earth. Short circuit faults are normally caused by a breakdown in wiring insulation, which allows a feed wire to touch either another wire, or an earthed component such as the bodyshell. A short circuit fault will normally cause the relevant circuit fuse to blow.

Finding an open circuit

9 To check for an open circuit, connect one lead of a circuit tester or voltmeter to either the negative battery terminal or a known good earth.

10 Connect the other lead to a connector in the circuit being tested, preferably nearest to the battery or fuse.

11 Switch on the circuit, bearing in mind that some circuits are live only when the ignition switch is moved to a particular position.

12 If voltage is present (indicated either by the tester bulb lighting or a voltmeter reading, as applicable), this means that the section of the circuit between the relevant connector and the battery is problem-free.

13 Continue to check the remainder of the circuit in the same fashion.

14 When a point is reached at which no voltage is present, the problem must lie between that point and the previous test point with voltage. Most problems can be traced to a broken, corroded or loose connection.

Finding a short circuit

15 To check for a short circuit, first disconnect the load(s) from the circuit (loads are the components which draw current from a circuit, such as bulbs, motors, heating elements, etc).

16 Remove the relevant fuse from the circuit, and connect a circuit tester or voltmeter to the fuse connections.

17 Switch on the circuit, bearing in mind that some circuits are live only when the ignition switch is moved to a particular position.

18 If voltage is present (indicated either by the tester bulb lighting or a voltmeter reading, as applicable), this means that there is a short circuit.

19 If no voltage is present, but the fuse still blows with the load(s) connected, this indicates an internal fault in the load(s).

Finding an earth fault

20 The battery negative terminal is connected to 'earth' – the metal of the engine/transmission and the vehicle body – and most systems are wired so that they only receive a positive feed, the current returning through the metal of the vehicle body **(see illustrations)**. This means that the component mounting and the body form part of that circuit. Loose or corroded mountings can therefore cause a range of electrical faults, ranging from total failure of a circuit, to a puzzling partial fault. In particular, lights may shine dimly (especially when another circuit sharing the same earth point is in operation), motors (eg, wiper motors or the radiator cooling fan motor) may run slowly, and the operation of one circuit may have an apparently unrelated effect on another. Note that on many vehicles, earth straps are used between certain components, such as the engine/transmission and the body, usually where there is no metal-to-metal contact between components due to flexible rubber mountings, etc.

21 To check whether a component is properly earthed, disconnect the battery and connect one lead of an ohmmeter to a known good earth point. Connect the other lead to

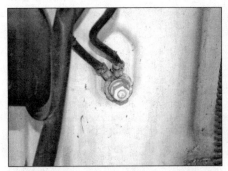

2.20a Earth connection behind both rear, upper lights...

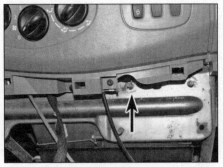

2.20b... beneath the heater control panel (arrowed)...

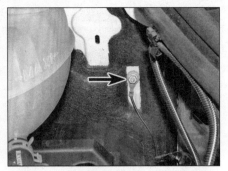

2.20c... in front of the coolant expansion tank (arrowed)...

2.20d... on the left-hand chassis member (arrowed) in the engine compartment...

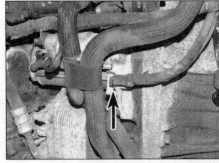

2.20e... on the starter motor mounting bolt (arrowed)...

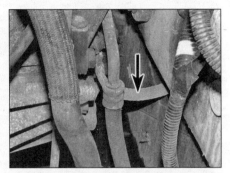

2.20f... between the transmission casing and vehicle body (arrowed)...

the wire or earth connection being tested. The resistance reading should be zero; if not, check the connection as follows.

22 If an earth connection is thought to be faulty, dismantle the connection and clean back to bare metal both the bodyshell and the wire terminal or the component earth connection mating surface. Be careful to remove all traces of dirt and corrosion, then use a knife to trim away any paint, so that a clean metal-to-metal joint is made. On reassembly, tighten the joint fasteners securely; if a wire terminal is being refitted, use serrated washers between the terminal and the bodyshell to ensure a clean and secure connection. When the connection is remade, prevent the onset of corrosion in the future by applying a coat of petroleum jelly or silicone-based grease or by spraying on (at regular intervals) a proprietary ignition sealer or a water dispersant lubricant.

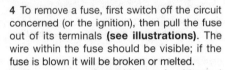

3 Fuses and relays – general information

Main fuses

1 The majority of the fuses are located at the passenger's end of the facia, whilst fusible links are located above the battery (2.0 litre models only), and 'maxi' fuses/relays are located in the electrical box at the left-hand end of the engine compartment (see illustrations).

2 To remove the main fusebox cover, prise open the ashtray panel from the facia.

3 A list of the circuits each fuse protects is given on the label attached to the inside of the main fusebox cover. A pair of tweezers for removing the fuses is also clipped to the fusebox cover.

4 To remove a fuse, first switch off the circuit concerned (or the ignition), then pull the fuse out of its terminals (see illustrations). The wire within the fuse should be visible; if the fuse is blown it will be broken or melted.

5 Always renew a fuse with one of an identical rating; never use a fuse with a different rating from the original or substitute anything else. Never renew a fuse more than once without tracing the source of the trouble. The fuse rating is stamped on top of the fuse; note that the fuses are also colour-coded for easy recognition.

6 If a new fuse blows immediately, find the cause before renewing it again; a short to earth as a result of faulty insulation is most likely. Where a fuse protects more than one circuit, try to isolate the defect by switching on each circuit in turn (if possible) until the fuse blows again. Always carry a supply of spare fuses of

3.1a Pull open the cover to access the main fusebox at the end of the facia

3.1b Fusible links are located above the battery (2.0 litre models only)

3.1c 'Maxi' fuses and relays are in the electrical box beneath the coolant expansion tank

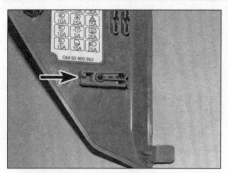

3.4a Use the tweezers (arrowed) clipped to the inside of the fusebox cover...

3.4b... to pull the fuse from the terminals

each relevant rating on the vehicle, a spare of each rating should be clipped into the base of the fusebox.

Relays

7 The majority of relays are located in the electrical box at the left-hand end of the engine compartment (see illustration 3.1c).

8 If a circuit or system controlled by a relay develops a fault and the relay is suspect, operate the system; if the relay is functioning it should be possible to hear it click as it is energised. If this is the case the fault lies with the components or wiring of the system. If the relay is not being energised then either the relay is not receiving a main supply or a switching voltage or the relay itself is faulty. Testing is by the substitution of a known good unit but be careful; while some relays are identical in appearance and in operation, others look similar but perform different functions.

9 To renew a relay first ensure that the ignition switch is off. The relay can then simply be pulled out from the socket and the new relay pressed in.

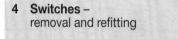

4   Switches –
    removal and refitting

Note: *Disconnect the battery negative lead (see Chapter 5) before removing any switch, and reconnect the lead after refitting the switch.*

Ignition switch lock cylinder

1 Renewal of the lock cylinder is described in Chapter 10, Section 21.

Steering column combination switch assembly

Note: *It is possible to remove some of the*

steering column switches individually, as described later in this Section.

2 Remove the steering wheel as described in Chapter 10, Section 19.

3 Undo the 2 screws and remove the steering column upper and lower shrouds (see illustrations).

4 On models with ESP, release the 4 retaining clips, disconnect the wiring plug and remove the steering angle sensor from the steering column.

5 Immobilise the airbag rotary contact unit by pushing the spring-loaded locking device upwards, then undoing the screw beneath till it's flush with the edge of the locking device (see illustration).

6 Note their fitted locations, then disconnect the various wiring plugs from the switch assembly (see illustration).

7 Release the retaining clip and slide the switch assembly upwards from the steering column (see illustration).

8 Refitting is a reversal of removal, but after fitting the switch assembly to the column, tighten the screw beneath the spring-loaded locking device to release it.

Windscreen wiper switch

9 Remove the steering wheel as described in Chapter 10, Section 19.

10 Undo the 2 screws and remove the steering column upper and lower shrouds (see illustrations 4.3a and 4.3b).

11 Release the 2 retaining clips, disconnect the wiring plug, and remove the switch (see illustration).

12 Refitting is the reverse of removal.

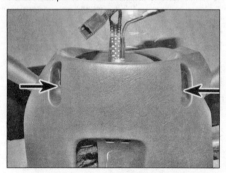

4.3a Undo the screws (arrowed)...

4.3b... and unclip the steering column shrouds

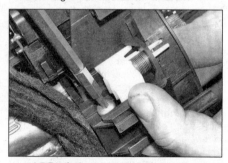

4.5 Push the sprung-loaded device upwards, and undo the locking screw to hold it in place/release the switch assembly

4.6 Disconnect the wiring plugs from the combination switch

4.7 Release the clips (arrowed) and slide the switch assembly from the column

4.11 Squeeze together the upper and lower clips (arrowed), then slide the wash/wiper switch from place

Direction indicator/ headlight dipping switch

13 Remove the steering wheel as described in Chapter 10, Section 19.
14 Undo the 2 screws and remove the steering column upper and lower shrouds (see illustrations 4.3a and 4.3b).
15 Release the 2 retaining clips, disconnect the wiring plug, and remove the switch (see illustration 4.11).
16 Refitting is the reverse of removal.

Hazard warning and central locking switches

17 Carefully prise up the gearchange lever gaiter from the centre console.
18 Undo the 4 screws, and remove the centre console rearwards a little (see illustration).
19 Disconnect the wiring plug, then release the clips and remove the switch.
20 Refitting is the reverse of removal.

Electric window and exterior mirror switches

21 Carefully prise the switch from the door panel to release the 3 retaining clips.
22 Disconnect the wiring plug(s) as the switch is withdrawn.
23 Refitting is the reverse of removal.

Clutch pedal switch

24 Removal of the switch is described in Chapter 6, Section 6.

Heated rear window, ESP and central locking switches

25 Using a flat-bladed, blunt tool, starting at the top edge, carefully prise the switch panel from the facia (see illustration).
26 Disconnect the wiring plug, then release the clips and remove the switch from the panel.
27 Refitting is a reversal of removal.

Heater blower motor switch

28 The switch is an integral part of the control unit and cannot be renewed. If the switch is faulty seek the advice of a dealer.

Air conditioning system switch

29 The switch is an integral part of the control unit and cannot be renewed. If the

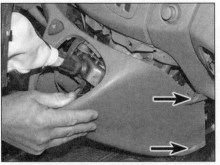
4.18 Undo the screws each side (arrowed) and pull the centre console rearwards

switch is faulty seek the advice of a Vauxhall or Renault dealer.

Heated front windscreen, headlight range control and parking distance sensor switches

30 Using a flat-bladed, blunt tool, carefully prise the switch panel from the facia (see illustration).
31 Disconnect the wiring plug, then release the clips and remove the switch from the panel.
32 Refitting is a reversal of removal.

Handbrake warning switch

33 Carefully prise up the handbrake lever gaiter (see illustration).
34 Disconnect the wiring connector then undo the screw and remove the switch (see illustration).

4.30 Starting at the top, carefully prise the switch panel from the facia

4.34 Undo the handbrake warning light switch retaining screw (arrowed)

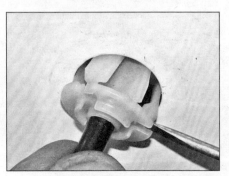
4.37a Press in the 3 clips...

4.25 Starting at the top, prise the switch panel from the facia

35 Refitting is the reverse of removal. Check the operation of the switch before refitting the gaiter.

Brake light switch

36 Refer to Chapter 9, Section 18.

Front courtesy light switches

37 Prise the cover from the switch, carefully depress the retaining clips and prise the switch from position (see illustrations). Disconnect the wiring plug as the switch is withdrawn.
38 Refitting is a reversal of removal.

Rear courtesy light switches

39 Carefully prise the switch from place, releasing the clips as it's withdrawn (see illustration). Disconnect the wiring plug as the switch is withdrawn.
40 Refitting is a reversal of removal.

4.33 Unclip the handbrake lever gaiter

4.37b... pull out the courtesy light switch and disconnect the wiring plug

4.39 Carefully prise the rear door courtesy light switch from place

4.41 Undo the screw (arrowed) and remove the side door contact unit

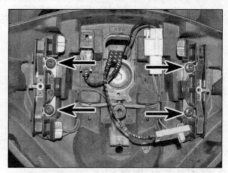

4.46 Undo the screws (arrowed) and remove the horn contact assemblies

Side door contact unit

41 Undo the 2 retaining screws, and remove the contact unit from position **(see illustration)**. Disconnect the wiring plug as the unit is withdrawn.

42 Refitting is a reversal of removal.

Steering wheel switches

43 Remove the airbag as described in Section 24.

Radio remote control switches

44 Undo the 4 retaining screws, and remove the switch assembly from the steering wheel. Disconnect the wiring plugs as the assembly is withdrawn.

45 Refitting is a reversal of removal.

Horn buttons

46 Undo the retaining screws and remove the

horn button contact assemblies **(see illustration)**.

47 Refitting is the reverse of removal.

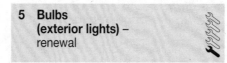

5 Bulbs (exterior lights) – renewal

General

1 Whenever a bulb is renewed, note the following points.
  a) *Remember that if the light has just been in use the bulb may be extremely hot.*
  b) *Always check the bulb contacts and holder, ensuring that there is clean metal-to-metal contact between the bulb and its live(s) and earth. Clean off any corrosion or dirt before fitting a new bulb.*

  c) *Wherever bayonet-type bulbs are fitted ensure that the live contact(s) bear firmly against the bulb contact.*
  d) *Always ensure that the new bulb is of the correct rating and that it is completely clean before fitting it; this applies particularly to headlight/foglight bulbs (see below).*

Headlight

2 Pull the wiring plug from the rear of the headlight.

3 Peel away the rubber cap from the rear of the headlight **(see illustration)**.

4 Release the retaining clip and remove the headlight bulb **(see illustrations)**.

5 When handling the new bulb, use a tissue or clean cloth to avoid touching the glass with the fingers; moisture and grease from the skin can cause blackening and rapid failure of this type of bulb. If the glass is accidentally touched, wipe it clean using methylated spirit.

6 Insert the new bulb into the headlight reflector, ensuring the locating lug engages correctly **(see illustration)**. Secure the retaining clip, refit the rubber cap and reconnect the wiring plug.

Front sidelight

7 Rotate the bulbholder 90° anti-clockwise and remove it from the headlight **(see illustration)**.

8 Pull the capless bulb from the holder **(see illustration)**.

9 Refitting is the reverse of removal.

5.3 Peel the rubber cap from the rear of the headlight

5.4a Press the retaining clip in the direction of the arrow...

5.4b... and fold the clip downwards

5.6 Ensure the lugs (arrowed) align with the slots in the reflector

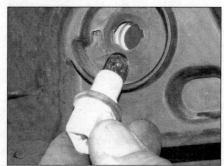

5.7 Rotate the sidelight bulbholder anti-clockwise to remove it

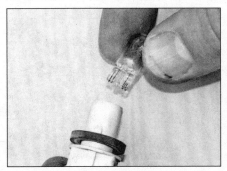

5.8 Pull the capless bulb from the holder

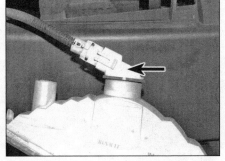

5.11 Rotate the indicator bulbholder anti-clockwise (arrowed)

5.14 Rotate the directional indicator bulbholder anti-clockwise to remove it

Front direction indicator

Bumper-mounted indicators

10 Remove the indicator as described in Section 7.

11 Rotate the bulbholder anti-clockwise and remove it from the rear of the light **(see illustration)**.

12 The bulb is a bayonet fitting in the holder. Push the bulb in slightly, then rotate it anti-clockwise and pull it from the holder.

13 Refitting is a reverse of the removal procedure.

Headlight-mounted indicators

14 Rotate the bulbholder 90° anti-clockwise and remove it from the headlight **(see illustration)**.

15 The bulb is a bayonet fitting in the holder. Push the bulb in slightly, then rotate it anti-clockwise and pull it from the holder. Note that the bulb bayonet pins are offset, and will only fit one way.

16 Refitting is a reverse of the removal procedure.

Side repeater

17 Open the bonnet, prise out the 2 clips. Close the bonnet, and manoeuvre the water deflector from the corner of the windscreen, releasing the upper clip as the deflector is withdrawn **(see illustrations)**.

18 Reach down through the aperture, squeeze together the retaining clips and pull the side repeater from the wing **(see illustrations)**.

19 Rotate the bulbholder anti-clockwise and pull it from the lens, pull the capless bulb it from the holder.

20 Refitting is a reverse of the removal procedure.

Front foglight

21 To improve access, raise the front of the vehicle, support it securely on axle stands (see *Jacking and vehicle support*).

Models up to 06/2006

22 Rotate the plastic cap 90° anti-clockwise and remove it from the rear of the foglight.

23 Disconnect the wiring from the bulbholder, then release the retaining clip and remove the bulb.

Models from 06/2006

24 Disconnect the wiring plug, then rotate the bulbholder 90° anti-clockwise and remove it from the rear of the foglight.

5.17a Undo the centre pin, prise out the clips...

5.17b... and remove the water deflector from the corner of the windscreen

25 Pull the bulb from the holder.

All models

26 When handling the new bulb, use a tissue or clean cloth to avoid touching the glass with the fingers; moisture and grease from the skin can cause blackening and rapid failure of this type of bulb. If the glass is accidentally touched, wipe it clean using methylated spirit.

27 Refitting is a reversal of removal. If necessary, adjust the aim of the light by rotating the adjusting screw adjacent to the lens **(see illustration)**.

Rear light cluster

Upper light cluster

28 Open the rear door(s), undo the 3 retaining screws, manoeuvre the light cluster from place, noting the locating pins at the outer

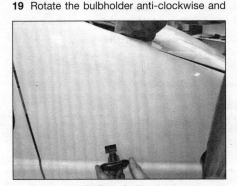

5.18a Reach down...

5.18b... and squeeze together the side repeater retaining clips (arrowed)

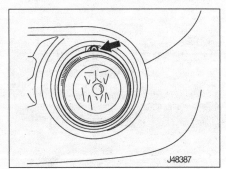

5.27 Foglight adjustment screw (arrowed)

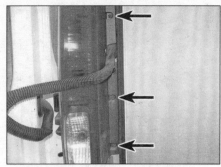

5.28a Rear upper light retaining screws (arrowed)

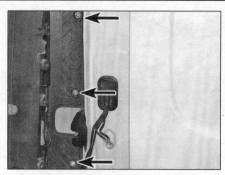

5.28b Note the locating pins (arrowed)

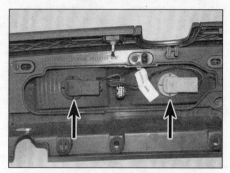

5.29 Rotate the bulbholders (arrowed) anti-clockwise

5.30 Press in the bulb and twist it anti-clockwise

5.32a Undo the lower rear light screws (arrowed)

5.32b Note the clips at the edge (arrowed)

edge **(see illustrations)**. Disconnect the wiring plug(s) as the cluster is withdrawn.
29 Rotate the relevant bulbholder anti-clockwise and pull it from the light cluster **(see illustration)**.

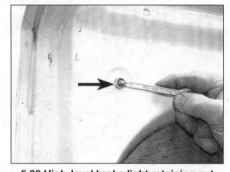

5.36 High-level brake light retaining nut (arrowed)

30 Press the relevant bulb in slightly, twist it anti-clockwise, and remove it from the bulbholder **(see illustration)**. **Note:** *If renewing the indicator bulb, the bayonet fitting pins are offset and will only fit in one way.*

5.37 Press in the bulb and twist it anti-clockwise

31 Refitting is a reversal of removal.

Lower light cluster

32 Open the rear door(s), undo the 2 retaining screws, and manoeuvre the light cluster from place, noting the locating clips at the outer edge **(see illustrations)**.
33 Rotate the bulbholder anti-clockwise and remove it from the tail light.
34 Press the relevant bulb in slightly, twist it anti-clockwise, and remove it from the bulbholder.
35 Refitting is a reversal of removal.

High-level brake light

36 Open the rear door(s), undo the nut and remove the high-level brake light **(see illustration)**. Disconnect the wiring plug as the light is withdrawn.
37 Press the relevant bulb in slightly, twist it anti-clockwise, and remove it from the bulbholder **(see illustration)**.
38 Refitting is a reversal of removal.

Number plate light

39 Undo the 2 retaining screws and remove the number plate light lens **(see illustrations)**.
40 Pull the capless bulb from the contacts.
41 Refitting is the reverse of removal.

5.39a Undo the number plate light screws (arrowed)...

5.39b... and remove the lens

6	Bulbs (interior lights) – renewal

General

1 Refer to Section 5, paragraph 1.

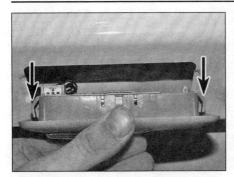

6.2 Press in the clip each side (arrowed) and pull down the ceiling light

6.3 Pull open the metal cover and remove the festoon bulb

6.10 Prise the front edge of the glovebox light lens downwards

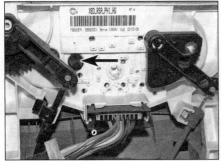

6.13 Rotate the heater control panel bulbholder (arrowed) anti-clockwise

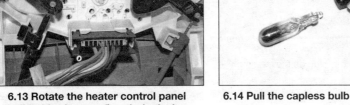

6.14 Pull the capless bulb from the holder

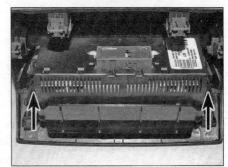

6.16 Undo the screws (arrowed) and detach the display unit from the panel

Ceiling lights

2 Using a wooden or plastic spatula, carefully prise down the interior light lens and remove it (see illustration).
3 Pull the festoon bulb from the contacts (see illustration).
4 Pull the relevant capless bulb from the holder.

Footwell lights

5 Carefully prise the light lens from place.
6 Two different versions of the light may be fitted. On the first, the capless bulb pulls from the holder. On the second, rotate the bulbholder anti-clockwise, then pull the capless bulb from place.

Luggage compartment light

7 Carefully prise the light unit from place (see illustration 6.2). Disconnect the wiring plug as the unit is withdrawn.
8 Hinge up the metal cover (where fitted) from the light unit, and prise out the festoon bulb (see illustration 6.3).

Instrument illumination/ warning lights

9 Instrument illumination is provided by integral LEDs. If faulty the instrument cluster may have to be renewed. Consult your dealer or specialist.

Glovebox illumination bulb

10 Open the glovebox and carefully prise the lens from the light unit (see illustration).
11 Pull the festoon bulb from the contacts.

Heater control panel illumination

12 Remove the heater control panel as described in Chapter 3.
13 Rotate the bulbholder anti-clockwise and remove it from the rear of the panel (see illustration).
14 Pull the capless bulb from the bulbholder (see illustration).

Switch illumination bulbs

15 All of the switches are fitted with LEDs. These LEDs are an integral part of the switch assembly and cannot be obtained separately. LED renewal will therefore require the renewal of the complete switch assembly.

Display unit bulb

16 Remove the information display unit as described in Section 10, then undo the screws

securing the unit to the surround panel (see illustration).
17 Rotate the bulbholder anti-clockwise and remove it from the rear of the unit (see illustration). Note that the bulbs are integral with the bulbholders.

7 Exterior light units – removal and refitting

Headlight

1 Remove the radiator grille as described in Chapter 11.
2 Undo the retaining screws and remove the headlight (see illustrations).
3 Manoeuvre the headlight from position. Note the locating lugs at the base of each headlight.

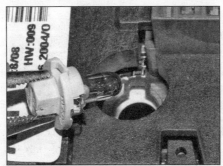
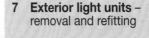

6.17 Rotate the bulbholder anti-clockwise and remove it from the rear of the display unit

7.2a Undo the 2 screws, lift the retaining pin at the top (arrowed – pre-06/2006 models)...

7.2b... then slide the lower mounting pin (arrowed) to the side to detach it from the clip

7.2c On models from 06/2006, the headlight is secured by screws at the top edge, inner edge (arrowed)...

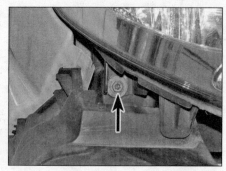

7.2d... and lower, outer edge (arrowed)

4 Disconnect the wiring plugs from the rear of the headlight **(see illustration)**.

5 Refitting is a direct reversal of the removal procedure. Lightly tighten the retaining screws and check the alignment of the headlight with the bumper and bonnet. Once the light unit is correctly positioned, securely tighten the retaining screws and check the headlight beam alignment using the information given in Section 8

Front direction indicator light

Note: *On models from 06/2006, the indicator is integral with the headlight unit.*

6 Use a small flat-bladed screwdriver to release the clip at the side, then remove the indicator light from the bumper **(see illustrations)**.

7 Rotate the bulbholder anti-clockwise and remove it from the light unit **(see illustration 5.14)**.

8 Refitting is a reversal of removal.

Front indicator side repeater

9 Removal of the side repeater is described in Section 5.

Front foglight

Models up to 06/2006

10 Undo the 2 retaining screws, and remove the foglight complete with surround panel. Disconnect the wiring plug as the assembly is withdrawn.

11 Undo the retaining bolt and separate the foglight from the panel.

Models from 06/2006

12 To improve access, raise the front of the vehicle, support it securely on axle stands (see *Jacking and vehicle support*).

13 Disconnect the wiring plug, the retaining screw, release the clip and remove the foglight.

All models

14 Refitting is a reversal of removal. If required, the foglight aim can be adjusted by rotating the adjuster screw adjacent to the foglight **(see illustration 5.27)**.

Rear light cluster

Upper light cluster

15 Open the rear door(s), undo the 3 retaining screws, manoeuvre the light cluster from place, noting the locating pins at the outer edge **(see illustrations 5.28a and 5.28b)**. Disconnect the wiring plug(s) as the cluster is withdrawn.

16 Refitting is a reversal of removal.

Lower light cluster

17 Open the rear door(s), undo the 2 retaining screws, and manoeuvre the light cluster from place, noting the locating pins at the outer edge **(see illustrations 5.32a and 5.32b)**. Disconnect the wiring plug as the cluster is removed **(see illustration)**.

18 Refitting is a reversal of removal.

Number plate light

19 Remove the door/tailgate inner trim panel as described in Section 8 of Chapter 11.

20 Disconnect the wiring plug, undo the 2 nuts and remove the number plate light unit.

21 Refitting is the reverse of removal.

High-level brake light

22 Open the rear door(s), undo the nut and remove the high-level brake light **(see illustration 5.36)**. Disconnect the wiring plug as the light is withdrawn.

23 Refitting is a reversal of removal.

8 Headlight beam alignment – general information

1 Accurate adjustment of the headlight beam is only possible using optical beam setting equipment and this work should therefore be carried out by a dealer or suitably-equipped workshop.

2 For reference, the headlights can be adjusted by rotating the adjuster screws on the top, rear of the headlight unit **(see**

7.4 Disconnect the wiring plugs from the rear of the headlight

7.6b... and pull the indicator from the bumper

7.6a Press in the clip at the inner edge...

7.17 Disconnect the lower rear light cluster wiring plug

illustration). The outer adjuster alters the horizontal position of the beam whilst the inner adjuster alters the vertical aim of the beam.

3 Some models have an electrically-operated headlight beam adjustment system which is controlled through the switch in the facia. On these models ensure that the switch is set to the off (0) position before adjusting the headlight aim.

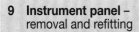

9 Instrument panel – removal and refitting

Removal

1 Disconnect the battery negative terminal (see Chapter 5).

2 Move the steering column down as far as it will go, and extend it completely.

3 Carefully prise the instrument panel surround trim rearwards to release the retaining clips **(see illustration)**.

4 Undo the 2 retaining screws at the lower edge, and manoeuvre the instrument panel rearwards **(see illustrations)**. Disconnect the wiring plugs as the panel is withdrawn.

5 At the time of writing, no individual components are available for the instrument panel and therefore the panel must be treated as a sealed unit. If there is a fault with one of the instruments, remove the panel as described and take it to your dealer or specialist for testing. They have access to a special diagnostic tester which will be able to locate the fault and will then be able to advise you on the best course of action.

Refitting

6 Refitting is the reverse of removal, making sure the instrument panel wiring is correctly reconnected and securely held in position by any retaining clips. On completion reconnect the battery and check the operation of the panel warning lights to ensure that they are functioning correctly. **Note:** *If the instrument cluster has been renewed at the same time as the Body Control Module, the new unit must be coded to match the vehicle. This can only be carried out by a dealer or suitably-equipped specialist.*

10 Display unit – removal and refitting

Removal

1 Carefully prise the information display unit upwards, releasing the 4 retaining clips **(see illustration)**. Disconnect the wiring plug as the unit is withdrawn.

2 If required, undo the 2 screws and detach the display unit from the cover **(see illustration 6.16)**.

Refitting

3 Refitting is a reversal of removal.

8.2 Headlight horizontal and vertical aim adjustment screws (arrowed)

9.3 Prise the instrument panel surround trim rearwards

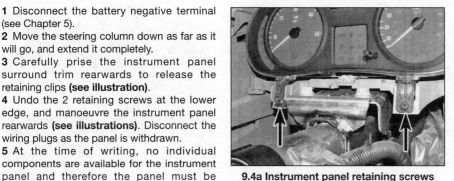 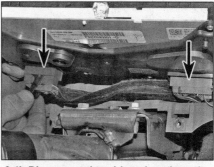

9.4a Instrument panel retaining screws (arrowed)

9.4b Disconnect the wiring plugs from the instrument panel (arrowed)

11 Body Control Module – removal and refitting

Removal

1 Remove the steering column as described in Chapter 10.

2 Unclip the plastic shield from the module (where fitted), then disconnect the accessible wiring plug, undo the clips securing the module in place **(see illustration)**.

3 Drill out the rivets securing the bracket to the module, then disconnect the remaining wiring plug **(see illustration)**.

Refitting

4 Refitting is a reversal of removal. **Note:** *If*

the Body Control Module has been renewed, the new unit must be initialised. This can only be carried out by a dealer or suitably-equipped specialist.

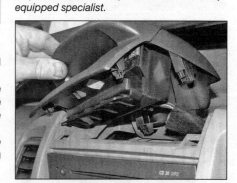

10.1 Prise the display unit upwards to release the clips

 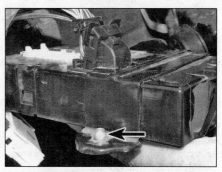

11.2 Disconnect the accessible Body Control Module wiring plug (arrowed)

11.3 Drill out the rivet (arrowed), remove the bracket, then disconnect the remaining wiring plug

12 Outside temperature sensor – removal and refitting
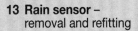

Removal

1 The outside temperature sensor is fitted to the lower section of the front bumper. Release the retaining clips, and remove the sensor from place. Disconnect the wiring plug as the sensor is withdrawn.

Refitting

2 Refitting is a reversal of the removal procedure, ensuring the wiring connector is securely reconnected.

13 Rain sensor – removal and refitting
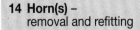

Removal

1 Carefully prise the plastic cover from the rear of the sensor, located at the top of the windscreen.
2 Disconnect the wiring plug, then release the 2 catches and remove the sensor.

Refitting

3 Refitting is a reversal of removal.

14 Horn(s) – removal and refitting

Removal

1 The horn(s) are located behind the left-hand end of the front bumper.
2 To gain access to the horn(s) from below, apply the handbrake then jack up the front of the vehicle and support it on axle stands (see *Jacking and vehicle support*). Undo the fasteners securing the front, lower section of the wheel arch liner.
3 Undo the retaining bolt and remove the horn, disconnecting the wiring plug as it become accessible **(see illustration)**.

Refitting

4 Refitting is the reverse of removal.

15 Wiper arm – removal and refitting
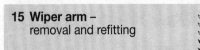

Removal

Front wiper arm

1 Operate the wiper motor, then switch it off so that the wiper arm returns to the 'at rest' position. Open the bonnet.
2 Stick a piece of masking tape along the edge of the wiper blade to use as an alignment aid on refitting.

14.3 Horn retaining bolt (arrowed – bumper removed for clarity)

15.3b... and remove the spindle nut

3 Prise off the wiper arm spindle nut cover(s) then slacken and remove the spindle nut(s). Lift the blade off the glass and pull the wiper arm off its spindle. If necessary the arm can be levered off the spindle using a suitable flat-bladed screwdriver or suitable puller **(see illustrations)**.

Rear wiper arm

4 Stick a piece of masking tape along the edge of the wiper blade to use as an alignment aid on refitting.
5 Pull the wiper arm cover from the spindle, undo the nut and remove the wiper arm.

Refitting

6 Ensure that the wiper arm and spindle splines are clean and dry then refit the arm to the spindle, aligning the wiper blade with the tape fitted on removal. Refit the spindle nut, tightening it to the specified torque setting, and clip the nut cover back in position.

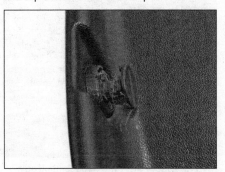
16.3a Prise out the centre pin, remove the middle...

15.3a Prise off the nut cover...

15.3c If necessary, use a puller to remove the arm

7 If the position of the front wiper arms has been lost, set the arms so the blades align with the triangles etched into the windscreen glass. The end of the rear wiper blade should be 30 mm above the window edge.

16 Windscreen wiper motor and linkage – removal and refitting

Removal

1 Disconnect the battery negative lead as described in Chapter 5.

Front windscreen wiper motor

2 Remove the wiper arms as described in Section 15.
3 Pull up the rubber sealing strip, then release the clips and remove the water deflector panels from each end of the scuttle **(see illustrations)**.

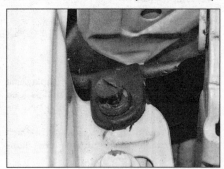
16.3b... and lower clip...

16.3c... then pull the water deflector panel upwards from the upper clip (arrowed)

16.4a Push in the centre pins and remove the clip at the each corner...

16.4b... then pull the scuttle panel upwards from the windscreen

4 Release the clips and pull the scuttle panel upwards from the base of the windscreen **(see illustrations)**. Disconnect the washer hoses as the panel is withdrawn.
5 Undo the retaining screw/nuts, disconnect the wiring plug and remove the heater fan housing from the engine compartment bulkhead **(see illustrations)**.
6 Disconnect the wiring plug, and unclip the harness from the motor/linkage.
7 Undo the nuts/washers and manoeuvre the motor/linkage from place **(see illustrations)**.

Rear windscreen wiper motor

8 Remove the wiper arm as described in Section 15.
9 Remove the rear door/tailgate trim panel as described in Chapter 11.
10 Disconnect the motor wiring plug.
11 Make alignment marks where the motor and bracket touch the door/tailgate, to aid

refitting. Undo the screws, and remove the wiper motor. Renew the spindle sealing ring.

Refitting

12 Refitting is the reverse of removal. On completion refit the wiper arms as described in Section 15.

17 Washer system components – removal and refitting

Washer system reservoir

1 The windscreen washer reservoir is situated in the engine compartment. On models equipped with rear screen washers, the reservoir also supplies the rear jets, using the same pump, rotating in the opposite direction.

2 Empty the contents of the reservoir or be prepared for fluid spillage.
3 Remove the front bumper as described in Chapter 11.
4 Undo the retaining bolt, and rotate the reservoir to access the pump.
5 Disconnect the wiring connector from the pump, unclip the wiring harness, then note their fitted locations, and disconnect the various hoses from the pump.
6 Manoeuvre the reservoir from position. Wash off any spilt fluid with cold water.
7 Refitting is a reversal of removal. Refill the reservoir and check for leakage.

Washer pump

8 Raise the front of the vehicle and support it securely on axle stands (see *Jacking and vehicle support*). Remove the right-hand front roadwheel.

16.5a The heater fan housing is secured by a nut on the right-hand side (arrowed)...

16.5b... on the left-hand side (arrowed)...

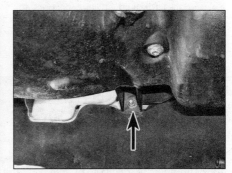

16.5c... underneath (arrowed)...

16.5d... and a screw on the top edge (arrowed)

16.7a Undo the spindle nuts, and recover the washers

16.7b Manoeuvre the wiper linkage/motor from place

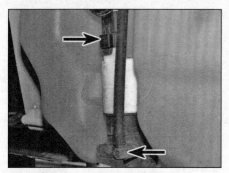

17.10 Disconnect the wiring plug and hose from the washer pump (arrowed)

17.12 Pull the washer jet from the scuttle panel

Removal

1 Disconnect the battery negative lead as described in Chapter 5.

Models without tachograph

2 Insert Vauxhall audio unit removal tools No KM 6067 or Renault tools MS1373 or MS1821 (depending on model) into the holes until they click into place **(see illustrations)**.
3 Pull the unit rearwards, and disconnect the various wiring plugs.

Models with tachograph

4 Carefully prise away the surround trim from the radio.
5 Insert the radio removal tools, then pull the unit rearwards from the facia.
6 Disconnect the various wiring plugs as the unit is withdrawn.

Refitting

7 Refitting is a reversal of removal.

18.2a Insert the radio removal tools into the holes (arrowed)...

18.2b... until they click into place, depressing the clip (arrowed)

19 Loudspeakers –
   removal and refitting

9 Undo the various fasteners and remove the front section of the wheel arch liner.
10 Disconnect the wiring connector and hose(s) from the washer pump. Carefully pull the pump up from the reservoir **(see illustration)**. Be prepared for fluid spillage. Inspect the pump sealing grommet for signs of damage or deterioration and renew if necessary.
11 Refitting is the reverse of removal, using a new sealing grommet if the original one shows signs of damage or deterioration. Refill the reservoir and check the pump grommet for leaks.

Windscreen washer jets

12 Open the bonnet and pull the jet from the scuttle panel. Disconnect the washer hose from the base of the jet **(see illustration)**.
13 Refitting is a reversal of removal. If necessary, adjust the aim of the jets using a pin inserted into the jet outlet hole.

Rear screen washer jet

14 Carefully prise the washer jet from place, and disconnect the washer hose.
15 Refitting is a reversal of removal.

18 Radio/cassette/CD player –
   removal and refitting

Note: *The following removal and refitting procedure is for some of the range of units which Vauxhall and Renault fit as standard equipment. Removal and refitting procedures of non-standard will differ slightly.*
Note: *Specific radio removal tools are required during these procedures. Although available from Vauxhall and Renault dealers, equivalent tools are readily available from automotive parts/audio specialists.*

Door main loudspeaker

1 Rotate the speaker grille anti-clockwise a little, and remove it to access the speaker **(see illustration)**.
2 Undo the retaining screws, manoeuvre the speaker from the door panel, and disconnect the wiring plug **(see illustration)**.
3 Refitting is the reverse of removal.

Treble loudspeaker

4 Rotate the speaker grille anti-clockwise a little and remove it **(see illustration)**.
5 Undo the 2 retaining screws and manoeuvre the speaker from the facia. Disconnect the wiring plug as the speaker is withdrawn.
6 Refitting is a reversal of removal.

20 Radio aerial –
   general information

The radio aerial is mounted on the cabin roof. In order to remove the aerial, the roof headlining

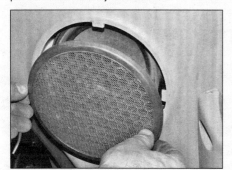

19.1 Rotate the speaker trim anti-clockwise a little

19.2 Speaker retaining screws (arrowed)

19.4 Rotate the facia speaker grille anti-clockwise and remove it

must be partially removed. This is an involved job, requiring patience, dexterity and a certain amount of experience in order to minimise damage. Consequently, we recommend this task is entrusted to an upholstery specialist.

21 Anti-theft alarm system – general information

All models are equipped with a sophisticated anti-theft alarm and immobiliser system. Should a fault develop, the system's self-diagnosis facility should be interrogated using dedicated test equipment. Consult your Vauxhall or Renault dealer or suitably-equipped specialist.

22 Fuel filler flap motor – removal and refitting

Removal

1 Remove the right-hand front seat belt inertia reel as described in Chapter 11.
2 Disconnect the wiring plug, then rotate the motor and pull it from the support bracket **(see illustration)**.
3 Open the filler flap, position the motor and rotate it into place. Reconnect the wiring plug

Refitting

4 Refit the seat belt inertia reel as described in Chapter 11.

23 Airbag system – general information and precautions

The models covered by this manual are equipped with a driver's airbag as standard equipment, mounted in the centre of the steering wheel, an optional passenger's airbag located behind the facia and two optional side airbags located in the front seat backrests. The airbag system comprises of the airbag unit(s) (complete with gas generators), impact sensors, the control unit and a warning light in the instrument panel.

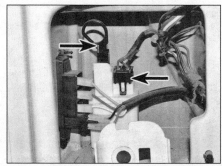

22.2 Fuel filler flap motor wiring plug and emergency release handle (arrowed)

The airbag system is triggered in the event of a heavy frontal or side impact above a predetermined force; depending on the point of impact, the airbag(s) is inflated within milliseconds and forms a safety cushion between the cabin occupants and the cabin interior, and therefore greatly reduces the risk of injury. The airbag then deflates almost immediately.

Every time the ignition is switched on, the airbag control unit performs a self-test. The self-test takes approximately 2 to 6 seconds and during this time the airbag warning light on the facia is illuminated. After the self-test has been completed the warning light should go out. If the warning light fails to come on, remains illuminated after the initial period, or comes on at any time when the vehicle is being driven, there is a fault in the airbag system. The vehicle should be taken to a dealer or suitably-equipped repairer for examination at the earliest possible opportunity.

⚠️ **Warning: Before carrying out any operations on the airbag system, disconnect the battery negative terminal, and wait for at least 2 minutes. This will allow the capacitors in the system to discharge. When operations are complete, make sure no one is inside the vehicle when the battery is reconnected.**
• **Note that the airbag(s) must not be subjected to temperatures in excess of 90°C. When the airbag is removed, ensure that it is stored the correct way up to prevent possible inflation (padded surface uppermost).**
• **Do not allow any solvents or cleaning**

agents to contact the airbag assemblies. They must be cleaned using only a damp cloth.
• **The airbags and control unit are both sensitive to impact. If either is dropped or damaged they should be renewed.**
• **Disconnect the airbag control unit wiring plug prior to using arc-welding equipment on the vehicle.**

24 Airbag system components – removal and refitting

Note: *Refer to the warnings in Section 23 before carrying out the following operations.*
1 Disconnect the battery negative terminal (see Chapter 5), then continue as described under the relevant heading.

Driver's airbag

2 With the wheels in the straight-ahead position, rotate the steering wheel 180°, insert a screwdriver into the hole in the base of the steering wheel boss until it contacts the retaining clip/spring. Press in the screwdriver to release the retaining clip, and slide the airbag from the steering wheel **(see illustrations)**. Rotate the steering wheel back to the straight-ahead position.
3 Carefully lift the airbag assembly away from the steering wheel. Note their fitted positions and disconnect the wiring plug(s) from the airbag unit **(see illustration)**. Note that the airbag must not be knocked or dropped and should be stored with its padded surface uppermost.
4 On refitting reconnect the wiring connector(s) and seat the airbag unit in the steering wheel, making sure the wire does not become trapped. Reconnect the battery as described in Chapter 5.

Passenger airbag

5 Open the glovebox to access the airbag, then undo the screws and remove the cover above the airbag.
6 The airbag is secured by 6 screws. Undo the screws, disconnect the wiring plugs and remove the airbag.
7 Refitting is a reversal of removal. Tighten

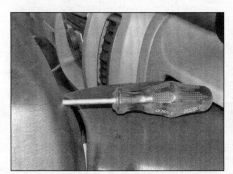

24.2a Insert a screwdriver into the hole in the steering wheel boss...

24.2b... until it releases the airbag retaining clip (arrowed)

24.3 Pull the wiring plug from the airbag

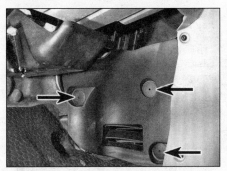

24.19 Prise out the clips (arrowed) and remove the footwell panel each side

24.21 Note the arrow on the airbag control unit indicating direction of travel (arrowed – heater removed for clarity)

the airbag retaining screws securely, and reconnect the battery negative terminal.

Rotary contact unit

8 Remove the airbag as described in this Section, ensure the steering wheel is in the 'straight-ahead' position, then remove the steering wheel as described in Chapter 10.

9 Undo the 2 screws, and remove the steering column lower and upper shrouds **(see illustration 4.3a and 4.3b)**.

10 On models with ESP, release the 4 retaining clips, disconnect the wiring plug and remove the steering angel sensor.

11 Push the locking device upwards, and rotate the locking screw anti-clockwise until it comes to a stop **(see illustration 4.5)**. This locks the contact unit, and prevents accidental rotation.

12 Disconnect the wiring plug from the immobiliser antenna around the ignition switch barrel, and the various connectors from the steering column switches.

13 Release the clips and slide the contact unit

upwards from the column **(see illustration 4.7)**. If required, the column switches can be detached from the contact unit as described in Section 4.

14 Refitting is a reversal of removal. Note that if a new contact unit is fitted on models with ESP, the steering angle sensor must be calibrated using Vauxhall or Renault diagnostic equipment. Entrust this task to a dealer or suitably-equipped repairer.

Side impact sensors

15 Undo the 2 outer bolts securing the passenger's seat, then undo the 4 retaining screws and remove the footwell treadplate.

16 Remove the plastic cover, disconnect the wiring plug, undo the bolt and remove the sensor.

17 Refitting is a reversal of removal.

Side airbags

18 Removal of the side airbags involves the removal of the seat backrest cover. We recommend this task is entrusted to a dealer or upholstery specialist.

Airbag central sensor/ control unit

19 Remove the centre console as described in Chapter 11, then prise out the clips and remove the footwell panel each side **(see illustration)**.

20 Release the clips and remove the air outlet duct each side.

21 Undo the retaining nuts and lift the module. Disconnect the wiring plug as the unit is withdrawn **(see illustration)**.

22 Refitting is the reverse of removal. Note that if a new unit is fitted, it must be programmed using Vauxhall or Renault diagnostic equipment. Entrust this task to a dealer or suitably-equipped specialist.

25 Wiring diagrams – general information

1 The wiring diagrams which follow only offer limited coverage of the electrical systems fitted to the Vauxhall Vivaro and Renault Trafic.

2 Due to the sheer volume of wiring circuits applicable for the Vivaro and Trafic, comprehensive coverage of all the vehicle's systems is not possible.

3 Bear in mind that, while wiring diagrams offer a useful quick-reference guide to the vehicle electrical systems, it is still possible to trace faults, and to check for supplies and earths, using a simple multimeter. Refer to the general fault finding methods described in Section 2 of this Chapter (ignoring the references to wiring diagrams if one is not provided for the system concerned).

Vauxhall Vivaro and Renault Trafic (up to 09/2006) wiring diagrams

Diagram 1

WARNING: *This vehicle is fitted with a supplemental restraint system (SRS) consisting of a combination of driver (and passenger) airbag(s), side impact protection airbags and seatbelt pre-tensioners. The use of electrical test equipment on any SRS wiring systems may cause the seatbelt pre-tensioners to abruptly retract and airbags to explosively deploy, resulting in potentially severe personal injury. Extreme care should be taken to correctly identify any circuits to be tested to avoid choosing any of the SRS wiring in error.*
For further information see airbag system precautions in body electrical systems chapter.
Note: The SRS wiring harness can normally be identified by yellow and/or orange harness or harness connectors.

Key to symbols

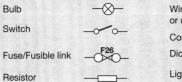

Bulb	⊗
Switch	⌐○
Fuse/Fusible link	F26
Resistor	▭
Variable resistor	
Variable resistor	

Wire splice, soldered joint, or unspecified connector	
Connecting wires	
Diode	
Light-emitting diode	
Item number	**12**
Motor/pump	Ⓜ
Heating element	

Solenoid actuator	
Earth point and location	E7
Dashed outline denotes part of a larger item, containing in this case an electronic or solid state device (pins 43 and 44 of a single connector designated x45).	x45/43 x45/44 Ⓚ
Wire colour (red with black tracer)	Rd/Bk

Earth locations

E1   Base of LH 'A' pillar
E2   Base of RH 'A' pillar
E3   Battery -ve terminal
E4   On bracket in front of gear lever
E5   Above master cylinder
E6   Above master cylinder
E7   Crossmember on underside of vehicle
E8   Crossmember on underside of vehicle
E9   Behind LH rear light
E10 Behind LH rear light
E11 RH side of engine compartment
E12 LH side of engine compartment
E13 LH side of engine compartment
E14 On gearbox
E15 On gearbox

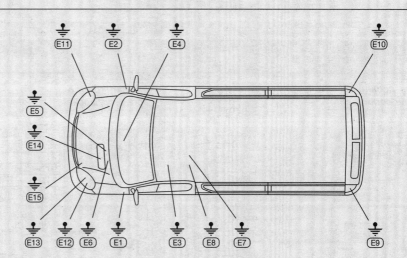

Engine fusebox ④

For fuse rating consult fusebox lid

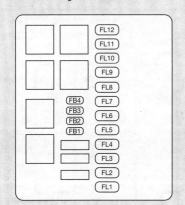

Passenger fusebox ⑤

For fuse rating consult fusebox lid

FC27	FC14	FC1
FC28	FC15	FC2
FC29	FC16	FC3
FC30	FC17	FC4
FC31	FC18	FC5
FC32	FC19	FC6
FC33	FC20	FC7
FC34	FC21	FC8
FC35	FC22	FC9
FC36	FC23	FC10
FC37	FC24	FC11
FC38	FC25	FC12
FC39	FC26	FC13

Key to circuits

Diagram 1   Information for wiring diagrams.
Diagram 2   Starting and charging, horn, engine cooling fan, cigar lighter and accessory socket, stop, reversing, side, tail and number plate lights.
Diagram 3   Headlights, foglights, direction indicators and hazard warning lights, headlight levelling and heater blower.
Diagram 4   Electric mirrors, electric windows, wash/wipe and interior lighting.
Diagram 5   Instrument cluster and central locking.
Diagram 6   Heated rear window, anti-lock brakes and audio system.

H47305

Wire colours

Bk	Black	Pk	Pink
Ye	Yellow	Vt	Violet
Bu	Blue	Og	Orange
Bn	Brown	Wh	White
Gn	Green	Lgn	Light Green
Gy	Grey	Lbu	Light Blue
Pu	Purple	Dgn	Dark Green
Bg	Beige	DBu	Dark Blue
Rd	Red		

Key to items

1 Battery
2 Alternator
3 Starter motor
4 Engine fusebox
5 Passenger fusebox
6 Ignition switch
7 Steering wheel contact unit
8 Horn switch
9 Horn
10 Steering column switch unit
  a = side/headlight
11 Engine cooling fan relay 1
12 Engine cooling fan relay 2
13 Engine cooling fan motor
14 Engine cooling fan resistor
15 Front accessory socket
16 Rear accessory socket
17 Cigar lighter
18 Stop light switch
19 Reversing light switch
20 High level stop light
21 LH tailgate light unit
  a = stop light
  b = tail light
22 LH rear light unit
  a = reversing light
23 RH tailgate light unit
  a = stop light
  b = tail light
24 RH rear light unit
  a = reversing light
25 LH front sidelight
26 RH front sidelight
27 Number plate light

Diagram 2

H47306

Starting & charging

FLA 150A | FLB 180A | FL5 60A
Rd Rd Rd Rd/Wh Rd/Wh Wh
Bk Bk
E7 E14
30 50 31 — 2 — B+ D+ B-
3

See diagram 5
Instrument cluster
(alternator warning light)

Horn

FLA 150A | FL4 60A
Rd
Bk Bk
E7 E14
x65/B6 x66 x65/A4
Rd Bk Bn
FC34 15A
Gy
8 7 x81/2 x81/1
9

Engine cooling fan - without air conditioning

FLA 150A | FL3 60A
Rd
Bk Bk
E7 E14
30 86 85 87 — K13
Rd Og Wh Gn
Gn Bk
E15
13

Engine management
control unit
(not shown)

Engine cooling fan - with air conditioning

FLA 150A | FL3 60A
Rd
Bk Bk
E7 E14
Wh Gn Pk — Engine management control unit (not shown)
Rd Pk Wh Gn — 30 86 85 87 K13
Rd Gn Wh Bn — 30 86 85 87 K14
Bn
Bk
E3
14 13

Cigar lighter & accessory sockets

FLA 150A | FL5 60A
Rd Rd/Wh
Bk Bk
E7 E14
30 15 15A 50
ST A M D
B1 A2 A1 B2
Ye FC26 15A Ye
Ye FC24 15A Ye
Ye FC16 15A Ye
Bn
E1
Ye Bn — 15
E9
Ye Bn — 16
17

Stop, reversing, side, tail & number plate lights

FLA 150A | FL4 60A | FL5 60A
Rd Rd/Wh Rd
Bk Bk
E7 E14
30 15 15A 50
ST A M D
B1 A2 A1 B2
x65/B6 a x65/B1
10
Ye FC16 15A
Ye FC14 25A
Bu FC32 10A Bu
Bu FC31 10A Bu
See diagram 6 ABS
18 B1 A3 | 19 2 1
Ye Wh Ye Og Og Wh Wh Bu Bu
Wh Vt Wh Bu Bu
x30/2 x30/6 x30/1 — 21
x31/2 x31/3 x30/3
25
Bk Pk Bk Bk
E12 | a 2 3 — 22 | E9
x32/2 x32/6 x32/1 — 23
x33/2 x33/3 x32/3
26
Bk Pk Bk Bk
E11 | 2 3 — 24 | E10
27 | 20 A1 A2
Bk Wh

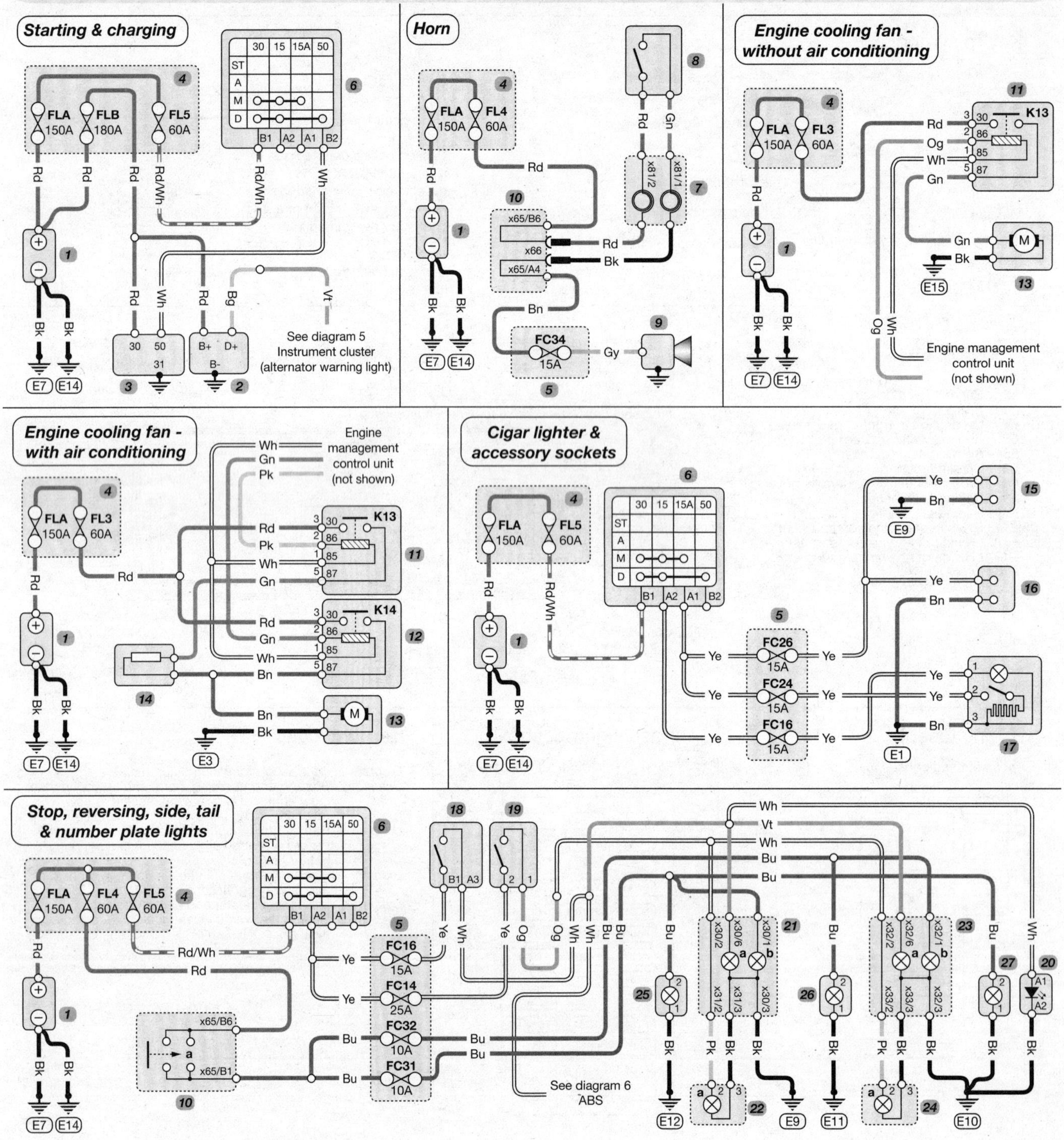

Wire colours

Bk	Black	Pk	Pink
Ye	Yellow	Vt	Violet
Bu	Blue	Og	Orange
Bn	Brown	Wh	White
Gn	Green	Lgn	Light Green
Gy	Grey	Lbu	Light Blue
Pu	Purple	Dgn	Dark Green
Bg	Beige	DBu	Dark Blue
Rd	Red		

Key to items

1 Battery
4 Engine fusebox
5 Passenger fusebox
6 Ignition switch
10 Steering column switch unit
  a = side/headlight
  b = headlight flasher
  c = dip main beam
  d = foglight switch
  e = direction indicator
21 LH tailgate light unit
  c = direction indicator

22 LH rear light unit
  b = foglight
23 RH tailgate light unit
  c = direction indicator
24 RH rear light unit
  b = foglight
30 LH headlight unit
  a = main beam
  b = dip beam
31 RH headlight unit
  a = main beam
  b = dip beam

32 LH front foglight
33 RH front foglight
34 Front foglight relay
35 Body control unit
36 Hazard warning switch
37 LH front direction indicator
38 RH front direction indicator
39 LH indicator side repeater
40 RH indicator side repeater
41 Headlight levelling switch
42 LH headlight levelling motor
43 RH headlight levelling motor

44 Heater blower switch
45 Heater blower resistor
46 Recirculation motor
47 Heater blower motor

Diagram 3

H47307

Headlights

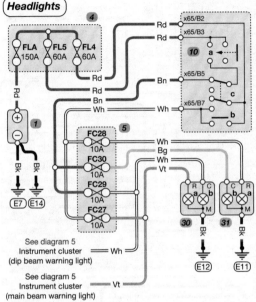

Fog lights

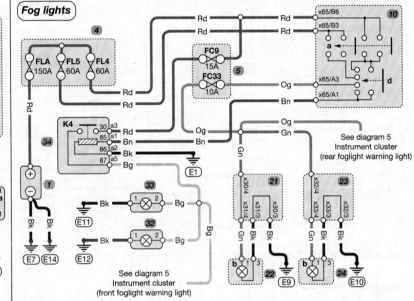

Direction indicators & hazard warning lights

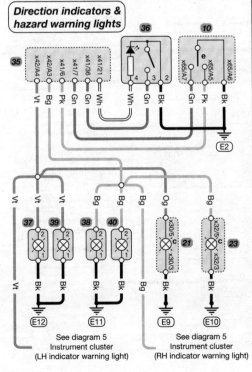

Headlight levelling

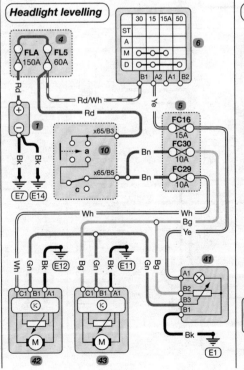

Heater blower

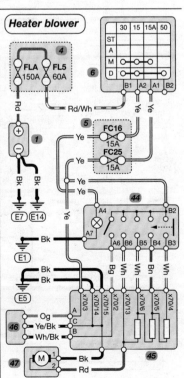

Wire colours

Bk	Black	Pk	Pink
Ye	Yellow	Vt	Violet
Bu	Blue	Og	Orange
Bn	Brown	Wh	White
Gn	Green	Lgn	Light Green
Gy	Grey	Lbu	Light Blue
Pu	Purple	Dgn	Dark Green
Bg	Beige	DBu	Dark Blue
Rd	Red		

Key to items

1 Battery
4 Engine fusebox
5 Passenger fusebox
6 Ignition switch
35 Body control unit
50 Driver's door contact switch
51 Passenger's door contact switch
52 Tailgate contact switch
53 Rear door contact switch
54 Front interior light
55 Passenger compartment light 1
56 Passenger compartment light 2
57 Luggage compartment light
58 Wash/wipe switch
  a = front wiper
  b = front washer
  c = rear wash/wipe
59 Front wiper motor
60 Rear wiper motor
61 Rear wiper relay
62 Rear wiper intermittent relay
63 Front/rear washer pump
64 LH sliding door switch
65 RH sliding door switch
66 Driver's window control unit
67 Terminal 15a relay
68 Driver's window switch
69 Passenger's window switch
70 Driver's window motor
71 Passenger's window motor
72 Electric mirror switch
73 LH electric mirror assembly
74 RH electric mirror assembly
75 Glovebox light

Diagram 4

H47308

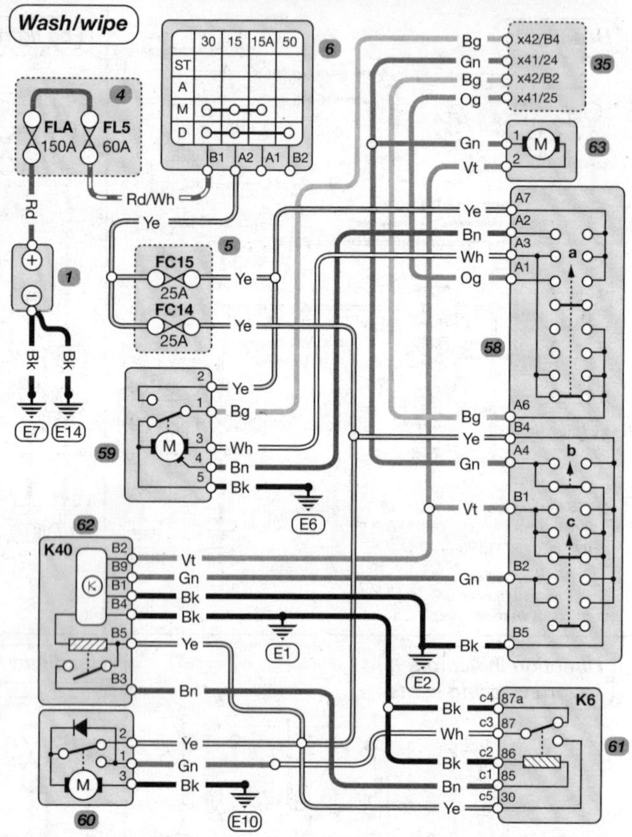

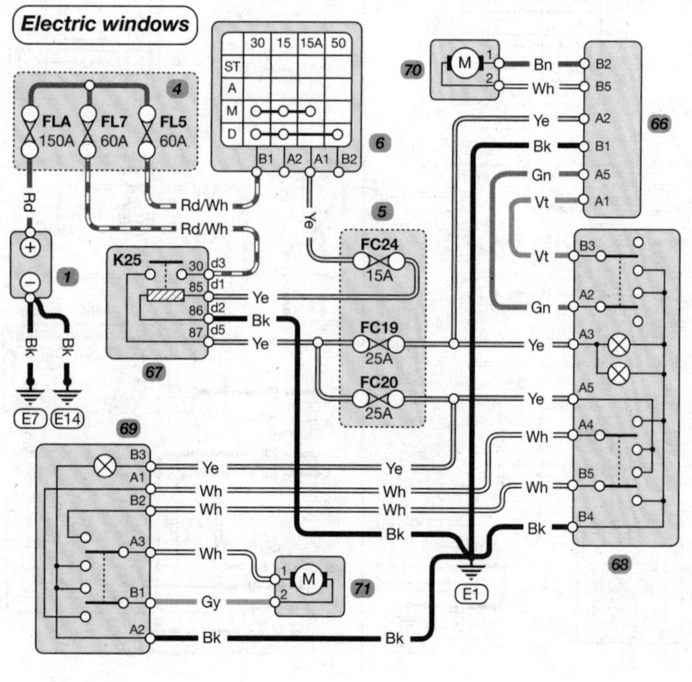

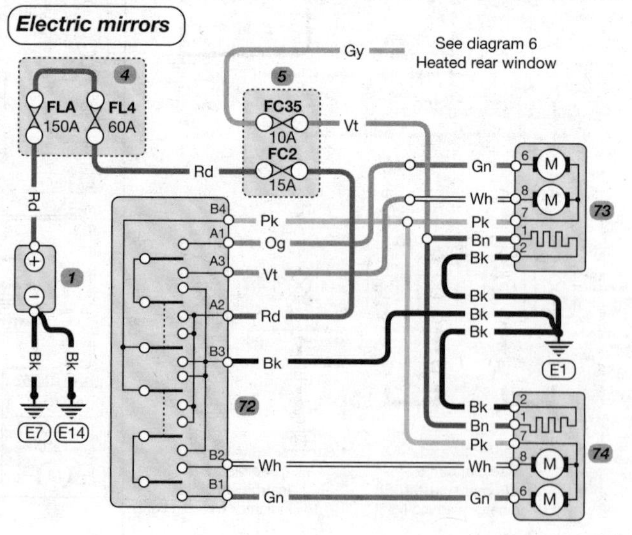

Interior lighting
Wash/wipe
Electric windows
Electric mirrors

See diagram 6
Heated rear window

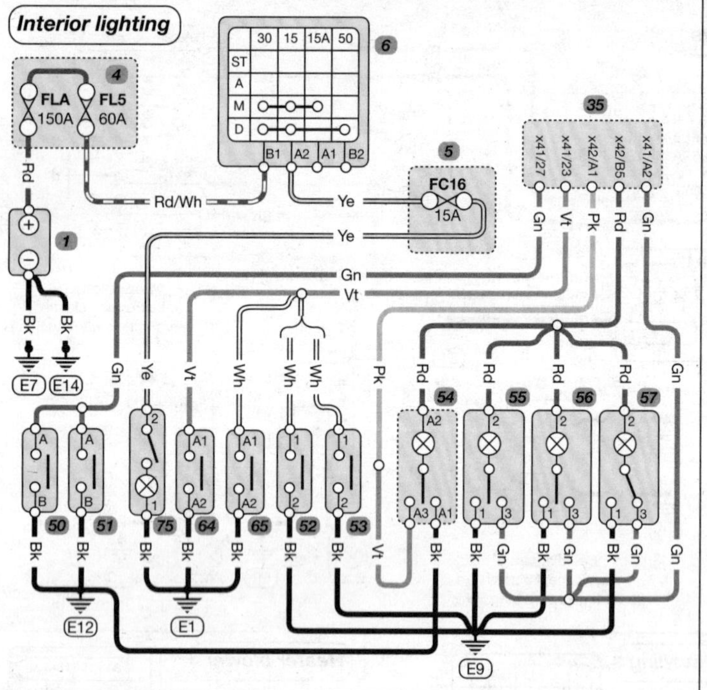

H47309

Wire colours

Bk	Black	Pk	Pink
Ye	Yellow	Vt	Violet
Bu	Blue	Og	Orange
Bn	Brown	Wh	White
Gn	Green	Lgn	Light Green
Gy	Grey	Lbu	Light Blue
Pu	Purple	Dgn	Dark Green
Bg	Beige	DBu	Dark Blue
Rd	Red		

Key to items

1 Battery
4 Engine fusebox
5 Passenger fusebox
6 Ignition switch
10 Steering column switch unit
   a   = side/headlight
35 Body control unit
79 Handbrake switch
80 Oil pressure switch
81 Low brake fluid switch
82 Fuel level sensor
83 Vehicle speed sensor

84 Oil level sensor
85 Instrument cluster
  a = alternator warning light
  b = brake system warning light
  c = stop warning light
  d = oil pressure warning light
  e = control unit
  f = immobiliser warning light
  g = airbag warning light
  h = seatbelt warning light
  i = main beam warning light
  j = dip beam warning light

k = rear foglight warning light
l = front foglight warning light
m = LH indicator warning light
n = RH indicator warning light
86 Central locking master switch
87 Driver's door lock
88 Passenger's door lock
89 LH sliding door lock
90 RH sliding door lock
91 Fuel filler flap motor
92 Tailgate lock motor
93 Rear door lock motor

Diagram 5

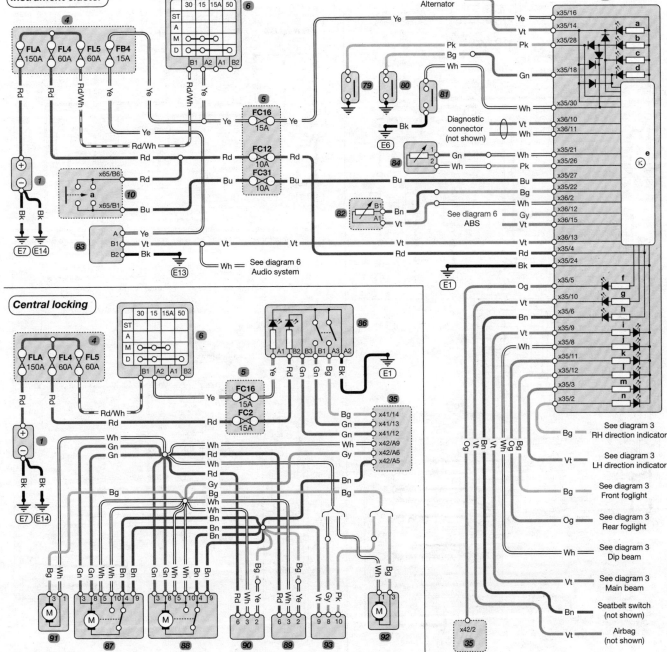

Wire colours

Bk	Black	Pk	Pink
Ye	Yellow	Vt	Violet
Bu	Blue	Og	Orange
Bn	Brown	Wh	White
Gn	Green	Lgn	Light Green
Gy	Grey	Lbu	Light Blue
Pu	Purple	Dgn	Dark Green
Bg	Beige	DBu	Dark Blue
Rd	Red		

Key to items

1 Battery
4 Engine fusebox
5 Passenger fusebox
6 Ignition switch
7 Steering wheel contact unit
10 Steering column switch unit
   a = side/headlight
35 Body control unit
95 Heated rear window relay
96 Heated rear window switch

97 LH heated rear window
98 RH heated rear window
99 Heated rear window (tailgate)
100 ABS control unit
101 LH front wheel sensor
102 RH front wheel sensor
103 LH rear wheel sensor
104 RH rear wheel sensor
105 Audio unit
106 Audio satellite controls

107 Outside air temperature sensor
108 Antenna
109 LH front speaker
110 LH front tweeter
111 RH front speaker
112 RH front tweeter
113 LH rear speaker
114 RH rear speaker

Diagram 6

H47310

Heated rear window

Audio system

Anti-lock brakes

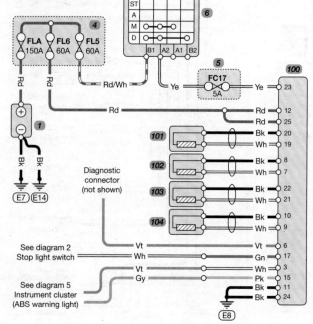

Vauxhall Vivaro and Renault Trafic (from 09/2006) wiring diagrams

Diagram 7

WARNING: This vehicle is fitted with a supplemental restraint system (SRS) consisting of a combination of driver (and passenger) airbag(s), side impact protection airbags and seatbelt pre-tensioners. The use of electrical test equipment on any SRS wiring systems may cause the seatbelt pre-tensioners to abruptly retract and airbags to explosively deploy, resulting in potentially severe personal injury. Extreme care should be taken to correctly identify any circuits to be tested to avoid choosing any of the SRS wiring in error.
For further information see airbag system precautions in body electrical systems chapter.
Note: The SRS wiring harness can normally be identified by yellow and/or orange harness or harness connectors.

Key to symbols

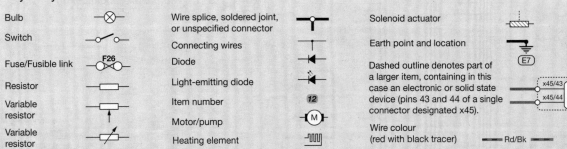

Bulb	Wire splice, soldered joint, or unspecified connector	Solenoid actuator
Switch	Connecting wires	Earth point and location
Fuse/Fusible link **F26**	Diode	Dashed outline denotes part of a larger item, containing in this case an electronic or solid state device (pins 43 and 44 of a single connector designated x45).
Resistor	Light-emitting diode	
Variable resistor	Item number **12**	
Variable resistor	Motor/pump	Wire colour (red with black tracer) Rd/Bk
	Heating element	

Earth locations

E1   Base of RH 'A' pillar
E2   Base of LH 'A' pillar
E3   Centre of top of windscreen
E4   Battery
E5   Gear lever bracket
E6   LH side behind cab (floor cab)
E7   LH side of engine compartment
E8   LH side of engine compartment
E9   Engine compartment, above master cylinder
E10   Engine compartment, above master cylinder
E11   Crossmember on underside of vehicle
E12   Crossmember on underside of vehicle
E13   Crossmember on underside of vehicle
E14   Behind LH rear light
E15   On panel near top of LH rear door
E16   Behind RH rear light
E17   Behind LH headlight
E18   Behind RH headlight
E19   On engine
E20   On engine

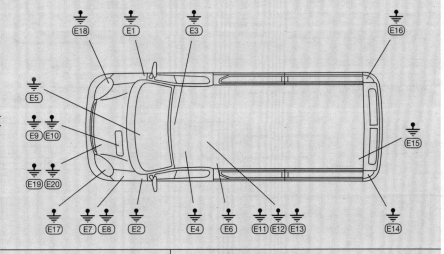

Engine fusebox ④

For fuse rating consult fusebox lid

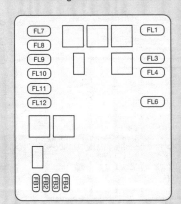

Passenger fusebox ⑤

For fuse rating consult fusebox lid

Key to circuits

Diagram 7   Information for wiring diagrams.
Diagram 8   Starting and charging, horn, engine cooling fan, cigar lighter and accessory socket, stop, reversing, side, tail and number plate lights.
Diagram 9   Headlights, foglights, direction indicators and hazard warning lights, headlight levelling and heater blower.
Diagram 10 Electric windows, wash/wipe and interior lighting.
Diagram 11 Instrument cluster and central locking.
Diagram 12 Heated rear window, electric mirrors and audio system.

H47311

Wire colours

Bk	Black	Pk	Pink
Ye	Yellow	Vt	Violet
Bu	Blue	Og	Orange
Bn	Brown	Wh	White
Gn	Green	Lgn	Light Green
Gy	Grey	Lbu	Light Blue
Pu	Purple	Dgn	Dark Green
Bg	Beige	DBu	Dark Blue
Rd	Red		

Key to items

1 Battery
2 Alternator
3 Starter motor
4 Engine fusebox
5 Passenger fusebox
6 Ignition switch
7 Steering wheel contact unit
8 Horn switch
9 Horn
10 Steering column switch unit
  a = side/headlight
11 Engine cooling fan relay 1
12 Engine cooling fan relay 2
13 Engine cooling fan motor
14 Engine cooling fan resistor
15 Front accessory socket
16 Rear accessory socket
17 Cigar lighter
18 Stop light switch
19 Reversing light switch
20 High level stop light
21 LH tailgate light unit
  a = stop light
  b = tail light
22 LH rear light unit
  a = reversing light
23 RH tailgate light unit
  a = stop light
  b = tail light
24 RH rear light unit
  a = reversing light
25 LH front sidelight
26 RH front sidelight
27 Number plate light

Diagram 8

H47312

Starting & charging

Horn

Engine cooling fan - without air conditioning

Engine cooling fan - with air conditioning

Cigar lighter & accessory sockets

Stop, reversing, side, tail & number plate lights

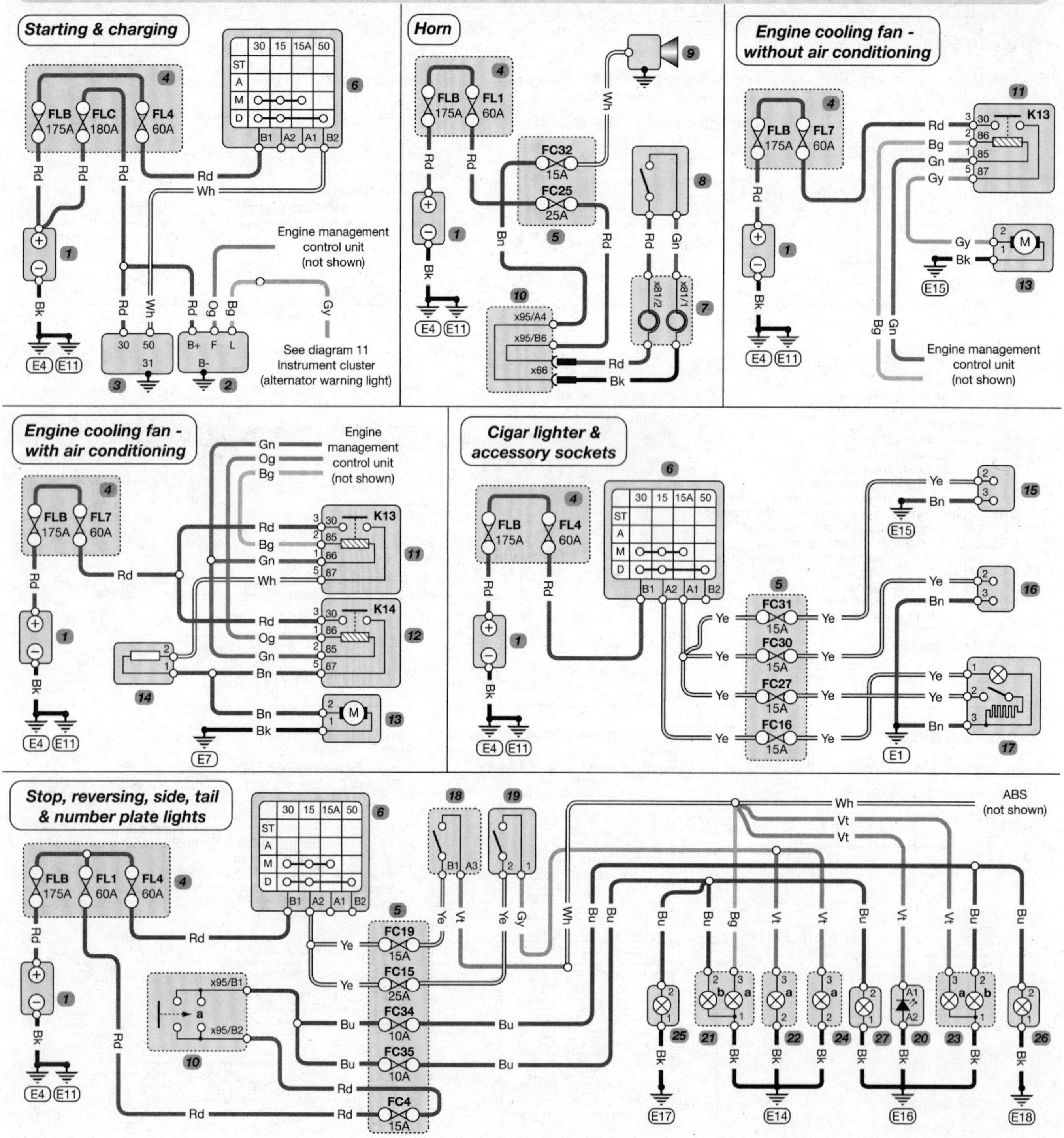

Wire colours

Bk	Black	Pk	Pink
Ye	Yellow	Vt	Violet
Bu	Blue	Og	Orange
Bn	Brown	Wh	White
Gn	Green	Lgn	Light Green
Gy	Grey	Lbu	Light Blue
Pu	Purple	Dgn	Dark Green
Bg	Beige	DBu	Dark Blue
Rd	Red		

Key to items

1 Battery
4 Engine fusebox
5 Passenger fusebox
6 Ignition switch
10 Steering column switch unit
  a = side/headlight
  b = headlight flasher
  c = dip main beam
  d = foglight switch
  e = direction indicator
21 LH tailgate light unit
  c = direction indicator
22 LH rear light unit
  b = foglight
23 RH tailgate light unit
  c = direction indicator
24 RH rear light unit
  b = foglight
30 LH headlight unit
  a = main beam
  b = dip beam
31 RH headlight unit
  a = main beam
  b = dip beam
32 LH front foglight
33 RH front foglight
34 Front foglight relay
35 Body control unit
36 Hazard warning switch
37 LH front direction indicator
38 RH front direction indicator
39 LH indicator side repeater
40 RH indicator side repeater
41 Headlight levelling switch
42 LH headlight levelling motor
43 RH headlight levelling motor
44 Heater blower switch
45 Heater blower resistor
46 Recirculation motor
47 Heater blower motor

Diagram 9

H47313

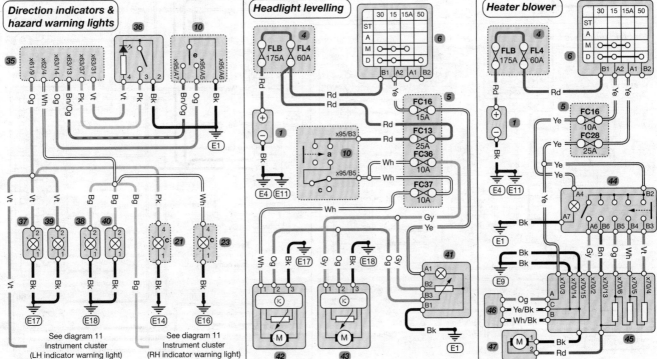

Wire colours

Bk	Black	Pk	Pink
Ye	Yellow	Vt	Violet
Bu	Blue	Og	Orange
Bn	Brown	Wh	White
Gn	Green	Lgn	Light Green
Gy	Grey	Lbu	Light Blue
Pu	Purple	Dgn	Dark Green
Bg	Beige	DBu	Dark Blue
Rd	Red		

Key to items

1 Battery
4 Engine fusebox
5 Passenger fusebox
6 Ignition switch
35 Body control unit
50 Driver's door contact switch
51 Passenger's door contact switch
52 Tailgate contact switch
53 Rear door contact switch
54 Front interior light
55 Passenger compartment light 1
56 Passenger compartment light 2
57 Luggage compartment light
58 Wash/wipe switch
 a = front wiper
 b = front washer
 c = rear wash/wipe
 d = trip computer switch
59 Front wiper motor
60 Rear wiper motor
61 Rear wiper relay
62 Rear wiper intermittent relay
63 Front/rear washer pump
64 LH sliding door switch
65 RH sliding door switch
68 Driver's window switch
69 Passenger's window switch
70 Driver's window motor
71 Passenger's window motor
72 Terminal 15 relay
73 Terminal 15 relay
74 Front wiper relay
75 Glovebox light

Diagram 10

H47314

Interior lighting

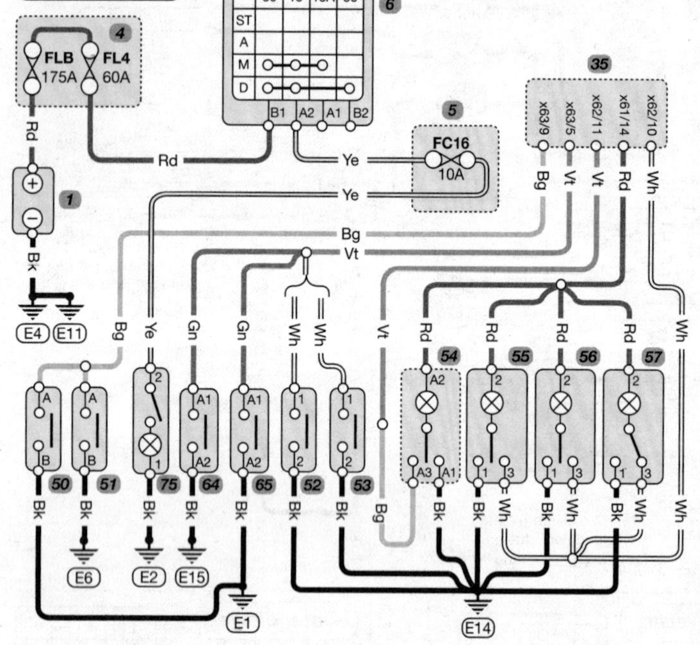

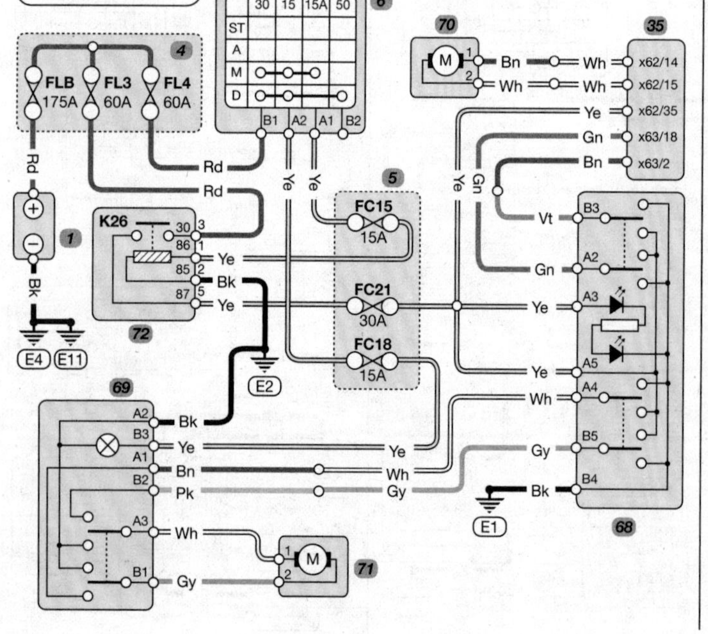

Wash/wipe

Electric windows

See diagram 11
Instrument cluster
(trip computer)

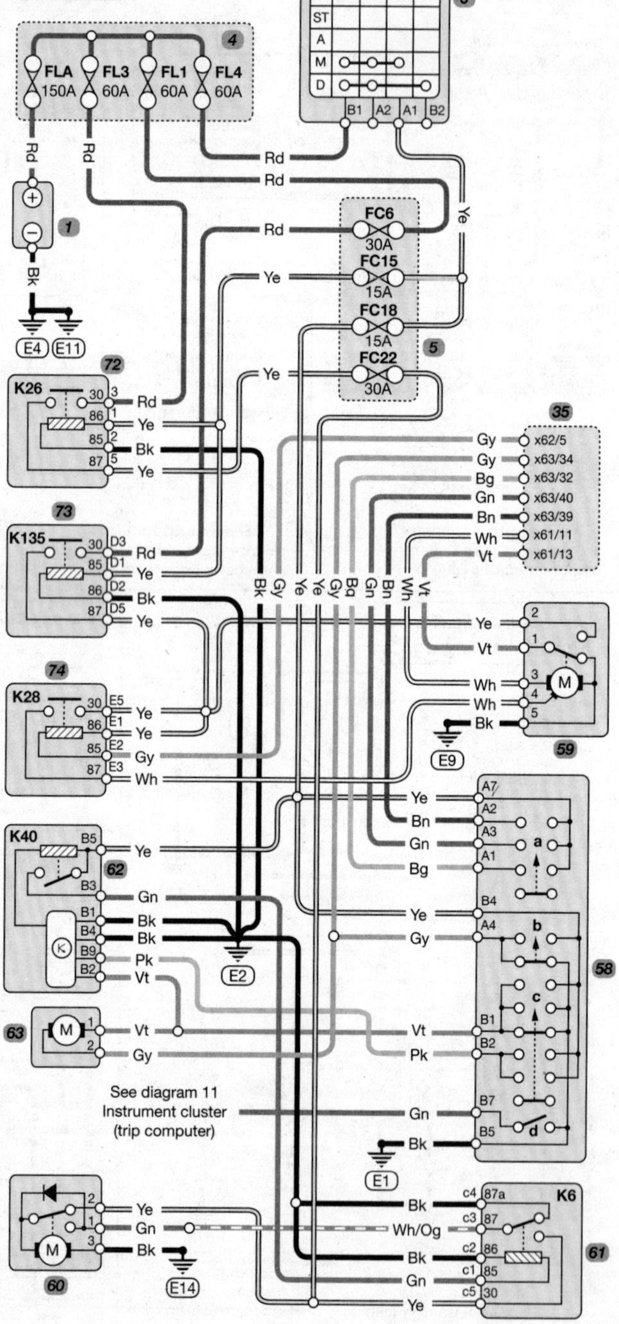

Wire colours

Bk Black
Ye Yellow
Bu Blue
Bn Brown
Gn Green
Gy Grey
Pu Purple
Bg Beige
Rd Red
Pk Pink
Vt Violet
Og Orange
Wh White
Lgn Light Green
Lbu Light Blue
Dgn Dark Green
DBu Dark Blue

Key to items

1 Battery
4 Engine fusebox
5 Passenger fusebox
6 Ignition switch
10 Steering column switch unit
  a = side/headlight
35 Body control unit
79 Handbrake switch
80 Oil pressure switch
81 Low brake fluid switch
82 Fuel level sensor
84 Oil level sensor

85 Instrument cluster
  a = alternator warning light
  b = brake system warnimg light
  c = stop warning light
  d = oil pressure warning light
  e = control unit
  f = immobiliser warning light
  h = seatbelt warning light
  i = main beam warning light
  j = dip beam warning light
  k = rear foglight warning light
  l = front foglight warning light

m = LH indicator warning light
n = RH indicator warning light
86 Central locking master switch
87 Driver's door lock
88 Passenger's door lock
89 LH sliding door lock
90 RH sliding door lock
91 Fuel filler flap motor
92 Tailgate lock motor
93 Rear door lock motor

Diagram 11

H47315

Instrument cluster

Central locking

See diagram 10
Wash/wipe switch
(trip computer switch)

See diagram 8
Alternator

FLB 175A FLD 40A FL1 60A FL4 60A

FC16 10A, FC9 10A, FC35 10A, FC4 15A

Speed sensor (not shown)

CAN Bus (not shown)

ABS (not shown)

See diagram 9 RH direction indicator
See diagram 9 LH direction indicator
See diagram 9 Front foglight
See diagram 9 Rear foglight
See diagram 9 Dip beam
See diagram 9 Main beam
Seatbelt switch (not shown)

91 87 90 88 89 93 92

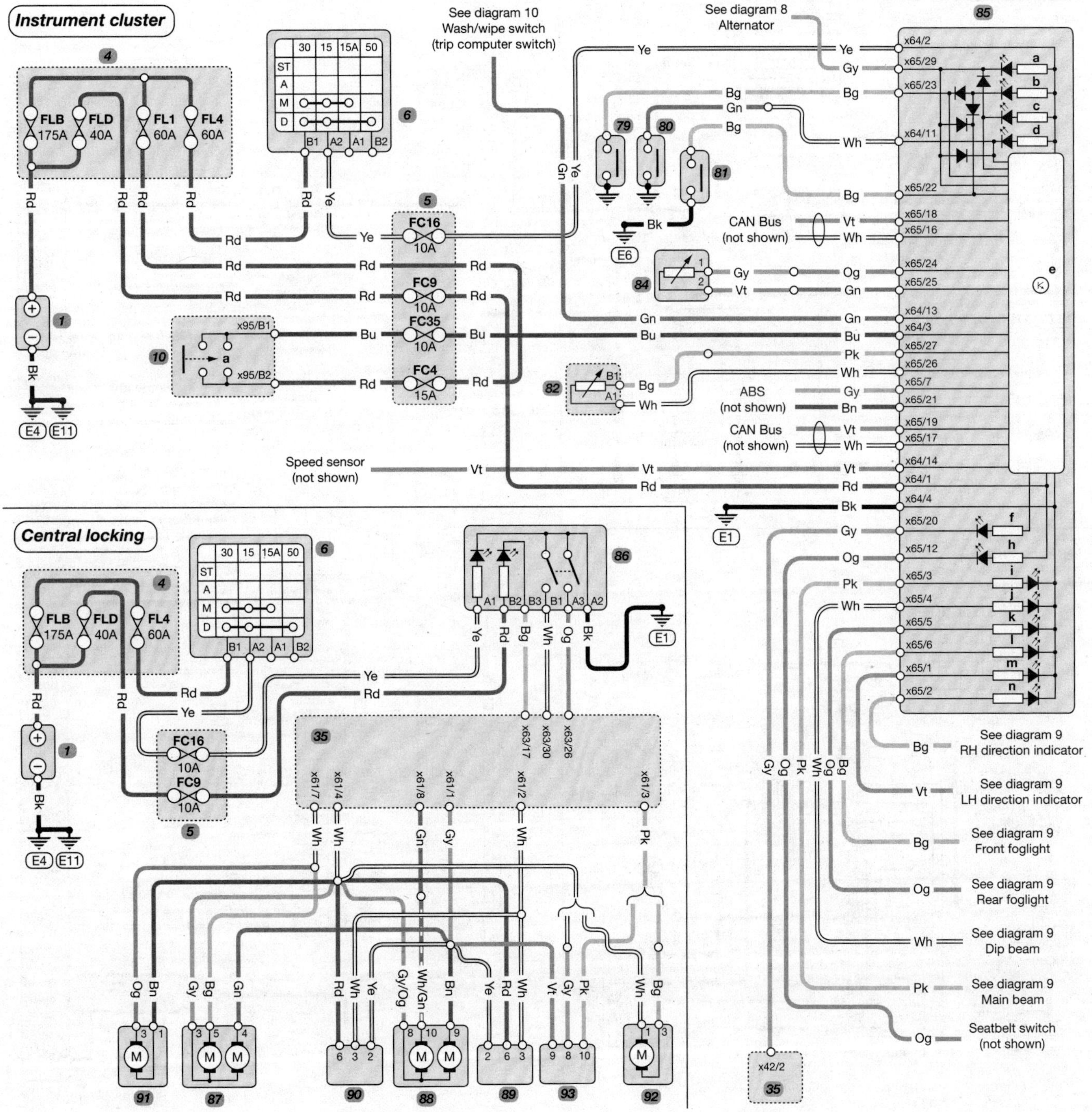

Wire colours

Bk	Black	**Pk**	Pink
Ye	Yellow	**Vt**	Violet
Bu	Blue	**Og**	Orange
Bn	Brown	**Wh**	White
Gn	Green	**Lgn**	Light Green
Gy	Grey	**Lbu**	Light Blue
Pu	Purple	**Dgn**	Dark Green
Bg	Beige	**DBu**	Dark Blue
Rd	Red		

Key to items

1   Battery
4   Engine fusebox
5   Passenger fusebox
6   Ignition switch
7   Steering wheel contact unit
35 Body control unit
95 Heated rear window relay
96 Heated rear window switch
97 LH heated rear window
98 RH heated rear window
99 Heated rear window (tailgate)
100 Electric mirror switch
101 LH electric mirror assembly
102 RH electric mirror assembly
105 Audio unit
106 Audio satellite controls
108 Antenna
109 LH front speaker
110 LH front tweeter
111 RH front speaker
112 RH front tweeter
113 LH rear speaker
114 RH rear speaker

Diagram 12

H47316

Heated rear window

Electric mirrors

Audio system

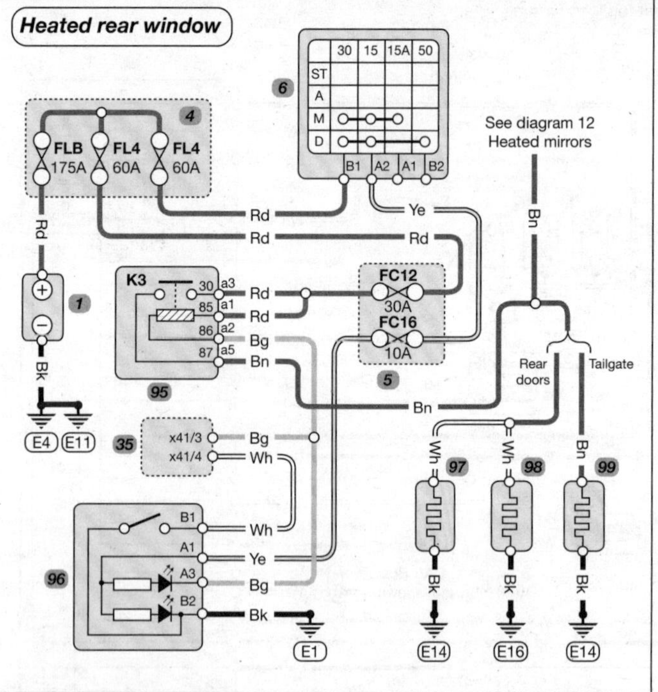

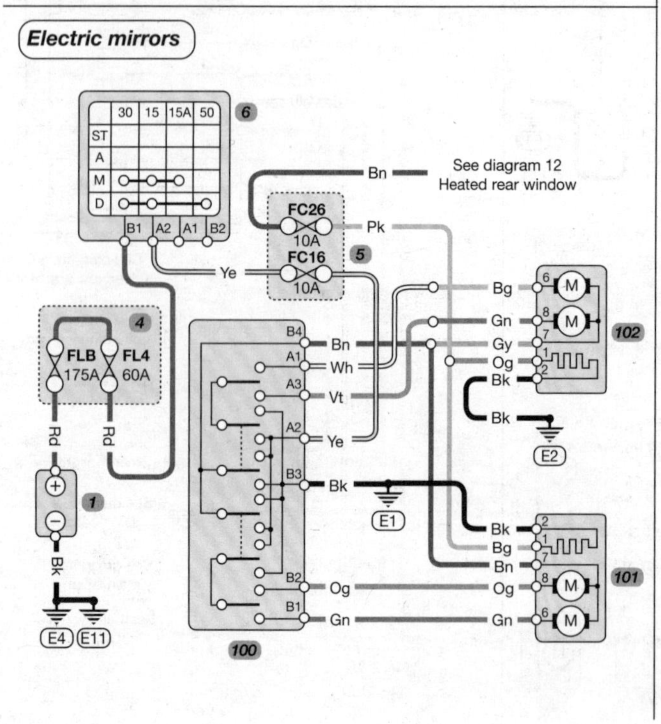

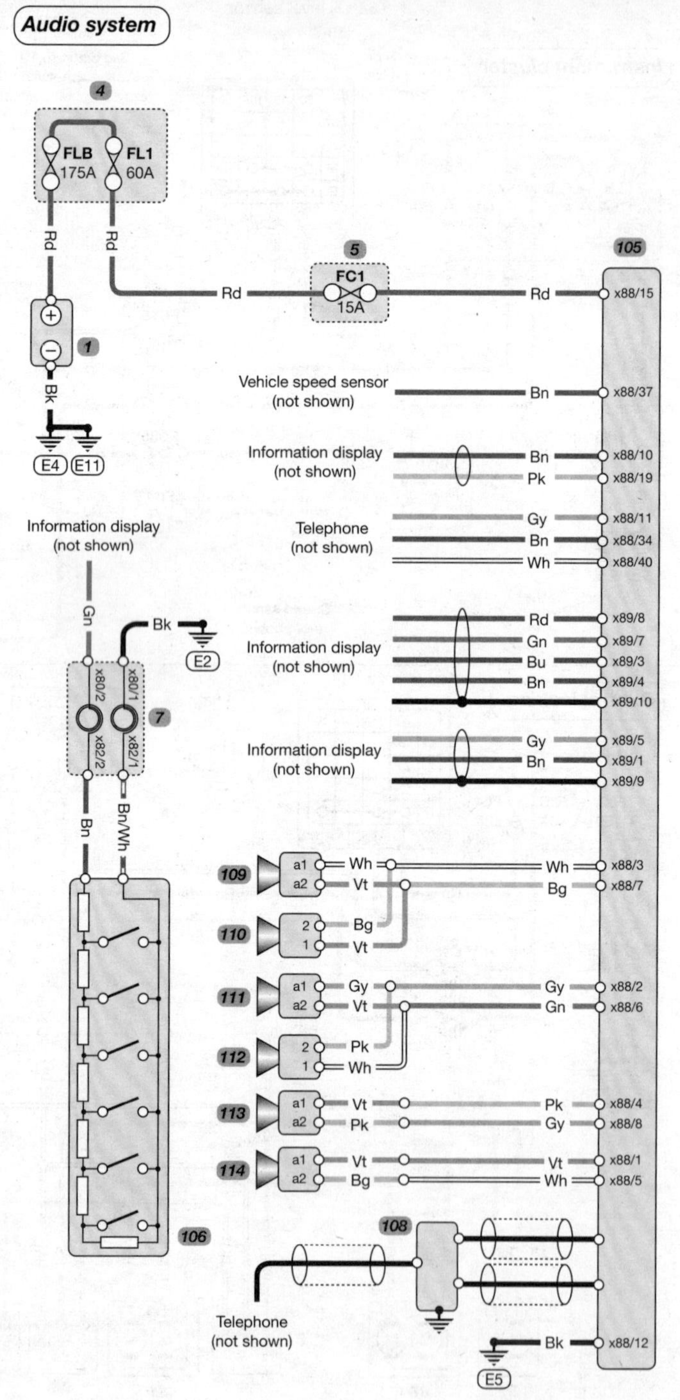

Dimensions and weights

Note: *All figures are approximate, and may vary according to model. Refer to manufacturer's data for exact figures.*

Dimensions

Overall length (depending on model):

    SWB van . . . . 4782 mm

    LWB van . . . . 5182 mm

Overall width:

    Without mirrors . . . . 1904 mm

    With mirrors . . . . 2232 mm

Overall height:

    Standard roof van . . . . 1968 mm

    High roof van . . . . 2492 mm

Wheelbase:

    SWB . . . . 3098 mm

    LWB . . . . 3498 mm

Weights

Kerb weight . . . . 1660 to 1954 kg

Maximum roof rack load . . . . 140 to 210 kg

Fuel economy

Although depreciation is still the biggest part of the cost of motoring for most car owners, the cost of fuel is more immediately noticeable. These pages give some tips on how to get the best fuel economy.

Working it out

Manufacturer's figures

Car manufacturers are required by law to provide fuel consumption information on all new vehicles sold. These 'official' figures are obtained by simulating various driving conditions on a rolling road or a test track. Real life conditions are different, so the fuel consumption actually achieved may not bear much resemblance to the quoted figures.

How to calculate it

Many cars now have trip computers which will

display fuel consumption, both instantaneous and average. Refer to the owner's handbook for details of how to use these.

To calculate consumption yourself (and maybe to check that the trip computer is accurate), proceed as follows.

1. Fill up with fuel and note the mileage, or zero the trip recorder.
2. Drive as usual until you need to fill up again.
3. Note the amount of fuel required to refill the tank, and the mileage covered since the previous fill-up.
4. Divide the mileage by the amount of fuel used to obtain the consumption figure.

For example:

Mileage at first fill-up (a) = 27,903
Mileage at second fill-up (b) = 28,346
Mileage covered (b - a) = 443
Fuel required at second fill-up = 48.6 litres

The half-completed changeover to metric units in the UK means that we buy our fuel

in litres, measure distances in miles and talk about fuel consumption in miles per gallon. There are two ways round this: the first is to convert the litres to gallons before doing the calculation (by dividing by 4.546, or see Table 1). So in the example:

48.6 litres ÷ 4.546 = 10.69 gallons
443 miles ÷ 10.69 gallons = 41.4 mpg

The second way is to calculate the consumption in miles per litre, then multiply that figure by 4.546 (or see Table 2).

So in the example, fuel consumption is:

443 miles ÷ 48.6 litres = 9.1 mpl
9.1 mpl x 4.546 = 41.4 mpg

The rest of Europe expresses fuel consumption in litres of fuel required to travel 100 km (l/100 km). For interest, the conversions are given in Table 3. In practice it doesn't matter what units you use, provided you know what your normal consumption is and can spot if it's getting better or worse.

Table 1: conversion of litres to Imperial gallons

litres	1	2	3	4	5	10	20	30	40	50	60	70
gallons	0.22	0.44	0.66	0.88	1.10	2.24	4.49	6.73	8.98	11.22	13.47	15.71

Table 2: conversion of miles per litre to miles per gallon

miles per litre	5	6	7	8	9	10	11	12	13	14
miles per gallon	23	27	32	36	41	46	50	55	59	64

Table 3: conversion of litres per 100 km to miles per gallon

litres per 100 km	4	4.5	5	5.5	6	6.5	7	8	9	10
miles per gallon	71	63	56	51	47	43	40	35	31	28

Maintenance

A well-maintained car uses less fuel and creates less pollution. In particular:

Filters

Change air and fuel filters at the specified intervals.

Oil

Use a good quality oil of the lowest viscosity specified by the vehicle manufacturer (see *Lubricants and fluids*). Check the level often and be careful not to overfill.

Spark plugs

When applicable, renew at the specified intervals.

Tyres

Check tyre pressures regularly. Under-inflated tyres have an increased rolling resistance. It is generally safe to use the higher pressures specified for full load conditions even when not fully laden, but keep an eye on the centre band of tread for signs of wear due to over-inflation.

When buying new tyres, consider the 'fuel saving' models which most manufacturers include in their ranges.

Driving style

Acceleration

Acceleration uses more fuel than driving at a steady speed. The best technique with modern cars is to accelerate reasonably briskly to the desired speed, changing up through the gears as soon as possible without making the engine labour.

Air conditioning

Air conditioning absorbs quite a bit of energy from the engine – typically 3 kW (4 hp) or so. The effect on fuel consumption is at its worst in slow traffic. Switch it off when not required.

Anticipation

Drive smoothly and try to read the traffic flow so as to avoid unnecessary acceleration and braking.

Automatic transmission

When accelerating in an automatic, avoid depressing the throttle so far as to make the transmission hold onto lower gears at higher speeds. Don't use the 'Sport' setting, if applicable.

When stationary with the engine running, select 'N' or 'P'. When moving, keep your left foot away from the brake.

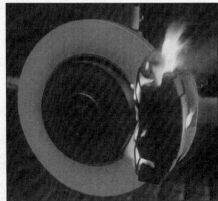

Braking

Braking converts the car's energy of motion into heat – essentially, it is wasted. Obviously some braking is always going to be necessary, but with good anticipation it is surprising how much can be avoided, especially on routes that you know well.

Carshare

Consider sharing lifts to work or to the shops. Even once a week will make a difference.

Electrical loads

Electricity is 'fuel' too; the alternator which charges the battery does so by converting some of the engine's energy of motion into electrical energy. The more electrical accessories are in use, the greater the load on the alternator. Switch off big consumers like the heated rear window when not required.

Freewheeling

Freewheeling (coasting) in neutral with the engine switched off is dangerous. The effort required to operate power-assisted brakes and steering increases when the engine is not running, with a potential lack of control in emergency situations.

In any case, modern fuel injection systems automatically cut off the engine's fuel supply on the overrun (moving and in gear, but with the accelerator pedal released).

Gadgets

Bolt-on devices claiming to save fuel have been around for nearly as long as the motor car itself. Those which worked were rapidly adopted as standard equipment by the vehicle manufacturers. Others worked only in certain situations, or saved fuel only at the expense of unacceptable effects on performance, driveability or the life of engine components.

The most effective fuel saving gadget is the driver's right foot.

Journey planning

Combine (eg) a trip to the supermarket with a visit to the recycling centre and the DIY store, rather than making separate journeys.

When possible choose a travelling time outside rush hours.

Load

The more heavily a car is laden, the greater the energy required to accelerate it to a given speed. Remove heavy items which you don't need to carry.

One load which is often overlooked is the contents of the fuel tank. A tankful of fuel (55 litres / 12 gallons) weighs 45 kg (100 lb) or so. Just half filling it may be worthwhile.

Lost?

At the risk of stating the obvious, if you're going somewhere new, have details of the route to hand. There's not much point in achieving record mpg if you also go miles out of your way.

Parking

If possible, carry out any reversing or turning manoeuvres when you arrive at a parking space so that you can drive straight out when you leave. Manoeuvering when the engine is cold uses a lot more fuel.

Driving around looking for free on-street parking may cost more in fuel than buying a car park ticket.

Premium fuel

Most major oil companies (and some supermarkets) have premium grades of fuel which are several pence a litre dearer than the standard grades. Reports vary, but the consensus seems to be that if these fuels improve economy at all, they do not do so by enough to justify their extra cost.

Roof rack

When loading a roof rack, try to produce a wedge shape with the narrow end at the front. Any cover should be securely fastened – if it flaps it's creating turbulence and absorbing energy.

Remove roof racks and boxes when not in use – they increase air resistance and can create a surprising amount of noise.

Short journeys

The engine is at its least efficient, and wear is highest, during the first few miles after a cold start. Consider walking, cycling or using public transport.

Speed

The engine is at its most efficient when running at a steady speed and load at the rpm where it develops maximum torque. (You can find this figure in the car's handbook.) For most cars this corresponds to between 55 and 65 mph in top gear.

Above the optimum cruising speed, fuel consumption starts to rise quite sharply. A car travelling at 80 mph will typically be using 30% more fuel than at 60 mph.

Supermarket fuel

It may be cheap but is it any good? In the UK all supermarket fuel must meet the relevant British Standard. The major oil companies will say that their branded fuels have better additive packages which may stop carbon and other deposits building up. A reasonable compromise might be to use one tank of branded fuel to three or four from the supermarket.

Switch off when stationary

Switch off the engine if you look like being stationary for more than 30 seconds or so. This is good for the environment as well as for your pocket. Be aware though that frequent restarts are hard on the battery and the starter motor.

Windows

Driving with the windows open increases air turbulence around the vehicle. Closing the windows promotes smooth airflow and

reduced resistance. The faster you go, the more significant this is.

And finally . . .

Driving techniques associated with good fuel economy tend to involve moderate acceleration and low top speeds. Be considerate to the needs of other road users who may need to make brisker progress; even if you do not agree with them this is not an excuse to be obstructive.

Safety must always take precedence over economy, whether it is a question of accelerating hard to complete an overtaking manoeuvre, killing your speed when confronted with a potential hazard or switching the lights on when it starts to get dark.

Conversion factors

Length (distance)

Inches (in)	x 25.4	= Millimetres (mm)	x 0.0394	= Inches (in)
Feet (ft)	x 0.305	= Metres (m)	x 3.281	= Feet (ft)
Miles	x 1.609	= Kilometres (km)	x 0.621	= Miles

Volume (capacity)

Cubic inches (cu in; in^3)	x 16.387	= Cubic centimetres (cc; cm^3)	x 0.061	= Cubic inches (cu in; in^3)
Imperial pints (Imp pt)	x 0.568	= Litres (l)	x 1.76	= Imperial pints (Imp pt)
Imperial quarts (Imp qt)	x 1.137	= Litres (l)	x 0.88	= Imperial quarts (Imp qt)
Imperial quarts (Imp qt)	x 1.201	= US quarts (US qt)	x 0.833	= Imperial quarts (Imp qt)
US quarts (US qt)	x 0.946	= Litres (l)	x 1.057	= US quarts (US qt)
Imperial gallons (Imp gal)	x 4.546	= Litres (l)	x 0.22	= Imperial gallons (Imp gal)
Imperial gallons (Imp gal)	x 1.201	= US gallons (US gal)	x 0.833	= Imperial gallons (Imp gal)
US gallons (US gal)	x 3.785	= Litres (l)	x 0.264	= US gallons (US gal)

Mass (weight)

Ounces (oz)	x 28.35	= Grams (g)	x 0.035	= Ounces (oz)
Pounds (lb)	x 0.454	= Kilograms (kg)	x 2.205	= Pounds (lb)

Force

Ounces-force (ozf; oz)	x 0.278	= Newtons (N)	x 3.6	= Ounces-force (ozf; oz)
Pounds-force (lbf; lb)	x 4.448	= Newtons (N)	x 0.225	= Pounds-force (lbf; lb)
Newtons (N)	x 0.1	= Kilograms-force (kgf; kg)	x 9.81	= Newtons (N)

Pressure

Pounds-force per square inch (psi; lbf/in^2; lb/in^2)	x 0.070	= Kilograms-force per square centimetre (kgf/cm^2; kg/cm^2)	x 14.223	= Pounds-force per square inch (psi; lbf/in^2; lb/in^2)
Pounds-force per square inch (psi; lbf/in^2; lb/in^2)	x 0.068	= Atmospheres (atm)	x 14.696	= Pounds-force per square inch (psi; lbf/in^2; lb/in^2)
Pounds-force per square inch (psi; lbf/in^2; lb/in^2)	x 0.069	= Bars	x 14.5	= Pounds-force per square inch (psi; lbf/in^2; lb/in^2)
Pounds-force per square inch (psi; lbf/in^2; lb/in^2)	x 6.895	= Kilopascals (kPa)	x 0.145	= Pounds-force per square inch (psi; lbf/in^2; lb/in^2)
Kilopascals (kPa)	x 0.01	= Kilograms-force per square centimetre (kgf/cm^2; kg/cm^2)	x 98.1	= Kilopascals (kPa)
Millibar (mbar)	x 100	= Pascals (Pa)	x 0.01	= Millibar (mbar)
Millibar (mbar)	x 0.0145	= Pounds-force per square inch (psi; lbf/in^2; lb/in^2)	x 68.947	= Millibar (mbar)
Millibar (mbar)	x 0.75	= Millimetres of mercury (mmHg)	x 1.333	= Millibar (mbar)
Millibar (mbar)	x 0.401	= Inches of water (inH$_2$O)	x 2.491	= Millibar (mbar)
Millimetres of mercury (mmHg)	x 0.535	= Inches of water (inH$_2$O)	x 1.868	= Millimetres of mercury (mmHg)
Inches of water (inH$_2$O)	x 0.036	= Pounds-force per square inch (psi; lbf/in^2; lb/in^2)	x 27.68	= Inches of water (inH$_2$O)

Torque (moment of force)

Pounds-force inches (lbf in; lb in)	x 1.152	= Kilograms-force centimetre (kgf cm; kg cm)	x 0.868	= Pounds-force inches (lbf in; lb in)
Pounds-force inches (lbf in; lb in)	x 0.113	= Newton metres (Nm)	x 8.85	= Pounds-force inches (lbf in; lb in)
Pounds-force inches (lbf in; lb in)	x 0.083	= Pounds-force feet (lbf ft; lb ft)	x 12	= Pounds-force inches (lbf in; lb in)
Pounds-force feet (lbf ft; lb ft)	x 0.138	= Kilograms-force metres (kgf m; kg m)	x 7.233	= Pounds-force feet (lbf ft; lb ft)
Pounds-force feet (lbf ft; lb ft)	x 1.356	= Newton metres (Nm)	x 0.738	= Pounds-force feet (lbf ft; lb ft)
Newton metres (Nm)	x 0.102	= Kilograms-force metres (kgf m; kg m)	x 9.804	= Newton metres (Nm)

Power

Horsepower (hp)	x 745.7	= Watts (W)	x 0.0013	= Horsepower (hp)

Velocity (speed)

Miles per hour (miles/hr; mph)	x 1.609	= Kilometres per hour (km/hr; kph)	x 0.621	= Miles per hour (miles/hr; mph)

Fuel consumption*

Miles per gallon, Imperial (mpg)	x 0.354	= Kilometres per litre (km/l)	x 2.825	= Miles per gallon, Imperial (mpg)
Miles per gallon, US (mpg)	x 0.425	= Kilometres per litre (km/l)	x 2.352	= Miles per gallon, US (mpg)

Temperature

Degrees Fahrenheit = (°C x 1.8) + 32   Degrees Celsius (Degrees Centigrade; °C) = (°F - 32) x 0.56

It is common practice to convert from miles per gallon (mpg) to litres/100 kilometres (l/100km), where mpg x l/100 km = 282

Spare parts are available from many sources, including maker's appointed garages, accessory shops, and motor factors. To be sure of obtaining the correct parts, it will sometimes be necessary to quote the vehicle identification number. If possible, it can also be useful to take the old parts along for positive identification. Items such as starter motors and alternators may be available under a service exchange scheme – any parts returned should be clean.

Our advice regarding spare parts is as follows.

Officially appointed garages

This is the best source of parts which are peculiar to your car, and which are not otherwise generally available (eg, badges, interior trim, certain body panels, etc). It is also the only place at which you should buy parts if the vehicle is still under warranty.

Accessory shops

These are very good places to buy materials and components needed for the maintenance of your vehicle (oil, air and fuel filters, light bulbs, drivebelts, greases, brake pads, touch-up paint, etc). Components of this nature sold by a reputable shop are usually of the same standard as those used by the vehicle manufacturer.

Besides components, these shops also sell tools and general accessories, usually have convenient opening hours, charge lower prices, and can often be found close to home. Some accessory shops have parts counters where components needed for almost any repair job can be purchased or ordered.

Motor factors

Good factors will stock all the more important components which wear out comparatively quickly, and can sometimes supply individual components needed for the overhaul of a larger assembly (eg, brake seals and hydraulic parts, bearing shells, pistons, valves). They may also handle work such as cylinder block reboring, crankshaft regrinding, etc.

Engine reconditioners

These specialise in engine overhaul and can also supply components. It is recommended that the establishment is a member of the Federation of Engine Re-Manufacturers, or a similar society.

Tyre and exhaust specialists

These outlets may be independent, or members of a local or national chain. They frequently offer competitive prices when compared with a main dealer or local garage, but it will pay to obtain several quotes before making a decision. When researching prices, also ask what extras may be added – for instance fitting a new valve, balancing the wheel and tyre disposal all both commonly charged on top of the price of a new tyre.

Other sources

Beware of parts or materials obtained from market stalls, car boot sales, on-line auctions or similar outlets. Such items are not invariably sub-standard, but there is little chance of compensation if they do prove unsatisfactory. In the case of safety-critical components such as brake pads, there is the risk not only of financial loss, but also of an accident causing injury or death.

Second-hand components or assemblies obtained from a car breaker can be a good buy in some circumstances, but this sort of purchase is best made by the experienced DIY mechanic.

Joint mating faces and gaskets

When separating components at their mating faces, never insert screwdrivers or similar implements into the joint between the faces in order to prise them apart. This can cause severe damage which results in oil leaks, coolant leaks, etc upon reassembly. Separation is usually achieved by tapping along the joint with a soft-faced hammer in order to break the seal. However, note that this method may not be suitable where dowels are used for component location.

Where a gasket is used between the mating faces of two components, a new one must be fitted on reassembly; fit it dry unless otherwise stated in the repair procedure. Make sure that the mating faces are clean and dry, with all traces of old gasket removed. When cleaning a joint face, use a tool which is unlikely to score or damage the face, and remove any burrs or nicks with an oilstone or fine file.

Make sure that tapped holes are cleaned with a pipe cleaner, and keep them free of jointing compound, if this is being used, unless specifically instructed otherwise.

Ensure that all orifices, channels or pipes are clear, and blow through them, preferably using compressed air.

Oil seals

Oil seals can be removed by levering them out with a wide flat-bladed screwdriver or similar implement. Alternatively, a number of self-tapping screws may be screwed into the seal, and these used as a purchase for pliers or some similar device in order to pull the seal free.

Whenever an oil seal is removed from its working location, either individually or as part of an assembly, it should be renewed.

The very fine sealing lip of the seal is easily damaged, and will not seal if the surface it contacts is not completely clean and free from scratches, nicks or grooves. If the original sealing surface of the component cannot be restored, and the manufacturer has not made provision for slight relocation of the seal relative to the sealing surface, the component should be renewed.

Protect the lips of the seal from any surface which may damage them in the course of fitting. Use tape or a conical sleeve where possible. Where indicated, lubricate the seal lips with oil before fitting and, on dual-lipped seals, fill the space between the lips with grease.

Unless otherwise stated, oil seals must be fitted with their sealing lips toward the lubricant to be sealed.

Use a tubular drift or block of wood of the appropriate size to install the seal and, if the seal housing is shouldered, drive the seal down to the shoulder. If the seal housing is unshouldered, the seal should be fitted with its face flush with the housing top face (unless otherwise instructed).

Screw threads and fastenings

Seized nuts, bolts and screws are quite a common occurrence where corrosion has set in, and the use of penetrating oil or releasing fluid will often overcome this problem if the offending item is soaked for a while before attempting to release it. The use of an impact driver may also provide a means of releasing such stubborn fastening devices, when used in conjunction with the appropriate screwdriver bit or socket. If none of these methods works, it may be necessary to resort to the careful application of heat, or the use of a hacksaw or nut splitter device. Before resorting to extreme methods, check that you are not dealing with a left-hand thread!

Studs are usually removed by locking two nuts together on the threaded part, and then using a spanner on the lower nut to unscrew the stud. Studs or bolts which have broken off below the surface of the component in which they are mounted can sometimes be removed using a stud extractor.

Always ensure that a blind tapped hole is completely free from oil, grease, water or other fluid before installing the bolt or stud. Failure to do this could cause the housing to crack due to the hydraulic action of the bolt or stud as it is screwed in.

For some screw fastenings, notably cylinder head bolts or nuts, torque wrench settings are no longer specified for the latter stages of tightening, "angle-tightening" being called up instead. Typically, a fairly low torque wrench setting will be applied to the bolts/nuts in the correct sequence, followed by one or more stages of tightening through specified angles.

When checking or retightening a nut or bolt to a specified torque setting, slacken the nut or bolt by a quarter of a turn, and then retighten to the specified setting. However, this should not be attempted where angular tightening has been used.

Locknuts, locktabs and washers

Any fastening which will rotate against a component or housing during tightening should always have a washer between it and the relevant component or housing.

Spring or split washers should always be renewed when they are used to lock a critical component such as a big-end bearing retaining bolt or nut. Locktabs which are folded over to retain a nut or bolt should always be renewed.

Self-locking nuts can be re-used in non-critical areas, providing resistance can be felt when the locking portion passes over the bolt or stud thread. However, it should be noted that self-locking stiffnuts tend to lose their effectiveness after long periods of use, and should then be renewed as a matter of course.

Split pins must always be replaced with new ones of the correct size for the hole.

When thread-locking compound is found on the threads of a fastener which is to be re-used, it should be cleaned off with a wire brush and solvent, and fresh compound applied on reassembly.

Special tools

Some repair procedures in this manual entail the use of special tools such as a press, two or three-legged pullers, spring compressors, etc. Wherever possible, suitable readily-available alternatives to the manufacturer's special tools are described, and are shown in use. In some instances, where no alternative is possible, it has been necessary to resort to the use of a manufacturer's tool, and this has been done for reasons of safety as well as the efficient completion of the repair operation. Unless you are highly-skilled and have a thorough understanding of the procedures described, never attempt to bypass the use of any special tool when the procedure described specifies its use. Not only is there a very great risk of personal injury, but expensive damage could be caused to the components involved.

Environmental considerations

When disposing of used engine oil, brake fluid, antifreeze, etc, give due consideration to any detrimental environmental effects. Do not, for instance, pour any of the above liquids down drains into the general sewage system, or onto the ground to soak away, as this is likely to pollute your local environment. Many local council refuse tips provide a facility for waste oil disposal, as do some garages. You can find your nearest disposal point by calling the Environment Agency on 03708 506 506 or by visiting www.oilbankline.org.uk.

Note: It is illegal and anti-social to dump oil down the drain. To find the location of your local oil recycling bank, call 03708 506 506 or visit www.oilbankline.org.uk.

Vehicle identification numbers REF•9

Modifications are a continuing and unpublicised process in vehicle manufacture, quite apart from major model changes. Spare parts manuals and lists are compiled upon a numerical basis, the individual vehicle identification numbers being essential to correct identification of the component concerned.

When ordering spare parts, always give as much information as possible. Quote the vehicle type and year, vehicle identification number (VIN), and engine number, as appropriate.

The vehicle identification number (VIN) appears on a metal plate attached to the right-hand door pillar. The model plate also gives vehicle loading details, engine type, and various trim and colour codes. The VIN also appears on a plastic tag attached to the passenger side of the facia panel, visible through the windscreen, and behind a plastic cover on the right-hand side door step **(see illustrations)**.

The engine number is stamped on the right-hand end of the cylinder block.

The transmission identification numbers are located on a plate attached to the top of the transmission casing, or cast into the casing itself.

The VIN plate is attached to the driver's side door pillar...

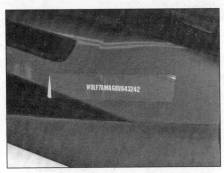

... is visible through the windscreen...

... and is stamped in to the vehicle body, behind a plastic cover on the driver's side door step

Jacking and vehicle support

The jack supplied with the vehicle tool kit should **only** be used for changing the roadwheels in an emergency – see *Wheel changing* at the front of this book. When carrying out any other kind of work, raise the vehicle using a heavy-duty hydraulic (or 'trolley') jack, and always supplement the jack with axle stands positioned under the vehicle jacking points. If the roadwheels do not have to be removed, consider using wheel ramps – if wished, these can be placed under the wheels once the vehicle has been raised using a hydraulic jack, and the vehicle lowered onto the ramps so that it is resting on its wheels.

Only ever jack the vehicle up on a solid, level surface. If there is even a slight slope, take great care that the vehicle cannot move as the wheels are lifted off the ground. Jacking up on an uneven or gravelled surface is not recommended, as the weight of the vehicle will not be evenly distributed, and the jack may slip as the vehicle is raised.

As far as possible, do not leave the vehicle unattended once it has been raised, particularly if children are playing nearby.

Before jacking up the front of the vehicle, ensure that the handbrake is firmly applied. When jacking up the rear of the vehicle, place wooden chocks in front of the front wheels, and engage first gear.

The jack supplied with the vehicle locates in lifting points adjacent to each wheel, inboard of the sills **(see illustration)**. Ensure that the jack head is correctly engaged before attempting to raise the vehicle.

When using a hydraulic jack or axle stands, the jack head or axle stand head may be placed under one of the four jacking points inboard of the door sills. When jacking or supporting the vehicle at these points, always use a block of wood between the jack head or axle stand, and the vehicle body. It is also considered good practice to use a large block of wood when supporting other areas, to spread the load over a wider area, and reduce the risk of damage to the underside of the vehicle (it also helps to prevent the underbody coating from being damaged by the jack or axle stand). **Do not** jack the vehicle under any other part of the sill, engine sump, floor pan, subframe, or directly under any of the steering or suspension components.

Never work under, around, or near a raised vehicle, unless it is adequately supported on stands. Do not rely on a jack alone, as even a hydraulic jack could fail under load. Makeshift methods should not be used to lift and support the vehicle during servicing work.

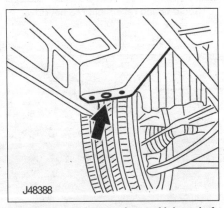

The jacking points are located inboard of the sills, adjacent to the wheels (arrowed)

Introduction

A selection of good tools is a fundamental requirement for anyone contemplating the maintenance and repair of a motor vehicle. For the owner who does not possess any, their purchase will prove a considerable expense, offsetting some of the savings made by doing-it-yourself. However, provided that the tools purchased meet the relevant national safety standards and are of good quality, they will last for many years and prove an extremely worthwhile investment.

To help the average owner to decide which tools are needed to carry out the various tasks detailed in this manual, we have compiled three lists of tools under the following headings: *Maintenance and minor repair, Repair and overhaul*, and *Special*. Newcomers to practical mechanics should start off with the *Maintenance and minor repair* tool kit, and confine themselves to the simpler jobs around the vehicle. Then, as confidence and experience grow, more difficult tasks can be undertaken, with extra tools being purchased as, and when, they are needed. In this way, a *Maintenance and minor repair* tool kit can be built up into a *Repair and overhaul* tool kit over a considerable period of time, without any major cash outlays. The experienced do-it-yourselfer will have a tool kit good enough for most repair and overhaul procedures, and will add tools from the *Special* category when it is felt that the expense is justified by the amount of use to which these tools will be put.

Maintenance and minor repair tool kit

The tools given in this list should be considered as a minimum requirement if routine maintenance, servicing and minor repair operations are to be undertaken. We recommend the purchase of combination spanners (ring one end, open-ended the other); although more expensive than open-ended ones, they do give the advantages of both types of spanner.

☐ *Combination spanners:*
  Metric - 8 to 19 mm inclusive
☐ *Adjustable spanner - 35 mm jaw (approx.)*
☐ *Spark plug spanner (with rubber insert) - petrol models*
☐ *Spark plug gap adjustment tool - petrol models*
☐ *Set of feeler gauges*
☐ *Brake bleed nipple spanner*
☐ *Screwdrivers:*
  Flat blade - 100 mm long x 6 mm dia
  Cross blade - 100 mm long x 6 mm dia
  Torx - various sizes (not all vehicles)
☐ *Combination pliers*
☐ *Hacksaw (junior)*
☐ *Tyre pump*
☐ *Tyre pressure gauge*
☐ *Oil can*
☐ *Oil filter removal tool (if applicable)*
☐ *Fine emery cloth*
☐ *Wire brush (small)*
☐ *Funnel (medium size)*
☐ *Sump drain plug key (not all vehicles)*

Repair and overhaul tool kit

These tools are virtually essential for anyone undertaking any major repairs to a motor vehicle, and are additional to those given in the *Maintenance and minor repair* list. Included in this list is a comprehensive set of sockets. Although these are expensive, they will be found invaluable as they are so versatile - particularly if various drives are included in the set. We recommend the half-inch square-drive type, as this can be used with most proprietary torque wrenches.

The tools in this list will sometimes need to be supplemented by tools from the *Special* list:

☐ *Sockets to cover range in previous list (including Torx sockets)*
☐ *Reversible ratchet drive (for use with sockets)*
☐ *Extension piece, 250 mm (for use with sockets)*
☐ *Universal joint (for use with sockets)*
☐ *Flexible handle or sliding T "breaker bar" (for use with sockets)*
☐ *Torque wrench (for use with sockets)*
☐ *Self-locking grips*
☐ *Ball pein hammer*
☐ *Soft-faced mallet (plastic or rubber)*
☐ *Screwdrivers:*
  Flat blade - long & sturdy, short (chubby), and narrow (electrician's) types
  Cross blade - long & sturdy, and short (chubby) types
☐ *Pliers:*
  Long-nosed
  Side cutters (electrician's)
  Circlip (internal and external)
☐ *Cold chisel - 25 mm*
☐ *Scriber*
☐ *Scraper*
☐ *Centre-punch*
☐ *Pin punch*
☐ *Hacksaw*
☐ *Brake hose clamp*
☐ *Brake/clutch bleeding kit*
☐ *Selection of twist drills*
☐ *Steel rule/straight-edge*
☐ *Allen keys (inc. splined/Torx type)*
☐ *Selection of files*
☐ *Wire brush*
☐ *Axle stands*
☐ *Jack (strong trolley or hydraulic type)*
☐ *Light with extension lead*
☐ *Universal electrical multi-meter*

Sockets and reversible ratchet drive

Brake bleeding kit

Torx key, socket and bit

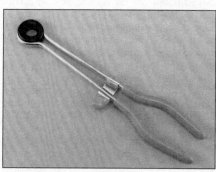

Hose clamp

Angular-tightening gauge

Special tools

The tools in this list are those which are not used regularly, are expensive to buy, or which need to be used in accordance with their manufacturers' instructions. Unless relatively difficult mechanical jobs are undertaken frequently, it will not be economic to buy many of these tools. Where this is the case, you could consider clubbing together with friends (or joining a motorists' club) to make a joint purchase, or borrowing the tools against a deposit from a local garage or tool hire specialist.

The following list contains only those tools and instruments freely available to the public, and not those special tools produced by the vehicle manufacturer specifically for its dealer network. You will find occasional references to these manufacturers' special tools in the text of this manual. Generally, an alternative method of doing the job without the vehicle manufacturers' special tool is given. However, sometimes there is no alternative to using them. Where this is the case and the relevant tool cannot be bought or borrowed, you will have to entrust the work to a dealer.

- ☐ Angular-tightening gauge
- ☐ Valve spring compressor
- ☐ Valve grinding tool
- ☐ Piston ring compressor
- ☐ Piston ring removal/installation tool
- ☐ Cylinder bore hone
- ☐ Balljoint separator
- ☐ Coil spring compressors (where applicable)
- ☐ Two/three-legged hub and bearing puller
- ☐ Impact screwdriver
- ☐ Micrometer and/or vernier calipers
- ☐ Dial gauge
- ☐ Tachometer
- ☐ Fault code reader
- ☐ Cylinder compression gauge
- ☐ Hand-operated vacuum pump and gauge
- ☐ Clutch plate alignment set
- ☐ Brake shoe steady spring cup removal tool
- ☐ Bush and bearing removal/installation set
- ☐ Stud extractors
- ☐ Tap and die set
- ☐ Lifting tackle

Buying tools

Reputable motor accessory shops and superstores often offer excellent quality tools at discount prices, so it pays to shop around.

Remember, you don't have to buy the most expensive items on the shelf, but it is always advisable to steer clear of the very cheap tools. Beware of 'bargains' offered on market stalls, on-line or at car boot sales. There are plenty of good tools around at reasonable prices, but always aim to purchase items which meet the relevant national safety standards. If in doubt, ask the proprietor or manager of the shop for advice before making a purchase.

Care and maintenance of tools

Having purchased a reasonable tool kit, it is necessary to keep the tools in a clean and serviceable condition. After use, always wipe off any dirt, grease and metal particles using a clean, dry cloth, before putting the tools away. Never leave them lying around after they have been used. A simple tool rack on the garage or workshop wall for items such as screwdrivers and pliers is a good idea. Store all normal spanners and sockets in a metal box. Any measuring instruments, gauges, meters, etc, must be carefully stored where they cannot be damaged or become rusty.

Take a little care when tools are used. Hammer heads inevitably become marked, and screwdrivers lose the keen edge on their blades from time to time. A little timely attention with emery cloth or a file will soon restore items like this to a good finish.

Working facilities

Not to be forgotten when discussing tools is the workshop itself. If anything more than routine maintenance is to be carried out, a suitable working area becomes essential.

It is appreciated that many an owner-mechanic is forced by circumstances to remove an engine or similar item without the benefit of a garage or workshop. Having done this, any repairs should always be done under the cover of a roof.

Wherever possible, any dismantling should be done on a clean, flat workbench or table at a suitable working height.

Any workbench needs a vice; one with a jaw opening of 100 mm is suitable for most jobs. As mentioned previously, some clean dry storage space is also required for tools, as well as for any lubricants, cleaning fluids, touch-up paints etc, which become necessary.

Another item which may be required, and which has a much more general usage, is an electric drill with a chuck capacity of at least 8 mm. This, together with a good range of twist drills, is virtually essential for fitting accessories.

Last, but not least, always keep a supply of old newspapers and clean, lint-free rags available, and try to keep any working area as clean as possible.

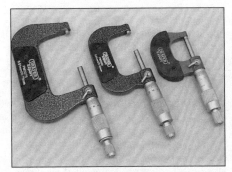

Micrometers

Dial test indicator ("dial gauge")

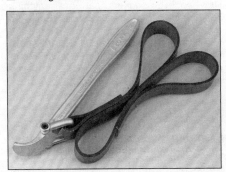

Oil filter removal tool (strap wrench type)

Compression tester

Bearing puller

This is a guide to getting your vehicle through the MOT test. Obviously it will not be possible to examine the vehicle to the same standard as the professional MOT tester. However, working through the following checks will enable you to identify any problem areas before submitting the vehicle for the test.

It has only been possible to summarise the test requirements here, based on the regulations in force at the time of printing. Test standards are becoming increasingly stringent, although there are some exemptions for older vehicles.

An assistant will be needed to help carry out some of these checks.

The checks have been sub-divided into four categories, as follows:

1 Checks carried out **FROM THE VEHICLE INTERIOR**

2 Checks carried out **WITH THE VEHICLE ON THE GROUND**

3 Checks carried out **WITH THE VEHICLE RAISED AND THE WHEELS FREE TO TURN**

4 Checks carried out on **YOUR VEHICLE'S EXHAUST EMISSION SYSTEM**

1 Checks carried out **FROM THE VEHICLE INTERIOR**

Handbrake (parking brake)

☐ Test the operation of the handbrake. Excessive travel (too many clicks) indicates incorrect brake or cable adjustment.

☐ Check that the handbrake cannot be released by tapping the lever sideways. Check the security of the lever mountings.

☐ If the parking brake is foot-operated, check that the pedal is secure and without excessive travel, and that the release mechanism operates correctly.

☐ Where applicable, test the operation of the electronic handbrake. The brake should engage and disengage without excessive delay. If the warning light does not extinguish, or a warning message is displayed when the brake is disengaged, this could indicate a fault which will need further investigation.

Footbrake

☐ Depress the brake pedal and check that it does not creep down to the floor, indicating a master cylinder fault. Release the pedal, wait a few seconds, then depress it again. If the pedal travels nearly to the floor before firm resistance is felt, brake adjustment or repair is necessary. If the pedal feels spongy, there is air in the hydraulic system which must be removed by bleeding.

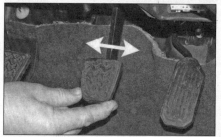

☐ Check that the brake pedal is secure and in good condition. Check also for signs of fluid leaks on the pedal, floor or carpets, which would indicate failed seals in the brake master cylinder.

☐ Check the servo unit (when applicable) by operating the brake pedal several times, then keeping the pedal depressed and starting the engine. As the engine starts, the pedal will move down. If not, the vacuum hose or the servo itself may be faulty.

Steering wheel and column

☐ Examine the steering wheel for fractures or looseness of the hub, spokes or rim.

☐ Move the steering wheel from side to side and then up and down. Check that the steering wheel is not loose on the column, indicating wear or a loose retaining nut. Continue moving the steering wheel as before, but also turn it slightly from left to right.

☐ Check that the steering wheel is not loose on the column, and that there is no abnormal movement of the steering wheel, indicating wear in the column support bearings or couplings.

☐ Check that the ignition lock (where fitted) engages and disengages correctly.

☐ Steering column adjustment mechanisms (where fitted) must be able to lock the column securely in place with no play evident.

Windscreen, mirrors and sunvisor

☐ The windscreen must be free of cracks or other significant damage within the 'swept area' of the windscreen. This is the area swept by the windscreen wipers. A second test area, known as 'Zone A', is the part of the swept area 290 mm wide, centred on the steering wheel centre line. Any damage in Zone A that cannot be contained in a 10 mm diameter circle, or any damage in the remainder of the swept area that cannot be contained in a 40 mm diameter circle, may cause the vehicle to fail the test.

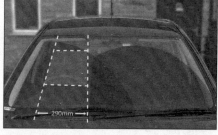

290mm

☐ Any items that may obscure the drivers view, such as stickers, sat-navs, anything hanging from the interior mirror, should be removed prior to the test.

☐ Vehicles registered after 1st August 1978 must have a drivers side mirror, and either an interior mirror, or a passenger's side mirror. Cameras (or indirect vision devices) may replace the mirrors, but they must function correctly.

☐ The driver's sunvisor must be capable of being stored in the "up" position.

Seat belts, seats and supplementary restraint systems (SRS)

Note: *The following checks are applicable to all seat belts, front and rear.*

☐ Examine the webbing of all the belts (including rear belts if fitted) for cuts, serious fraying or deterioration. Fasten and unfasten each belt to check the buckles. If applicable, check the retracting mechanism. Check the security of all seat belt mountings accessible from inside the vehicle, ensuring any height adjustable mountings lock securely in place.

☐ Where the seat belt is attached to a seat, the frame and mountings of the seat form part of the belt mountings, and are to be inspected as such.

☐ Any airbag, or SRS warning light must extinguish a few seconds after the ignition is switched on. Failure to do so indicates a fault which must be investigated.

☐ Seat belts with pre-tensioners, once activated, have a "flag" or similar showing on the seat belt stalk. This, in itself, is a reason for test failure.

☐ Check that the original airbag(s) is/are present, and not obviously defective.

☐ The seats themselves must be securely attached and the backrests must lock in the upright position. The driver's seat must also be able to slide forwards/rearwards, and lock in several positions.

Doors

☐ Both front doors must be able to be opened and closed from outside and inside, and must latch securely when closed.

☐ The rear doors must open from the outside.

☐ Examine all door hinges, catches and striker plates for missing, deteriorated, or insecure parts that could effect the opening and closing of the doors.

Speedometer

☐ The vehicle speedometer must be present, and appear operative. The figures on the speedometer must be legible, and illuminated when the lights are switched on.

2 Checks carried out WITH THE VEHICLE ON THE GROUND

Vehicle identification

☐ Number plates must be in good condition, secure and legible, with letters and numbers correctly spaced – spacing at (A) should be 33 mm and at (B) 11 mm. At the front, digits must be black on a white background and at the rear

black on a yellow background. Other background designs (such as honeycomb) are not permitted.

☐ The VIN plate and/or homologation plate must be permanently displayed and legible.

Electrical equipment

☐ Switch on the ignition and check the operation of the horn.

☐ Check the windscreen washers and wipers, examining the wiper blades; renew damaged or perished blades. The wiper blades must clear a large enough area of the windscreen to provide an 'adequate' view of the road, and be able to be parked in a position where they will not affect the drivers' view.

☐ On vehicles first used from 1st September 2009, the headlight washers (where fitted) must operate correctly.

☐ Check the operation of the stop-lights. This includes any lights that appear to be connected – Eg. high-level lights.

☐ Check the operation of the sidelights and number plate lights. The lenses and reflectors must be secure, clean and undamaged.

☐ Check the operation and alignment of the headlights. The headlight reflectors must not be tarnished and the lenses must be undamaged. Where plastic lenses are fitted, check they haven't deteriorated to the extent where they affect the light ouput or beam image. It's often possible to restore the plastic lens using a suitable polish or aftermarket treatment.

☐ Where HID or LED headlights are fitted, check the operation of the cleaning and self-levelling functions.

☐ The headlight main beam warning lamp must be functional.

☐ On vehicles first used from 1st March 2018, the daytime running lights (where fitted) must operate correctly.

☐ Switch on the ignition and check the operation of the direction indicators (including the instrument panel tell-tale) and the hazard warning lights. Operation of the sidelights and stop-lights must not affect the indicators – if it does, the cause is usually a bad earth at the rear light cluster. Indicators should flash at a rate of between 60 and 120 times per minute – faster or slower than this could indicate a fault with the flasher unit or a bad earth at one of the light units.

☐ The hazard warning lights must operate with the ignition on and off.

☐ Check the operation of the rear foglight(s), including the warning light on the instrument panel or in the switch. Note that the foglight

must be positioned in the centre or driver's side of the vehicle. If only the passenger's side illuminates, the test will fail.

☐ The warning lights must illuminate in accordance with the manufacturers' design (this includes any warning messages). For most vehicles, the ABS and other warning lights should illuminate when the ignition is switched on, and (if the system is operating properly) extinguish after a few seconds. Refer to the owner's handbook.

☐ On vehicles first used from 1st September 2009, the reversing lights must operate correctly when reverse gear is selected.

☐ Check the vehicle battery for security and leakage.

☐ Check the visible/accessible vehicle wiring is adequately supported, with no evidence of damage or deterioration that could result in a short-circuit.

Footbrake

☐ Examine the master cylinder, brake pipes and servo unit for leaks, loose mountings, corrosion or other damage. If ABS is fitted, this unit should also be examined for signs of leaks or corrosion.

☐ The fluid reservoir must be secure and the fluid level must be between the upper (A) and lower (B) markings.

☐ Check the fluid in the reservoir for signs of contamination.

☐ Inspect both front brake flexible hoses for cracks or deterioration of the rubber. Turn the steering from lock to lock, and ensure that the hoses do not contact the wheel, tyre, or any part of the steering or suspension mechanism. With the brake pedal firmly depressed, check the hoses for bulges or leaks under pressure.

Steering and suspension

☐ Have your assistant turn the steering wheel from side to side slightly, up to the point where the steering gear just begins to transmit this movement to the roadwheels. Check for excessive free play between the steering wheel and the steering gear, indicating wear or insecurity of the steering column joints, the column-to-steering gear coupling, or the steering gear itself. With a standard (380 mm diameter) steering wheel, there should be no more than 13 mm of free play for rack-and-pinion systems, and no more than 75 mm for non-rack-and-pinion designs.

☐ Have your assistant turn the steering

wheel more vigorously in each direction, so that the roadwheels just begin to turn. As this is done, examine all the steering joints, linkages, fittings and attachments. Renew any component that shows signs of wear or damage. On vehicles with hydraulic power steering, check the security and condition of the steering pump, drivebelt and hoses.

☐ Note that all movement checks on power steering systems are carried out with the engine running.

☐ Check that the vehicle is standing level, and at approximately the correct ride height.

Exhaust system

☐ Start the engine. With your assistant holding a rag over the tailpipe, check the entire system for leaks. Repair or renew leaking sections.

3 Checks carried out
WITH THE VEHICLE RAISED AND THE WHEELS FREE TO TURN

Jack up the front and rear of the vehicle, and securely support it on axle stands. Position the stands clear of the suspension assemblies. Ensure that the wheels are clear of the ground and that the steering can be turned from lock to lock.

Steering mechanism

☐ Have your assistant turn the steering from lock to lock. Check that the steering turns smoothly, and that no part of the steering mechanism, including a wheel or tyre, fouls any brake hose or pipe or any part of the body structure.

☐ Examine the steering rack rubber gaiters for damage or insecurity of the retaining clips. If power steering is fitted, check for signs of damage or leakage of the fluid hoses, pipes or connections. Also check for excessive stiffness or binding of the steering, a missing split pin or locking device, or severe corrosion of the body structure within 30 cm of any steering component attachment point.

☐ Check the track rod end ball joint dust covers. Any covers that are missing, seriously damaged, deteriorated or insecure, may fail inspection.

Front and rear suspension and wheel bearings

☐ Starting at the front right-hand side, grasp the roadwheel at the 3 o'clock and 9 o'clock positions and rock gently but firmly. Check for free play or insecurity at the wheel bearings, suspension balljoints, or suspension mountings, pivots and attachments.

☐ Now grasp the wheel at the 12 o'clock and 6 o'clock positions and repeat the previous inspection. Spin the wheel, and check for roughness or tightness of the front wheel bearing.

☐ If excess free play is suspected at a component pivot point, this can be confirmed by using a large screwdriver or similar tool and levering between the mounting and the component attachment. This will confirm whether the wear is in the pivot bush, its retaining bolt, or in the mounting itself (the bolt holes can often become elongated).

☐ Carry out all the above checks at the other front wheel, and then at both rear wheels.

Springs and shock absorbers

☐ Examine the suspension struts (when applicable) for serious fluid leakage, corrosion, or damage to the casing. Also check the security of the mounting points.

☐ If coil springs are fitted, check that the spring ends locate in their seats, and that the spring is not corroded, cracked or broken.

☐ If leaf springs are fitted, check that all leaves are intact, that the axle is securely attached to each spring, and that there is no deterioration of the spring eye mountings, bushes, and shackles.

☐ The same general checks apply to vehicles fitted with other suspension types, such as torsion bars, hydraulic displacer units, etc. Ensure that all mountings and attachments are secure, that there are no signs of excessive wear, corrosion or damage, and (on hydraulic types) that there are no fluid leaks or damaged pipes.

☐ Check any suspension and anti-roll bar link ball joint dust covers. Any covers that are missing, seriously damaged, deteriorated or insecure, may fail inspection.

☐ Examine each shock absorber for signs of leakage, corrosion of the casing, missing, detached or worn pivots and/or rubber bushes.

Driveshafts (fwd vehicles only)

☐ Rotate each front wheel in turn and inspect the inner and outer joint gaiters for splits or damage. Also check that each driveshaft is straight and undamaged.

Braking system

☐ If possible without dismantling, check brake pad wear and disc condition. Ensure that the friction lining material has not worn excessively, (A) and that the discs are not fractured, pitted, scored or badly worn (B). As a general rule, if the friction material is less than 1.5 mm thick, the inspection will fail.

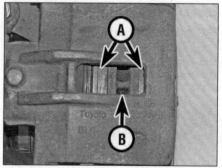

☐ Examine all the rigid brake pipes underneath the vehicle, and the flexible hose(s) at the rear. Look for corrosion, chafing or insecurity of the pipes, and for signs of bulging under pressure, chafing, splits or deterioration of the flexible hoses.

☐ Look for signs of fluid leaks at the brake calipers or on the brake backplates. Repair or renew leaking components.

☐ Slowly spin each wheel, while your assistant depresses and releases the footbrake. Ensure that each brake is operating and does not bind when the pedal is released.

☐ Examine the handbrake mechanism, checking for frayed or broken cables, excessive corrosion, or wear or insecurity of the linkage. Check that the mechanism works on each relevant wheel, and releases fully, without binding.

☐ Check the ABS sensors' wiring for signs of damage, deterioration or insecurity.

☐ It is not possible to test brake efficiency without special equipment, but a road test can be carried out later to check that the vehicle pulls up in a straight line.

Fuel and exhaust systems

☐ Inspect the fuel tank (including the filler cap), fuel pipes, hoses and unions. All components must be secure and free from leaks. Locking fuel caps must lock securely and the key must be provided for the MOT test.

☐ Examine the exhaust system over its entire length, checking for any damaged, broken or missing mountings, security of the retaining clamps and rust or corrosion.

☐ If the vehicle was originally equipped with a catalytic converter or particulate filter, one must be fitted.

Wheels and tyres

☐ Examine the sidewalls and tread area of each tyre in turn. Check for cuts, tears, lumps, bulges, separation of the tread, and exposure of the ply or cord due to wear or damage. Check that the tyre bead is correctly seated on the wheel rim, that the valve is sound and properly seated, and that the wheel is not distorted or damaged.

☐ Check that the tyres are of the correct size for the vehicle, that they are of the same size and type on each axle, and that the pressures are correct. The vehicle will fail the test if the tyres are obviously under-inflated.

☐ Check the tyre tread depth. The legal minimum at the time of writing is 1.6 mm over the central three-quarters of the tread width. Abnormal tread wear may indicate incorrect front wheel alignment or wear in steering or suspension components.

☐ Check that all wheel bolts/nuts are present.

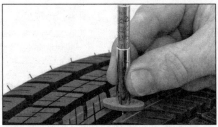

☐ If the spare wheel is fitted externally or in a separate carrier beneath the vehicle, check that mountings are secure and free of excessive corrosion.

Body corrosion

☐ Check the condition of the entire vehicle structure for signs of corrosion in load-bearing areas. (These include chassis box sections, side sills, cross-members, pillars, and all suspension, steering, braking system and seat belt mountings and anchorages.) Any corrosion which has seriously reduced the thickness of a load-bearing area (or is within 30 cm of safety-related components such as steering or suspension) is likely to cause the vehicle to fail. In this case professional repairs are likely to be needed.

☐ Damage or corrosion which causes sharp or otherwise dangerous edges to be exposed will also cause the vehicle to fail.

Towbars

☐ Check the condition of mounting points (both beneath the vehicle and within boot/hatchback areas) for signs of corrosion, ensuring that all fixings are secure and not worn or damaged. There must be no excessive play in detachable tow ball arms or quick-release mechanisms.

☐ Examine the security and condition of the towbar electrics socket. If the later 13-pin socket is fitted, the MOT tester will check its' wiring functions/connections are correct.

General leaks

☐ The vehicle will fail the test if there is a fluid leak of any kind that poses an environmental risk.

4 Checks carried out on **YOUR VEHICLE'S EXHAUST EMISSION SYSTEM**

Petrol models

☐ The engine should be warmed up, and running well (ignition system in good order, air filter element clean, etc).

☐ Before testing, run the engine at around 2500 rpm for 20 seconds. Let the engine drop to idle, and watch for smoke from the exhaust. If the idle speed is too high, or if dense blue or black smoke emerges for more than 5 seconds, the vehicle will fail. Typically, blue smoke signifies oil burning (engine wear); black smoke means unburnt fuel (dirty air cleaner element, or other fuel system fault).

☐ An exhaust gas analyser for measuring carbon monoxide (CO) and hydrocarbons (HC) is now needed. If one cannot be hired or borrowed, have a local garage perform the check.

CO emissions (mixture)

☐ The MOT tester has access to the CO limits for all vehicles from 1st August 1992. The CO level is measured at idle speed, and at 'fast idle' (2500 to 3000 rpm). The following limits are given as a general guide:

At idle speed – Less than 0.3% CO
At 'fast idle' – Less than 0.2% CO
Lambda reading – 0.97 to 1.03

☐ If the CO level is too high, this may point to poor maintenance, a fuel injection system problem, faulty lambda (oxygen) sensor or catalytic converter. Try an injector cleaning treatment, and check the vehicle's ECU for fault codes.

HC emissions

☐ The MOT tester has access to HC limits for all vehicles. The HC level is measured at 'fast idle' (2500 to 3000 rpm). The following limits are given as a general guide:

At 'fast idle' – Less than 200 ppm

☐ Excessive HC emissions are typically caused by oil being burnt (worn engine), or by a blocked crankcase ventilation system ('breather'). If the engine oil is old and thin, an oil change may help. If the engine is running badly, check the vehicle's ECU for fault codes.

Diesel models

☐ If the vehicle was fitted with a DPF (Diesel Particulate Filter) when it left the factory, it will fail the test if the MOT tester can see smoke of any colour emitting from the exhaust, or finds evidence that the filter has been tampered with.

☐ The only emission test for diesel engines is measuring exhaust smoke density, using a calibrated smoke meter.

☐ This test involves accelerating the engine to its maximum unloaded speed a minimum of once, and a maximum of 6 times. With the smoke meter connected, the engine is accelerated quickly to its maximum speed. If the smoke level is at or below the limit specified, the vehicle will pass. If the level is more than the specified limit then two further accelerations are carried out, and an average of the readings calculated. If the vehicle is still over the limit, a further three accelerations are carried out, with the average of the last three calculated after each check.

Note: *On engines with a timing belt, it is VITAL that the belt is in good condition before the test is carried out.*

Vehicles registered after 1st July 2008
Smoke level must not exceed 1.5m-1 – Turbo-charged and non-Turbocharged engines

Vehicles registered before 1st July 2008
Smoke level must not exceed 2.5m-1 – Non-turbo vehicles
Smoke level must not exceed 3.0m-1 – Turbocharged vehicles:

☐ If excess smoke is produced, try fitting a new air cleaner element, or using an injector cleaning treatment. If the engine is running badly, where applicable, check the vehicle's ECU for fault codes. Also check the vehicle's EGR system, where applicable. At high mileages, the injectors may require professional attention.

Engine

- ☐ Engine fails to rotate when attempting to start
- ☐ Engine rotates, but will not start
- ☐ Engine difficult to start when cold
- ☐ Engine difficult to start when hot
- ☐ Starter motor noisy or excessively-rough in engagement
- ☐ Engine starts, but stops immediately
- ☐ Engine idles erratically
- ☐ Engine misfires at idle speed
- ☐ Engine misfires throughout the driving speed range
- ☐ Engine hesitates on acceleration
- ☐ Engine stalls
- ☐ Engine lacks power
- ☐ Engine backfires
- ☐ Oil pressure warning light illuminated with engine running
- ☐ Engine runs-on after switching off
- ☐ Engine noises

Cooling system

- ☐ Overheating
- ☐ Overcooling
- ☐ External coolant leakage
- ☐ Internal coolant leakage
- ☐ Corrosion

Fuel and exhaust systems

- ☐ Excessive fuel consumption
- ☐ Fuel leakage and/or fuel odour
- ☐ Excessive noise or fumes from exhaust system

Clutch

- ☐ Pedal travels to floor – no pressure or very little resistance
- ☐ Clutch fails to disengage (unable to select gears)
- ☐ Clutch slips (engine speed increases, with no increase in vehicle speed)
- ☐ Judder as clutch is engaged
- ☐ Noise when depressing or releasing clutch pedal

Manual transmission

- ☐ Noisy in neutral with engine running
- ☐ Noisy in one particular gear
- ☐ Difficulty engaging gears
- ☐ Jumps out of gear
- ☐ Vibration
- ☐ Lubricant leaks

Driveshafts

- ☐ Vibration when accelerating or decelerating
- ☐ Clicking or knocking noise on turns (at slow speed on full-lock)

Braking system

- ☐ Vehicle pulls to one side under braking
- ☐ Noise (grinding or high-pitched squeal) when brakes applied
- ☐ Excessive brake pedal travel
- ☐ Brake pedal feels spongy when depressed
- ☐ Excessive brake pedal effort required to stop vehicle
- ☐ Judder felt through brake pedal or steering wheel when braking
- ☐ Brakes binding
- ☐ Rear wheels locking under normal braking

Suspension and steering

- ☐ Vehicle pulls to one side
- ☐ Wheel wobble and vibration
- ☐ Excessive pitching and/or rolling around corners, or during braking
- ☐ Wandering or general instability
- ☐ Excessively-stiff steering
- ☐ Excessive play in steering
- ☐ Lack of power assistance
- ☐ Tyre wear excessive

Electrical system

- ☐ Battery will not hold a charge for more than a few days
- ☐ Ignition/no-charge warning light remains illuminated with engine running
- ☐ Ignition/no-charge warning light fails to come on
- ☐ Lights inoperative
- ☐ Instrument readings inaccurate or erratic
- ☐ Horn inoperative, or unsatisfactory in operation
- ☐ Windscreen wipers inoperative, or unsatisfactory in operation
- ☐ Windscreen washers inoperative, or unsatisfactory in operation
- ☐ Electric windows inoperative, or unsatisfactory in operation
- ☐ Central locking system inoperative, or unsatisfactory in operation

Introduction

The vehicle owner who does his or her own maintenance according to the recommended service schedules should not have to use this section of the manual very often. Modern component reliability is such that, provided those items subject to wear or deterioration are inspected or renewed at the specified intervals, sudden failure is comparatively rare. Faults do not usually just happen as a result of sudden failure, but develop over a period of time. Major mechanical failures in particular are usually preceded by characteristic symptoms over hundreds or even thousands of miles. Those components which do occasionally fail without warning are often small and easily carried in the vehicle.

With any fault finding, the first step is to decide where to begin investigations. Sometimes this is obvious, but on other occasions, a little detective work will be necessary. The owner who makes half a dozen haphazard adjustments or replacements may be successful in curing a fault (or its symptoms), but will be none the wiser if the fault recurs, and ultimately may have spent more time and money than was necessary. A calm and logical approach will be found to be more satisfactory in the long run. Always take into account any warning signs or abnormalities that may have been noticed in the period preceding the fault – power loss, high or low gauge readings,

unusual smells, etc – and remember that failure of components such as fuses or spark plugs may only be pointers to some underlying fault.

The pages which follow provide an easy-reference guide to the more common problems which may occur during the operation of the vehicle. These problems and their possible causes are grouped under headings denoting various components or systems, such as Engine, Cooling system, etc. The Chapter and/or Section which deals with the problem is also shown in brackets. Whatever the fault, certain basic principles apply. These are as follows:

Verify the fault. This is simply a matter of

being sure that you know what the symptoms are before starting work. This is particularly important if you are investigating a fault for someone else, who may not have described it very accurately.

Don't overlook the obvious. For example, if the vehicle won't start, is there fuel in the tank? (Don't take anyone else's word on this particular point, and don't trust the fuel gauge either). If an electrical fault is indicated, look for loose or broken wires before digging out the test gear.

Cure the disease, not the symptom. Substituting a flat battery with a fully-charged one will get you off the hard shoulder, but if the underlying cause is not attended to, the new battery will go the same way. Similarly, changing oil-fouled spark plugs for a new set will get you moving again, but remember that the reason for the fouling (if it wasn't simply an incorrect grade of plug) will have to be established and corrected.

Don't take anything for granted. Particularly, don't forget that a 'new' component may itself be defective (especially if it's been rattling around in the boot for months), and don't leave components out of a fault diagnosis sequence just because they are new or recently-fitted. When you do finally diagnose a difficult fault, you'll probably realise that all the evidence was there from the start.

Consider what work, if any, has recently been carried out. Many faults arise through careless or hurried work. For instance, if any work has been performed under the bonnet, could some of the wiring have been dislodged or incorrectly routed, or a hose trapped? Have all the fasteners been properly tightened? Were new, genuine parts and new gaskets used? There is often a certain amount of detective work to be done in this case, as an apparently-unrelated task can have far-reaching consequences.

Diesel engine fault finding

The majority of starting problems on small diesel engines are electrical in origin. The mechanic who is familiar with petrol engines but less so with diesel may be inclined to view the diesel's injectors and pump in the same light as the spark plugs and distributor, but this is generally a mistake.

When investigating complaints of difficult starting for someone else, make sure that the correct starting procedure is understood and is being followed. Some drivers are unaware of the significance of the preheating warning light – many modern engines are sufficiently forgiving for this not to matter in mild weather, but with the onset of winter, problems begin. Glow plugs in particular are often neglected – just one faulty plug will make cold-weather starting very difficult.

As a rule of thumb, if the engine is difficult to start but runs well when it has finally got going, the problem is electrical (battery, starter motor or preheating system). If poor performance is combined with difficult starting, the problem is likely to be in the fuel system. The low-pressure (supply) side of the fuel system should be checked before suspecting the injectors and high-pressure pump. The most common fuel supply problem is air getting into the system, and any pipe from the fuel tank forwards must be scrutinised if air leakage is suspected.

Engine

Engine fails to rotate when attempting to start

- [ ] Battery terminal connections loose or corroded (see *Weekly checks*)
- [ ] Battery discharged or faulty (Chapter 5)
- [ ] Broken, loose or disconnected wiring in the starting circuit (Chapter 5)
- [ ] Defective starter solenoid or ignition switch (Chapter 5 or 12)
- [ ] Defective starter motor (Chapter 5)
- [ ] Starter pinion or flywheel ring gear teeth loose or broken (Chapter 2A, 2B or 5)
- [ ] Engine earth strap broken or disconnected (Chapter 5 or 12)
- [ ] Engine suffering 'hydraulic lock' (eg, from water ingested after traversing flooded roads, or from a serious internal coolant leak) – consult a Vauxhall or Renault dealer or specialist for advice

Engine rotates, but will not start

- [ ] Fuel tank empty
- [ ] Battery discharged (engine rotates slowly) (Chapter 5)
- [ ] Battery terminal connections loose or corroded (see *Weekly checks*)
- [ ] Immobiliser fault, or 'uncoded' ignition key being used (Chapter 12 or *Roadside repairs*)
- [ ] Crankshaft sensor fault (Chapter 4A)
- [ ] Preheating system faulty (Chapter 5)
- [ ] Fuel injection system fault (Chapter 4A)
- [ ] Air in fuel system (Chapter 4A)
- [ ] Major mechanical failure (eg, timing belt/chain snapped) (Chapter 2A or 2B)

Engine difficult to start when cold

- [ ] Battery discharged (Chapter 5)
- [ ] Battery terminal connections loose or corroded (see *Weekly checks*)
- [ ] Preheating system faulty (Chapter 5)
- [ ] Fuel injection system fault (Chapter 4A)
- [ ] Wrong grade of engine oil used (*Weekly checks*, Chapter 1)
- [ ] Low cylinder compression (Chapter 2A or 2B)

Engine difficult to start when hot

- [ ] Air filter element dirty or clogged (Chapter 1)
- [ ] Fuel injection system fault (Chapter 4A)
- [ ] Low cylinder compression (Chapter 2A or 2B)

Starter motor noisy or excessively-rough in engagement

- [ ] Starter pinion or flywheel ring gear teeth loose or broken (Chapter 2A, 2B or 5)
- [ ] Starter motor mounting bolts loose or missing (Chapter 5)
- [ ] Starter motor internal components worn or damaged (Chapter 5)

Engine starts, but stops immediately

- [ ] Blocked injectors/fuel injection system fault (Chapter 4A)
- [ ] Air in fuel, possibly due to loose fuel line connection (Chapter 4A)

Engine idles erratically

- [ ] Air filter element clogged (Chapter 1)
- [ ] Valve clearances incorrect (Chapter 2A)
- [ ] Uneven or low cylinder compression (Chapter 2A or 2B)
- [ ] Camshaft lobes worn (Chapter 2A or 2B)
- [ ] Timing/chain belt incorrectly fitted (Chapter 2A)
- [ ] Blocked injectors/fuel injection system fault (Chapter 4A)
- [ ] Air in fuel, possibly due to loose fuel line connection (Chapter 4A)

Engine misfires at idle speed

- [ ] Blocked injectors/fuel injection system fault (Chapter 4A)
- [ ] Faulty injector(s) (Chapter 4A)
- [ ] Uneven or low cylinder compression (Chapter 2A or 2B)
- [ ] Disconnected, leaking, or perished crankcase ventilation hoses (Chapter 4B)

Engine (continued)

Engine misfires throughout the driving speed range

- ☐ Fuel filter choked (Chapter 1)
- ☐ Fuel tank vent blocked, or fuel pipes restricted (Chapter 4A)
- ☐ Faulty injector(s) (Chapter 4A)
- ☐ Uneven or low cylinder compression (Chapter 2A or 2B)
- ☐ Blocked injector/fuel injection system fault (Chapter 4A)
- ☐ Blocked catalytic converter (Chapter 4A)
- ☐ Engine overheating (Chapter 3)
- ☐ Fuel tank level low (Chapter 4A)

Engine hesitates on acceleration

- ☐ Blocked injectors/fuel injection system fault (Chapter 4A)
- ☐ Faulty injector(s) (Chapter 4A)
- ☐ Faulty clutch pedal switch (Chapter 6)

Engine stalls

- ☐ Fuel filter choked (Chapter 1)
- ☐ Fuel pump faulty, or delivery pressure low (Chapter 4A)
- ☐ Fuel tank vent blocked, or fuel pipes restricted (Chapter 4A)
- ☐ Blocked injectors/fuel injection system fault (Chapter 4A)
- ☐ Faulty injector(s) (Chapter 4A)

Engine lacks power

- ☐ Air filter element blocked (Chapter)
- ☐ Fuel filter choked (Chapter 1)
- ☐ Fuel pipes blocked or restricted (Chapter 4A)
- ☐ Valve clearances incorrect (Chapter 2A)
- ☐ Engine overheating (Chapter 3)
- ☐ Fuel tank level low (Chapter 4A)
- ☐ Accelerator position sensor faulty (Chapter 4A)
- ☐ Blocked injectors/fuel injection system fault (Chapter 4A)
- ☐ Faulty injector(s) (Chapter 4A)
- ☐ Timing belt/chain incorrectly fitted (Chapter 2A)
- ☐ Fuel pump faulty, or delivery pressure low (Chapter 4A)
- ☐ Uneven or low cylinder compression (Chapter 2A or 2B)
- ☐ Blocked catalytic converter (Chapter 4A)
- ☐ Brakes binding (Chapter 1 or 9)
- ☐ Clutch slipping (Chapter 6)

Engine backfires

- ☐ Timing belt/chain incorrectly fitted (Chapter 2A or 2B)
- ☐ Blocked injectors/fuel injection system fault (Chapter 4A)
- ☐ Blocked catalytic converter (Chapter 4A)

Oil pressure warning light illuminated with engine running

- ☐ Low oil level, or incorrect oil grade (see *Weekly checks*)
- ☐ Faulty oil pressure sensor, or wiring damaged (Chapter 12)
- ☐ Worn engine bearings and/or oil pump (Chapter 2A, 2B or 2C)
- ☐ High engine operating temperature (Chapter 3)
- ☐ Oil pump pressure relief valve defective (Chapter 2A or 2B)
- ☐ Oil pump pick-up strainer clogged (Chapter 2A or 2B)

Engine runs-on after switching off

- ☐ Excessive carbon build-up in engine (Chapter 2A or 2B)
- ☐ High engine operating temperature (Chapter 3)
- ☐ Fuel injection system fault (Chapter 4A)

Engine noises

Pre-ignition (pinking) or knocking during acceleration or under load

- ☐ Incorrect grade of fuel (Chapter 4)
- ☐ Excessive carbon build-up in engine (Chapter 2A, 2B or 2C)
- ☐ Blocked injector/fuel injection system fault (Chapter 4A)
- ☐ Faulty injector(s) (Chapter 4A)

Whistling or wheezing noises

- ☐ Leaking exhaust manifold gasket or pipe-to-manifold joint (Chapter 4A)
- ☐ Leaking vacuum hose (Chapter 4A or 9)
- ☐ Blowing cylinder head gasket (Chapter 2A or 2B)
- ☐ Partially blocked or leaking crankcase ventilation system (Chapter 4B)

Tapping or rattling noises

- ☐ Valve clearances incorrect (Chapter 2A)
- ☐ Worn valve gear or camshaft (Chapter 2A or 2B)
- ☐ Ancillary component fault (coolant pump, alternator, etc) (Chapter 3, 5, etc)

Knocking or thumping noises

- ☐ Worn big-end bearings (regular heavy knocking, perhaps less under load) (Chapter 2C)
- ☐ Worn main bearings (rumbling and knocking, perhaps worsening under load) (Chapter 2C)
- ☐ Piston slap – most noticeable when cold, caused by piston/bore wear (Chapter 2C)
- ☐ Ancillary component fault (coolant pump, alternator, etc) (Chapter 3, 5, etc)
- ☐ Engine mountings worn or defective (Chapter 2A or 2B)
- ☐ Front suspension or steering components worn (Chapter 10)

Cooling system

Overheating

- ☐ Insufficient coolant in system (see *Weekly checks*)
- ☐ Thermostat faulty (Chapter 3)
- ☐ Radiator core blocked, or grille restricted (Chapter 3)
- ☐ Cooling fan faulty, or control module fault (Chapter 3)
- ☐ Inaccurate coolant temperature sender (Chapter 3)
- ☐ Airlock in cooling system (Chapter 3)
- ☐ Expansion tank pressure cap faulty (Chapter 3)
- ☐ Engine management system fault (Chapter 4A)

Overcooling

- ☐ Thermostat faulty (Chapter 3)
- ☐ Inaccurate coolant temperature sender (Chapter 3)
- ☐ Cooling fan faulty (Chapter 3)
- ☐ Engine management system fault (Chapter 4A)

External coolant leakage

- ☐ Deteriorated or damaged hoses or hose clips (Chapter 1)
- ☐ Radiator core or heater matrix leaking (Chapter 3)
- ☐ Expansion tank pressure cap faulty (Chapter 1)
- ☐ Coolant pump internal seal leaking (Chapter 3)
- ☐ Coolant pump gasket leaking (Chapter 3)
- ☐ Boiling due to overheating (Chapter 3)
- ☐ Cylinder block core plug leaking (Chapter 2C)

Internal coolant leakage

- ☐ Leaking cylinder head gasket (Chapter 2A or 2B)
- ☐ Cracked cylinder head or cylinder block (Chapter 2A or 2B)

Corrosion

- ☐ Infrequent draining and flushing (Chapter 1)
- ☐ Incorrect coolant mixture or inappropriate coolant type (see *Weekly checks*)

Fuel and exhaust systems

Excessive fuel consumption

- ☐ Air filter element dirty or clogged (Chapter 1)
- ☐ Fuel injection system fault (Chapter 4A)
- ☐ Engine management system fault (Chapter 4A)
- ☐ Crankcase ventilation system blocked (Chapter 4B)
- ☐ Tyres under-inflated (see *Weekly checks*)
- ☐ Brakes binding (Chapter 1 or 9)
- ☐ Fuel leak, causing apparent high consumption (Chapter 1 or 4A)

Fuel leakage and/or fuel odour

- ☐ Damaged or corroded fuel tank, pipes or connections (Chapter 4A)

Excessive noise or fumes from exhaust system

- ☐ Leaking exhaust system or manifold joints (Chapter 1 or 4A)
- ☐ Leaking, corroded or damaged silencers or pipe (Chapter 1 or 4A)
- ☐ Broken mountings causing body or suspension contact (Chapter 1)

Clutch

Pedal travels to floor – no pressure or very little resistance

☐ Air in hydraulic system/faulty master or slave cylinder (Chapter 6)
☐ Faulty hydraulic release system (Chapter 6)
☐ Clutch pedal return spring detached or broken (Chapter 6)
☐ Broken clutch release bearing or fork (Chapter 6)
☐ Broken diaphragm spring in clutch pressure plate (Chapter 6)

Clutch fails to disengage (unable to select gears)

☐ Air in hydraulic system/faulty master or slave cylinder (Chapter 6)
☐ Faulty hydraulic release system (Chapter 6)
☐ Clutch disc sticking on transmission input shaft splines (Chapter 6)
☐ Clutch disc sticking to flywheel or pressure plate (Chapter 6)
☐ Faulty pressure plate assembly (Chapter 6)
☐ Clutch release mechanism worn or incorrectly assembled (Chapter 6)

Clutch slips (engine speed increases, with no increase in vehicle speed)

☐ Faulty hydraulic release system (Chapter 6)
☐ Clutch disc linings excessively worn (Chapter 6)
☐ Clutch disc linings contaminated with oil or grease (Chapter 6)
☐ Faulty pressure plate or weak diaphragm spring (Chapter 6)

Judder as clutch is engaged

☐ Clutch disc linings contaminated with oil or grease (Chapter 6)
☐ Clutch disc linings excessively worn (Chapter 6)
☐ Faulty or distorted pressure plate or diaphragm spring (Chapter 6).
☐ Worn or loose engine or transmission mountings (Chapter 2A or 2B)
☐ Clutch disc hub or transmission input shaft splines worn (Chapter 6)

Noise when depressing or releasing clutch pedal

☐ Worn clutch release bearing (Chapter 6)
☐ Worn or dry clutch pedal bushes (Chapter 6)
☐ Worn or dry clutch master cylinder piston (Chapter 6)
☐ Faulty pressure plate assembly (Chapter 6)
☐ Pressure plate diaphragm spring broken (Chapter 6)
☐ Broken clutch disc cushioning springs (Chapter 6)

Manual transmission

Noisy in neutral with engine running

☐ Lack of oil (Chapter 1)
☐ Input shaft bearings worn (noise apparent with clutch pedal released, but not when depressed) (Chapter 7)*
☐ Clutch release bearing worn (noise apparent with clutch pedal depressed, possibly less when released) (Chapter 6)

Noisy in one particular gear

☐ Worn, damaged or chipped gear teeth (Chapter 7)*

Difficulty engaging gears

☐ Clutch fault (Chapter 6)
☐ Worn or damaged gearchange cables (Chapter 7)
☐ Lack of oil (Chapter 7)
☐ Worn synchroniser units (Chapter 7)*

Jumps out of gear

☐ Worn or damaged gearchange cables (Chapter 7)
☐ Worn synchroniser units (Chapter 7)*
☐ Worn selector forks (Chapter 7)*

Vibration

☐ Lack of oil (Chapter 1)
☐ Worn bearings (Chapter 7)*

Lubricant leaks

☐ Leaking driveshaft or selector shaft oil seal (Chapter 7)
☐ Leaking housing joint (Chapter 7)*
☐ Leaking input shaft oil seal (Chapter 7)*

Although the corrective action necessary to remedy the symptoms described is beyond the scope of the home mechanic, the above information should be helpful in isolating the cause of the condition, so that the owner can communicate clearly with a professional mechanic.

Driveshafts

Vibration when accelerating or decelerating

☐ Worn inner constant velocity joint (Chapter 8)
☐ Bent or distorted driveshaft (Chapter 8)
☐ Worn intermediate bearing (Chapter 8)

Clicking or knocking noise on turns (at slow speed on full-lock)

☐ Worn outer constant velocity joint (Chapter 8)
☐ Lack of constant velocity joint lubricant, possibly due to damaged gaiter (Chapter 8)
☐ Worn intermediate bearing (Chapter 8)

Braking system

Note: *Before assuming that a brake problem exists, make sure that the tyres are in good condition and correctly inflated, that the front wheel alignment is correct, and that the vehicle is not loaded with weight in an unequal manner. Apart from checking the condition of all pipe and hose connections, any faults occurring on the anti-lock braking system should be referred to a dealer or specialist for diagnosis.*

Vehicle pulls to one side under braking

☐ Worn, defective, damaged or contaminated brake pads on one side (Chapter 1 or 9)
☐ Seized or partially-seized brake caliper piston (Chapter 1 or 9)
☐ A mixture of brake pad lining materials fitted between sides (Chapter 1 or 9)
☐ Brake caliper mounting bolts loose (Chapter 9)
☐ Worn or damaged steering or suspension components (Chapter 1 or 10)

Noise (grinding or high-pitched squeal) when brakes applied

☐ Brake pad friction lining material worn down to metal backing (Chapter 1 or 9)
☐ Excessive corrosion of brake disc (may be apparent after the vehicle has been standing for some time (Chapter 1 or 9)
☐ Foreign object (stone chipping, etc) trapped between brake disc and shield (Chapter 1 or 9)

Excessive brake pedal travel

☐ Faulty master cylinder (Chapter 9)
☐ Air in hydraulic system (Chapter 1, 6 or 9)
☐ Faulty vacuum servo unit (Chapter 9)

Brake pedal feels spongy when depressed

☐ Air in hydraulic system (Chapter 1, 6 or 9)
☐ Deteriorated flexible rubber brake hoses (Chapter 1 or 9)
☐ Master cylinder mounting nuts loose (Chapter 9)
☐ Faulty master cylinder (Chapter 9)

Excessive brake pedal effort required to stop vehicle

☐ Faulty vacuum servo unit (Chapter 9)
☐ Faulty vacuum pump (Chapter 9)
☐ Disconnected, damaged or insecure brake servo vacuum hose (Chapter 9)
☐ Primary or secondary hydraulic circuit failure (Chapter 9)
☐ Seized brake caliper piston (Chapter 9)
☐ Brake pads incorrectly fitted (Chapter 9)
☐ Incorrect grade of brake pads fitted (Chapter 9)
☐ Brake pad linings contaminated (Chapter 1 or 9)

Judder felt through brake pedal or steering wheel when braking

Note: *Under heavy braking on models equipped with ABS, vibration may be felt through the brake pedal. This is a normal feature of ABS operation, and does not constitute a fault*

☐ Excessive run-out or distortion of discs (Chapter 1 or 9)
☐ Brake pad linings worn (Chapter 1 or 9)
☐ Brake caliper mounting bolts loose (Chapter 9)
☐ Wear in suspension or steering components or mountings (Chapter 1 or 10)
☐ Front wheels out of balance (see *Weekly checks*)

Brakes binding

☐ Seized brake caliper piston (Chapter 9)
☐ Incorrectly-adjusted handbrake mechanism (Chapter 9)
☐ Faulty master cylinder (Chapter 9)

Rear wheels locking under normal braking

☐ Rear brake pad linings contaminated or damaged (Chapter 1 or 9)
☐ Rear brake discs warped (Chapter 1 or 9)

Suspension and steering

Note: *Before diagnosing suspension or steering faults, be sure that the trouble is not due to incorrect tyre pressures, mixtures of tyre types, or binding brakes.*

Vehicle pulls to one side

- [ ] Defective tyre (see *Weekly checks*)
- [ ] Excessive wear in suspension or steering components (Chapter 1 or 10)
- [ ] Incorrect front wheel alignment (Chapter 10)
- [ ] Accident damage to steering or suspension components (Chapter 10)

Wheel wobble and vibration

- [ ] Front wheels out of balance (vibration felt mainly through the steering wheel) (see *Weekly checks*)
- [ ] Rear wheels out of balance (vibration felt throughout the vehicle) (see *Weekly checks*)
- [ ] Roadwheels damaged or distorted (see *Weekly checks*)
- [ ] Faulty or damaged tyre (see *Weekly checks*)
- [ ] Worn steering or suspension joints, bushes or components (Chapter 1 or 10)
- [ ] Wheel bolts loose (Chapter 1)

Excessive pitching and/or rolling around corners, or during braking

- [ ] Defective shock absorbers (Chapter 1 or 10)
- [ ] Broken or weak spring and/or suspension component (Chapter 1 or 10)
- [ ] Worn or damaged anti-roll bar or mountings (Chapter 1 or 10)

Wandering or general instability

- [ ] Incorrect front wheel alignment (Chapter 10)
- [ ] Worn steering or suspension joints, bushes or components (Chapter 1 or 10)
- [ ] Roadwheels out of balance (see *Weekly checks*)
- [ ] Faulty or damaged tyre (see *Weekly checks*)
- [ ] Wheel bolts loose (Chapter 1)
- [ ] Defective shock absorbers (Chapter 1 or 10)

Excessively-stiff steering

- [ ] Seized steering linkage balljoint or suspension balljoint (Chapter 1 or 10)
- [ ] Broken or incorrectly-adjusted auxiliary drivebelt (Chapter 1)
- [ ] Incorrect front wheel alignment (Chapter 10)
- [ ] Steering rack damaged (Chapter 10)

Excessive play in steering

- [ ] Worn steering column/intermediate shaft joints (Chapter 10)
- [ ] Worn track rod balljoints (Chapter 1 or 10)
- [ ] Worn steering rack (Chapter 10)
- [ ] Worn steering or suspension joints, bushes or components (Chapter 1 or 10)

Lack of power assistance

- [ ] Broken or incorrectly-adjusted auxiliary drivebelt (Chapter 1)
- [ ] Incorrect power steering fluid level (see *Weekly checks*)
- [ ] Restriction in power steering fluid hoses (Chapter 1)
- [ ] Faulty power steering pump (Chapter 10)
- [ ] Faulty steering rack (Chapter 10)

Tyre wear excessive

Tyres worn on inside or outside edges

- [ ] Tyres under-inflated (wear on both edges) (see *Weekly checks*)
- [ ] Incorrect camber or castor angles (wear on one edge only) (Chapter 10)
- [ ] Worn steering or suspension joints, bushes or components (Chapter 1 or 10)
- [ ] Excessively-hard cornering or braking
- [ ] Accident damage

Tyre treads exhibit feathered edges

- [ ] Incorrect toe-setting (Chapter 10)

Tyres worn in centre of tread

- [ ] Tyres over-inflated (see *Weekly checks*)

Tyres worn on inside and outside edges

- [ ] Tyres under-inflated (see *Weekly checks*)

Tyres worn unevenly

- [ ] Tyres/wheels out of balance (see *Weekly checks*)
- [ ] Excessive wheel or tyre run-out
- [ ] Worn shock absorbers (Chapter 1 or 10)
- [ ] Faulty tyre (see *Weekly checks*)

Electrical system

Note: *For problems associated with the starting system, refer to the faults listed under 'Engine' earlier in this Section.*

Battery will not hold a charge for more than a few days

☐ Battery defective internally (Chapter 5)
☐ Battery terminal connections loose or corroded (see *Weekly checks*)
☐ Auxiliary drivebelt worn or incorrectly adjusted (Chapter 1)
☐ Alternator not charging at correct output (Chapter 5)
☐ Alternator or voltage regulator faulty (Chapter 5)
☐ Short-circuit causing continual battery drain (Chapter 5 or 12)

Ignition/no-charge warning light remains illuminated with engine running

☐ Auxiliary drivebelt broken, worn, or incorrectly adjusted (Chapter 1)
☐ Internal fault in alternator or voltage regulator (Chapter 5)
☐ Broken, disconnected, or loose wiring in charging circuit (Chapter 5 or 12)

Ignition/no-charge warning light fails to come on

☐ Warning light bulb blown (Chapter 12)
☐ Broken, disconnected, or loose wiring in warning light circuit (Chapter 5 or 12)
☐ Alternator faulty (Chapter 5)

Lights inoperative

☐ Bulb blown (Chapter 12)
☐ Corrosion of bulb or bulbholder contacts (Chapter 12)
☐ Blown fuse (Chapter 12)
☐ Faulty relay (Chapter 12)
☐ Broken, loose, or disconnected wiring (Chapter 12)
☐ Faulty switch (Chapter 12)

Instrument readings inaccurate or erratic

Fuel or temperature gauges give no reading

☐ Faulty gauge sender unit (Chapter 3 or 4A)
☐ Wiring open-circuit (Chapter 12)
☐ Faulty instrument cluster (Chapter 12)

Fuel or temperature gauges give continuous maximum reading

☐ Faulty gauge sender unit (Chapter 3 or 4A)
☐ Wiring short-circuit (Chapter 12)
☐ Faulty instrument cluster (Chapter 12)

Horn inoperative, or unsatisfactory in operation

Horn operates all the time

☐ Horn push either earthed or stuck down (Chapter 12)
☐ Horn cable-to-horn push earthed (Chapter 12)

Horn fails to operate

☐ Blown fuse (Chapter 12)
☐ Cable or connections loose, broken or disconnected (Chapter 12)
☐ Faulty horn (Chapter 12)

Horn emits intermittent or unsatisfactory sound

☐ Cable connections loose (Chapter 12)
☐ Horn mountings loose (Chapter 12)
☐ Faulty horn (Chapter 12)

Windscreen wipers inoperative, or unsatisfactory in operation

Wipers fail to operate, or operate very slowly

☐ Wiper blades stuck to screen, or linkage seized or binding (Chapter 12)
☐ Blown fuse (Chapter 12)
☐ Battery discharged (Chapter 5)
☐ Cable or connections loose, broken or disconnected (Chapter 12)
☐ Faulty wiper motor (Chapter 12)

Wiper blades sweep over too large or too small an area of the glass

☐ Wiper blades incorrectly fitted, or wrong size used (see *Weekly checks*)
☐ Wiper arms incorrectly positioned on spindles (Chapter 12)
☐ Excessive wear of wiper linkage (Chapter 12)
☐ Wiper motor or linkage mountings loose or insecure (Chapter 12)

Wiper blades fail to clean the glass effectively

☐ Wiper blade rubbers dirty, worn or perished (see *Weekly checks*)
☐ Wiper blades incorrectly fitted, or wrong size used (see *Weekly checks*)
☐ Wiper arm tension springs broken, or arm pivots seized (Chapter 12)
☐ Insufficient windscreen washer additive to adequately remove road film (see *Weekly checks*)

Electrical system (continued)

Windscreen washers inoperative, or unsatisfactory in operation

One or more washer jets inoperative

- [ ] Blocked washer jet
- [ ] Disconnected, kinked or restricted fluid hose (Chapter 12)
- [ ] Insufficient fluid in washer reservoir (see *Weekly checks*)

Washer pump fails to operate

- [ ] Broken or disconnected wiring or connections (Chapter 12)
- [ ] Blown fuse (Chapter 12)
- [ ] Faulty washer switch (Chapter 12)
- [ ] Faulty washer pump (Chapter 12)

Washer pump runs for some time before fluid is emitted from jets

- [ ] Faulty one-way valve in fluid supply hose (Chapter 12)

Electric windows inoperative, or unsatisfactory in operation

Window glass will only move in one direction

- [ ] Faulty switch (Chapter 12)

Window glass slow to move

- [ ] Battery discharged (Chapter 5)
- [ ] Regulator seized or damaged, or in need of lubrication (Chapter 11)
- [ ] Door internal components or trim fouling regulator (Chapter 11)
- [ ] Faulty motor (Chapter 11)

Window glass fails to move

- [ ] Blown fuse (Chapter 12)
- [ ] Faulty relay (Chapter 12)
- [ ] Broken or disconnected wiring or connections (Chapter 12)
- [ ] Faulty motor (Chapter 11)
- [ ] Faulty control module (Chapter 12)

Central locking system inoperative, or unsatisfactory in operation

Complete system failure

- [ ] Remote handset battery discharged, where applicable
- [ ] Blown fuse (Chapter 12)
- [ ] Defective control module (Chapter 12)
- [ ] Broken or disconnected wiring or connections (Chapter 12)
- [ ] Faulty motor (Chapter 11)

Latch locks but will not unlock, or unlocks but will not lock

- [ ] Remote handset battery discharged, where applicable
- [ ] Faulty master switch (Chapter 12)
- [ ] Broken or disconnected latch operating rods or levers (Chapter 11)
- [ ] Faulty control module (Chapter 12)
- [ ] Faulty motor (Chapter 11)

One solenoid/motor fails to operate

- [ ] Broken or disconnected wiring or connections (Chapter 12)
- [ ] Faulty operating assembly (Chapter 11)
- [ ] Broken, binding or disconnected latch operating rods or levers (Chapter 11)
- [ ] Fault in door latch (Chapter 11)

A

ABS (Anti-lock brake system) A system, usually electronically controlled, that senses incipient wheel lockup during braking and relieves hydraulic pressure at wheels that are about to skid.

Air bag An inflatable bag hidden in the steering wheel (driver's side) or the dash or glovebox (passenger side). In a head-on collision, the bags inflate, preventing the driver and front passenger from being thrown forward into the steering wheel or windscreen.

Air cleaner A metal or plastic housing, containing a filter element, which removes dust and dirt from the air being drawn into the engine.

Air filter element The actual filter in an air cleaner system, usually manufactured from pleated paper and requiring renewal at regular intervals.

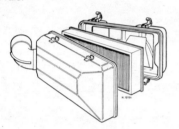
Air filter

Allen key A hexagonal wrench which fits into a recessed hexagonal hole.

Alligator clip A long-nosed spring-loaded metal clip with meshing teeth. Used to make temporary electrical connections.

Alternator A component in the electrical system which converts mechanical energy from a drivebelt into electrical energy to charge the battery and to operate the starting system, ignition system and electrical accessories.

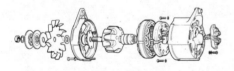
Alternator (exploded view)

Ampere (amp) A unit of measurement for the flow of electric current. One amp is the amount of current produced by one volt acting through a resistance of one ohm.

Anaerobic sealer A substance used to prevent bolts and screws from loosening. Anaerobic means that it does not require oxygen for activation. The Loctite brand is widely used.

Antifreeze A substance (usually ethylene glycol) mixed with water, and added to a vehicle's cooling system, to prevent freezing of the coolant in winter. Antifreeze also contains chemicals to inhibit corrosion and the formation of rust and other deposits that

would tend to clog the radiator and coolant passages and reduce cooling efficiency.

Anti-seize compound A coating that reduces the risk of seizing on fasteners that are subjected to high temperatures, such as exhaust manifold bolts and nuts.

Anti-seize compound

Asbestos A natural fibrous mineral with great heat resistance, commonly used in the composition of brake friction materials. Asbestos is a health hazard and the dust created by brake systems should never be inhaled or ingested.

Axle A shaft on which a wheel revolves, or which revolves with a wheel. Also, a solid beam that connects the two wheels at one end of the vehicle. An axle which also transmits power to the wheels is known as a live axle.

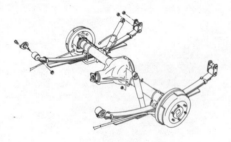
Axle assembly

Axleshaft A single rotating shaft, on either side of the differential, which delivers power from the final drive assembly to the drive wheels. Also called a driveshaft or a halfshaft.

B

Ball bearing An anti-friction bearing consisting of a hardened inner and outer race with hardened steel balls between two races.

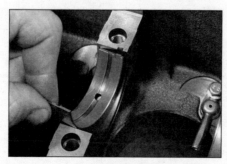
Bearing

Bearing The curved surface on a shaft or in a bore, or the part assembled into either, that permits relative motion between them with minimum wear and friction.

Big-end bearing The bearing in the end of the connecting rod that's attached to the crankshaft.

Bleed nipple A valve on a brake wheel cylinder, caliper or other hydraulic component that is opened to purge the hydraulic system of air. Also called a bleed screw.

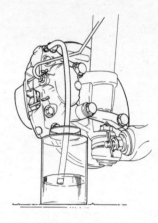
Brake bleeding

Brake bleeding Procedure for removing air from lines of a hydraulic brake system.

Brake disc The component of a disc brake that rotates with the wheels.

Brake drum The component of a drum brake that rotates with the wheels.

Brake linings The friction material which contacts the brake disc or drum to retard the vehicle's speed. The linings are bonded or riveted to the brake pads or shoes.

Brake pads The replaceable friction pads that pinch the brake disc when the brakes are applied. Brake pads consist of a friction material bonded or riveted to a rigid backing plate.

Brake shoe The crescent-shaped carrier to which the brake linings are mounted and which forces the lining against the rotating drum during braking.

Braking systems For more information on braking systems, consult the *Haynes Automotive Brake Manual*.

Breaker bar A long socket wrench handle providing greater leverage.

Bulkhead The insulated partition between the engine and the passenger compartment.

C

Caliper The non-rotating part of a disc-brake assembly that straddles the disc and carries the brake pads. The caliper also contains the hydraulic components that cause the pads to pinch the disc when the brakes are applied. A caliper is also a measuring tool that can be set to measure inside or outside dimensions of an object.

Camshaft A rotating shaft on which a series of cam lobes operate the valve mechanisms. The camshaft may be driven by gears, by sprockets and chain or by sprockets and a belt.

Canister A container in an evaporative emission control system; contains activated charcoal granules to trap vapours from the fuel system.

Canister

Carburettor A device which mixes fuel with air in the proper proportions to provide a desired power output from a spark ignition internal combustion engine.

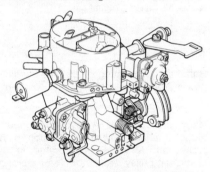

Carburettor

Castellated Resembling the parapets along the top of a castle wall. For example, a castellated balljoint stud nut.

Castellated nut

Castor In wheel alignment, the backward or forward tilt of the steering axis. Castor is positive when the steering axis is inclined rearward at the top.

Catalytic converter A silencer-like device in the exhaust system which converts certain pollutants in the exhaust gases into less harmful substances.

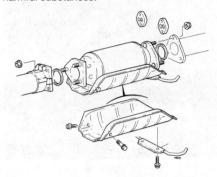

Catalytic converter

Circlip A ring-shaped clip used to prevent endwise movement of cylindrical parts and shafts. An internal circlip is installed in a groove in a housing; an external circlip fits into a groove on the outside of a cylindrical piece such as a shaft.

Clearance The amount of space between two parts. For example, between a piston and a cylinder, between a bearing and a journal, etc.

Coil spring A spiral of elastic steel found in various sizes throughout a vehicle, for example as a springing medium in the suspension and in the valve train.

Compression Reduction in volume, and increase in pressure and temperature, of a gas, caused by squeezing it into a smaller space.

Compression ratio The relationship between cylinder volume when the piston is at top dead centre and cylinder volume when the piston is at bottom dead centre.

Constant velocity (CV) joint A type of universal joint that cancels out vibrations caused by driving power being transmitted through an angle.

Core plug A disc or cup-shaped metal device inserted in a hole in a casting through which core was removed when the casting was formed. Also known as a freeze plug or expansion plug.

Crankcase The lower part of the engine block in which the crankshaft rotates.

Crankshaft The main rotating member, or shaft, running the length of the crankcase, with offset "throws" to which the connecting rods are attached.

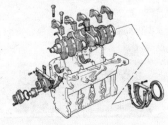

Crankshaft assembly

Crocodile clip See Alligator clip

D

Diagnostic code Code numbers obtained by accessing the diagnostic mode of an engine management computer. This code can be used to determine the area in the system where a malfunction may be located.

Disc brake A brake design incorporating a rotating disc onto which brake pads are squeezed. The resulting friction converts the energy of a moving vehicle into heat.

Double-overhead cam (DOHC) An engine that uses two overhead camshafts, usually one for the intake valves and one for the exhaust valves.

Drivebelt(s) The belt(s) used to drive accessories such as the alternator, water pump, power steering pump, air conditioning compressor, etc. off the crankshaft pulley.

Accessory drivebelts

Driveshaft Any shaft used to transmit motion. Commonly used when referring to the axleshafts on a front wheel drive vehicle.

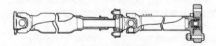

Driveshaft

Drum brake A type of brake using a drum-shaped metal cylinder attached to the inner surface of the wheel. When the brake pedal is pressed, curved brake shoes with friction linings press against the inside of the drum to slow or stop the vehicle.

Drum brake assembly

E

EGR valve A valve used to introduce exhaust gases into the intake air stream.

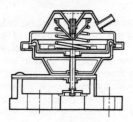

EGR valve

Electronic control unit (ECU) A computer which controls (for instance) ignition and fuel injection systems, or an anti-lock braking system. For more information refer to the *Haynes Automotive Electrical and Electronic Systems Manual.*

Electronic Fuel Injection (EFI) A computer controlled fuel system that distributes fuel through an injector located in each intake port of the engine.

Emergency brake A braking system, independent of the main hydraulic system, that can be used to slow or stop the vehicle if the primary brakes fail, or to hold the vehicle stationary even though the brake pedal isn't depressed. It usually consists of a hand lever that actuates either front or rear brakes mechanically through a series of cables and linkages. Also known as a handbrake or parking brake.

Endfloat The amount of lengthwise movement between two parts. As applied to a crankshaft, the distance that the crankshaft can move forward and back in the cylinder block.

Engine management system (EMS) A computer controlled system which manages the fuel injection and the ignition systems in an integrated fashion.

Exhaust manifold A part with several passages through which exhaust gases leave the engine combustion chambers and enter the exhaust pipe.

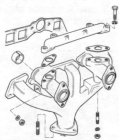

Exhaust manifold

F

Fan clutch A viscous (fluid) drive coupling device which permits variable engine fan speeds in relation to engine speeds.

Feeler blade A thin strip or blade of hardened steel, ground to an exact thickness, used to check or measure clearances between parts.

Feeler blade

Firing order The order in which the engine cylinders fire, or deliver their power strokes, beginning with the number one cylinder.

Flywheel A heavy spinning wheel in which energy is absorbed and stored by means of momentum. On cars, the flywheel is attached to the crankshaft to smooth out firing impulses.

Free play The amount of travel before any action takes place. The "looseness" in a linkage, or an assembly of parts, between the initial application of force and actual movement. For example, the distance the brake pedal moves before the pistons in the master cylinder are actuated.

Fuse An electrical device which protects a circuit against accidental overload. The typical fuse contains a soft piece of metal which is calibrated to melt at a predetermined current flow (expressed as amps) and break the circuit.

Fusible link A circuit protection device consisting of a conductor surrounded by heat-resistant insulation. The conductor is smaller than the wire it protects, so it acts as the weakest link in the circuit. Unlike a blown fuse, a failed fusible link must frequently be cut from the wire for replacement.

G

Gap The distance the spark must travel in jumping from the centre electrode to the side

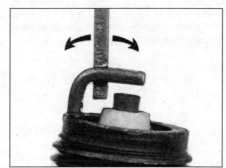

Adjusting spark plug gap

electrode in a spark plug. Also refers to the spacing between the points in a contact breaker assembly in a conventional points-type ignition, or to the distance between the reluctor or rotor and the pickup coil in an electronic ignition.

Gasket Any thin, soft material - usually cork, cardboard, asbestos or soft metal - installed between two metal surfaces to ensure a good seal. For instance, the cylinder head gasket seals the joint between the block and the cylinder head.

Gasket

Gauge An instrument panel display used to monitor engine conditions. A gauge with a movable pointer on a dial or a fixed scale is an analogue gauge. A gauge with a numerical readout is called a digital gauge.

H

Halfshaft A rotating shaft that transmits power from the final drive unit to a drive wheel, usually when referring to a live rear axle.

Harmonic balancer A device designed to reduce torsion or twisting vibration in the crankshaft. May be incorporated in the crankshaft pulley. Also known as a vibration damper.

Hone An abrasive tool for correcting small irregularities or differences in diameter in an engine cylinder, brake cylinder, etc.

Hydraulic tappet A tappet that utilises hydraulic pressure from the engine's lubrication system to maintain zero clearance (constant contact with both camshaft and valve stem). Automatically adjusts to variation in valve stem length. Hydraulic tappets also reduce valve noise.

I

Ignition timing The moment at which the spark plug fires, usually expressed in the number of crankshaft degrees before the piston reaches the top of its stroke.

Inlet manifold A tube or housing with passages through which flows the air-fuel mixture (carburettor vehicles and vehicles with throttle body injection) or air only (port fuel-injected vehicles) to the port openings in the cylinder head.

J

Jump start Starting the engine of a vehicle with a discharged or weak battery by attaching jump leads from the weak battery to a charged or helper battery.

L

Load Sensing Proportioning Valve (LSPV) A brake hydraulic system control valve that works like a proportioning valve, but also takes into consideration the amount of weight carried by the rear axle.

Locknut A nut used to lock an adjustment nut, or other threaded component, in place. For example, a locknut is employed to keep the adjusting nut on the rocker arm in position.

Lockwasher A form of washer designed to prevent an attaching nut from working loose.

M

MacPherson strut A type of front suspension system devised by Earle MacPherson at Ford of England. In its original form, a simple lateral link with the anti-roll bar creates the lower control arm. A long strut - an integral coil spring and shock absorber - is mounted between the body and the steering knuckle. Many modern so-called MacPherson strut systems use a conventional lower A-arm and don't rely on the anti-roll bar for location.

Multimeter An electrical test instrument with the capability to measure voltage, current and resistance.

N

NOx Oxides of Nitrogen. A common toxic pollutant emitted by petrol and diesel engines at higher temperatures.

O

Ohm The unit of electrical resistance. One volt applied to a resistance of one ohm will produce a current of one amp.

Ohmmeter An instrument for measuring electrical resistance.

O-ring A type of sealing ring made of a special rubber-like material; in use, the O-ring is compressed into a groove to provide the sealing action.

O-ring

Overhead cam (ohc) engine An engine with the camshaft(s) located on top of the cylinder head(s).

Overhead valve (ohv) engine An engine with the valves located in the cylinder head, but with the camshaft located in the engine block.

Oxygen sensor A device installed in the engine exhaust manifold, which senses the oxygen content in the exhaust and converts this information into an electric current. Also called a Lambda sensor.

P

Phillips screw A type of screw head having a cross instead of a slot for a corresponding type of screwdriver.

Plastigage A thin strip of plastic thread, available in different sizes, used for measuring clearances. For example, a strip of Plastigage is laid across a bearing journal. The parts are assembled and dismantled; the width of the crushed strip indicates the clearance between journal and bearing.

Plastigage

Propeller shaft The long hollow tube with universal joints at both ends that carries power from the transmission to the differential on front-engined rear wheel drive vehicles.

Proportioning valve A hydraulic control valve which limits the amount of pressure to the rear brakes during panic stops to prevent wheel lock-up.

R

Rack-and-pinion steering A steering system with a pinion gear on the end of the steering shaft that mates with a rack (think of a geared wheel opened up and laid flat). When the steering wheel is turned, the pinion turns, moving the rack to the left or right. This movement is transmitted through the track rods to the steering arms at the wheels.

Radiator A liquid-to-air heat transfer device designed to reduce the temperature of the coolant in an internal combustion engine cooling system.

Refrigerant Any substance used as a heat transfer agent in an air-conditioning system. R-12 has been the principle refrigerant for many years; recently, however, manufacturers have begun using R-134a, a non-CFC substance that is considered less harmful to the ozone in the upper atmosphere.

Rocker arm A lever arm that rocks on a shaft or pivots on a stud. In an overhead valve engine, the rocker arm converts the upward movement of the pushrod into a downward movement to open a valve.

Rotor In a distributor, the rotating device inside the cap that connects the centre electrode and the outer terminals as it turns, distributing the high voltage from the coil secondary winding to the proper spark plug. Also, that part of an alternator which rotates inside the stator. Also, the rotating assembly of a turbocharger, including the compressor wheel, shaft and turbine wheel.

Runout The amount of wobble (in-and-out movement) of a gear or wheel as it's rotated. The amount a shaft rotates "out-of-true." The out-of-round condition of a rotating part.

S

Sealant A liquid or paste used to prevent leakage at a joint. Sometimes used in conjunction with a gasket.

Sealed beam lamp An older headlight design which integrates the reflector, lens and filaments into a hermetically-sealed one-piece unit. When a filament burns out or the lens cracks, the entire unit is simply replaced.

Serpentine drivebelt A single, long, wide accessory drivebelt that's used on some newer vehicles to drive all the accessories, instead of a series of smaller, shorter belts. Serpentine drivebelts are usually tensioned by an automatic tensioner.

Serpentine drivebelt

Shim Thin spacer, commonly used to adjust the clearance or relative positions between two parts. For example, shims inserted into or under bucket tappets control valve clearances. Clearance is adjusted by changing the thickness of the shim.

Slide hammer A special puller that screws into or hooks onto a component such as a shaft or bearing; a heavy sliding handle on the shaft bottoms against the end of the shaft to knock the component free.

Sprocket A tooth or projection on the periphery of a wheel, shaped to engage with a chain or drivebelt. Commonly used to refer to the sprocket wheel itself.

Starter inhibitor switch On vehicles with an automatic transmission, a switch that prevents starting if the vehicle is not in Neutral or Park.

Strut See MacPherson strut.

T

Tappet A cylindrical component which transmits motion from the cam to the valve stem, either directly or via a pushrod and rocker arm. Also called a cam follower.

Thermostat A heat-controlled valve that regulates the flow of coolant between the cylinder block and the radiator, so maintaining optimum engine operating temperature. A thermostat is also used in some air cleaners in which the temperature is regulated.

Thrust bearing The bearing in the clutch assembly that is moved in to the release levers by clutch pedal action to disengage the clutch. Also referred to as a release bearing.

Timing belt A toothed belt which drives the camshaft. Serious engine damage may result if it breaks in service.

Timing chain A chain which drives the camshaft.

Toe-in The amount the front wheels are closer together at the front than at the rear. On rear wheel drive vehicles, a slight amount of toe-in is usually specified to keep the front wheels running parallel on the road by offsetting other forces that tend to spread the wheels apart.

Toe-out The amount the front wheels are closer together at the rear than at the front. On front wheel drive vehicles, a slight amount of toe-out is usually specified.

Tools For full information on choosing and using tools, refer to the *Haynes Automotive Tools Manual.*

Tracer A stripe of a second colour applied to a wire insulator to distinguish that wire from another one with the same colour insulator.

Tune-up A process of accurate and careful adjustments and parts replacement to obtain the best possible engine performance.

Turbocharger A centrifugal device, driven by exhaust gases, that pressurises the intake air. Normally used to increase the power output from a given engine displacement, but can also be used primarily to reduce exhaust emissions (as on VW's "Umwelt" Diesel engine).

U

Universal joint or U-joint A double-pivoted connection for transmitting power from a driving to a driven shaft through an angle. A U-joint consists of two Y-shaped yokes and a cross-shaped member called the spider.

V

Valve A device through which the flow of liquid, gas, vacuum, or loose material in bulk may be started, stopped, or regulated by a movable part that opens, shuts, or partially obstructs one or more ports or passageways. A valve is also the movable part of such a device.

Valve clearance The clearance between the valve tip (the end of the valve stem) and the rocker arm or tappet. The valve clearance is measured when the valve is closed.

Vernier caliper A precision measuring instrument that measures inside and outside dimensions. Not quite as accurate as a micrometer, but more convenient.

Viscosity The thickness of a liquid or its resistance to flow.

Volt A unit for expressing electrical "pressure" in a circuit. One volt that will produce a current of one ampere through a resistance of one ohm.

W

Welding Various processes used to join metal items by heating the areas to be joined to a molten state and fusing them together. For more information refer to the *Haynes Automotive Welding Manual.*

Wiring diagram A drawing portraying the components and wires in a vehicle's electrical system, using standardised symbols. For more information refer to the *Haynes Automotive Electrical and Electronic Systems Manual.*

Note: *References throughout this index are in the form* "**Chapter number**" • "**Page number**". *So, for example, 2C•15 refers to page 15 of Chapter 2C.*

Note: *References throughout this index are in the form* **"Chapter number"** • **"Page number"**. *So, for example, 2C•15 refers to page 15 of Chapter 2C.*

Note: *References throughout this index are in the form* **"Chapter number"** • **"Page number"**. *So, for example, 2C•15 refers to page 15 of Chapter 2C.*

Note: *References throughout this index are in the form* "**Chapter number**" • "**Page number**". *So, for example, 2C•15 refers to page 15 of Chapter 2C.*

Note: *References throughout this index are in the form "**Chapter number**" • "**Page number**". So, for example, 2C•15 refers to page 15 of Chapter 2C.*

Preserving Our Motoring Heritage

> The Model J Duesenberg Derham Tourster. Only eight of these magnificent cars were ever built – this is the only example to be found outside the United States of America

Almost every car you've ever loved, loathed or desired is gathered under one roof at the Haynes Motor Museum. Over 300 immaculately presented cars and motorbikes represent every aspect of our motoring heritage, from elegant reminders of bygone days, such as the superb Model J Duesenberg to curiosities like the bug-eyed BMW Isetta. There are also many old friends and flames. Perhaps you remember the 1959 Ford Popular that you did your courting in? The magnificent 'Red Collection' is a spectacle of classic sports cars including AC, Alfa Romeo, Austin Healey, Ferrari, Lamborghini, Maserati, MG, Riley, Porsche and Triumph.

A Perfect Day Out

Each and every vehicle at the Haynes Motor Museum has played its part in the history and culture of Motoring. Today, they make a wonderful spectacle and a great day out for all the family. Bring the kids, bring Mum and Dad, but above all bring your camera to capture those golden memories for ever. You will also find an impressive array of motoring memorabilia, a comfortable 70 seat video cinema and one of the most extensive transport book shops in Britain. The Pit Stop Cafe serves everything from a cup of tea to wholesome, home-made meals or, if you prefer, you can enjoy the large picnic area nestled in the beautiful rural surroundings of Somerset.

> John Haynes O.B.E., Founder and Chairman of the museum at the wheel of a Haynes Light 12.

> Graham Hill's Lola Cosworth Formula 1 car next to a 1934 Riley Sports.

The Museum is situated on the A359 Yeovil to Frome road at Sparkford, just off the A303 in Somerset. It is about 40 miles south of Bristol, and 25 minutes drive from the M5 intersection at Taunton.
Open 9.30am - 5.30pm (10.00am - 4.00pm Winter) 7 days a week, *except Christmas Day, Boxing Day and New Years Day*
Special rates available for schools, coach parties and outings Charitable Trust No. 292048